Trails & Tales
of
Yosemite & the Central Sierra

Climb the mountains and get their good tidings.
Nature's peace will flow into you as sunshine flows into trees.
The winds will blow their own freshness into you,
and the storms their energy,
while cares will drop off like autumn leaves.

~ John Muir

Trails & Tales
of
Yosemite & the Central Sierra

A GUIDE FOR HIKERS & HISTORY BUFFS

Exploring
The Gold Country
North, West & South of Yosemite Park
Yosemite National Park
The Eastern Sierra

Sharon Giacomazzi

BORED FEET PRESS
MENDOCINO, CALIFORNIA
2001

© 2001 by Sharon Giacomazzi
First Printing, September 2001
Printed in the United States of America with soy based inks
on 30% recycled acid-free paper

Cover illustration, *Yosemite Valley (El Capitan and Bridal Veil Falls)* by
Thomas Hill used by permission of Oakland Museum of California, Bequest of
Dr. Cecil E. Nixon
Edited by Donna Bettencourt & Bob Lorentzen
Maps by Marsha Mello
Cover and book design by Elizabeth Petersen
Composition by Linda Richmond & Carlos Olivares

Most of the articles in this book appeared in somewhat different form between
1992 to 2001 in three periodicals, *Sierra Heritage, California Explorer* and the
Yosemite Highway Herald.

Published and Distributed by
Bored Feet Press
Post Office Box 1832
Mendocino, CA 95460
(707)964-6629, (888)336-6199

Library of Congress Cataloging-in-Publication Data
Giacomazzi, Sharon
    Trails and tales of Yosemite and the central Sierra: a guide for hikers and
history buffs/ Sharon Giacomazzi. : foreword by Caetlin O'Riordan
        p. cm.
    Includes bibliographical references and index.
    ISBN 0-939431-25-4 : $16.00

ISBN 0-939431-25-4

10 9 8 7 6 5 4 3 2 1

Dedication

Dedicated to Lois Perry—I couldn't have done it without you.

Two roads diverged in a wood, and I took the one
less traveled by, and that has made all the difference.

~Robert Frost

Acknowledgments

Many dear Sierra friends—you know who you are—contributed in some special way to every facet of this book. For your generous encouragement, expertise and enthusiasm, I am deeply grateful. Please know what a joy it is to have each of you in my life.

In particular, I offer thanks to Ardeth Huntington, Caetlin O'Riordan, Kathy Seaton, Dodie Heiny, Kay Graves, Leroy Radanovich, Linda Eade, Noel Walter Perry and John Muir, my posthumous mentor. Moveover, I am indebted to all of the scholars and historians of Yosemite National Park and the Sierra Nevada, past and present, for their invaluable work.

Illustration Credits

Page	Description	Artist/Source
Cover	Yosemite Valley	Thomas Hill/permission of Oakland Museum
2	Parker Lake	Sharon Giacomazzi
16	Woman and bear	Courtesy of Yosemite Research Library
18	Bridalveil Falls	Courtesy of Yosemite Concession Services
22	Oaks and grasslands	Leroy Radanovich, Courtesy of the artist
24	Murphys 1853	Courtesy of Murphys Old Timers Museum
26	Calaveras Big Trees Hotel	Courtesy of Murphys Old Timers Museum
34	Bagby, circa 1905	Courtesy of Mariposa Cty. Historical Society
41	N. Fork Merced cascade	Sharon Giacomazzi
45	Residents of Hornitos	Courtesy of Leroy Radanovich Collection
49	Mount Ophir, 1860	Courtesy of Leroy Radanovich Collection
51	Ruins of Trabucco's Store	Sharon Giacomazzi
53	Mount Ophir stamp mill	Courtesy of Leroy Radanovich Collection
55	View from Fremont Peak	Sharon Giacomazzi
57	Jessie Fremont, 1856	Courtesy of Mariposa Cty. Historical Society
61	Big Table Mountain	Sharon Giacomazzi
67	Camels in Calaveras Gr.	E. Vischer/Courtesy, Murphys Old Timers Mus.
76	Bourland Trestle, 1924	Courtesy of Stanislaus National Forest
82	Preston Falls	Sharon Giacomazzi
88	Peach & Fig engine	Courtesy of City of San Francisco
92	Rainbow Pool, 1936	Courtesy of Bill Foster
94	Rainbow Pool today	Sharon Giacomazzi
98	Bower Cave, 1920s	Courtesy of Caroline Wenger Korn

continued on page 293

Contents

Foreword

by Caetlin O'Riordan
Editor, **Sierra Heritage** *magazine 1991-2000*

As an architect of words, Sharon Giacomazzi quotes the truth of history and the rhythm of poets. Bridging the two gives us a new breadth in experiencing Yosemite and its environs.

It is a rare manuscript that weaves history, travel, environmental concerns and the voice of a caring heart into a tapestry to be read in the comfort of a favorite chair or by the light of a Sierra campfire. Such are the narratives penned by Sharon. As astronauts have explored the cosmos, she explores the soul and past of Yosemite and the surrounding region.

Through these pages we find a portrait of how the Central Sierra region came to be, its personalities, growing pains, accessibility, and its need for stewardship. Continually awed by nature's capacity for renewal, change and ever-higher order, Sharon is almost painfully open about her passion and devotion for things natural: hiking, exploring and environmental paradigms. She guides us on easy strolls and tough hikes, places us in the footsteps of our pioneer ancestors, tells us where to stalk the ultimate lemon meringue pie, and advises when best to view a spectacular panorama of wildflowers. On a practical note, Sharon is one of the most attentive-to-detail persons I've ever met; when she says it's 1.6 miles to the next fork in the trail, you can bet the farm that she's right.

One of the truths of our time is people's abiding passion to develop a stronger relationship with nature. Carefully, without preaching, Sharon's book takes us there. Those who read these stories will find what so many of us yearn for. Embarking on the adventures outlined here, whether on foot or simply by imagining, will take you on transformative journeys and evoke symbols, language and feelings unique to your own experience. The book offers guidance for inner and outward discovery and does so with grace and intellectual rigor.

May your explorations of Yosemite and the Central Sierra Nevada be fired by these caring, encouraging, informative tales.

Yosemite and the Central Sierra

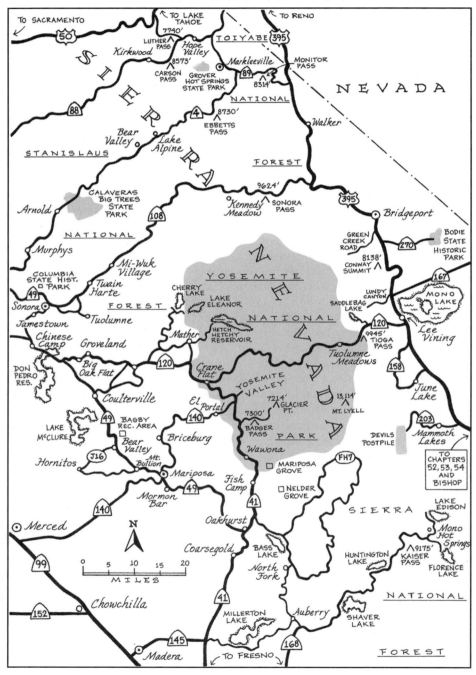

Introduction

The Sierra Nevada range was born millions of years ago in the volcanic fury of a cataclysmic upthrust of a stupendous block of granite that tilted downward toward the coast, creating the gradual 50- to 80-mile western slope and the abrupt 10-mile drop off on the eastern side. Over the millennia, Mother Nature continued to work on her 400-mile long masterpiece. Rivers of ice chiseled and sculpted bedrock into exquisite geological formations, and the less violent actions of weather, wind and water fine-tuned the range into what we see today. These refinements continue in an ongoing process.

Essentially, the Sierra Nevada is one colossal mountain which covers a vast portion of California and a tiny corner of Nevada around Lake Tahoe. From the gold country foothill lowlands to the rarefied heights of its baker's dozen 14,000-foot peaks, the range extends along California's east side from the Tehachapi Mountains in the south to Lassen Peak in the north. Comprising the backbone of the state's complex and diverse geography, it is indeed one of California's most dominant features.

The name Sierra Nevada (meaning snow-covered range) was recorded for the first time in 1776 while 13 fledgling colonies on the Atlantic coast bravely declared their independence from England. Spanish missionary Pedro Font stood atop a hill near the mouth of the Sacramento River and wrote in his journal: " . . . At the opposite end of an immense plain about 40 leagues off, we saw a great snow-covered range (un gran sierra nevada) which seemed to run south-southeast to north-northwest." The snowy sawtooth mountains were called other names, but Font's descriptive name prevailed on maps.

Poetically called "The Range of Light" by naturalist John Muir, the Sierra Nevada mountain chain is home to very impressive statistics. It's the highest, longest and the most thoroughly trailed and traveled range in the contiguous United States. It harbors America's greatest diversity of plant habitats, and contains its largest trees and tallest waterfalls, its most profound canyons, the highest mountain in the lower 48 states, and has had its deepest recorded snowpack.

Moreover, the range was the site of the first large public park—Yosemite Valley and Mariposa Grove of Big Trees—established by the federal government and receded to California in 1864. Additionally, the High Sierra peaks are California's principal weather-makers and the source of its life-giving water supply. In a sense the lungs of California are the range's great forests and woodlands which discharge huge amounts of oxygen into the atmosphere. The range also includes most of the climatic and geological zones of the earth. And, for better or worse, it was the discovery of Sierra gold that drastically transformed California from a pristine wilderness to the most populous American state.

This guidebook covers the heart of that marvelously gorgeous range, the Central Sierra, an area of about 12,000 square miles. Many highways and backroads wind into the range on both its western and eastern sides. Four of those highways traverse the crest of this part of the Sierra Nevada, although they are all closed by snow in winter, with some, especially Tioga Pass, generally closed until June. From north to south those roads and their passes are Highway 88 and Carson Pass, Highway 4 and Ebbetts Pass, Highway 108 and Sonora Pass, and Highway 120 and Tioga Pass.

Of course Yosemite National Park is the much loved centerpiece of this wild and rugged land, with the Park's 1190 square miles alone being nearly the size of the state of Rhode Island. The largest number of this book's trails are within Yosemite Park, with several other hikes snuggling close to its perimeter. That leaves more than 10,000 square miles of lesser known Sierra scenery that this guidebook explores in varying depth.

Reading books about the Sierra Nevada is most certainly an enriching and rewarding activity, and you'll learn many fascinating facts about this magnificent piece of unrivaled California real estate. Still, the amazing facts and statistics about this spectacular mountain range do not touch its essence. Words are simply too small to describe its intrinsic character and world class scenery.

If you really want to know the Sierra, you must get out of your car. While the Sierra's many tremendously scenic roads, eye-popping vistas and little known byways offer sumptuous visual feasts, you will never experience the Sierra's essence until you walk some of its trails. To feel its pulse and know it with your heart involves more than passively and quickly looking at them through a windshield or snapping a photo at a turnout. To fully appreciate these mountains, you must walk among them.

Trails and Tales of Yosemite and the Central Sierra encourages you to sample from 54 historical journeys, ranging from easy to strenuous, to get personally acquainted with its glorious foothills, forests and uplands. Before long you'll find that dry Sierra facts, though intriguing, will pass right out of your head while you're out there mingling with the natural world.

You don't need to know how old the warm chunk of granite is that you're resting against, or how tall that waterfall is, or the name of the peak across the canyon. All that matters is that you are in the moment experiencing one of the world's most classically beautiful mountain ranges, personally and with all of your senses. So get out and explore the marvelous Central Sierra.

How to Use this Book

The basic purpose of this book is to help you select from a variety of 54 hikes in the Central Sierra the ones that fit best with your needs such as physical condition, time available, energy and interests. Although the focus is on day hikes, many of the outings can be incorporated into backpacking trips.

Essentially, this book provides a broad sample of hikes for a broad range of hiking abilities. It's oriented toward novice and average hikers of all ages who have a yearning to explore the natural wonders and cultural heritage of one of the most dramatically beautiful and diverse landscapes on earth. This book especially serves hikers—or armchair travelers—interested in the region's history. Hiking through history offers a deeper experience by linking us with a colorful past that is all too swiftly slipping through the cracks of time. This book is really not intended as a guide for rock jocks, long-distance backpackers, expert off-trail trekkers, mountaineers or thunder-thighed tri-athletes who burn up a vertical slope solely for exercise and rapid transit between two points.

The hikes in this book are grouped geographically into five sections of the Central Sierra Nevada, with Yosemite National Park in the center: I) the Gold Country, II) the Western Slope: trails north, west and south of Yosemite, III) Yosemite National Park/Yosemite Valley, IV) Yosemite National Park outside of the Valley, and V) the Eastern Sierra. An overview previews each of these regions.

You'll find summary information about the hike starting each chapter. This overview details how to find the trailhead, nearby camping and lodging options, hike distance, difficulty rating, the best time to go, cautions about hazards you may encounter or restrictions on use, the starting elevation and the gain on the hike, maps, and where to get further information.

Excluding Half Dome, the hikes range between one and ten miles long, with many having several choices of varying length. All the hikes lead you to some special niche in the Sierra landscape: jawdropping vistas, rugged river canyons, the grandeur of giant Sequoias, shimmering alpine lakes, mountain tops and handsome Gold Country locations.

A word about rating a hike's difficulty: This is rather tricky business because the difficulty or ease of any trek depends primarily on the hiker's fitness level. As a rule, physical condition has little to do with age. I know fit senior citizens who can walk circles around 30-year-olds. It follows then that no qualitative evaluation fits everyone. This book uses a choice of five adjectives to assess each journey: easy, moderate, moderately strenuous, strenuous, and very strenuous.

The bottom line is that none of these journeys should be a death march. Hiking is simply taking one step at a time at your pace in the direction of your choice. Nothing is carved in stone that says you must get to the end of a trail. In fact, the destination is exactly where you decide to stop. Hike, or walk if that word is less daunting, only as far as your ability and desire dictate.

As readers will discover, hiking the Sierra Nevada encompasses much more territory than just High Country trails during summer months. This magnificent "Range of Light" is a vast and varied playground, a destination for all seasons, depending on elevation. We sometimes forget that its glorious foothills, forests and river gorges afford superb hiking opportunities too.

Besides awesome scenery, the Sierra Nevada harbors many intriguing tales from yesteryear. To make the journeys more alluring and meaningful, each hike is accompanied by an in-depth historical account of the area it passes through. This historical essay is followed by a short description of the hike, providing enough information to set the tone, help you avoid trouble and discover the best features, but not so much detail that you can't make some discoveries yourself.

At the heart of this book is the hope that, by enticing you to explore these unimaginably scenic and historic routes, you will realize the urgency and importance of protecting what is left of our natural world and cultural heritage. If one individual like John Muir can make such a difference in preserving wilderness, think about the enormous impact thousands and thousands of people like you can have who gain a similar environmental respect and sense of stewardship.

I truly believe that taking a hike can be a catalyst for great personal change, eventually global change. John Muir said it another way. "Between every two pine trees is a doorway leading to a new life." To be a wise caretaker of the environment doesn't mean you have to take on the entire planet. Just begin where you are, right now, today.

Map Legend

Ⓣ	Trailhead
▬▬▬	Paved Road/ Hwy.
═══	Unpaved Road
= = = =	Unimproved Road
▬•▬•▬	Shuttle Bus Route
– – –	Described Trail
··········	Other Trail
∿∿	River/ Creek
·∿··∿··	Seasonal Creek
〜⌇〜	Waterfall
—·—·—	Park Boundary
∧	Summit/ Peak
◊	Spring
o—o	Gate
⇧	Lodging
⇧	Ranger Station
▲	Campground
□	Point of Interest
Ⓟ	Parking
⊐⊏	Tunnel
⤙	Mine Site
⤬	Picnic Area

The Dangers:
Hiker's Ten Commandments

When on the trail, always keep your senses wide open so that you can best appreciate nature's pleasures as well as her dangers. Don't let nature lull you into complacency. Here are ten rules to keep you out of danger and enhance your journey so that you may safely enjoy nature's beauty.

1. DON'T LITTER. Most of these places are unspoiled. Do your part to keep them that way. Show your appreciation by hiking with a trash bag which you can fill with any trash you find in otherwise pristine places, even cigarette butts, matches and bottle caps.

2. LEAVE NO TRACE. Tread lightly! Make every effort to leave no trace of your visit. Accept personal responsibility for your impact on the environment. Human waste: When there is no toilet, find a spot at least 200 feet from water and dig a hole six inches deep, then cover thoroughly when done. Do not bury toilet paper, tampons, diapers; pack them out in ziplock plastic bags. **Do not** remove, deface or destroy natural features. Don't walk in wet meadows. Please always leave historical artifacts in place; they have much more value connected with the landscape. Excessive noise (radios, cell phones, hollering, etc.) ruins the natural experience for everyone—including wildlife.

3. FIRE. Be extremely careful with it. Don't smoke on trails. Always extinguish campfires until cold to the touch. You generally need a free campfire permit to have a fire outside a developed campground. Fires may be banned altogether during the dry season. Wood fires are prohibited above 9600 feet. Because of wildfire danger, campfires are not encouraged even at lower elevations. If you must build a fire (when permitted), keep it very small and use only downed wood.

4. CLIFFS AND FORDS. Nature provides plenty of inherent dangers. These are two of the worst. CLIFFS: The Central Sierra, especially Yosemite, has many treacherous precipices. Don't get too close to the cliff's edge, keep children in control near them, and never climb on cliffs unless there is a safe trail. Polished granite can be very slippery, especially when wet as it is near waterfalls. FORDS: Surging waters can overcome even experienced hikers. Never cross a ford that seems unsafe. Always use a hiking stick or two, unbuckle your pack's waist belt and loosen shoulder straps ready to free yourself in case of a slip, and proceed carefully on a 45 degree angle downstream to cross moving streams. Even small creeks can become dangerous after rains or during snowmelt.

5. WILD THINGS: ANIMAL. Bears are wild animals. Never tempt a bear or any wild animal with food or try to resist a bear that is raiding your camp, car or pack. Keep food put away (never in your tent!) when not eating and clean uten-

sils promptly. In Yosemite the Park Service deems it your responsibility to store food properly, and you're liable for a fine if it isn't. **Never** leave food or scented items (gum, soda, trash, lotion, etc.) **anywhere** in your car. Where available, always store food and related items in bear-proof metal storage boxes located in parking lots and at trailheads. Mountain lions and even deer can also be dangerous.

Never run from a mountain lion; stand tall with arms spread and wave a big stick. Most pests are much smaller. Watch out for ticks and check yourself after a hike. Some carry Lyme disease. Also watch for wasps, mosquitoes, biting spiders, scorpions and rattlesnakes. Human animals can be the most dangerous, particularly outside of parks during hunting seasons where you should listen for gunfire and wear bright clothing.

6. WILD THINGS: PLANT. These mean business too, especially poison oak which can get you with the slightest touch. Many other plants are poisonous. It's best not to touch any plants unless you know by positive identification that they're safe. This is most important with mushrooms. Please never pick or trample wildflowers or other vegetation. Leave them to re-seed and for others to enjoy.

7. TRAIL COURTESY & SAFETY. Stay on established trails; always avoid making new ones. Never cut switchbacks. Limit groups to 15, fewer is always better. Dogs aren't allowed on trails in Yosemite. They can and do harass and frighten wildlife and other hikers. In national forest wilderness areas, dogs are permitted but not encouraged. Do not drink untreated stream or lake water. Either carry and use a lightweight water filter, treat it with iodine or boil it to prevent debilitating intestinal illness. Equestrians always have the right of way on trails, because you can move aside for a horse much more easily than its rider can yield to you. Mountain bikers must stay on trails open to them, yield to hikers and horses, and slow to walking speed on blind corners. Bikes can cause serious injury when other trail users don't know one is coming. **Bikes and other wheeled vehicles are not allowed on Yosemite trails or in wilderness areas.** Bikes are permitted in Yosemite Valley only on paved bikeways or roads. Wilderness permits are required year round for all overnight stays in Yosemite and Forest

Service backcountry locations. They are not required for day hikes.

8. TRAFFIC. Mountain and park roads are difficult and sometimes crowded. Drive carefully and courteously. Please turn out for faster traffic. You'll enjoy the journey more if you do. If you stop, pull safely off the road.

9. CRIME. Be sure to lock your car when you park it at the trailhead. Leave valuables out of sight, or better yet, back at your lodging.

10. **ALWAYS TAKE RESPONSIBILITY FOR YOURSELF AND YOUR PARTY.** The author cannot and will not be responsible for you in the wilds. Information contained in this book is correct to the best of the author's knowledge at press time. Author and publisher assume no liability for damages arising from errors or omissions. **You must take the responsibility for your safety and health while on these trails.** These are wild places. Safety conditions of trails vary with the seasons. Be cautious, heed the above warnings and cautions about each specific trail, and always check on local conditions. It is safer to hike with a friend and to give your itinerary to someone not on the hike. Know where you can get help in case of an emergency.

The Climate

The Sierra Nevada range exhibits a wide diversity of weather patterns. Temperatures and precipitation vary greatly between foothill and summit areas. As a rule in the lowlands and foothills, winter is the wet season and summer is usually hot and dry. That means spring and autumn often offer the best hiking, although winter can be pleasant between storms.

In the High Country (subalpine and alpine zones), the mountains are weather makers. Winter is cold, and periods of clear skies alternate with snow storms. By late November, High Country access closes to motorists and hikers until late spring. Summer is usually dry with warm days and chilly nights. However, afternoon thunderstorms, generally short-lived, can build with incredible speed. Sometimes these fast-moving squalls are accompanied by violent hailstorms or a few inches of snow. Don't take a sunny day for granted. Bring a variety of clothing when traveling in higher elevations. Even when thunderstorms strike, the storm clouds usually disappear by dusk.

The 400-mile-long Sierra Nevada has several climates, depending on elevation and on which side of the Sierra you're considering. The eastern slope is much more arid because moisture-laden clouds drop most of their water as they ascend the western slope. By the time wet air masses reach the crest and arrive on the eastern escarpment, most of the moisture has been squeezed from them.

Take note that the winter snow pack can have a big impact on your summer hiking plans. In years with a heavy snowfall, many high trails won't be clear until mid-August. If snowfall is light, the same trails may be open by July 1st. Be advised that spring runoff after a heavy winter equals dangerous and/or impossible stream crossings, often until mid-summer.

Be prepared before you hit the trail! Get as much weather information as possible before and during you visit. Contact local Forest Service ranger stations or National Park Service information for current weather and trail conditions. Be flexible and use common sense. Change your hiking destination, abort it en route or even postpone it, if conditions are hazardous and weather is threatening.

Bridalveil Falls

1

Off to See the Elephant
🐻 THE GOLD COUNTRY 🐻

THE MOTHER LODE is a narrow belt of land in east-central California ranging in elevation between 700 and 3000 feet. Called La Veta Madre (The Mother Vein) by Mexican miners, it snuggles along the western slope of the Sierra Nevada for about 250 miles between Mariposa and Sierra City and encompasses some of the most beautiful scenery in the state. From gently rolling, chaparral-covered foothills, alive with wildflowers in spring and lion-colored grasses in summer, to slender river gorges and wooded valleys, the scenery offers pure visual delights.

The eight chapters in this section explore hidden corners of that beauty and offer a lively exploration of its colorful history. They lead you to one of its oldest boom towns in Murphys, to one of its best preserved towns at Jamestown where steam trains still ride the rails, to one of the many early ghost towns and a compelling mystery of a lost fortune at Mount Ophir, and to the now sleepy backwater Gold Rush town of Hornitos, hideout of the notorious bandido Joaquin Murietta. Other hikes in the section explore the marvelous Sequoia groves of Calaveras Big Trees State Park, the lower Merced River along the old Yosemite Valley Railroad line, the one-time camp of colorful pioneer and presidential candidate John Fremont where High Sierra vistas enthrall, and the fascinating, wildflower-rich volcanic tablelands of a little known preserve.

Make no mistake about it, the Mother Lode was not always the peaceful landscape we see today. At the peak of the Gold Rush in the 1850s, several hundred thousand miners were prowling the hills and slogging through streams seeking their fortunes. The siren call of gold seduced men away from all walks of life, from all over the globe. The Mother Lode was the destination of one of the most frantic and phenomenal migrations mankind has ever witnessed, and it certainly was among the most significant events in California history.

Sparked by James Marshall's 1848 discovery of gold along the American River, California rocketed from an obscure territory to statehood just two years later. Towns, rough mining camps in reality, sprouted everywhere gold was found and were as quickly abandoned when the strike was over. It was an era characterized by flux and impermanence.

One Gold Rush scholar commented, "The discovery of gold brought changes far out of proportion to the value of the metal itself." In one short year, California changed completely and dramatically from a backward, peaceful agricultural community of about 2000 Americans to a society of transients and strangers. By 1849 some 90,000 miners had invaded this wilderness and set in motion astonishing technological, financial and societal changes felt across the nation and around the world.

"Off to see the elephant!" was a universal expression of the Gold Rush, symbolizing the exotic and unequaled adventure of a lifetime, going to California to strike it rich in the gold fields. Later, after experiencing the harsh realities of the journey and then life in mining camps, "to see the elephant" meant suffering great hardships, overcoming misfortune and coming to grips with the disappointment of not finding gold.

The gold seekers were not true pioneers or settlers. They came as adventurous transients, concerned only with taking rather than building. Most of them had no interest in California's future. Their sole focus was to make a large amount of money in the shortest possible time and then head back home. This horde of restless strangers wanted no roots or the burden of responsibility. Like soldiers in a foreign land, they easily shed the moral and social codes instilled in them by family, friends and church. No watchdogs monitored their behavior; this was a land without law, government or religion.

Of the estimated 546 mining camp towns in the Mother Lode, about 300 have disappeared. Some of the survivors, not much more than ghost towns in progress or just names on a map, call attention to the area's colorful past: Rough and Ready, Volcano, Hornitos, Moccasin and Dutch Flat. These rural hamlets still beckon travelers and invite exploration.

The towns of the Gold Rush existed only to supply the needs of the miners. When the miners moved on, the towns often vanished, with a new camp springing up elsewhere. Then came the saloon-keepers, with the sporting ladies right on their heels. Next came the merchants who built stores and sold their goods at astronomically inflated prices. Only a small number of miners ever became wealthy. The real fat cats were the merchants and gamblers who mined the miners.

These years were rowdy and wild and brawling, a time that brought out the best and too often the worst in men. This was essentially a world of men and explosive masculine energy. They were young, in their 20s and 30s for the most part, and bloated with ambition, optimism and the dream of easy riches. Except for the painted ladies, few women chose to set up housekeeping in this crude, untamed frontier. They stayed home, waiting and worrying about their men folk.

Gold camp life was not the romantic picture many Hollywood films have led us to believe it was. Lodgings at best were primitive, and health and sanitary conditions were poor. The labor was tedious and back-breaking, malnutrition common, doctors and medicine almost nonexistent, and law and order were often dispensed at the end of a rope or gun.

Furthermore, miners found California in a period of turmoil. The region was in the slow process of changing hands from Mexican authority to U.S. jurisdiction. Although officially annexed to the United States by treaty in February 1848, California's vast frontier was not yet firmly governed by U.S. authorities. Washington was 3000 miles away and had little influence on daily life. In the southern section of the Mother Lode between Mariposa and Sonora, where so many foreigners had gathered, racial tension was especially strong. Many of the Americans had recently returned from the war with Mexico and their prejudices were still intense. The American-born miner believed that foreigners had no right to "their" gold, and many hostile and deadly confrontations occurred, particularly with Latin and Chinese miners.

As early as 1850, rapid advances in mining methods began taking hold in the gold fields. As placer mining generally proved inefficient and unprofitable, science replaced Lady Luck in coaxing the Mother Lode out of her treasure. Gold was still in abundance, but the time had come for the pick, pan and shovel to stand aside for complex and long-term operations involving expensive machinery, technical expertise and considerable financial backing.

Thus began the years when gold was mined from deep shafts, quartz veins, tunnels and hydraulic claims. Looking for gold was big business, and the romance and adventure of the miners of '48 and '49 came to an end. By the time of the Civil War in 1861, the Gold Rush was essentially over, although mining activity continued here and there in varying degrees of success until the end of the century.

In truth, tens of thousands of weary, homesick, discouraged men, after "seeing the elephant," gave up their quest and returned to their origins. The vast majority of these men, who had been farmers or city dwellers, knew absolutely nothing about mining or were not the least bit prepared for the long and dangerous sea or overland journey to California and the miserable living conditions once they arrived.

Ironically the "bust following the boom" created the Mother Lode we see today. When the gold petered out, masses of miners abandoned the diggings, allowing Mother Nature to begin healing the ugly wounds they left behind. The miners had actually changed the character of rivers, gophered into the earth in places a mile or more, and blasted away topsoil with dredges and high-powered hoses, in their search for gold bearing gravel beneath the land.

During the phenomenon of the Gold Rush, California symbolized freedom and change, excitement and unimaginable opportunities. Thousands of ex-gold seekers returned to California because they became restless and dissatisfied with their conventional lifestyle in the East. They came this time with their families to settle and build and put down roots.

Following Highway 49 can be your passport to the Gold Country. Whether you visit it in sections or in full, exploring the Mother Lode gives a tremendous sense of being linked with our past because it has changed very little over the years. A few of the old mining camps, such as Sonora or Placerville, have become bustling little cities, but the vast majority are small communities with a handful of residents. One can find many old buildings still standing and in use, deserted mines, crumbling walls and foundations, old boom towns preserved as state parks and places like Coulterville where the whole town is a living museum. If you're not a history buff, then Highway 49 offers a journey through some of the West's most magnificent and photogenic countryside. Bookstores and libraries have volumes of interesting books on Gold Rush history and other things to do and see.

For me, the romance of the '49er wandering the hills is still very much alive. Now and then gold fever grabs hold, and I find myself wading into some remote streambed, gold pan in hand, looking for another small nugget to complete a set of earrings. Whether I find it or not is of little importance. Just being out there in the solitude and peace of the foothills, connecting with days gone by, is more than enough. Once you've "seen the elephant," you're never the same.

1
Murphys & Calaveras Big Trees State Park
A Well Preserved Gold Rush Town & Some Mighty Grand Trees

■ THE DETAILS

Getting There: Murphys lies 59 miles east of Stockton on Highway 4 (9 miles east of Angels Camp at the junction of Highways 49 and 4), where you turn north on Main Street to enter town. Calaveras Big Trees State Park is 15 miles east of Murphys up Highway 4.

Nearest Campgrounds: Calaveras Big Trees State Park has two campgrounds (one open year round) with a total of 105 sites.

Lodging: Many choices in Murphys.

Further Info: Calaveras Big Trees State Park 209-795-3840. Calaveras County Chamber of Commerce 209-736-2580.

Hike Distance: North Grove: one-mile loop, South Grove: 5-mile loop.

Difficulty: Easy for North Grove. Moderate for South Grove.

Best Time to Go: May through October.

Cautions: None.

Starting Elevation: Murphys: 2171 feet. Calaveras Big Trees State Park: 4800 feet.

Other Maps: USGS Boards Crossing 7.5 minute topo or state park map.

Tucked into the rolling foothills of eastern Calaveras County is Murphys, an exceptionally captivating and well preserved Mother Lode town. Huge oak, sycamore and black locust trees spread dappled sunlight over Main Street, home to more than a dozen, ancient brick and stone structures as well as to more recent ones. The Murphys Hotel and the Peter Travers (Old Timers Museum) buildings are the oldest in town, dating to 1855 and 1856. In all, you can see over 70 historic buildings in the handsome, compact downtown area. Originally called Murphys Diggings and Murphys Camp, it was founded in 1848 by the Murphy boys. Their story could be put in a nutshell: they came, they saw, they conquered, and they left as young millionaires within a year.

How John and Daniel Murphy arrived in California is just as significant as how they left their name on this picturesque hamlet. By the late 1830s the era of mountain men and fur trapping was drawing to a close, while that of the farmer-settler was about to begin. Oregon and California became meccas for restless pioneers

Murphys, 1855, the earliest known photograph. The 1859 fire destroyed all these buildings.

like the Murphy family, eagerly seeking new lands. Starting in Missouri these forerunners of the great Western movement ended their epic journey at Sutter's Fort near today's Sacramento. The Murphy brothers came West in 1844 with the historic Murphy-Stevens-Townsend wagon train, the first emigrant party to bring wagons across the Sierra Nevada. Their 60-year-old father, Martin Murphy Sr., was co-leader of the party. Martin Murphy Sr. settled in Santa Clara County on a large land grant near the present-day town of Morgan Hill. John and Daniel later left the rancho to make their own way on the California frontier.

The Murphy brothers began as Indian traders but turned to prospecting after the discovery of gold on the American River in 1848. Lured to the Mother Lode by the irresistible call of gold, John and Daniel teamed up with the Stockton Mining Company along with Henry Angel (Angels Creek) and James Carson (Carson Hill Mine). Working their way south from the Sacramento area, the Company dipped their pans in every potential stream. When they reached a stream now known both as Murphys and as Angels Creek, Angel dropped out to mine and open a tent store.

Carson and a few others left to try their luck on Carson Creek, while the Murphys dawdled for a short time on Coyote Creek (Vallecito). Later they wandered a few miles north to a promising location on Angels Creek where they hit a rich placer strike in 1848. After putting 150 Indians to work on their claims, John and Daniel opened a trading post that garnered $400 per day in gold dust.

By the end of 1848 the Murphys had acquired a fortune and wisely left town and the Gold Rush scene with their fortune intact.

Twenty-three year old John Murphy became one of the first and youngest millionaires of the Gold Rush. Brother Daniel moved to the San Jose area to buy land. He helped his father run the vast Las Llagas Rancho and assumed ownership of it after Murphy Sr. died in 1865. He went on to own far-reaching tracts of land and immense herds of cattle in California, Arizona, Nevada and Mexico. By the time of his death in 1882, Daniel had amassed an enormous fortune.

The gold camp continued to prosper after the Murphy brothers left with their treasure, and by 1859 the local Wells Fargo office had shipped out over $15 million in gold. At its zenith Murphys boasted 5000 inhabitants. As a consequence of major fires in 1859, 1874 and 1893, people began to use stone and brick for their buildings, many of which have survived for the modern visitor to enjoy.

Closely allied with the history of Murphys is the famed Calaveras Grove of Big Trees located 15 miles to the northeast. These mammoth specimens at Calaveras were first seen by pioneer John Bidwell in 1841. Before the account of the 1833 Joseph Walker expedition came to light, Bidwell was credited as the first white man to have seen the Tree Giants. For a number of years it was thought that the Calaveras Grove was the only stand in existence. We now know that the Walker Party, while in the Yosemite region, was the first to note the Big Trees. By 1850 a few miners came across them, but because they concentrated on finding gold and struggled to stay alive in the wilderness, their discoveries went largely unnoticed.

Then in spring 1852, a hunter named Augustus Dowd found himself in an unfamiliar forest while pursuing a wounded grizzly. Dowd was employed by Union Water Company of Murphys to supply its workers with fresh meat. He soon forgot the bear as he gaped in awe at the monstrously big trees. Before returning to his camp above Murphys, he spent the rest of the day exploring the area. His excited tale of these impossibly huge trees was met with ridicule and much rolling of eyes until he finally persuaded a group of men to make the 20-mile hike into the mountains to see for themselves.

Almost overnight the news of the Tree Giants spread like wildfire, and curious visitors began traveling up the crude path from Murphys to what became known as Calaveras North Grove. Soon word spread across the continent and even to Europe. Although Dowd was not the first to have seen them, it was really his discovery that riveted public attention on *Sequoiadendron giganteum*, attracting fascinated visitors from all over the globe.

It didn't take long for speculators and ambitious lumbermen to become interested in the trees' commercial potential. In 1853 the gargantuan tree first seen by Dowd was stripped of its bark to a height of 30 feet and felled by a promoter. The Discovery Tree bark was shipped to the East coast, reassembled and then exhibited from New York to London. To make the senseless desecration even worse, fire destroyed the traveling exhibit a year later. The enormous stump of the Discovery Tree, six feet high and 96 feet in circumference, was smoothed and used as a dance floor. To put its size in perspective, during a Fourth of July celebration in 1854, 32 people and musicians danced the night away on its surface. The fallen trunk was so huge that a two-lane bowling alley and a saloon were eventually built atop it.

Aside from hitting pay dirt and quickly stockpiling a sizable fortune, the Murphys did little for the town that is their namesake. James Sperry, on the other hand, arrived in Murphys in 1850 and put down deep roots. Over the years he became a respected, prominent citizen and a driving force in the community. Sperry, co-owner of the first hotel in town, shrewdly realized that a stampede of tourists would soon be coming to the North Calaveras Grove.

With this in mind, Sperry and partner John Perry bought the Mammoth Tree Ranch from A.S. Haynes in 1858. The property included a small hotel built by Haynes to "accommodate tourists who had made the trip by stagecoach from Stockton." By the time Sperry bought out his partner, they had increased the land holdings to 2300 acres. Due to the steady growth of sightseers passing through Murphys en route to the grove, Sperry built the stately Calaveras Big Trees Hotel in 1867. Clean and comfortable lodging for 75 guests and good food in a spectacular and unique setting magnetized tourists from all over the world.

The luxurious two-story hotel in Calaveras Grove was financed by James Sperry in the early 1860s. It burned to the ground in 1943.

The hotel, under different ownerships, was a fixture in the grove until it was destroyed by fire on August 17, 1943.

In addition to the hotel business, James Sperry was involved in many community projects. He was a director and leading stockholder of the Murphys Flat Fluming Company, an impressive venture created in 1857 to drain the mines of excess water. He also owned an iron mine near town and was the promoter and president of the Carson Valley Turnpike Company which built the Ebbetts Pass Road in 1864. Sperry was elected president of the Murphys Board of Trustees in 1876 and affixed his signature on all deeds given to property holders. After nearly 40 years in Calaveras County, James Sperry retired from the business world. He and Mrs. Sperry moved to Berkeley where they resided until their deaths in 1902 and 1911, respectively.

You'll find a wealth of things to do and see in Murphys and the Calaveras Grove. Because of their intertwined histories and close physical proximity, it would be a shame to visit one and not the other. Murphys is blessed with a peaceful atmosphere, somehow blending its 153-year-old Gold Rush heritage with its more modern influence. The town is wonderfully suited for a leisurely stroll through the shaded downtown area and side streets to see the dozens of venerable structures, many of which are still in use. In spite of its laidback charm, Murphys is not a hayseed town. Tasteful, low-key shops and very good restaurants add an intriguing contrast to one of the very oldest settlements in the Mother Lode. Nearby attractions include wineries and two fascinating caves. Both Moaning and Mercer Caverns offer guided tours at reasonable rates. If you opt to extend your stay, you have a number of excellent choices to hang your hat for the night.

To reach Calaveras Grove, take the beautiful drive up Highway 4. Only 15 miles northeast of Murphys you'll find Calaveras Big Trees State Park, elevation 4800 feet. The North Grove was protected as a state park in 1931, finally calling a halt to the commercial exploitation and destruction of these patriarchs of the forest. The much more extensive South Grove was included in 1967. Calaveras Big Trees State Park protects 6073 acres, with the only stands of giant Sequoias sheltered within a state park. Many other tree species also thrive here. Among them are pine, dogwood, maple, cedar, oak, alder and white fir. The grove is in two sections: the North Grove lies within Calaveras County while adjoining Tuolumne County claims the South Grove.

■ THE HIKES

An easy, one-mile long interpretive trail loops through North Grove. The path is well planned and remarkably appealing. Lightly visited South Grove is much larger and more primeval. A signed, paved road past the entrance station takes you to its trailhead, where the trail winds a mile along Big Trees Creek to reach the grove's western edge. Trails through this pristine, undeveloped wilderness

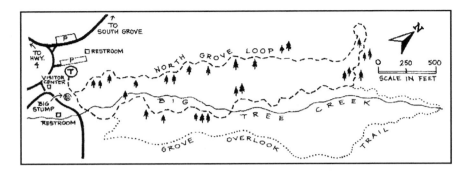

offer the hiker an intimate experience among these "ambassadors from another time." Other park trails lead to isolated sections of the North Fork Stanislaus River and up through an interesting lava flow. An inexpensive guide booklet to the grove shows the trails and provides useful information. The park also offers picnic tables and two campgrounds.

Touring Murphys and the Big Trees provides exceptional history and great scenery. You can make this an all-day outing, or better yet, take lodging in Murphys or camp in the magnificent grove of Sequoias. This uncrowded locale is definitely a spot in the Sierra you won't want to rush through. Both sites invite lingering and unhurried exploration. An eloquent passage from Kahlil Gibran's **The Prophet** might move you to get out of the car and slow the pace. "And forget not that the earth delights to feel your bare feet and the winds long to play with your hair."

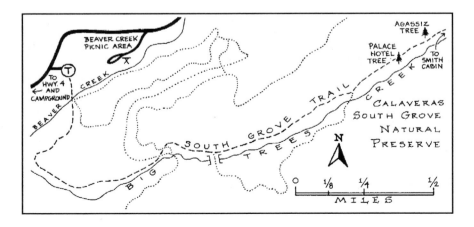

2
Jamestown & the Sierra Railway
Steam Trains Still Chug through the Foothills

■ THE DETAILS

Getting There: Jamestown lies on Highway 49 and Highway 108 just 4 miles southwest of Sonora.

Nearest Campground: Tuttletown Recreation Area 209-536-9094 on New Melones Reservoir has 155 year-round sites and showers.

Lodging: Jamestown has a few choices and Sonora has several.

Further Info: Railtown 1897 State Historic Park 209-984-3953, 209-984-1600, or write Box 1250, Jamestown, CA 95327.

Hike Distance: Short walk around historic town.

Difficulty: Easy.

Best Time to Go: Trains run hourly from 11 to 3 on Saturdays, Sundays and holidays only from April through October. Depot open daily with scheduled roundhouse tours.

Cautions: None.

Starting Elevation: 1405 feet.

Map: Compass Map of Calaveras & Tuolumne Counties.

Not yet am I a true "choo-choo junkie," but it could happen. My primary addiction is hiking, which in a roundabout fashion led to an interest in railroads. Not the giant companies, but the short lines of the Sierra Nevada grabbed my attention. As some of you know, abandoned railroad grades afford wonderful hiking opportunities. These old routes allow one to be part of incredibly beautiful scenery in often remote and otherwise inaccessible country. Some years ago, while walking in the Merced River canyon on the long-defunct Yosemite Valley Railroad grade from Bagby to Briceburg (see chapters 3 & 4), I became hooked. Then and there my goal was to plant my boots on as many of them as possible. It wasn't enough to just walk on them. Curiosity led to research, providing information about their history to complete the experience.

The Sierra Railway was not a short-lived venture, as so many short lines were. It was adaptable, and through the far-sighted and crafty leadership of its creators, the Sierra bridged many tough periods of potential extinction. Furthermore, many private railroads were spawned from the Sierra tracks in the Southern Mother Lode. The Yosemite Short Line, Hetch Hetchy Railroad, West Side Lumber Company Railroad, Empire City Railroad and Pickering Lumber Company Railroad all spun off from Sierra Railroad. Many towns built a railroad and flourished only as briefly as spring wildflowers because their economic base was chiefly dependent upon mining and then lumbering. Once the miners wandered off to richer digs and the loggers cut down their livelihood, towns woke up one morning to find that their trains were no longer needed.

The Sierra Railway, headquartered in Jamestown, was incorporated in February 1897, nearly 50 years after the Gold Rush and mining boom in California. Before the 1849 gold frenzy, Tuolumne County was relatively unknown and thinly inhabited. However, the county did certainly explode into being as a result of the '49 rush when gold was discovered near Columbia. Thousands upon thousands stampeded into the area, and towns sprouted like weeds. Although the furious excitement was essentially over by the early 1860s, a new breed of settler slowly began moving into the county. Farmers, ranchers and merchants replaced the transient miners and loggers. In fact, Tuolumne County didn't really show signs of progress until the 1890s.

Even though numerous mines were still working profitably, lumbering was barely in its infancy. By the Gay Nineties, the California mining industry had become listless, largely due to the nation's depression and lack of modern mining techniques. Incidentally, during that period state-of-the-art mining technology came to us from highly successful operations in South Africa. During this era three wealthy promoters decided that Tuolumne County needed a railroad to inject life into sagging mining operations and to develop the timber industry. To be sure, their intentions were slightly to the left of real benevolence. Nevertheless, the Sierra Railway was extremely important in providing an isolated, rural community with virtually their only contact with the outside world by connecting it with the Southern Pacific. The "Big Three" included Prince Andre Poniatowski, William Crocker and Thomas Bullock. Poniatowski was the mouthpiece for several groups of European investors who had heavily invested in California gold mines. Crocker was a bank president and principal in numerous California developments and was by no means a newcomer to railroads. His father, Charles Crocker, was one of the prime movers behind Central Pacific Railroad. Bullock was a speculator and investor who had built railroads in the southwest and Mexico. The depression forced his Arizona line out of business, leaving him with a lot of idle equipment and looking for a new location. Bullock met Poniatowski in 1896 when he moved to Stockton, and together they conceived the Sierra Railway.

Construction was underway by March 1897 from a connection with the Southern Pacific at Oakdale in the San Joaquin Valley. Originally, the short line's terminus was Jamestown, 41 miles distant. Here the railway's roundhouse, maintenance facilities, business office and a plush, new hotel were built. Jamestown, almost overnight, became the hub of the county's economic and social life. In August 1899, a four-mile branch was completed to Sonora, and by February 1900, an additional 12 miles of track were added to reach the town of Tuolumne to service the West Side Flume and Lumber Company recently purchased by Bullock, Poniatowski and Crocker. The 19 miles from Jamestown to Angels Camp were in full operation by the summer of 1902. This marked the end of new tracks laid and solely owned by the Sierra Railway. However, during the 1920s a few temporary spur branches were built to serve the construction requirements of dams being installed on the Tuolumne and Stanislaus Rivers.

The Sierra Railway was never a big money-maker even though it prospered through the 1920s. The construction finale of the monumental dam projects followed by the belt-tightening times of the Great Depression led to bankruptcy in 1932. The Angels Camp branch was shut down in 1935, and the last passenger run steamed out of Tuolumne City in March 1939.

Ironically, a heavy player in their bankruptcy was the Yosemite Short Line Railway, brainchild of Thomas Bullock. The line was built to serve the southern Tuolumne mines, provide transit between there and Mariposa County and to and from Yosemite. Also a factor was Bullock and Poniatowski's ownership of a 66,000-acre tract of timberland near the line's route. Though they were self-serving, the Sierra Railway creators were ambitious, inventive and astute entrepreneurs on a grand scale.

Unfortunately, Mother Nature intervened in these best laid plans on April 18, 1906. After six miles of line were in operation, just shy of Bullock Lumber Company holdings, the San Francisco earthquake struck with disastrous consequences reaching all the way to Tuolumne County. Bullock and Crocker suffered major financial losses, Poniatowski withdrew his French investors' support and Bullock's Lumber Company went belly-up, forcing the discontinuation of the Yosemite Short Line. Along with paying off its own bonds, the Sierra grimly faced making payments on the Yosemite Short Line for the next three decades. In 1935 the bondholders, spearheaded by William Crocker, took control of the Sierra Railway, and formed the Sierra Railroad Company.

In the 1950s another hard punch was dealt the Sierra. Railroads throughout the nation replaced their steam locomotives with diesel engines. By 1955 diesel engines came to stay, although a few steam locomotives were kept by the Sierra as back-ups and for movie contracts. A direct spin-off of this transition was that the Jamestown facilities were not equipped to adequately service the new diesels. Accordingly, the decision was made to move their maintenance shops to Oakdale while keeping the Jamestown shops to service the remaining steamers. The latter proved to be a very significant resolution; the Jamestown operations remained virtually unchanged and effectively preserved as "one of the last original, fully functional steam locomotive complexes in North America." Today these shops are basically as they were in the era when steam was the power source for trains.

In so many ways the Sierra Railway's story is a great tale of a versatile and tough little survivor. To add to its accomplishments, it first became a movie star in 1919 when the producers of **The Red Glove** needed a passenger train for a robbery scene. During the next ten years, great numbers of silent movies were shot on the line. Film history was made in 1929 with **The Virginian**, starring Gary Cooper, when the first talkie was filmed away from the studio. Nearly 300 films have been shot on the Sierra since then. To mention a sampling that you'll no doubt recognize: **My Little Chickadee, Duel in the Sun, High Noon, Pale Rider** and **Back to the Future III**. In addition to feature-length movies, numerous scenes for popular, long-running TV shows have used the Sierra: **Petticoat Junction, Gunsmoke, Bonanza** and **Little House on the Prairie**.

Besides starring in movies, the Sierra ran steam-powered excursion tours for a few years in the late 1950s and early 1960s. Unfortunately in October 1963, these popular trips came to a halt when Engine #28 derailed and almost tipped over. The owners decided immediately to use the steamers for movie work only. During the 1960s, the Sierra realized falling revenues and rising costs. To put new energy and profit in the line, Crocker, Sierra's president, developed a theme park in Jamestown and revived the steam excursions. On May 1, 1971 his "Rail Town 1897" became a reality.

Once again, the Sierra became a pioneering role model with the concept of these trips, later to be imitated throughout the nation. In spite of ups and downs, including the destruction by fire of the depot and office buildings in 1978, the Sierra survives today. Although the owners sold the freight and track operations in 1980 to Silverfoot Inc. of Illinois, the 26-acre Jamestown complex was sold to the California Department of Parks and Recreation. "Rail Town 1897 State Historic Park," offering guided tours and steam-powered trips, reopened in 1983 and today provides avid rail fans and other visitors with the excitement and nostalgia of the days when steam was king in the Mother Lode.

No one can of course predict what the future will bring to the railroad. If it's true that history tends to repeat itself, then the odds seem to favor the Sierra Railway finding yet another creative way to survive as it has for over 100 years. It's well worth your time to visit the park, take a guided tour, poke around in the visitor center and book shop, and best of all step back in time for an hour or two and ride one or more of the excursion trains. Who knows? Perhaps a "choo-choo junkie" lurks inside you, too.

3
Bagby & the Merced River Trail
Hiking in Hell's Hollow

■ THE DETAILS

Getting There: The site of Bagby lies 16 miles north of Mariposa (12 miles south of Coulterville) on Highway 49 on the east side of the highway and the north bank of the river near the head of McClure Reservoir.

Nearest Campground: Bagby Recreation Area (800-468-8889 for reservations) on the reservoir's south bank opposite the trail has about 30 sites, open year round, with piped water.

Lodging: Mariposa has several choices from budget to elegant and Coulterville has a few.

Further Info: Mariposa Chamber of Commerce 209-966-2456.

Hike Distance: Merced River Trail: up to 14 miles (or more) round trip, 7.5 miles round trip to North Fork Cascades.

Difficulty: Easy to moderate. Moderately strenuous for round trip to North Fork.

Best Time to Go: Early spring, winter.

Cautions: At peak run-off, first mile of trail may be underwater or inaccessible. Watch for rattlesnakes. Very hot in summer.

Starting Elevation: 816 feet. Gain to North Fork: 130 feet.

Other Maps: USGS Coulterville and Bear Valley 7.5 minute topos.

At the southern end of the Mother Lode, just off Highway 49, the site of Bagby lies 16 miles north of Mariposa. Not far from the graceful bridge spanning the river, a few rusted metal scraps and concrete foundations are the lone survivors of a Yosemite Valley Railroad station and a tiny town alongside the Merced River. From here, a 7-mile walk on the abandoned railroad bed leads to the confluence with the North Fork Merced. However, it's up to you how far you want to stroll. As you proceed, remind yourself it's the journey, not the destination, that counts. No one is keeping score of how many miles you walk, and no rule says you must reach the North Fork to have a satisfying experience in this wild and scenic canyon.

If you're partial to solitary, streamside walks in canyon environments, this is the place for you before snow melt raises the water level. During peak run-off, the old grade penetrating this rugged, seldom-traveled gorge is covered with water along its west end. Except for the sighting of an occasional railroad spike, faint tie shadows, and trestle ruins, nothing remains to suggest the 38-year existence of a rail line that carried passengers from Merced to Yosemite's doorstep.

From a ridgetop about 12 miles out from Mariposa, the 1000-foot, corkscrewing road descent into Hell's Hollow, as it's known locally, is utterly spectacular and even daunting to flatland motorists. The hollow at the bottom of an awesome chasm was named for its hot-as-the-hinges-of-hell summer temperatures, steep drop-offs and dangerous access.

In the late 1850s, Jessie Benton Fremont described it without wasting words by saying, "A fall into it was Death." Another less ominous account of the four-mile-long plunge into the heart of Merced River canyon portrays it as "a sight different from all other grades, with a play of light and shadow, rolling contour upon rolling contour until lost to sight in the long distance."

Bagby was originally the location of Ridley's Ferry between 1850 and 1859. Later, a dam and John C. Fremont's water-powered stamp mills were built there. Fremont, owner of the 44,000-acre Las Mariposas Land Grant, named it Benton Mills for his prominent father-in-law, Senator Thomas Benton of Missouri. Still later, Benjamin Bagby built a store, hotel, saloon and boarding house on the north side of the river.

In 1897 when a post office was to be established at Benton Mills, someone discovered that a Mono County mining town had the same name. Instead, the Mother Lode settlement was dubbed Bagby. After the turn of the century, Bagby's history was intertwined with the Yosemite Valley Railroad which operated from

At Bagby, circa 1905, the powerhouse at right center supplied electricity to Mariposa 15 miles south.

1907 to 1945. After the railroad ceased operations, Bagby managed to survive as a fisherman's resort until the New Exchequer Dam was completed in 1966. Then the waters of the Merced River backed up into the canyon and created McClure Reservoir.

Before flooding began, a turntable, twin water towers, and the quaint wooden Bagby Station were removed and relocated to El Portal. After remodeling, the historic depot became headquarters for the Yosemite Association. Other buildings and an old bridge were burned in 1966. The lake makers named Bagby Recreation Area in memory of the drowned town. Presently, two campgrounds, launch ramp, boat rentals and a small store cater primarily to anglers.

■ THE HIKE

To get started on this hike, park your car at the north end of the bridge and walk east down the slope to river's edge. You'll have to rock hop across a sidestream to access the railroad grade. Usually in March, the water level is still low enough to ford this stream without difficulty. Scramble up the bank, turn right and head up river. Known locally as the lower river below Briceburg, the Merced becomes relatively calm below its confluence with the North Fork. The Merced loses the hard-charging energy and whitewater rapids so prevalent upstream, although it still runs swift during snowmelt season. In late summer and autumn the river ambles in its diminished flow into the head of the reservoir near the trailhead. Heading up the canyon, you'll soon see the Bagby site marked by concrete foundations across the river. Pause here awhile to imagine the bustling mining community that once went about its business.

Instead of the small marina, hear the racket of powerful stamp mills crushing gold-laden rock. Look up and imagine the rumble of ore carts carrying high grade rock down from the Pine Tree and Josephine mines on the ridge far above you. Discovered in 1849, these two mines yielded $4 million in gold. Cornishmen did the blasting, and Chinese laborers built Fremont's tramway in two weeks. Ore cars descended by gravity and then were towed back up by mules. Picture a dam and hydroelectric plant during the property's foreign ownership between 1898 and 1907. The plant supplied 15,000 volts of electricity to mines between here and Mariposa 15 miles away.

Mother Nature has been taking care of business in the hollow these past 150 years, healing the ugly mining scars on her chaparral-covered hillsides. A few years ago a huge Canadian mining company caused an uproar in Mariposa County. Millions of dollars were spent in exploration and preparation to reopen the Pine Tree and Josephine which were last worked profitably in 1944 when they were forced to close because of World War II. Among other negative environmental impacts, a cyanide roasting process ignited a lengthy conflict. In the end, the company threw in the towel and left the area.

Except for the old railroad bed and trestle ruins spanning the wide mouths of side canyons, the terrain is much the same as it was before the Gold Rush. By March, especially if it has been warm, you'll be treated to a nice variety of wildflowers at this low elevation. You can expect to see red maids, fiddlenecks, shooting stars, baby blue eyes, Sierra wallflowers, poppies and more.

Around 1.8 miles you'll come to the first of three major washed-out bridges. The only things left of these big spans are concrete piers and abutments. Detour down and then up the slope to regain the railroad bed. Driftwood deposited on the grade is courtesy of the 100-year flood in January 1997. Remnants of another missing bridge are about a mile farther on. Here, nearly 3 miles from Bagby, is a good place to stop if you choose to abbreviate the journey.

Before retracing your steps, walk up the ravine for a few minutes. You are in a wide, picturesque gulch with some evidence of past prospecting and mining activity. Pick a spot near the creek and enjoy absolute peace and quiet while you have lunch. The Merced and its tributaries harbor a wide variety of birds. Among others, finches, quail, dippers, red-winged blackbirds, cliff swallows, and red-tailed hawks make their homes here. The common merganser duck often rests along the river, and occasionally, a majestic bald eagle can be seen skimming the water.

The railroad grade/trail stays close to the river until it takes a lazy, southerly bend, looking somewhat like the top of a question mark, before straightening out again. You'll notice that this area is different from the previous terrain because it's grassy and shaded. Beyond this moist stretch you'll see several mining claim markers, and big piles of rock speak of past dredging operations.

Just 1.25 miles before the main stem of Merced's confluence with its North Fork, the stream across the canyon from you is Sherlock Creek. The rich diggings all along it attracted many Argonauts. To this day, modern miners still work this narrow gorge from time to time. By now, you've probably been aware of walnut-sized rock on the grade, more plentiful in some places than in others. This is nonindigenous material called ballast on top of which the tracks were laid. Please don't remove any artifacts from mining or railroading days that you might find.

At trail's end, a grassy flat where the two rivers merge invites hikers to linger before returning to Bagby in Hell's Hollow. A hefty trestle once bridged the gap created by the North Fork Merced, a swift sidestream which may not be crossable during wet weather or snow run-off months. One of the Merced's two primary tributaries, the North Fork begins life on Pilot Ridge in Stanislaus National Forest, some 20 miles to the north. It dashes through a pristine canyon accessed by a vague path on the south side.

The main stem was named El Rio Nuestra Señora de la Merced, the River of Our Lady of Mercy, by Gabriel Moraga of the Mexican army in 1806 in gratitude for coming upon its waters at the end of a 40-mile march. Originating in Yosemite on the Sierra Crest, the Merced flows wild and free until it reaches Lake McClure, formed by Exchequer Dam near Merced Falls. From the reservoir, the river flows into the San Joaquin Valley, joining the San Joaquin River near Newman.

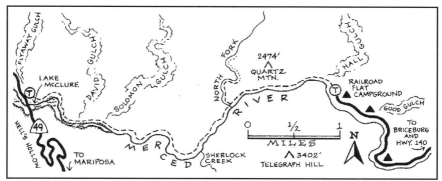

Chapters 3 and 4

On your return journey, be on the lookout for a pair of beaver just below the confluence. Though not abundant, the Merced corridor is home to both beaver and bobcat. The mostly level Yosemite Valley Railroad right-of-way along the Merced's north bank provides hikers of all ages and abilities a wonderful opportunity to explore a beautiful, rugged canyon. This is a good location to introduce children to the great outdoors, offering easy walking with plenty to see.

4

A Merced River Trail Ramble

Exploring Briceburg & the Yosemite Valley Railroad Line

■ THE DETAILS

Getting There: From Mariposa, drive 14 miles north on Highway 140. Turn left (west) at the Merced River Recreation Area sign, cross a suspension bridge, go left again and continue about 5 miles downstream to trailhead.

Nearest Campgrounds: Three small shaded campgrounds line the river below Briceburg, all first come-first serve, with no drinking water.

Lodging: Mariposa has several choices.

Further Info: Bureau of Land Management 209-966-3192, Sierra National Forest 209-966-2456.

Hike Distance: 5 miles round trip to North Fork Merced River, 7.5 miles round trip to the North Fork cascade. Up to 9.5 miles one way to Bagby on Highway 49.

Difficulty: Easy. Moderate to North Fork cascades or Bagby.

Best Time to Go: March and April for wildflowers, winter for mild temperatures.

Cautions: Temperatures can be hot between May and October. Although rarely seen, rattlesnakes live in the canyon. Trail up the North Fork to cascades is not maintained, so beware of poison oak. Do not attempt to ford the North Fork at peak run-off.

Starting Elevation: 1050 feet. Gain for round trip to North Fork cascade: 320 feet.

Map: See Chapter 3, page 37.

Other Maps: USGS Feliciana Mountain and Bear Valley 7.5 minute topos.

The western approach to Yosemite via Highway 140 through the Merced River Canyon is utterly captivating. The lower canyon as well offers a glorious landscape to celebrate the beauty of Yosemite's lower mountains. A side trip to the rarely visited, pristine North Fork Merced River canyon awaits you. Although many visitors prefer spring when the river is running full and wildflowers blanket slopes in an extravaganza of color, the canyon provides a visual feast during any season. In spring, revitalized by snowmelt and warming temperatures, the canyon seethes with life and energy, thrilling newcomers and returning hikers. Laced with joyful streams and riotously verdant hillsides starred with flowers, spring's first wave in these water-cut gorges offers a feast for winter-weary eyes. Wildflowers begin blooming as early as February, with ever changing species as the days warm up. Besides offering a glorious landscape, the rugged and scenic gorge is the locale of many important historical events and intriguing human stories. While streamside walking on the abandoned Yosemite Valley Railroad (YVRR) grade, hikers can only imagine the momentous history that unfolded here.

Centuries before European-Americans came and obliterated their way of life, the Miwok people lived in the canyon. The shameful Mariposa Indian War erupted in 1850 at Savage's Trading Post upstream. Gold was a powerful magnet during the latter half of the 19th century along with logging, barium mining, and produce farming. This became the industrial section of Mariposa County. The Yosemite Valley Railroad, sometimes called "the short line to paradise," snaked through the canyon from 1906 to 1945. Logging, the railroad, mining and satellite businesses here provided jobs for more than a third of the county's population, but today you'll find scarce evidence that almost 2000 people lived and worked in the canyon during those years.

Because of Yosemite's phenomenal tourist appeal since its discovery in 1851, a group of Oakland and San Francisco entrepreneurs decided to finance a railroad running through the Merced River Canyon. To see Yosemite's fabled grandeur before the railroad, visitors had to endure days of fatiguing travel by stagecoach. By capitalizing on the park's skyrocketing popularity and providing a vastly more comfortable and expedient means of transportation, YVRR financiers anticipated a lucrative and long-lasting revenue source.

Taking into account all facets of construction, rights-of-way, equipment, and property, YVRR cost about $3.3 million to put into operation. With a puzzling lack of hoopla, on May 15, 1907 the first full-length run left Merced, chugging into El Portal four hours later carrying only 12 passengers. In spite of an unceremonious debut, the arrival of the Iron Horse heralded a new era in transportation and launched the tourist boom in Yosemite. From its inception, the pioneer YVRR demonstrated steady growth in passenger and freight revenue for 20 years.

The abandoned Yosemite Valley Railroad grade is your passport to the lower Merced River Canyon. You can connect with it at the former settlement of Briceburg. Long before realtors coined the cardinal rules for buying property—location, location, location—the Brices chose the right spot to do business. Their choices demonstrated foresight and coincided with two influential events in the Central Sierra—building the railroad and later the popularity of the automobile.

Before becoming a canyon dweller, William Brice operated a general merchandising store at Colorow, a mining camp in Midpines. The gold camp and store thrived, but Brice knew that when the mines petered out so would his profits. Shortly after the YVRR was completed, the canny merchant decided to move his store to a site near the railroad along the north bank of the Merced across from its confluence with Bear Creek. Brice dismantled the buildings at Colorow, and along with all the inventory and household goods, traveled with his wife and infant son to the canyon in July 1906. Brice reassembled the store first so that he could conduct business while the house and other buildings were finished.

By October 1909 a post office was established in the store, and Briceburg became a regular stop for passengers and freight on the railroad and provided needed goods for miners and ranchers scattered throughout the hills and along the river. The Mountain King and Clearinghouse Mines were important customers. These mines each had about 50 families who welcomed the many goods available at Brice's.

William Brice's death in 1917 thrust his eldest son Maxwell into premature responsibility at age seven. By age 14, however, he was capably running the whole operation with his mother Elsie.

In a sense, Max was robbed of his childhood and does not harbor many fond memories of life at Briceburg. When interviewed recently, Max reminisced, "It was a valuable experience, but the hard work and long hours were just too great for a boy."

One event would prove momentous for the future of Briceburg but disastrous for the railroad. The opening of Highway 140 in 1926 affected the fate of the entire Merced River Canyon. In the railroad's 40-year life span, the opening of the highway was most detrimental. Passenger revenue plummeted 38% the first year, then continued dropping. What the railroad did so quickly to the stagecoach two decades earlier, the automobile did to the railroad. Moreover, a flood of epic proportions destroyed the Bagby Bridge and 30 miles of track in the canyon in 1937. In addition, industries that provided substantial revenues for YVRR ceased operation. On August 24, 1945, as quietly as it had begun, Yosemite Valley Railroad passed into history as its last run left Merced. Happily, the railroad bed now serves us doubly as a 9.5-mile hiking trail and road access to three pleasant campgrounds.

The highway building project brought work crews into the canyon. By October 1923, a supervisor and 30 laborers established a work camp on the Merced River opposite Brice's store.

Frank Dovidio, the superb Italian chef for the crew, courted and married the widow Brice. Because of Elsie Brice Dovidio's shrewdness, Briceburg changed from a generalized service center for a small far-flung colony of local residents into a specialized enterprise oriented toward automobile travel. With a sharp eye on the future, Elsie anticipated the damaging consequences the new highway would have on the railroad. For her business to remain vital, she would have to relocate and restructure the establishment on the highway side of the river. In August 1926, she applied for a mining patent on a 20-acre parcel across the river, but rather than engage in mining, her objective was to create a business to attract Yosemite visitors traveling by car.

Frank Dovidio designed and built a beautiful granite structure known as River View Tavern. They also added a family residence behind the tavern. The tavern, gas station, and fine Italian restaurant opened when the highway was paved in 1927. Only the tavern and a graceful, curving rock wall and steps leading to the house survived a 1950 fire. Across the river, portions of the mortarless slate foundations of the original house and outbuildings are still visible.

After the Dovidios separated in 1928, Elsie moved with her two sons to the Bay Area to begin a new life. Over the next 30 years a series of lessees ran the business and added an inn, auto repair shop, campground and a new residence. Commercial use of the property ceased in 1958, but it continued to be occupied until 1989. In that year, Max Brice sold it to the BLM to aid their efforts to upgrade the scenic and recreational qualities along the lower Merced River. The granite structure of River View Tavern was sandblasted and restored to its former state, and then converted into a BLM information center. The unusual, handsome stone building stands as a solid monument to the ingenuity and vision of the pioneering Brice family.

■ THE HIKE

To get acquainted with the area, cross the suspension bridge and drive about 5 miles downstream to where the railroad grade is closed to vehicles and park. Your goal is to walk to the confluence with the North Fork Merced River, an easy 2.5 miles on the gentle YVRR grade. For a special treat, the rarely seen cascades in the North Fork canyon wilds add 1.25 miles to your riparian outing. Unless it's peak spring run-off time, you can also ford the North Fork and continue downstream to Bagby (see Chapter 3). If you do, you'll want to shuttle a car to that end or have someone pick you up there. Only hikers, equestrians and mountain bikers are permitted beyond the gate, and soon the old grade becomes more of a trail. Not much remains to suggest YVRR's 38-year tenure in the Sierra. Past the gate, walk on the defunct, flat grade heading for the confluence with the North Fork. This section is especially scenic and gives the feeling of real wilderness because only nonmotorized

This two-tiered cascade races through the wild and remote North Fork Merced River Canyon.

traffic is allowed.

After crossing a restored trestle built by current owners of the Mountain King Mine property, note the ruins of a slate foundation marking the mining colony near their small house. Beyond the trestle, the rampaging Merced in January 1997 deposited debris and roughened up the old grade for about .75 mile. Farther downstream, you'll see a collapsed flume on the south side of the river. During the 1920s, it carried water to run an electric plant which supplied power to the mine and its community of 50 people.

Near the North Fork you will see two sets of curious looking pipes running downslope to the river. Rafters use these to portage around a dangerous stretch of whitewater. The North Fork confluence offers an excellent spot for a trail lunch.

After a break, you have three choices. With a car shuttle in place, hikers can rock hop across the North Fork after peak run-off and continue downstream 7 miles to Bagby at the head of Lake McClure beside Highway 49. Otherwise, either retrace your steps, or wander up the North Fork and absorb the gentle wildness of this remote, infrequently visited branch of the Merced. Walk down to a huge, spreading oak beside the North Fork, and pass the stone foundation of a miner's cabin. Turn uphill at the butt end of a large, fallen tree. A couple of rock cairns mark the way.

Often indistinct and sometimes disappearing, an ancient trail contours 100 feet or so above the water. Should you lose the faint path, don't worry. You can't get lost. Just keep well above the river and head upstream. Most years a riotous wildflower pageant graces the grassy slopes. Beneath the intense, young green of California Buckeyes you pass rocks thickly carpeted with lush moss.

Ferns and waterfall buttercups sprout from moist nooks and crannies in the canyon wall as you near the falls. About 1.25 miles from the cabin ruins, a lovely three-tiered cascade sprints through a colorful rocky defile. Nearby are some granite perches, perfect for listening to the water music and viewing the unspoiled beauty of this Sierra gorge.

Whether for a day or a week, an exploration of the wild and scenic Merced River Canyon will reward you. The area's rugged beauty, abundant hiking, and diverse recreational opportunities will capture your interest, tempting you to return again and again to this historic niche in the Sierra Nevada foothills.

Designated "wild and scenic" in 1988, the Merced has two significant branches. The South Fork tumbles through Wawona to join the main stem at Savage's Trading Post on Highway 140. Born in Yosemite's High Sierra, the Merced's main stem rolls through Yosemite Valley, continues down the canyon and eventually reaches the San Joaquin Valley near Newman. Smaller and little known, the North Fork Merced begins in the Pilot Ridge region of Stanislaus National Forest and converges with the main stem seven miles below the suspension bridge at Briceburg. You'll find other hikes in the various canyons of the Merced in Chapters 3, 15, 16, 17, 29, 40 and 41.

5
Hornitos

A Remnant of Old California

■ THE DETAILS

Getting There: Hornitos lies in the foothills west of Mariposa on Highway 49. Several backroads lead there (see loop drive described below), but for the easiest route to Hornitos, turn west off Highway 49 at tiny Bear Valley 11 miles north of Mariposa (17 miles south of Coulterville) onto Bear Valley Road, which winds 11 miles down to Hornitos. Park near the town square.

Nearest Campground: Lake McSwain Recreation Area has 112 sites and showers on a small reservoir 7 miles west of Hornitos via Hornitos Road.

Lodging: In Coulterville, Hotel Jeffery 209-878-3471, Yosemite Gold Country Motel 209-8783400. In Mariposa, Mariposa Lodge 209-966-3607, Mother Lode Lodge 209-966-2521, Best Western Yosemite Way Station 800-321-5261, Miner's Inn 209-742-7777, Whispering Pines 209-966-5253, Yosemite Gold Rush Inn 800-321-5261.

Further Info: Chamber of Commerce (Main Street), P.O. Box 333, Coulterville, CA 95311, 209-878-3074. Chamber of Commerce, P.O. Box 425, Mariposa, CA 95338, 209-966-7081.

Hike Distance: Up to 2 miles of town rambling.

Difficulty: Easy.

Best Time to Go: Early spring is ideal, late fall and winter also pleasant.

Cautions: Very hot in summer.

Starting Elevation: 821 feet.

Map: USGS Hornitos 7.5 minute topo.

Encompassing some of the most historically significant and beautiful scenery in California, State Highway 49 threads through the heart of the Mother Lode. As the road climbs, dips and snakes through foothills and mountains, many fascinating old mining camps and tiny Gold Rush communities beckon the traveler, inviting exploration. Today, it's difficult to imagine that these bucolic and sparsely-populated hinterlands were once a lodestar to several hundred thousand miners hoping to strike it rich. It's still harder to believe that some of these wee villages once swarmed with thousands of inhabitants. According to historians, of the estimated 546 mining-camp towns, about 300 have disappeared. Some of the remaining towns are little more than wide spots in the road, and each year brings less to see.

Just off Highway 49, some 20 miles west of Mariposa, one of the oldest survivors in the southern Mother Lode dozes peacefully in virtual obscurity. Hornitos offers a step backward in time and a rewarding look at California's Gold Rush heritage. The town is absolutely unblemished by contrived restoration, gift shops and gimmicks to lure tourists to spend their time and money. Although relics of yesteryear are everywhere, it's up to the visitor to seek them out.

Hornitos, Spanish for "little ovens," seems appropriately named if you were to pay a visit in summer. Indeed, oven-like temperatures are common in this Sierra lowland nestled at the bottom of a picturesque valley. Dropping down into Hornitos takes us through an unmistakable California landscape. A rich tapestry of typical foothill flora spreads before you. Ruby-barked manzanita, the cheerful yellow of mustard in bloom, feathery chemise bushes, pungent, green tarweed giving the illusion of lushness, purple-blossomed yerba santa, and an eternity of rolling hills covered with soft, tawny grasses and dotted with live oaks provide a visual feast. Even poison oak's shiny scarlet and russet leaves make one forget its potential misery. Easterners often remark that the scene is drab, dull and dry, underlining the truth of beauty being in the eye of the beholder.

Spring is perhaps the most delightful time to explore this sleepy little town. Between late February and May temperatures are mild, the dun-colored grasses are transformed to a luxuriant, bright green, and wildflowers sprinkle the hills. Herds of fat, sassy cattle wander the fields in an orgy of grazing. Regardless of the season, to a native Californian this countryside offers a handsome and familiar sight, distilling the very essence of Sierra foothill scenery. To us it is a colorful montage and evokes a deep pioneer sense of solitude, wide-open spaces and freedom.

Except for a few mining scars, an occasional ranch or house and tree stumps, the land has changed very little since the days of Mexican dominion. Blessedly, after the fever of the Gold Rush waned, California's growth and development burgeoned elsewhere in the state. As a result, places like Hornitos afford the opportunity to recapture the flavor of Old California. The region abounds with remnants of local history and of our rollicking, frontier days.

Because Hornitos is off the beaten path and has no lodging, restaurants or curio shops, you needn't fret about crowds. Only a few visitors roam the streets in any season. The collection of modest houses and ancient stone and adobe buildings comprising Hornitos stretches the definition of a town. A saloon and a post office offer the only services. And, not surprising to kindred lovers of small, rural communities, the 75 residents are most content with their life in the very slow lane.

Arriving in this drowsy hamlet, one finds it almost incredible to learn that in its prime 15,000 people lived in this settlement along Burns Creek. Mexican miners explored and settled Hornitos around 1850 after they were driven out of

Residents of Hornitos pose in front of Reeb's Butcher Shop circa 1880. Today it's the Plaza Bar, one of the few signs of life in the town.

their diggings at nearby Quartzburg. The name Hornitos derives from the Mexican practice of burying the dead in above-ground tombs made of rock and adobe. Below-ground interment was difficult due to the hard, rocky earth. To the unknowing these burial mounds resembled little outdoor ovens. It was a hell-roaring society with a nasty reputation for vice and violence. During the Gold Rush strong racial prejudices were rife in the southern Mother Lode. All foreigners, especially those from Latin countries, suffered abuse and persecution.

The Hornitos environs proved extremely rich in placer (surface) and hard rock gold. When some of the outcasts traded gold for supplies in Mariposa, they triggered a rush. The rough collection of outlaws, thieves, saloons and "sinful dives" of Quartzburg quickly moved to the place of "little ovens" a couple of miles away. The town grew rapidly, becoming one of the most rowdy and prosperous mining camps in the Mother Lode. At its peak the thriving population supported 12 hotels, 32 saloons, many stores, numerous fandango (dance) halls, opium dens, six fraternal lodges and various satellite businesses. The first express office in the country, Wells Fargo, opened in 1853 in Hornitos and for a time shipped $40,000 in gold a day. It was a fabulously wealthy town; records reveal that nuggets as hefty as 34 pounds were unearthed nearby.

In the early years, as you'd expect, it was a wild-and-woolly, lawless environment. Gold magnetized people to Hornitos from all walks of life and classes of society. The good, the bad and the ugly were all represented here. Joaquin Murietta, notorious killer and primo bandido of the gold country in the 1850s, was a frequent visitor to Hornitos bars and fandango-hall señoritas.

Domenico Ghirardelli, later to become the "Chocolate King" in San Francisco, got his start in Hornitos. John Studebaker worked here as a blacksmith.

After putting together a grubstake, he moved to Placerville and began making wheelbarrows. Ultimately, Studebaker moved to Indiana and became the nation's most famous and largest wagon maker, eventually developing the Studebaker car. The originators of the renowned Visalia Stock Saddle, Jesus Salazar and his partner, began their business in Hornitos, moving it to Visalia in 1863.

A definite Mexican atmosphere runs through Hornitos. In fact, it shows their influence more than any other gold country settlement. The town was originally fashioned around a central plaza. Its narrow streets were lined with adobe buildings with walls three feet thick, many with iron doors and shutters. In the beginning, because of no timber or sawmills in the area, some of the saloons and fandango halls were built underground. Cockfights and bull vs. bear death duels were popular spectacles. On the lighter side, frequent fiestas in the plaza and exciting horse races also provided entertainment. The fandango halls and their "sporting ladies" were well patronized avenues of diversion for more lusty pursuits.

In time, although reluctantly, this rough settlement outgrew its violent youth. In 1870 Hornitos became the first and only incorporated city in Mariposa County. Curiously, of all the social ills to remedy, the first two laws dealt with the licensing of dogs and the prohibition of cattle running free in the streets. Later, other social abuses were addressed. Finally, as Hornitos matured, it became safe for law-abiding citizens to walk the streets.

As the gold deposits dwindled, so did the population. Most of the transient miners moved on. Similar to most mining towns after the diggings were abandoned, Hornitos began the slow process of deterioration. By the early 1870s it began to fade as a principle town in the Mother Lode. One by one the merchants shut down as the population wandered away.

By 1896 only two of the 32 saloons were in business. The once-prosperous Gagliardo store survived for over a century of continuous operation until it closed in 1960. On the shelves remain hundreds of dusty items dating back to the early years of Hornitos. Roy's Cafe, a general store, gas station and tiny motel managed to hang on into the 1980s. Only the Plaza Bar survives today. Mrs. Ortiz, owner and bartender for nearly 50 years, indeed has many tales to share with visitors.

A loop driving tour is the best way to get acquainted with the land of little ovens, allowing you to slow your pace and savor the handsome countryside. Using either Coulterville or Mariposa as a base of operations will further enhance your journey. Both towns are among the oldest in the Mother Lode, offering many intriguing things to do and see. Visit their Chamber of Commerce offices for maps, books and information on each town.

After leaving Coulterville, southbound motorists can start the loop by leaving Highway 49 in the tiny hamlet of Bear Valley. Turn right on County Road J16 to Hornitos, and via Old Toll Road rejoin Highway 49 at Mt. Bullion, an even smaller village. For northbound drivers the order is reversed. Turn left on Old Toll Road to Hornitos, then follow Road J16 out to Highway 49. From Mt. Bullion it is 13 miles to Hornitos, then 11 miles back to Highway 49 at Bear Valley.

■ THE HIKE

When you get to Hornitos, be sure to stop in the sleepy little town's center. Park your car and take a rambling walk around the town, keeping your eyes peeled for the remnants of this Gold Rush boom/bust settlement. If the day is mild, end your walk by climbing the hill to St. Catherine's Church and exploring its historic cemetery, perhaps reading the dates and inscriptions on some of the 19th century tombstones and investigating the two remaining hornitos or crypts.

The old plaza in front of the post office is a good place to start your stroll through the village. Among the interesting buildings are a former fandango hall facing the square, the ruins of the Ghirardelli store built in 1855 and the jail with two-foot thick granite walls and an iron door imported from England. The Masonic Lodge, established in 1855, one of the earliest in the state, is still in use. It has the distinction of being the only lodge permitted to conduct meetings on the ground floor. A sealed tunnel at the corner of High Street and Bear Valley Road was used by Murietta as an escape route when lawmen came to town. The tunnel led from Rosie's fandango hall to the home of one of the dancers across the street, only a dash from the corral where Murietta's horses were kept ready.

The Chinese population of 2000 had their own community of dwellings, stores, gambling halls and opium dens in a four-square block area on the eastern edge of town. An opium den building still stands in that corner of town.

St. Catherine's Church and cemetery sits on a knoll above town to the east. Years ago stone buttresses were added to reinforce the tired wooden walls of the 1863 building. Mass is held twice a year, and on November 2, the Mexican religious custom to honor the dead on All Souls Day draws many participants to the solemn, candlelit procession. Toward the back of the cemetery among the ancient gravestones you'll find the two remaining hornitos. It is here, perhaps, as the wind prowls among the tombstones, that the aura of history surrounding the crumbling ruins and sagging buildings is most palpable.

Whether you are a native Californian or a transplant, a trip to this special place and its eye-pleasing countryside is rewarding. It affords the visitor a rare opportunity to experience our rapidly vanishing past. Hornitos is a tough old man of a town, down but not out. Some say it is merely a ghost town waiting to happen. Plan to see it before it disappears.

6

The Legend of Mount Ophir
Of Lost Treasure & Minted Gold

■ THE DETAILS

Getting There: Turn off Highway 49 onto Mount Ophir Road 6 miles north of Mariposa. About midway along this short loop, park near the E Clampus Vitus monument.

Nearest Campground: Bagby Recreation Area (see Chapter 3).

Lodging: Mariposa has numerous choices, see Chapter 5.

Further Info: None.

Hike Distance: One mile round trip or 2.5-mile loop.

Difficulty: Easy.

Best Time to Go: Spring, autumn, winter.

Cautions: Always use caution around mine tailings. When exploring abandoned mining areas, watch where you put your feet. Be alert for uncovered shafts and stay out of tunnels.

Starting Elevation: 1950 feet.

Map: USGS Bear Valley 7.5 minute topo.

Typical of many Gold Country locations, Mariposa County teems with downright curious place names. Places like Ben Hur, Fly Away, Bootjack, Forlorn Hope, Dog Town, Hell's Hollow, Pendola Garden and Chili Gulch are among the many towns and places colorfully named by our pioneer forebears more than a century ago. We've inherited a rich legacy of peculiar, amusing monikers whose historical significance has fallen through the cracks of time.

Six miles north of Mariposa, near the hamlet of Mount Bullion, a sign indicates a road called Mount Ophir. Ophir (rhymes with gopher) is an odd name even among odd names. If you have an inquisitive bent and like to find where such a road leads, veer off the highway here. You might be disappointed because nothing catches your eye and the road goes nowhere except to loop back to Highway 49 in a mile or so. However, if you are observant and drive slowly, you might spot two crumbling slate walls in a scrub oak thicket . . . and herein lies the tale.

You might not realize, like most motorists who pass the flanks of an unremarkable, rather low, chaparral-covered hill pockmarked with mining scars, that

This 1860 photo of the town of Mount Ophir (wrongly labelled 1854) by Carleton Watkins was commissioned for the Mariposa Grant series, a portfolio to present to Eastern investors.

you've just scooted by one of California's famous but forgotten ties with the past. Largely unheard of today, Mount Ophir was the site of a fabulous gold strike in the southern Mother Lode. The settlement and surroundings swarmed with about 5000 miners in its prime.

California's first federally authorized private mint was built here in 1850. The decaying fieldstone walls are remnants of Louis Trabucco's General Store in the town of Ophir; for years they were incorrectly believed to be from an assay office. From Mount Ophir came the raw gold which was turned into unusual, hexagonal $50 slugs, the first official coins issued in the state. Some 300 of these coins cost a man his life and gave rise to one of the best legends of lost treasure in the Mother Lode.

Regrettably, the recorded historical information about Mount Ophir is scanty. We have no chronicle of who first discovered the gold-bearing quartz in this brush-covered hill above Bear Creek, nor do we know who dubbed it Mount Ophir. Whoever named it, however, was acquainted with the Bible. The Biblical Ophir was a land of great opulence from whence came the gold to adorn King Solomon's temple (refer to 1 Kings, verses 10 and 11). Mount Ophir's reputation spread quickly and lured thousands of Argonauts to the area, hoping to become as rich as Croesus.

Among those bewitched by the Mother Lode Ophir's glittering reputation was John L. Moffat, a geologist and experienced miner in the Georgia gold fields. He came to San Francisco in 1850 with a Presidential appointment as United

States Assayer for California, and is also known as the inventor of a radical improvement for the California mining cradle. After an inspection tour through the Mariposa district, he immediately filed a claim at Mount Ophir. In the same year, Moffat received permission to establish a mint at Ophir, the first private mint ever authorized by the U. S. Government.

Moffat recognized the need for uniformity in the purchasing power of gold. At that time a miner bought what he needed with nuggets, gold dust or chunks of gold-veined quartz, and no one knew whether he was paying too much or too little. Although other private companies minted coins in the early years of the Gold Rush, the coins were not legal tender even though accepted in local communities as a more convenient medium of exchange than gold dust. With the authorization of Moffat's Mint, miners and providers of services and supplies were assured a consistency of exchange throughout the state.

The first coins issued were hexagonal $50 gold pieces. Later, Moffat minted other denominations. An article in an 1852 San Francisco newspaper described the first coins as "hexagonal with an American eagle in the center of the face. Around the edge is stamped United States of America and just above the eagle are numerals 887 thous. (indicating the purity of the gold). The obverse side is stamped with rays radiating from a common center, between which are the numerals 50. The name of the U.S. Assayer is lettered close to the milled edge."

Moffat's mine and mint prospered for two years, but by an act of Congress in 1852, the authorization of private mints was revoked, and Moffat's mint closed. The mine continued to operate successfully until 1859 when John Fremont gerrymandered the boundaries of his 44,000-acre floating land grant, Las Mariposas, to include the mine at Mount Ophir. After Fremont's takeover, the mine was worked sporadically until its final closing in 1914. The estimated total production of the Mount Ophir Mine was $300,000. However, geological experts concluded in 1954 that by no means had its gold ore been exhausted.

A 149-year-old mystery of missing $50 slugs still clings to the aura of Mount Ophir. Since 1852 many people have searched, presumably without success, for this vanished treasure. Each newly minted, uncirculated rare coin would be worth a small fortune today. In 1933 a historian reported, "One of these slugs, could it be found, would probably be valued at $10,000." Historical accounts of their disappearance are inconclusive, posing more questions than answers.

The bare bones of the story state that in late December 1851, Joseph Marre stopped at Moffat's Mint on his tax-collecting circuit in Mariposa County. When Marre reached Mount Ophir, weather conditions were severe. The creeks were swollen and turbulent from unusually heavy rains, and a cloudburst was in full force the afternoon he left the mint en route to Mariposa. A few days later on December 30, 1851, his body and his dead horse were found in Mariposa Creek where they had drowned attempting to cross the raging stream. The horse's saddlebags and Marre's pockets were empty, and the tax collector was not wearing his money belt. Three hundred (some accounts say 200) gold coins from the mint, valued at $15,000, were missing without a trace. No signs of foul play were evident at the scene.

End of story. Maybe.

To armchair detectives fascinated by this tale of lost treasure, that will never be the end of the story. A number of feasible circumstances occurring around the time of Marre's death gave rise to some provocative theories. Although these scenarios are quite credible, too many years have passed and too many pieces of the puzzle are missing. We'll probably never know how the final chapter played out, but this mix of ingredients is all part of romancing the Sierra, the stuff that dreams and legends are made of.

To begin with, other than that Joseph Marre was a U.S. Tax Collector, we

Two slate walls in a scrub oak thicket are remnants of Trabucco's General Store, the only sign of the town, Mount Ophir.

know nothing about him. Whether he picked up 200 or 300 gold coins at Moffat's Mint is not clear, nor is why or where he was taking them. We can assume the mint was tax exempt due to its government status. Undoubtedly, profits from the mine were taxable, explaining Marre's presence at Ophir. However, a report by the Court of Sessions regarding Marre's death did not mention the missing $15,000. Surely such a huge sum of tax monies would have been included in an official statement of a tax collector's demise.

One theory advocates that he was not collecting taxes but was transporting monies to a safer location. The infamous bandido Joaquin Murietta was active in the area at the time, foraying out of his hangout at Hornitos whenever he smelled gold. Like everyone else, Murietta knew that coins and mint-ready gold were kept in a vault at Ophir. Conceivably, Moffat was apprehensive about having so much gold in storage or had actually received a tip about a Murietta raid and used Marre to move the coins to either the county seat at Agua Fria or to Mariposa. It is plausible that Joaquin got wind of the transfer, chased Marre down, robbed him and forced him to ford the rampaging creek which claimed his life.

Indeed, weather was an important element in the mystery. Lending credence to speculation that he was not at Ophir to collect taxes is the fact that Marre was in an extreme hurry. Rather than wait for the storm to abate, he chose to leave amidst a tremendous downpour. It would not seem likely that collecting taxes would fill him with such an urgency to depart so shortly after his arrival. Whatever his reasons were to come to Ophir from San Francisco during a violent storm to pick up a very large sum of money and ride out in such a lather remain an enigma.

Yet another explanation reasonably maintains that when Marre saw the creek at flood, he decided not to chance crossing it with his heavy and valuable cargo. Instead, he stashed Moffat's coins and his own money in a safe cache to return for them later. Bolstering this conjecture is a news item which reported that heavy rainfall in December 1851 unleashed a king-size mud slide on the slope above Mariposa Creek. Apparently it spread over two acres and was 50 feet deep in places. For more than a hundred years this supposition has spurred thousands of fortune hunters to dig in the banks and hillsides along Mariposa Creek.

Whether Marre was a victim of foul play or lost his life by accident is not provable. Whether he was picking up $15,000 in taxes from the Mount Ophir Mine or transferring the money to another location because Moffat was jittery of a robbery is also not verifiable. All that is known for certain is a tax collector drowned, and a fortune in gold coins has never turned up on the open market or in rare coin collections.

In August 1995 a provocative article appeared in the **Mariposa Gazette** which sparked a flurry of renewed interest among seekers of Mount Ophir's $50 slugs. A woman panning for gold "somewhere in Mariposa Creek" (note the vagueness of location so characteristic of prospectors) found a quarter-dollar, octagonal, gold coin minted in 1854. While not part of Ophir's vanished fortune, it is nonetheless tantalizing that a 147-year-old gold piece materialized in the same creek where Marre lost his life and the rare coins.

The tale of Mount Ophir is one example of forgotten Mother Lode communities whose lively history, like an old photograph, has faded with time. Each year the life story of these once colorful places becomes more obscure, further severing the connection to the past. Sadly, documentation in many cases is meager or nonexistent, and the old-timers are gone. In the case of Mount Ophir, we owe much to historian Doris Scovell for researching its history.

Should you be moved to explore the easily-accessible Mount Ophir environs, you'll quickly sense that the imprint of human endeavor and occupation is very faint. Walking around the site of this historically important region reveals no clues to its feverish activity during the 1850s and 1860s. Only the disintegrating walls of Trabucco's emporium and mine tailings offer a hint of its habitation. We find it difficult to imagine that this place was home to a sizable population, prosperous gold mine, mint, smelter, twelve-stamp mill, hotel, sawmill and dwellings.

Abraham Lincoln cautioned us: "A country with no regard for its past will have little worth remembering in the future." Perhaps you have stories from your grandmother, great uncle Fred, old snapshots, maps, letters, diaries, post-cards or newspaper clippings that would help fill in the gaps of history. What better way to keep history alive than to donate copies to local museums and history centers. Your contribution could be a priceless gift to future generations.

■ THE HIKE

Locating the site of Ophir and its mining-scarred mountain is easy. The hard part is finding anything once you're there. Don't expect much more than the ruins of the store. Your best bet is to combine a visit with other villages between Coulterville and Mariposa.

About midway along the short loop called Mount Ophir Road, park near the E Clampus Vitus monument and the two remaining walls of Trabucco's store just off the road. Look behind the stone historical marker for an unofficial path. Follow it for 150 feet across a seasonal creek, then pass slate foundations and mounds of rock. You quickly connect with a dirt road leading up a gentle slope. The community of Ophir was on the narrow flat to the right. The low rise of mining-scarred Mount Ophir lies directly ahead. Moffat's Mint and vault were situated near its base in a slightly elevated clearing.

The path reaches the base of Mount Ophir around .4 mile. You can continue to the summit, about a 400-foot climb, although the path becomes more brushy. You'll see several five-foot-wide strips of cleared vegetation from the base to the top. The summit offers a good view of the area. Return the way you came or walk back on the other side of the flat on an old road that leads to the slate ruins of Trabucco's store.

Mount Ophir's 12-stamp mill as shot by Carleton Watkins for the Mariposa Grant series in 1860. The summit of Mount Ophir rises in the background.

7
Fremont Peak
A Scenic Hike to Nearly Forgotten Camp Jessie

■ THE DETAILS

Getting There: From Mariposa, drive 4 miles north on Highway 49. Turn right at the Mt. Bullion Youth Conservation Camp sign onto the paved road winding up the western slope of Mt. Bullion. Go 3.1 miles to a three-way split in the road. Bear left and park away from the gate. Note that the dirt road is closed to automobile traffic. Keep the access clear and the gate closed. On the hike you will pass two more gates; leave them as you find them.

Nearest Campgrounds: Yosemite-Mariposa KOA in Midpines has 90 sites 209-966-2201. Or try Jerseydale Campground, 10 primitive sites, 13.5 miles northeast of Mariposa in Sierra National Forest 209-966-2456.

Lodging: Mariposa has many choices.

Further Info: Chamber of Commerce 209-966-7081, Interagency Visitor Center, P.O.Box 747, Mariposa, CA 95338, 209-966-3638.

Hike Distance: 7 miles round trip.

Difficulty: Moderate.

Best Time to Go: Winter, early spring, late autumn.

Cautions: Keep gates closed. Do not park blocking gate. No dogs.

Starting Elevation: 3200 feet. Elevation gain to Fremont Peak: 1000 feet.

Other Map: USGS Bear Valley 7.5 minute topo.

For hikers with an interest in Gold Rush history, this little known peak in Mariposa County is sure to satisfy. Fremont Peak, a few miles north of Mariposa, provides a scenic trek through a handsome foothill landscape. At 4199 feet elevation, the peak is the highest point on a long, massive ridge known as Mount Bullion. Views of the San Joaquin Valley and Merced River canyon below and successive amphitheaters of mountains rising ever upward to the snowy crest of Yosemite's High Country are breathtaking. The prominences of Half Dome, El Capitan, Cloud's Rest, and 35-mile distant Mount Clark (11,522 feet) appear considerably closer from this unobstructed vantage point. Late winter and early spring are ideal months to explore this seldom visited area.

Little known even among locals, Fremont Peak was the site of Camp Jessie, the

Though the lush environment around Fremont Spring is gone, the Sierra view eastward that captivated Jessie Fremont and inspired her to headquarter her household here in the blistering summer of 1859 remains the same.

summer encampment of prominent citizens John and Jessie Fremont during the two years they lived full-time in Bear Valley. Indeed, this could be called "Fremont country." In Mariposa County, John C. Fremont is almost a household word. Few who live here are unaware of his fabulous Las Mariposas (The Butterflies) land grant, his influence on California's history, or his role in opening the West to settlement. Driving through Mariposa town and environs reveals reminders of his formidable presence during the 1850s and 1860s. Buildings, streets, a town, mine, and natural formations bear his name or those of his in-laws.

The vast Mexican rancho did not come into Fremont's hands because of shrewd business acumen; it is no secret that a strong business sense was never one of John Fremont's aptitudes. Fremont was at his best in the wilderness. Outside of that arena, "The Pathfinder" invariably ran into difficulty. In 1847 he entrusted his agent, U.S. Consul Thomas Larkin, with $3000 to buy a large parcel of land southeast of San Francisco. Larkin, instead, inexplicably purchased nearly 45,000 acres from ex-Governor Juan Alvarado in what is now Mariposa County.

Fremont was livid to learn that he owned an enormous tract of worthless, dry land in the middle of nowhere. His wrath quickly evaporated, however, when 13 months later he heard of the January 1848 gold discovery. Immediately Colonel Fremont became hopeful, then confident, that his "worthless" estate in the Sierra foothills would prove to be El Dorado. He hired 28 Mexican miners to prospect and work his land on a share basis. Within a few months it was obvious that Las Mariposas was incredibly rich with gold-bearing rock.

Rancho Las Mariposas, a 70-square-mile chunk of real estate, was a "floating grant" with no clearly defined boundaries. The grant included mountains, foothills, and flat grazing or farm lands. About 25 square miles of this immense empire were within the Mother Lode. Fremont took advantage of the vague property lines when he heard that gold had been discovered in the nearby settlement of Logtown (Mariposa) in 1848, and he simply floated or shifted his boundaries to include the area. When it was to his advantage, Colonel Fremont continued to float his rancho's boundaries far from the original claim to include other gold-bearing properties. Ultimately his gerrymandering led to great public hostility, serious disputes, and expensive litigation.

After California became a state in 1850, Mariposa County occupied 30,000 square miles or one-fifth of the total land area. Mariposa, the new county seat, and the numerous settlements and mines surrounding it, prospered. However, Fremont, most often an absentee landlord, did not. He spent much of his time in the East pursuing several disastrous business schemes and running for president in 1856. While he was away, the majority of profits were lost to mismanagement, employee theft, squatters, expansion projects, astronomical legal fees and court costs.

Defeated for the presidency by James Buchanan, Fremont decided to settle down and move to Las Mariposas to manage and develop the mines personally. In 1858 Fremont and his family moved to the rancho's headquarters at Bear Valley. In spite of his full-time attention to Las Mariposas, its fabulous wealth continued to slip through his fingers. A portion of his estate was deeded to an associate to repay a debt. Fremont's lack of business judgment, ignorance of sound mining practices, and financial irresponsibility resulted in a $2,500,000 indebtedness.

By January 1863, he had no choice but to sell his estate to a New York banker. Fremont received $1,500,000 in cash and the balance in Las Mariposas stock. Soon after, the estate was purchased by a Wall Street consortium that became insolvent after a few years of mismanagement and stock manipulation. By then Fremont had squandered all of the cash payment through high-living and failed, scandalous railroad ventures. With the dissolution of the Wall Street corporation in 1870, his $5 million in stock was worthless, and he was bankrupt. Living in genteel poverty for 20 years, only Jessie's skill at writing books and articles kept them afloat. John died penniless in New York City in 1890. Jessie moved to Los Angeles and died there in 1902.

To wander in the Sierra footsteps of the Fremonts, begin in the wee village of Mount Bullion. Both the town and the mountain were named in honor of Senator Thomas Benton, Fremont's father-in-law, whose nickname was Old Bullion. Looming over the town is the hulking mass of Mount Bullion where the Fremonts camped during the blistering summer months of 1859. Except for the location of Fremont Spring noted on a topo map, absolutely nothing remains of idyllic Camp Jessie. The pool, once a lovely miniature lake, is now used to water cattle.

Camp Jessie was originally found quite by accident. While horseback riding

Jessie Benton Fremont (1824-1902) as painted in 1856. Called the Abigail Adams of the American West, Jessie became the first presidential candidate's wife to assume an active role in a political campaign.

along the crest one torrid day with a household employee-bodyguard, Jessie looked to the west and down upon the shimmering heat waves in the narrow valley where they lived. But on the east side, just below the ridgetop, she noticed a "green and cool-looking ledge of rocks and large-leafed oaks." Attracted by its coolness, they dismounted to explore this shaded oasis. About 50 yards downslope from the ledge in a cluster of oaks, they "shouted for joy" at the discovery of a fine spring which emptied into a large pool. Inevitably, it became known as Fremont Spring.

That summer was so hot that Jessie wrote of having to make leather shoes for the dogs to keep their paws from burning, and that eggs buried in the dust would cook in 18 minutes. When the temperature at sunset was still 104 degrees at their Bear Valley cottage, they grew desperate, and she decided to move the entire family up to Fremont Spring. Within 48 hours two of Fremont's men constructed a huge tent with a planked floor in the dense shade of an oak grove. It was open on three sides and furnished with a writing desk, work boxes and mattresses filled with oak leaves and fragrant bear clover.

According to Jessie's writings, the sun's rays never reached camp until 6 p.m., upslope breezes were always refreshingly cool, and the views of Yosemite's cliffs and chasms were awesome. Smaller, roofless, and floorless canvas enclosures made dressing rooms, and bathing was possible in India rubber bathtubs. Walking, horseback riding, and reading were their favorite entertainments. Fremont arose at 5 a.m. to go to his work at nearby Josephine and Pine Tree Mines, returning in time for the evening meal.

The days at Camp Jessie, in spite of turbulent events, were a particularly contented and happy time in their life, but it was short-lived. In August friendly Indians warned that warriors from a neighboring tribe would be passing through and could cause trouble. The Fremonts broke camp and returned to Bear Valley's punishing heat. By mid-1860 the hot weather had so seriously affected Jessie's health that Fremont sent her and the children to San Francisco. The Las Mariposas chapter of their story drew to a close, although Fremont commuted back and forth to Bear Valley until the outbreak of the Civil War in 1861. John accepted a commission as Major General in command of the West, and the family joined him at headquarters in St. Louis, Missouri.

■ THE HIKE

The 3.5-mile hike to Fremont Peak and the almost forgotten site of Camp Jessie offers a highly scenic cameo of a historically significant period in California's early years. The peaceful and spectacular vistas offer superb sensory appeal, but perhaps the most rewarding aspect of the journey is the sense of connection it provides with our rich heritage. A few "No Trespassing" signs are posted in the area, primarily aimed at game poachers and illegal wood cutters, but the owner has no objection to responsible hikers armed only with daypack and camera.

The hike to Fremont Peak begins at the gate at the three-way split in the road.

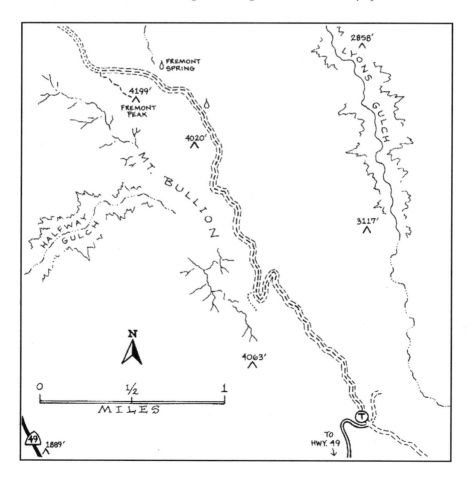

From the gate walk up the road 2.5 miles to find a cattle corral on your right. Several cow paths there descend 300 feet to a pond fed by Fremont Spring. Although the lush environment is gone, the view eastward that mesmerized Jessie Fremont remains the same. Pause here for awhile to absorb the magnificent scenery spreading before you. From the Merced River Canyon 2800 feet below to the Sierra Crest on the horizon, the panorama is spectacular. On especially clear days, you can see Carson Peak in Alpine County.

To reach Fremont Peak, continue walking up the road .25 mile to a fork, bear left and ascend the road .5 mile to the summit. This highest point on Mount Bullion is home to a clutch of communication towers. You get to decide which portion of the 360-degree view you want to take in while on your lunch break. West lies the narrow valley hemming in the hamlets of Mount Bullion and Bear Valley, the San Joaquin plains, and the Coast Range in the far view. To the east lie innumerable waves of foothills and mountains marching skyward. These quiet and stunning views are described in Jessie Fremont's words, "Nature could not be more beautiful. It was all peaceful and beautiful beyond telling. It was God's own free gift."

Besides the little known history surrounding it, Fremont Peak is a dramatically beautiful and infrequently visited area. Between January and the end of April it is at its best, with an eternity of mountains culminating at the snow-capped crest of the Sierra Nevada, wildflower-strewn slopes, and forever views in every direction—a worthy destination several times a year.

8
Big Table Mountain Preserve
Guided Hikes to a Remnant of Prehistoric California

A fragment of a primeval and once extensive landscape in California can be found less than an hour's drive south from Oakhurst or northeast from Fresno. Looking east from Highway 41, a disconnected series of long, table-topped mountains grab one's attention in this lowland setting of the Sierra Nevada. Not exactly typical mountains and certainly not foothills, their bold and blocky presence appears incongruous among softly rolling hills. More reminiscent of mesa formations in the desert southwest, they seem curiously out of place in central California.

Rising above the terrain like a chain of islands, the vertical tops tower more than 1000 feet over pastoral rangelands. Their origins are ancient, dating back ten million years when lava flowed sinuously through the original San Joaquin River channel. Subtropically vegetated hills that once lined the banks of the oxbow stream eroded away and formed rocky, flat-topped buttes. In the far-distant past, enormous rifts appeared, leaving the broken links of a former uninterrupted mass of lava. Nearby is the present-day San Joaquin River. Similar archipelagoes of volcanic plateaus can be seen near Sonora and Oroville.

Representing much more than unusual visual appeal in an otherwise unremarkable, low elevation landscape, the mesas are home to a highly distinctive biological community, including rare, threatened, or endangered species. Vernal (springtime) pools here host many plant species found nowhere else in California or, in some cases, the world. In the aquatic or wet phase, vernal pools also harbor a diverse and unique animal population, such as fairy and tadpole shrimp and the California tiger salamander.

Explorers intrigued by offbeat excursions will want to add Big Table Mountain Preserve to their list. Led by knowledgeable guides, field trip participants have an opportunity to leisurely investigate an extraordinary ecological niche. Besides providing a pleasurable walk in an unspoiled environment far from the madding crowd, the plateau appeals to a variety of interests in the natural world. Wildflowers, both rare and plentiful, and the uncommon beauty of vernal pools in a seldom-seen environment are among the treasures of this pristine habitat.

By definition, vernal pools are created when rainwater collects in shallow depressions underlaid by impenetrable soils (clay, hardpan or bedrock). Winter and early spring rainfall accumulate and produce a pool of standing water that lasts for several weeks to months, until it evaporates as summer approaches. The pools vary greatly in size and depth, ranging from muddy puddles covering a few square feet to lakelets several acres in size. Although their greatest numbers are found in grassland settings within the state's Central Valley, they are present in other regions of California, including sagebrush scrub, mixed forest, and chaparral environments.

Whether recognized or not by name or for their singular plant and animal colonists, vernal pools have long delighted hikers during spring. A profusion of wildflowers outlining a pool boundary in concentric rings of glorious color is, indeed, a visual feast. The stunning floral display changes as the season progresses. Different species bloom and fade as the weather warms and the water level shrinks.

What doesn't meet the eye is the extraordinary specialization peculiar to species living in and around vernal pools. All of its inhabitants, in order to survive, must be ingeniously adapted to long periods of both flooding and desiccation. Some thrive in the aquatic phase and endure the arid; others hang on through the wet months but flourish when the temperature rises and the ground dries out. Vernal pool tenants must also be able to make critical adjustments for annual variations in air temperatures and the amount and distribution of rainfall.

Vernal pools are known by a variety of names: hog wallows, prairie potholes, vernal lakes, holes in the grass, springtime pools, pasture puddles, winter pools and vernal ponds. No matter how they are described, late summer finds them bone dry, and the flowers have set seed and dried back. Creatures, such as the inch-long shrimp, which have laid their eggs during the wet stage, die en masse as the pool evaporates. The minuscule eggs fall into cracks or nestle among the dried grasses that rim the vanished pool. Both dormant seeds and eggs must abide heat, drought, and frost until the rains come again, be it next season or five years later, to begin anew the cycle of life.

Vernal pools and their hardy, amazingly resourceful residents are in great peril

Ten million years ago a volcano erupted upstream on the ancestral San Joaquin River. Lava flowed downstream and solidified. Later uplift and erosion exposed these granitic rocks at the surface. What was once an old stream bed is now a mountain top, a classic example of inverted topography.

of extinction. Not surprisingly, humankind is their greatest threat. Scientists estimate that more than 90 percent of them have been destroyed when land was plowed or leveled for agricultural development and drainage patterns were altered. Additionally, urban sprawl continues to encroach upon these extremely fragile environments as real estate developers and road builders push city limits into the countryside. Unfortunately, much of the remaining vernal pool habitat in California is also choice development land.

Once the pools have been manipulated or eradicated, they are incapable of regeneration or relocation and are gone forever. If we are to save the remaining two to five percent and their place-sensitive denizens, we must surround them with permanent legal protection. Since 1980, various agencies and environmental organizations, such as the Department of Fish and Game and the Sierra Foothill Conservancy, have recognized the threats to vernal pools and their adjacent grasslands. Concerted and ongoing programs to acquire pool habitat and to educate the general public as to their rarity and imperiled status are major elements in the effort to ensure their survival.

One of the most dramatic and extraordinary locations in California to witness the springtime grandeur of vernal pools is atop McKenzie Big Table Mountain, about 35 miles northeast of Fresno in the Lake Millerton hinterlands. Big Table Mountain Preserve was willed to the Nature Conservancy by the late Ruth McKenzie. A long-time rancher in the area, Ruth had the vision to realize that the incomparable features of her land had to be preserved rather than developed. The property included 2300 acres of oak woodland, grassland and basaltic table formation. Later, another 700 acres of contiguous land were acquired and added to the Preserve.

Each spring the Sierra Foothill Conservancy sponsors popular field trips to this ancient volcanic setting overlooking the San Joaquin River with vistas into the High Sierra. Experienced naturalists lead unhurried walks across the flat, mile-long plateau, exploring and discussing the rich biological and geological features that make these pristine table-topped preserves so special.

More than a century ago, John Muir called attention to human ruination of the natural environment in the pursuit of profit. On the cutting edge of the new conservation movement, he observed, "We must live together with the rest of nature, or we will die together with the rest of nature." Prophetically, Muir knew a time would surely come when it would be even more difficult to protect the environment than it was then. He ardently believed that wild places and wild things should be protected simply because they exist. He was also perceptive enough to know that wild beauty is never safe, that it needs as vigilant stewardship today and tomorrow as it did yesterday.

Join one of the guided walks to Big Table Mountain Preserve and see for yourself the striking beauty and ecological significance of this priceless and irreplaceable piece of our California heritage. You CANNOT visit the Preserve on your own. For specific information about hikes and classes, write Sierra Foothill Conservancy, Box 529, Prather, CA 93651, or call 559-855-3473.

II

Waving Seas of Evergreens
🐻 WESTERN SLOPE 🐻
TRAILS NORTH, WEST & SOUTH OF YOSEMITE

H ERE WE SAMPLE the highlights of vast portions of three national forests, Stanislaus, Toiyabe and Sierra. Tree-covered mountain terrain defines this beautiful and varied landscape, featuring some of the most diverse conifer forests in the world. Except near the rugged Sierra Crest, this is largely a gentle and rolling landscape, but one cut by the deep canyons of seven rivers and many high glacier-carved ridges. The area is so immense and convoluted that one could spend a lifetime exploring it.

Historically the area provided its native peoples an abundance of game and the natural fruits of the land. The several tribes that called the western slope of the Central Sierra home generally lived in peace, visiting and trading regularly with their neighbors both near and far. When the first trickle of Euro-American settlers came overland to California, they needed to find routes to get their wagons and stock over this rugged Sierra landscape. Fortunately early explorers had established several such routes, many of which followed essentially the same courses as do today's highways. With the discovery of gold in 1848, the trickle of immigrants quickly grew to flood proportions, changing the face of California.

Over the next 60 years the wilderness nature of the western slope gradually gave way to pockets of commerce. Of course early mines and gold camps extended into this region, but it was the growth of lumbering and its supporting network of logging railways that really changed the nature of the western slope. Still vast forests remained intact in many of the more remote corners of the region.

After the dawn of the 20th century, the federal government created the national forests to administer the vast mountain lands. Recreation soon began drawing greatly increasing numbers of visitors as California residents began to discover the joys of camping, hiking, riding and fishing in the Sierra Nevada. Of course John Muir and the Sierra Club he founded had a big part in popularizing the recreational uses of the range. Still it wasn't until 1964 that vast portions of the Sierra Nevada in general and its western slope in particular began to be set aside in their natural state as wilderness areas. Today the western slope of the Central Sierra includes seven wilderness areas that preserve its pristine untrammeled nature. From north to south they are the Mokelumne, Carson-Iceberg, Emigrant,

Ansel Adams, Kaiser, Dinkey Lakes and John Muir wilderness areas, which together protect 1.25 million acres.

This section has 15 chapters exploring the western slope. The first of these takes our explorations to their northern limit, exploring Highway 4 over Ebbetts Pass and Highway 88 over Carson Pass where you can explore mining areas, pioneer routes and Grover Hot Springs State Park as well as take a short hike on the Pacific Crest Trail.

The next eight chapters investigate the area directly west of Yosemite National Park, leading you to lightly traveled trails in the middle elevations on the way to the Park or a short drive from it. They lead you to great swimming holes, a historic cave, one of John Muir's least visited spiritual places, a rich mining area in a river canyon that still has one of the state's great spring wildflower pageants, two historic railroad lines you can walk, the story of a battle to save one of California's few remaining wild rivers, and the story of how Yosemite Valley's twin was flooded to provide water for San Francisco, and more.

The final six chapters in this section explore the gorgeous region just south of the Park. There you'll find an excursion train with roots in one of central California's most innovative timber companies, a lightly visited Sequoia grove where you can camp, two streamside trails exploring waterfalls and history, a trek to gorgeous lakes in the Ansel Adams Wilderness, and a hot springs resort surrounded by wilderness and more great hiking.

9
Exploring Alpine County
Hiking the Pacific Crest Trail to Noble Lake

■ THE DETAILS

Getting There: Drive Highway 4 east to Ebbetts Pass, 14 miles beyond Lake Alpine, and park in the turnout on the right (south) side of the highway. Find the Pacific Crest Trail sign on the right side of the road just east of the summit.

Nearest Campgrounds: Hermit Valley Campground 5 miles west of Ebbetts Pass has 6 sites with no piped water, while Silver Creek Campground 6 miles east has 22 sites with piped water, both open June to October. Grover Hot Springs State Park near Markleeville has year-round camping.

Lodging: Markleeville and nearby Woodfords have several choices. Or try delightful Sorenson's Resort on Highway 88 in Hope Valley 12 miles northwest of Markleeville.

Further Info: Alpine County Chamber of Commerce, Box 265, Markleeville, CA 96120, 530-694-2475, Toiyabe National Forest's Carson Ranger District 775-882-2766.

Hike Distance: 8 miles round trip.

Difficulty: Moderate.

Best Time to Go: July through October.

Cautions: None.

Starting Elevation: 8700 feet. Elevation gain to Noble Lake: 1500 feet.

Other Maps: USGS Ebbetts Pass 7.5 minute topo, Wilderness Press **Carson-Iceberg Wilderness** Map.

A leisurely ramble through tiny Alpine County is sure to satisfy. Ebbetts Pass Corridor, encompassing the area along Highway 4 between Murphys and Markleeville, provides your ticket to this stunning and uncrowded region. If you crave flaming fall foliage, a bounty of autumn drama awaits in this tranquil corner of the Sierra nudging the Nevada border. Few places in California surpass its mountain grandeur and glorious autumn finale. Highly scenic and lightly-used byways over Ebbetts, Carson, Monitor and Luther passes offer memorable excursions that appeal to a broad spectrum of interests.

Sightseers, nature enthusiasts, history buffs, sportsmen and adventurers can choose from a multitude of activities within 800 square miles of territory known as the California Alps. Scores of hiking trailheads, 60 lakes, headwaters of three major rivers, 30 campgrounds, two downhill/cross-country ski centers, a variety of trails and terrain for cyclists, and Grover Hot Springs State Park are on Alpine County's year-round recreational menu. Quiet resorts and inns and quaint villages offer unpretentious accommodations for motorists. Exploring some of the numerous historical sites will lend a sense of discovery to your journey, perhaps through stands of aspen and cottonwood aglow with autumn's fiery spectacle.

Named for its similarity to Europe's alpine country, Alpine County was established in 1864 as a result of a silver bonanza. The glittering success of Nevada's fabulous Comstock Lode lured miners east over the Sierra to Carson Valley and other promising silver ledges nearby. Bisected by the Sierra Crest, Alpine was created from parts of Mono, El Dorado, Amador, Tuolumne and Calaveras counties. Alpine is California's least populated county. The 1990 census found fewer than 1200 people residing within its borders, and the county seat of Markleeville has only 100 inhabitants. More than 95 percent of Alpine County is public land, almost all of it within Stanislaus, El Dorado and Toiyabe national forests and Carson-Iceberg and Mokelumne wilderness areas. Every primary road is designated a scenic highway.

Ironically, Ebbetts Pass was named for a man who never set foot on it. In 1852 John Ebbetts led a surveying party of 17 men in search of a trans-Sierra passage for the Atlantic-Pacific Railroad. From a peak about 11 miles distant, Ebbetts pointed to the pass he had "discovered" in 1850 as the best place for a railroad alignment. Despite considerable interest in building a transcontinental railroad at the time, plans for the Atlantic-Pacific never left the drawing board. Curiously, the pass Ebbetts proposed for the railroad is not the one that bears his name. In 1955 the California Historical Society published a carefully researched article by Stewart Mitchell who had analyzed Ebbetts' expedition diary. Based on the recorded data and topographical descriptions, Mitchell concluded that Ebbetts actually "discovered" Border Ruffian Pass.

The Washo people, centered around Lake Tahoe, inhabited Alpine County prior to the Gold Rush. They lived in permanent communities near present day Woodfords and Markleeville and other valleys. By the late 1840s, huge numbers of pioneers were on the move, leaving their homes east of the Mississippi for California. The California or Overland Emigrant Trail was in fact several different routes across the Sierra Nevada. The emigrant trail through Ebbetts Pass to Angels Camp opened in the 1850s, but no actual road was completed until 1864. At that time, great activity in Nevada's Comstock Lode prompted construction of a toll route known as Big Tree-Carson Valley Turnpike.

Forerunner of Highway 4, the Big Tree route was traversed by thousands of emigrants and provided a shortcut to the southern mines around Murphys, Angels Camp, Columbia and Sonora. Because the route offered the most direct approach to the river port of Stockton, pack trains and freight wagons hauling supplies to the Virginia City mines used it heavily.

Undoubtedly, the most exotic feet to tread Ebbetts Pass belonged to Bactrian (two-humped) camels from Mongolia. In 1861 O.H. Frank of Virginia City bought nine camels to transport freight across the desert and to carry salt from the Walker River salt marshes to the mines for use in processing silver ore. Journeying with the herd from San Francisco, artist Edward Vischer sketched the strange procession along the way. His most famous one depicted them passing through the Calaveras Grove of Big Trees. Before a law prohibited them from public highways in Nevada in 1875, camel trains periodically traveled over Ebbetts Pass.

En route to Ebbetts Pass hinterlands, you might wander the streets of Murphys, one of the most picturesque survivors of the Gold Rush, and visit Calaveras Big Trees State Park, both described in Chapter One. Above the Big Trees, Highway 4 climbs past Dorrington, Camp

Detail from Edward Vischer's 1861 sketch of the Bactrian camels in Calaveras Grove. They were imported from Mongolia to carry freight in the desert.

Connell, and Cottage Springs to Bear Valley just across Alpine County line. Once the site of the main toll station for Big Tree-Carson Valley Turnpike, today this village provides lodging for summer and winter recreationists plus various restaurants and seasonal activities.

Beyond Bear Valley, note a turn-off to Mount Reba Ski area, completed in 1967. Highway 4 gets plowed as far as Mount Reba Ski Bowl during winter. Serene Lake Alpine, elevation 7400 feet, was created when PG&E dammed Silver Creek, a tributary of the Stanislaus River. Boat rentals, rustic cabins, a small store and a good restaurant with lake views invite lingering. The old Emigrant Road passing through Silver Creek Valley is now beneath the lake.

State Route 4 east of Lake Alpine becomes a slender, sinuous ribbon through enchanting scenery as it meanders up and over Ebbetts Pass. A sign cautions, "VEHICLES OVER 25 FEET NOT ADVISED." Between Lake Alpine west of the Sierra Crest and Silver Creek on the east, the road is too narrow for a center dividing line.

At Pacific Summit, elevation 8050 feet, two artificial lakes present a lovely Kodak moment. Across from Mosquito Lakes and to the left of the highway you can see a small segment of old Emigrant Road. Pull off the road and look for an obvious cut through the pines. A short walk on this ancient dirt track leads to its end at a stunning vista, giving you a feel for the rigors early travelers had to deal with.

Highway 4 dips through Hermit Valley, crosses the North Fork Mokelumne River, then climbs to Ebbetts Pass, elevation 8730 feet, where you cross the Pacific Crest Trail, site of this chapter's hike to Noble Lake. The descent east of the pass follows Cascade and Silver Creeks to the East Fork Carson River near Markleeville. Across the canyon to the northwest, look for the remains of formidable switchbacks old-timers call "Double S" grade, where several fatalities occurred. It was a hazardous part of the Big Tree-Carson Valley Turnpike until the road was brought into the state highway system in 1911 and the present grade was established.

Highway 4 passes the site of Silver Mountain City, originally called Konisberg by Scandinavian miners who founded it in 1858. Between 1860 and 1880 Silver Mountain City was a prosperous town, population 3500 at its peak. The only remnants of the bustling settlement are a few stone blocks from the walls of the jail and the smelter's forlorn brick chimney.

The success of mining in Alpine County was insignificant compared to the fabulous Comstock Lode, primarily because of the difficulty and expense in recovering the silver. Although Alpine's ore was comparable to the assays of Comstock ore, it was said, "it required a gold mine to operate a silver mine."

Not far from Silver Mountain, the remains of the Exchequer Quartz Mill adjacent to the Chalmers Mansion comes into view. Lord Lewis Chalmers arrived in Alpine County in 1867 to manage and develop mining properties in the Silver Mountain District for London investors. Chalmers entertained lavishly in his beautifully appointed home on Silver Creek. London investors poured vast sums of money into the county, but the big bonanza never happened. Chalmers returned to England in 1885 to rally more funds, but while there he died suddenly.

A major blow to silver mining came with the demonetization of silver in 1873. The silver dollar was removed from the official coinage and replaced by the gold standard, virtually shutting down all mining activity in the area and making Silver Mountain City a ghost town. With the rapid decline of mining, Alpine County's population plummeted to about 10 percent of its earlier numbers. In 1875 Markleeville succeeded Silver Mountain as the county seat.

Sleepy, laidback Markleeville and nearby Grover Hot Springs State Park can serve as your turn-around point, but if you're interested in seeing new country, loop back on Highway 88. Jacob Marklee founded the town in 1861 but was killed in a shoot-out two years later over a land dispute. On the site of his cabin stands Alpine County's handsome courthouse, built in 1928 of native stone. A disastrous fire in 1886 destroyed many of the original 168 structures which were not replaced after the Silver Rush ended. It's a friendly, quiet village to stroll through, and the Alpine County Historical Complex merits a visit. Perched on a knoll, the Complex overlooks the town and beautiful surrounding meadows and peaks.

No excursion through Alpine County would be complete without a visit to Grover Hot Springs State Park, about four miles west of Markleeville. Although used by the Washo for centuries, John C. Fremont was the first Euro-American to discover the springs in 1844 on his second military expedition. Ten years later, rancher John Hawkins took squatter's rights to the spring and meadows. In 1878 he sold to the Grover family who built a hotel in Markleeville, and the hot springs became a resort. The property changed hands twice in the 1900s, and in 1959 the state finally bought it for $12,000 for a state park. Besides the hot pool, the complex has a full-sized cold pool, hiking trails and an all-year campground.

The nooks and crannies of Alpine County can take years to fully explore, but it's small enough to sample during a weekend. Enhancing its spectacular natural features and stunning fall foliage is the absence of crowds. Ebbetts Pass via Highway 4 is the least publicized Sierra crossing, perhaps because the road is so narrow and curvy, especially east of Lake Alpine. On the plus side, a slower pace allows you to savor the scenery.

■ THE HIKE

Barely outside the Carson-Iceberg Wilderness, the hike to Noble Lake offers a fine way to sample this rugged subalpine country. Besides forests and meadows, the region harbors a striking potpourri of volcanic and granitic features. At .3 mile your trail meets a trail on your left. Stay to the right here, following the Pacific Crest Trail east. If you prefer a shorter hike than the trek to Noble Lake, stop somewhere between 2 and 2.5 miles along a spectacular series of wildflower gardens. In season, these wild beauties thrive in ancient mudflow gullies. The last garden marks the hike's low point at 8300 feet.

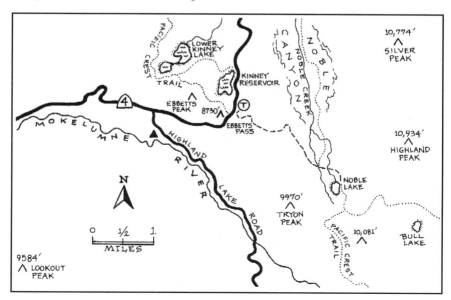

Beyond the flowery gullies the roller coaster trail continues, offering great views of the peaks north of Ebbetts Pass. Volcanic boulders, called lahar, lie scattered everywhere in a landscape deeply forested in some places, wide open in others. After negotiating the unrelenting zigzags above Noble Creek, you're once again rewarded with splendid vistas.

From the rounded hilltop, take the turnoff trail to your right to reach petite, flower-blessed Noble Lake. Hikers accustomed to Sierra granite might find the volcanic scenery somewhat bleak and forbidding. Nevertheless, it has a unique beauty that becomes less surreal with familiarity. Little Noble Lake adds a soft touch to this stern environment. Retrace your steps to the trailhead.

10
The Clavey River & God's Bath
A River Wild

We must save the heart of the Sierra while we may . . . Solitude, that greatest healer of the soul of man, is his great necessity. He will, he must, have the place where it may be found, and that place is the Sierra.

~Henry Saylor, 1920

■ THE DETAILS

Getting There: From Sonora, drive Highway 108 east about 3 miles and turn right onto Tuolumne Road. Go 7 miles to Tuolumne City and turn left toward River Ranch onto Carter Street. At .3 miles turn right onto Buchanan Mine Road, then immediately bear left toward the Clavey and Cherry Lake on Forest Service Road 1N04, Cottonwood Road. Drive 14 curvy miles to Cottonwood bridge spanning the Clavey and park on the east side.

Nearest Campground: River Ranch Campground 209-928-3708, a private facility, has 55 sites with showers on the North Fork Tuolumne River 6 miles east of Tuolumne City.

Lodging: None in Tuolumne. Sonora has several choices.

Further Info: District Office, Stanislaus National Forest, 19777 Greenley Road, Sonora, CA 95370, 209-532-3671.

Hike Distance: One mile round trip.

Difficulty: Easy.

Best Time to Go: Early summer.

Warnings: Beware of poison oak and rattlesnakes as you scramble over rocks to these beautiful swimming and fishing holes.

Starting Elevation: 2400 feet.

Maps: USGS Hull Creek 7.5 minute or Tuolumne 15 minute topo, Stanislaus National Forest map.

The Clavey still runs wild and free, precisely what a resolute group of advocates in the Central Sierra has fought for. The Clavey River Preservation Coalition, based in Groveland, engaged in a battle royal with the Turlock Irrigation District for ten long years to save the river from a massive hydroelectric project. It's a battle worth fighting since the Clavey belongs to an elite fraternity of free-flowing rivers. In the entire Sierra Nevada, only the Clavey, Cosumnes, Middle Fork Cosumnes and South Fork Merced remain undammed.

Unlike the American or Yuba Rivers, the Clavey is a low profile stream, and the reason for its anonymity is simple. Its remote location makes it not an easy river to befriend. No highways cross or parallel it, and it's so far off the beaten path that only three Forest Service roads, two of them primitive dirt tracks, lead to it. Even hiking access is relatively difficult. Except for a handful of world class whitewater aficionados, a smattering of ardent fishermen, serious bushwhacking, boulder-hopping hikers, and collectors of obscure backcountry destinations, few Californians know it exists.

The Clavey's headwaters lie in the Emigrant Wilderness north of Yosemite Park. Starting unceremoniously as a mere trickle from snow melt and underground springs, it flows through Stanislaus National Forest, and as it picks up volume and power from many wild feeder streams, it begins to resemble a river. It slides over slick granite and sprints through meadows and forests, including 8000 acres of California's last stands of old growth forests.

Farther downstream, on its 7000-foot, 47-mile descent to its confluence with the Tuolumne River, the Clavey plunges into a slender, V-shaped gorge that defines the remainder of its hell-bent journey. Ten million years in the making, the lower canyon is utterly primeval, a paradise of extraordinary beauty. Unbelievably, the scene becomes even more rugged as the Clavey careens through the heart of this awesome, boulder-choked abyss.

The Clavey is a feisty, banty rooster river of intense whitewater with foaming chutes, spitfire rapids and hissing, writhing swirls—"wahoo" water in kayaker jargon. Finally, the river's wild energy reaches a crescendo as it hurtles over Clavey Falls and sacrifices its identity to the Tuolumne River. Clavey Falls isn't famous for a huge drop, but the tremendous force and volume of the colliding rivers create a dangerous, technically tricky Class V rapid during spring runoff.

Its free-flowing state provides reason enough to spare the Clavey from being humbled by dams, reservoirs and tunnels. However, the extensive watershed represents much more than a vanishing breed of virgin California stream. The Clavey's basin provides a rich habitat for thousands of widely diverse forest and riparian creatures and plants. Bald and golden eagles, pine martens, spotted owls, fishers, peregrine falcons, wolverines, red foxes and other wildlife inhabit the forests and fields along the Clavey's banks. Fifteen species on the federal endangered list abide within these grand old growth forests and the largest stands of aspen in the Central Sierra.

The Clavey offers a winter haven for a populous Yosemite deer herd, as well as a crucial wildlife corridor between high and low elevations for many other species. Designated one of California's few Wild Trout Streams in 1968, the Clavey travels through six of seven Sierra ecological zones, all but true alpine. It has important sites of historic and cultural significance to the Tuolumne Miwok people.

This same obscure, unspoiled ecosystem also lured hydroelectric power developers whose vision of its value stemmed from a far different perspective. For decades the rivermeisters of Turlock and Modesto Irrigation Districts and the City and County of San Francisco viewed its unharnessed waters as wasted energy and potential profit. When Turlock Irrigation District (TID) among others sought to dam the Tuolumne River in the early 1980s, their billion dollar project was scrapped when Congress designated parts of the Tuolumne wild and scenic in 1984.

Although this was a stunning victory for battle-scarred Tuolumne River Preservation Trust and other groups, a compromise exempted the Clavey and its tributaries from federal protection. Almost immediately, TID formed a partnership with Tuolumne County and began planning a hydroelectric facility on the Clavey, the Tuolumne's major tributary. Modesto and San Francisco passed on developing the Clavey, citing "serious concerns about its economic feasibility." Since 1986, TID and Tuolumne County alone have tried to plumb and plug the Clavey.

A decade-long water fight ensued when TID unveiled its $707 million Clavey River Project to generate electricity for homes, businesses and farms in the San Joaquin Valley. TID's complex plans included five dams, many miles of tunnels and transmission lines, underground powerhouse, tributary diversion pipelines plus access and construction roads. The 2.8-mile-long primary reservoir created by a 423-foot-high dam (tenth tallest in the state) would have flooded 655 acres of old growth forest and meadows 20 miles above the Clavey's confluence with the Tuolumne. A 105-foot-high dam at the bottom of the system would've drowned another 180 acres, with three smaller dams on significant tributaries. In total, 19 miles of the Clavey would've been dewatered by nearly 90 percent, and another three miles would've been underwater. After applying for a license to build in 1986, TID spent nearly $9 million on project development.

The impending ecological catastrophe appalled river preservationists, but other realities further outraged the public. Namely, the captured water would benefit customers out of the county of origin mainly to run air conditioners during the blistering summer in towns like Ceres and Turlock. The project was never intended to provide drinking or irrigation water or prevent floods. Tuolumne County wouldn't get one drop of water from the plan. Instead, they'd get some revenue from surplus power sales, if any, to develop and/or improve their own inadequate water system.

The California Energy Commission and other impartial economists and energy analysts concluded that TID's hydro facility "was not economically feasible and would never pay for itself." Nevertheless, the utility district staunchly maintained that it was necessary to gain independence from PG&E and other power companies, and that the Clavey Project was the least expensive way to supply electricity to its customers.

TID hoped to ensure public support and tranquilize Sierra watchdogs by cloaking its proposal in ecologically benign terms, emphasizing that hydroelectricity is a "cheap, clean, nonpolluting, renewable energy resource." However, they budgeted $60 million for 355 measures to "mitigate environmental damage" and buy 1000 acres elsewhere for habitat preservation.

Realizing that a mitigated disaster is still a disaster and that no amount of money spent on cosmetically patching up Mother Nature would ever justify the project's catastrophic consequences on a healthy, intact ecosystem, a huge groundswell of opposition emerged to protest damming the Clavey. Saving substitute habitat elsewhere was an unacceptable trade-off for damming a rare, free-flowing river and the loss of an unsullied wilderness and all its life forms.

An amazing array of organizations, businesses, citizens and environmental groups stepped up to the plate, mounting a long campaign against the powerful resources of TID, the Forest Service and others favoring Clavey development. To save the unspoiled Clavey ecosystem, broad community support was essential.

In 1986 fourth generation rancher Wally Anker pulled everyone together and mobilized one of the Sierra's most diverse and effective grassroots organizations, the Clavey River Preservation Coalition. With unflagging dedication for nearly ten years, the Coalition spread the word in every conceivable fashion, educating and recruiting allies throughout Tuolumne and Stanislaus counties. Anker related, "The key was to take anyone we could on a walk up the river. Once they saw it, they could easily understand the issues." Through the efforts of committed volunteers, the Clavey's plight elevated from a local issue to a statewide and national audience and grabbed the attention of lawmakers making decisions about the Clavey's destiny.

As the campaign intensified, TID's defense of their five-dam proposal became difficult to understand in light of the many cost-effective alternatives and model energy programs in use by other California companies. Consultants advised that instituting conservation and energy efficient programs, all but non-existent in the district, would actually save as much electricity as Clavey hydropower could produce, lower rates and eliminate the need for the project.

In a surprise move, the Federal Energy Regulatory Commission (FERC) pulled the plug on the Clavey River dam project. On March 15, 1995 FERC, the agency in charge of reviewing and licensing large hydroprojects, finalized its recommendation against TID's controversial plan. The executive summary denied licensing because of "insufficient public benefits to justify the wide range of negative environmental consequences . . . even measures beyond those planned would not make the proposal acceptable." Despite strong development opposition by other state and federal resource agencies, FERC's decision was unexpected given their long history of approving both environmentally and financially questionable projects.

TID's venture is officially dead, but the final chapter on the Clavey's fate can only be written by an act of Congress. The next goal is to secure permanent protection under the federal Wild and Scenic Rivers Act. In the wake of TID's time-consuming and costly defeat, it seems unlikely that other proposals will imperil the Clavey because of heightened environmental awareness. However, without permanent protection, we have no guarantees that this virgin river basin will remain free of man's intrusion.

If nothing else, the fight to save the untouched, thriving Clavey River ecosystem teaches us that wild beauty is a fragile thing and never completely safe. The Clavey is a metaphor for all wilderness that is threatened by an out-of-sight, out-of-mind mentality and a dollar-sign land ethic. One hydropower advocate called it "just a win for tree-hugging, wacko environmentalists," but it was much more. Saving the Clavey represents a triumph for all of us. The victory is a symbol of what we can do and must do to protect our vanishing heritage.

Many readers will never experience this pristine landscape, but perhaps you can appreciate that a place has been saved for innumerable living things that can't survive anywhere else and for those humans who come in need of its gifts of spiritual renewal and solitude.

A wise person once said we need to be reminded that neither California nor the rest of America is rich enough to lose any more wilderness or poor enough to need to. As each one of us becomes a steward of the earth and fully embraces the fundamental truth that wild things and wild places should be preserved simply because they exist, there will be no more eco-battles.

■ THE HIKE

At Cottonwood Bridge, park on the east side. Walk cautiously down the steep path on the south side of the bridge. Follow a faint upstream trail with some boulder hopping about .5 mile to a steep-walled grotto of exquisite, river-sculpted granite pools known locally as God's Bath. Chapter 11 also explores the Clavey River country.

11
Bourland Trestle &
the West Side Lumber Co. Railroad
Magnificent Remnant of Early Railroading

■ THE DETAILS

Getting There: From Sonora, follow directions to the Clavey River in Chapter 10, then continue 7 miles. Turn left on Road 2N14 (the sign is up the road from the junction) and follow it about 5.5 miles to a fork. Bear right on Road 2N29 and park.

Nearest Campground: Hull Creek Campground, northwest on Forest Road 31, has 20 sites and piped water. Also see Chapters 10 and 12.

Lodging: Try Sonora, a full-service town.

Further Info: Mi-Wuk Ranger District, Stanislaus National Forest 209-586-3234.

Hike Distance: 6.4 miles round trip to Bourland Trestle, 4 miles round trip to Clavey Trestle site.

Difficulty: Easy.

Best Time to Go: Summer, after the roads are clear of snow.

Cautions: Do not walk on the trestle. Do not disturb historic artifacts.

Starting Elevation: 5400 feet, negligible gain.

Other Maps: USGS Hull Creek and Cherry Lake North 7.5 minute topos.

The first time I saw Bourland Trestle, I gasped in astonishment. Pam Conners, my guide and Stanislaus National Forest historian, mentioned having a similar visceral reaction when she first saw the trestle. Stalking our historic prey, we walked on a carpet of pine needles covering earth still damp from a recent downpour, savoring playful forest breezes, concerts of song birds, warm sun, and diamond-clear air. Suddenly we came upon it, as jungle explorers might stumble across a pre-Colombian ruin. A 315-foot-long, 76-foot-tall wooden trestle in the middle of nowhere is a stunning and formidable sight.

I stared in disbelief at the towering, gracefully curved structure spanning a deep ravine cut by Bourland Creek. A labyrinth of massive, crisscrossing timbers created intricate geometric patterns, looking like a colossal piece of abstract art.

Bourland Trestle's size dwarfs the locomotive crossing it in this 1924 photo.

Out of time, but not out of place, this grand work of architecture seemed to grow from the forest floor and fit beautifully into the woodsy setting. For a moment, my inner ear heard the frisky, ratchety sound of a steam engine echoing through the hills. Out of several dozen railroad trestles that once bridged gorges in Stanislaus National Forest (StNF), Bourland is the only one still standing.

Speaking quietly, not wanting to break the spell of my discovery, Pam supplied words to my thoughts: "Even if, as you walked to the trestle, you recognized that the gentle road gradient and broad, sweeping curves were telltale signs of a railroad, even if you knew that these woods had been the 'green gold' of the West Side Flume and Lumber Company during the first half of the 20th century, even if you expressly knew you were going to see an old bridge across Bourland Creek, it still takes your breath away, time after time."

Besides the 79-year old Bourland Trestle, my tour provided a glimpse into StNF's rich railroad logging history. In the first half of the 20th century, the Stanislaus was home to four railroad logging operations: the West Side Lumber Company, Standard Lumber Company, Yosemite Sugar Pine Lumber Company, and California Peach and Fig Growers Company. Here our focus is on the West Side Lumber Company (WSLC) whose railroad logging web included 70 miles of mainline and 250 miles of temporary spurs. Stretching from Tuolumne City east of Sonora to within six miles of Hetch Hetchy Valley in Yosemite Park, the WSLC and its railroad played a major role in the Central Sierra's economy and character between 1900 and 1960. "It's really an icon for the entire railroad logging history that shaped this area," stated Conners.

The West Side Flume and Lumber Company was incorporated in 1899 by

Thomas Bullock and Henry and William Crocker. Designed to reach abundant virgin pine in the Tuolumne River watershed, their narrow gauge railroad reached the seemingly endless resources of this land of steep ridgetops and deep drainages. By connecting with Sierra Railway and Southern Pacific, WSLC delivered lumber from the isolated StNF to state and national markets.

The West Side's railroad was incorporated as the Hetch Hetchy and Yosemite Valleys Railway in August 1900, so named due to Bullock's (unrealized) dream of combining a logging operation with tourist trade to Hetch Hetchy and Yosemite Valleys. In 1903 Henry Crocker sold the West Side and its Tuolumne City mill to a Michigan/Wisconsin consortium for $4 million. The new owners immediately changed the name to the West Side Lumber Company. Caring little for any anticipated tourist traffic, they terminated the scant passenger service in 1904.

Large and small trestles were pivotal to WSLC operations. As the mainline grade pushed deeper into the woods, WSLC had to cross several steep canyons. The four largest are well documented. Beginning in 1899 with River Bridge over the North Fork Tuolumne, these four were between 300 and 318 feet in length and 54 to 76 feet in height. Less substantial trestles were needed to cross many smaller drainages, while earth fills and culverts were used over others.

Trestles such as the Bourland built in 1922 were extremely important to the company and in constant use after their construction. The loss of even one caused down time and financial crisis. A full-time watchman resided at each major trestle to scrutinize passing engines and check for flying embers. Besides fire danger, the company worried about the effect of floods during spring thaw on these tall, massive structures, even though they stood on sizable concrete footings. At Bourland, the trestle tender's cabin stood west of the creek until it burned in the early 1980s.

Bourland Trestle was designed by Fred Ellis, who routed most of the logging grade as well. Timber trestles, rather than expensive steel, were typical for most large-scale spans in the West. Conners related, "The operational life span of these trestles was approximately 10 to 15 years with maintenance. All of them realized a longevity much greater than what they were designed for, and Bourland was in continuous use from its completion in 1922 until 1958."

By the mid-1940s, WSLC changed the pattern of its railroad logging procedures. After they built the final spur line in 1943 which nearly reached Yosemite's northwestern boundary, trucks began replacing spur lines due largely to the growing number of Forest Service roads. Ironically, logging trucks were too heavy to license for public roads. They had to be piggybacked through the woods on the same railroad flatcars they would soon eliminate. Throughout the 1950s, only the mainline was used as logging trucks hauled trees from the stump to primary landings.

Although surviving longer than most, WSLC fell victim to a combination of increasingly efficient truck use and the decreasing amount of logging land available. "As early as the 1930s," Conners explained, "the West Side sold their logged-over lands and relied more and more on Forest Service timber sales." As available land accessible by railroad shrank, profitable operations became impossible. Except for a four-year hiatus between 1930 and 1934 during the Great Depression, the company remained viable for 61 years. The end of an era came on October 28, 1960, when the last train of logs rolled into the mill at Tuolumne City.

After railroad logging ceased, the Forest Service took a hard look at the system's remnants scattered across public lands. Though the railroad grades, stripped of rails and ties, made excellent logging and fire access roads, the railroad left behind "a trail of abandoned camps, garbage dumps, buildings, wide-spread debris, steam donkey activity areas, and a string of bridges." Viewed as unsightly or safety hazards, these reminders of a bygone way of life alarmed officials. "Insufficient time had elapsed for the historic nature of trestles and related railroad properties even to enter agency consciousness," explained Conners. Bourland Trestle, instead of a monument to Sierra railroad logging, was considered a hazardous liability.

Although required by the 1966 National Historic Preservation Act to "locate, identify and evaluate the significance of historic properties," StNF focussed on prehistoric archaeology at first. With few exceptions, Forest Service archaeologists rarely gave equal attention to historic-era resources. Said Conners, "This was evident when in 1978 we contracted with a California State University archaeology department to identify and record cultural resources preparatory to a proposed timber sale. While scores of resources were located in the area encompassing Bourland Trestle and archaeologists were duly impressed by Bourland Trestle, [the railroad relics] were not recorded."

In 1985, five years after being hired as StNF's first historian, Pam Conners recorded the considerable cultural resources surrounding and including Bourland Trestle while scouting the area for a proposed timber sale. She nominated the trestle and eight other properties of the former WSLC for inclusion on the National Register of Historic Places, with eligibility established in 1986. Until 1992, management of the ancient trestle was one of "benign neglect" because funds were virtually non-existent for stabilization, restoration, or interpretation of historic resources.

What spared Bourland Trestle from being "removed and cleaned up" is not clear. Whether it was a burgeoning nostalgia, lack of money and commitment to do the job, sheer luck, or some unrelated motivation, happily the Forest Service did not enforce destruction of this mighty relic. The great Clavey and North Fork Tuolumne Trestles were long gone, lost to fire or the elements. In 1981, two-thirds of Niagara Trestle collapsed primarily because chainsaw vandals weakened its structural integrity. "Showing progressively alarming signs of failure," by 1985 Bourland was the sole surviving West Side trestle.

Unlike the National Park Service, Forest Service funding for large historic projects is rare. In 1992, a Bourland Trestle stabilization proposal was awarded $50,000 from President Bush's America's Great Outdoors Program. Barely enough for simple stabilization and far from complete restoration, it did keep the trestle from falling down and provided a "preservation window" for long-range planning and decision making.

Ingenious and highly skilled professionals from High Country Builders completed Phase I (about 10 percent) stabilization in August 1995. They painstakingly replaced 125 rotten timbers using rock climbing methods, including rappelling, to reach sections of the rickety trestle. Total cost for minimum stabilization totaled $74,000.

Unfortunately the January 1997 storm of the century sent flood-swollen waters raging down Bourland Creek, slamming logs and debris against the old trestle. The Forest Service worried that the weight of the logjam against support timbers would collapse the structure. Amazingly, it held together. Mother Nature, however, wasn't quite finished. The strong Markleeville earthquake of 1998 collapsed the weakened middle third of Bourland Trestle.

Even with a gap, Bourland Trestle continues to stand as an icon for railroad logging in the West. At press time the trestle project remains on hold. Various alternatives are being explored, ranging from demolition to full restoration. Funding continues to be an obstacle. Recognizing the trestle's historic significance, the Forest Service accepts responsibility for its preservation. While acknowledging their commitment, the project isn't high on their list because the trestle is a low traffic area. Ironically, Bourland Trestle's obscurity is a big part of its magic and allure.

Stanislaus National Forest envisions Bourland Trestle, fully restored and

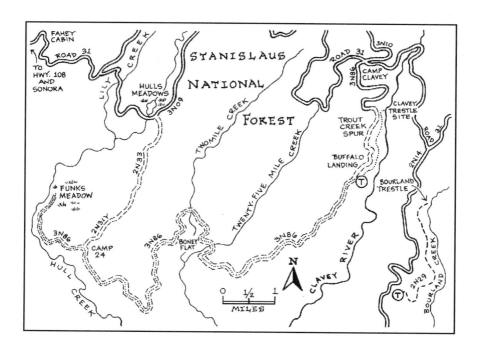

adapted for pedestrian use, as the centerpiece of a 45-mile Rails-to-Trails experience over the mainline of the West Side's railroad logging system from Hull Creek (northeast of Mi-Wuk Village) to Cherry Valley near Yosemite. To date, the first 18-mile segment is already a reality. A well-crafted, colorful brochure keyed to a dozen tourposts guides visitors on an expedition to a vanished era where donkey doctors, gandy dancers, whistle punks, flunkies, hoggers, powder monkeys, and other colorfully named railroad logging men earned a living.

■ THE HIKES

From the trailhead, walk 3.2 nearly level miles on the abandoned West Side Railroad grade (Road 2N29) to find Bourland Trestle. Caution! Do not walk on the trestle! Until it is fully restored, you risk bodily harm and can damage the structure. Return the way you came.

To explore a nearby stretch of the West Side Lumber Company's mainline, drive north on Road 24N14 to its end. Turn left and follow Forest Road 31 (3N01) west, crossing the Clavey River after 2 miles and meeting Road 3N86 on the left around 4 miles. Turn left and follow Road 3N86 south 4 miles to the site of Buffalo Landing, marked by Tourpost 12. You drove in on the Trout Creek spur. Look east to find the mainline downslope of the spur. You can walk the mainline grade northeast and north for about 2 miles to the site of the Clavey River Trestle. Though the trestle burned, some of its support structure is clearly visible. The bridge tender's camp and a water tank once stood west of the river here and the remains of a flat car are nearby.

When you return to your vehicle, consider that you can walk or mountain bike the railroad's mainline (now Road 3N86) west from here, encountering minimal vehicle traffic. If you do, it's about 7 miles to Twomile Creek, almost 13 miles to the rail trail's west end near Hull Creek.

12
Lake Eleanor & Preston Falls

The Hetch Hetchy Project & Early Intake Powerhouse

■ THE DETAILS

Getting There: From Groveland drive Highway 120 east 15 miles and turn left on paved Cherry Lake Road. Proceed about 25 miles to Cherry Lake. Continue across the dam, bear right, and follow the dirt road 4 miles to a small parking area at the Yosemite Park boundary.

Nearest Campground: Cherry Valley Campground at Cherry Lake, open April through October, has 46 sites with piped water in summer.

Lodging: Closest beds are on Highway 120 in Buck Meadows or Groveland.

Further Info: Stanislaus National Forest Groveland Ranger District 209-962-7825, Yosemite National Park 209-372-0200.

Hike Distance: 9 miles round trip to Preston Falls from Early Intake. One mile round trip to Lake Eleanor dam.

Facilities: Restrooms and picnic area at Preston Falls Trailhead.

Difficulty: Moderate to Preston Falls. Easy to Lake Eleanor dam.

Best Time to Go: Late spring for Preston Falls. Late spring to summer for Lake Eleanor.

Cautions: The road across Cherry Lake Dam is closed to vehicles from September 15 to May 1.

Starting Elevation: 2400 feet at Early Intake, 4900 feet at Lake Eleanor Trailhead.

Other Maps: USGS Lake Eleanor 15 minute topo, Stanislaus National Forest map.

In a handsome, cozy setting worthy of an artist's brush, Lake Eleanor (elevation 4657 feet) lies barely inside the northwestern boundary of Yosemite National Park. Hemmed by pine-thatched slopes, the three-mile-long lake is dotted with a few small islands on its western end and occupies a quiet, infrequently visited corner of the park. It was named for Eleanor Whitney, daughter of Josiah Whitney, geologist-chief of the first California State Geological Survey in the early 1860s.

Elevations in this neck of the woods are generally below 7000 feet, but the absence of sky-kissing peaks is amply offset by spectacular canyons separating heavily wooded ridges. In this gentle wilderness, summer arrives earlier and winter comes later than in loftier areas of Yosemite. To avoid midsummer heat, the most comfortable times to visit are autumn and spring.

Besides its serenity and beauty, the Lake Eleanor region is packed with history. For a time its environs were the nucleus of the monumental Hetch Hetchy Project, focus of one of the most controversial, prolonged and stormiest environmental battles in the West. Both Lake Eleanor and Early Intake Powerhouse were pivotal elements in San Francisco's far-reaching water plans.

Nearly 60 years before the vast project began to bring Sierra water to San Francisco, Horace Kibbe, pioneer settler and cattleman, found the lake and its valley in 1860. At that time the lake was a little, shallow body of water filling a depression scooped out by glacial action. Kibbe (also Kibbie) homesteaded 175 acres now covered by the waters of Eleanor Reservoir. In addition to ranching, he "stocked the lake with fish from Cherry Creek, carrying them in coal oil cans." During the warm months Kibbe lived in a cabin at Frog Creek, one of the lake's three inlet streams, well into old age. In the early years of the 20th century, a small fish hatchery was located at Frog Creek; some evidence of the operation is visible today.

Years before President Wilson signed the Raker Bill in 1913 allowing the Hetch Hetchy project to proceed, San Francisco engineers prowled the Sierra in search of water. Fourteen locations were studied, but the 654-square-mile Tuolumne watershed was deemed the best possible source.

At the heart of the ingenious, incredibly complex plan was the installation of a massive dam within Yosemite National Park. An eight-mile-long reservoir would be created when pristine Hetch Hetchy Valley became flooded by impounding the Tuolumne's natural flow. Although the invasion and violation of national park lands outraged an entire nation and sparked heated debates for 12 years, San Francisco ultimately succeeded in obtaining water rights.

Subsequent to lengthy, complicated planning and survey stages to deliver Sierra water to San Francisco 150 miles distant, two early priorities were established. First, a railroad was needed to transport men, machinery, materials and supplies to construction sites in the mountains. Second, a dependable electricity source was essential to operate a staggering array of equipment.

With the passage of the Raker Bill, tiny and obscure Lake Eleanor catapulted into the limelight preparatory to constructing the enormous Hetch Hetchy Project. Its captured water would provide the energy to generate a reliable electricity supply. At the bottom of the isolated Tuolumne River canyon, where the present road to Cherry Lake crosses the river, a small hydroelectric plant was built to power all the machinery used at the Hetch Hetchy dam site. A 19-mile

Preston Falls on the Tuolumne River tumbles into a green pool.

tunnel between Early Intake and Priest Reservoir, railroad shops and hospital in Groveland, construction camps and offices were also built.

Water to run the turbines first came from Cherry Creek, but to ensure an adequate year-round supply, a dam was built at Lake Eleanor. Water from the reservoir was released to augment Cherry Creek's natural flow. A little diversion dam was placed in Cherry Creek from which the combined Cherry and Eleanor water traveled 3.5 miles to the powerhouse through a system of flumes, pipes, tunnels and canals. Early Intake was the first of Hetch Hetchy's three power plants.

Between 1917 and 1918 a graceful, multiple-arch, concrete dam was built a mile downstream from existing Lake Eleanor. Resting on solid granite, the 1260-foot long, 70-foot high dam created a vastly larger lake with a capacity of 28,000 acre-feet. Water storage began in June 1918 when its outlet gates were closed, and by August Early Intake's three Pelton turbines were humming with 22,000 volts of electricity. Serving 25 different points, electricity was transmitted eastward 11 miles to the Hetch Hetchy dam site and 22 miles westward to Moccasin on power lines supported by wooden poles.

Before Lake Eleanor was dammed, a terror-breathing, 12-mile construction road was chiseled out of the canyon wall and ridge north of the future Hetch Hetchy dam location. A 168-foot truss bridge spanned the Tuolumne River, and a 12.5 percent grade snaked 1800 feet up the mountain via 13 dangerous switchbacks. The road continued, but on a longer and lesser grade, down to Lake Eleanor. Truck drivers needed steely nerves to negotiate the terrible turns, especially during inclement weather. Some men drove it only once and then quit.

When the Lake Eleanor Road was finished in September 1917, trucks began lugging sacked cement to the Eleanor work site, the first major dam in Hetch Hetchy's master plan. "Trains of six trucks made three round trips each 24 hours; 400 runs were required for the job." The road has long been closed to vehicle traffic, but fans of old roads can still walk the historic 9.5-mile track between Eleanor and O'Shaughnessy Dams.

As trees were felled from the reservoir area, a sawmill processed them into lumber for a variety of building needs. Even retired horses from San Francisco's fire departments were pressed into service for hauling jobs at the site. The earliest use of the Hetch Hetchy Railroad was to carry and dump concrete over a very short, narrow gauge line at the dam site from 1917 to 1918. The unusual, gracefully arched dam at Lake Eleanor began storing water only ten months after construction began.

Meanwhile, over the ridge from Eleanor, concurrent work on Early Intake Powerhouse and its diversion dam began by August 1917. The bustling community included employee tent houses, guest and office tents, garage, shops, cookhouse and dining room. Workers paid $1.25 per day for room and board. Later, more comfortable, permanent wood buildings replaced the canvas structures. The powerhouse, originally intended to be temporary, actually operated until 1965.

Gouged out of a steep mountainside in 1916, the so-called road down to Intake from a Hetch Hetchy Railroad station on the canyon rim was a narrow and treacherous nightmare. "Built where no road should have been," it was so hellish and inadequate for heavy drayage that an inclined tramway was constructed in 1918 to transport virtually all equipment, supplies and passengers. Although much safer and convenient, the tramway's 3700-foot plunge into the gorge, part of it on a 70 percent grade, provided riders with the thrill of a lifetime.

In October 1934 a gala ceremony marked the first Sierra water flowing into San Francisco. It was indeed the culmination of a long journey, both in distance and in decades of planning and construction. O'Shaughnessy Dam was raised 85 feet between 1936 and 1938 to its present height of 430 feet above bedrock.

Of the many Hetchy construction camps needed throughout the 25-year building project, a few became permanent settlements, or company towns, such as Moccasin and Early Intake. Long gone, however, is the work camp at Lake Eleanor.

Water from Lake Eleanor no longer flows to Early Intake. Instead, a mile-long tunnel punched through Kibbie Ridge in 1960 connects Eleanor with Cherry Lake. Their combined flow drives the turbines at Holm Powerhouse six miles below near the confluence of Cherry Creek and the Tuolumne River. Holm came online in August 1960. Today, both Kirkwood and Holm are operated by remote control from the state-of-the-art Moccasin plant 20 miles to the west. The temporary power plant at Intake that closed in 1965 was replaced in 1967 by Kirkwood Powerhouse, a much larger facility just upstream. The company town on the Tuolumne River, however, is still known as Early Intake.

■ THE HIKES

The soft, mellow days of spring or autumn are perfect for an outing to Early Intake and the Lake Eleanor region. Even if history isn't your cup of tea, you'll certainly enjoy the scenic drive on Sierra byways. Gas up the family flivver, pack a picnic and plan on a full day in the mountains. Your passport to this interesting backcountry is Cherry Lake Road, Road 1N07, 14 miles east of Groveland.

For orientation, pick up a Stanislaus National Forest map at Groveland Ranger Station. Follow paved Cherry Lake Road 8 miles to Early Intake. The now tamed route down the rugged canyon after the junction with Hetch Hetchy Road offers you a wee hint of what the 1916 dirt track must have been like. At Early Intake turn right and drive through the tiny community of San Francisco housing along the Tuolumne River. Just beyond Kirkwood Powerhouse is a large parking area. A trail starting near the restrooms follows the river upstream 4.5 miles to Preston Falls, an absolutely gorgeous hike, especially in spring when the Tuolumne is rampaging through its canyon. If you feel like a stretch, follow the path for a few minutes before heading on.

Continue on Cherry Lake Road to Cherry Lake, about 16 miles distant over hill and dale. Not far up the road from Early Intake, take note of an unsigned road on your left which leads to nearby Holm Powerhouse. You'll find fine spots along the river here for a picnic. Dammed by San Francisco in 1956, Cherry Lake Reservoir stores 268,000

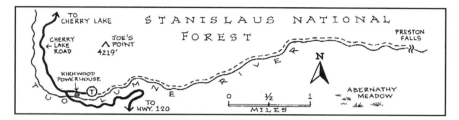

acre-feet at full capacity. After its waters leave Holm Powerhouse, they travel far downstream to Don Pedro Reservoir. Cherry Lake offers an outstanding place to camp, fish and hike. A pack station is close if you'd rather see the country from horseback. Check the map for many side road exploration possibilities.

To investigate more of the huge reservoir's shoreline or to reach lovely Lake Eleanor, drive across the .5-mile-long dam. With map in hand, bear right and follow a good dirt road about 4 miles to the Yosemite Park boundary, blocked by a gate. Park your car and walk only .5 mile down to Eleanor.

The tranquil, picturesque setting is complete with a rustic backcountry Ranger Station. Near the shoreline, one of the few remaining old ice houses in the Sierra reminds us of a bygone era. If you were to continue walking on this road, you'd reach Hetch Hetchy in 9.5 miles. Many spots along the shore invite lingering or casting your line for trout.

Return the way you came, or detour on the Hetch Hetchy Road uphill from Early Intake. A jaunt to O'Shaughnessy Dam (see Chapter 31) rewards the few extra miles, giving a sense of completion and underlining the reason behind everything you've seen on this golden day in the Sierra.

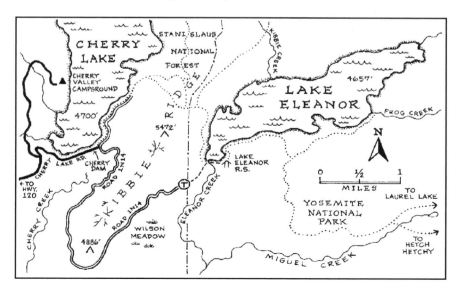

13
The Peach & Fig Growers Railroad
The Story of Camp Mather & Vicinity

■ THE DETAILS

Getting There: Follow Highway 120 toward Yosemite Park. Just 25 miles east of Groveland and one mile before the Park's Big Oak Flat Entrance Station, turn north onto Evergreen Road and go 5 miles to Middle Fork Picnic/Day Use Area.

Nearest Campground: Dimond "O" campground, one mile farther up Evergreen Road, has 38 sites and piped water, open April through October.

Lodging: Several choices in Groveland and Buck Meadows.

Further Info: Stanislaus National Forest Groveland Ranger District 209-962-7825.

Hike Distance: 3.3 miles round trip from Middle Fork. Up to 4 miles round trip from Peach Growers Tract.

Difficulty: Easy.

Best Time to Go: Late spring through autumn.

Cautions: Please leave all artifacts in place.

Starting Elevation: 4385 feet.

Other Maps: Lake Eleanor 15 minute topo or Stanislaus National Forest map.

The annals of the Sierra are rich with the stuff that dreams are made of. Its history brims with stories of daring and adventurous souls, dreamers and schemers, ingenious entrepreneurs, outlaws and heroes who embarked on creative but doomed ventures. What attracted these people to California was an unprecedented phenomenon. During the 1840s the national mood simmered with excitement, restlessness and a lust for adventure. The spirit of Manifest Destiny, one nation from the Atlantic to the Pacific, infected the population on all levels. And the spark that ignited the wildfire of the most massive migration in history was the 1848 discovery of gold at Coloma.

The excesses and wildness of Gold Rush society didn't last long; the big spree was all but over by the mid-1850s. As miners and new arrivals began to sense that this vast frontier's real potential lay in farming, they replaced their picks and pans with plows. Although California slowly settled down and changed to an agricultural-based economy, the essence of the free-wheeling gold seeker was never fully extinguished. Instead of plundering the Sierra of its gold, men tapped other resources to garner fame and fortune. For decades after the Gold Rush, California remained the Big Rock Candy Mountain for opportunity, freedom and the fulfillment of one's wildest dreams.

Such was the case of the California Peach and Fig Growers Railroad, one of many creative but flawed ventures in the Sierra. If you've never heard of it, take heart. Except for the most avid railroad buff, neither has 99.9 percent of the rest of California. This obscure short line chugged through the mountains near Hetch Hetchy between 1918 and 1925. Its six miles of tracks were laid in the heavily forested region near the former Middle Fork Campground, now a day-use picnic area, on the Middle Fork Tuolumne River. Less than a mile north of the campground was the lumber camp, millpond, yard and sawmill. An additional two miles of tracks connected the sawmill with Hetch Hetchy Railroad (HHRR) just outside the boundary of Yosemite. As we shall see, the HHRR was the kingpin in the company's operation.

The railroad was the brainchild of the newly organized California Peach Growers Association in 1916. From a corporate viewpoint, especially in that era, getting into the railroad business was a smart move and essentially a good idea. Primary goals of the Fresno-based group were having a reliable source of box materials in huge quantities and promoting and marketing their product. The San Joaquin Valley fig growers joined the Association in 1921, swelling their ranks to an impressive 7000 members. Several Fresno bigwigs were officers in the concern; the first president was the publisher of two newspapers, and the first secretary was the mayor.

When the Peach and Fig Growers had difficulty getting box materials, they approached the Forest Service about timber sales. At that time, the Forest Service was in its infancy and also in a promotional role. Their not very future-oriented motto, "the greatest good for the greatest number in the long run," dovetailed nicely with the needs of the Association. Because of its inexperience, the Forest Service had some hard lessons to learn about responsible timber management. What was good for the greatest number often did not result in the greatest good for the natural resources. A deal was struck, and the California Peach and Fig Growers Association was granted permission to occupy, build on and purchase timber in Stanislaus National Forest.

The original agreement included 100 million board feet from the Stanislaus and 54 million board feet of adjacent private timber. Built in 1916, the two-band sawmill could turn out 50,000 board feet of lumber per day. Logging was accomplished by chutes, donkey engines and Big Wheels. The Big Wheels were unique and quite simple pieces of equipment. Logs were balanced on an axle attached to two 20-foot wheels and pulled by mules or horses—simple but tricky. The proper loading and balancing of enormous logs were the key ingredients to their effectiveness. A donkey engine was basically a huge, steam-powered winch on a sled. From the sawmill the lumber was taken to Mather on the two-mile connector line. At Mather the lumber was processed into shipping crates used by

The Peach & Fig Growers Railroad connected with Hetch Hetchy Railroad at Mather, hauling lumber from the sawmill two miles south.

the Association and then hauled out of the mountains on the HHRR, ultimately reaching Fresno via the Sierra, Santa Fe and Central Pacific lines. Total cost for the railroad, mill, yard and camp was only $150,000, a relatively inexpensive investment.

Starting with its management, the California Peach and Fig Growers Railroad had troubles almost from day one. The Association's Board of Supervisors directed all logging operations, and their management was poor. Although it's understandable that they wanted to keep a tight rein, it was a mistake. These men knew a lot more about peaches and figs than about running a railroad and logging. Management changed hands six times, adding to their problems.

The sawmill's location was another adverse factor. The mill was uphill from most of the timber, making it difficult to transport logs to it and especially problematic for the Big Wheels with their touchy balance. Big Wheels were thought to be cost effective and cause less damage to the terrain, but they were scrapped in 1922 due to poor handling by inexperienced loggers.

At the end of the cutting season in 1919 only a fraction of the original 1918 timber sale had been cut. Although the Association contracted for more timber, they never harvested their quotas. By 1922 mismanagement was a large problem, with slumping sales of their products making it worse. Further erosion of the Association's operations developed in 1919 when the City of San Francisco bought the Camp Mather property and built their own sawmill to serve the gigantic Hetch Hetchy project. The HHRR, then operating as a common carrier, was pivotal to the success, or failure, of the Peach and Fig Growers enterprise. In addition to hauling their box materials and lumber out of the mountains, the tiny railroad used the Hetch Hetchy's Groveland shop for maintenance on a contract basis. The Association tried but failed to negotiate a reduction in freight rates, no more that a band-aid to mounting difficulties.

The HHRR was never meant to be a money-maker, only to make a costly construction job less expensive. When the dam was completed in 1923, the Hetch Hetchy Railroad announced that it would cease operating as a common carrier as of 1925. That was the last straw for the little railroad that thought it could. Without the HHRR the growers' logging operations were land-locked with no way to transport their products to a railhead. Finally, the Peach and Fig Growers sawmill burned in 1925 under suspicious circumstances. That ended a creative Sierra business scheme, failed due to poor management and reliance on another railroad that didn't need them.

The Oakland Boy Scouts Council bought the buildings and some equipment in November 1925 when Stanislaus National Forest granted them a permit to convert 13 acres from a logging camp to a Boy Scout Camp. The Scouts used the property until 1972. The Forest Service issued special use permits on lots for 27 cabins in 1927. Called the Peach Growers Tract, nine cabins were finally occupied. Similar to Foresta in Yosemite (see Chapter 34), residents don't own the land and must comply with government regulations. The permits pass to heirs, reverting to the Forest Service when there are no heirs. The private cabins, located just below the sawmill site, are still in use.

The historic and long-abandoned Peach and Fig Growers Railroad camp area saw new life in 1994 when Stanislaus National Forest began work on a campground project on the former Boy Scout/lumber mill site. Middle Fork Campground, originally a Civilian Conservation Corps camp site in the 1930s, was permanently closed due to being tired and worn after years of use and abuse. To allow the once beautiful riparian environment to heal, it was closed to vehicles and open only for picnic and day use. "Dimond O," the new campground, sits near the river but far enough away to prevent stream bank erosion, plant trampling and water pollution. A wiser, more experienced Forest Service is learning that "the greatest good for the greatest number in the long run" must include protection of precious and fragile resources.

■ THE HIKES

To get your boots on a one-mile section of the defunct logging railroad, drive to Middle Fork Day Use Area and park. Behind the restroom, follow an old road (closed to vehicles) that winds through the former campground. Near its end at .4 mile, look up a short rise to your left to find a concrete foundation. Walk up the slope to reach the old railroad grade 150 feet behind the foundation. Veer to the right, following the obvious route, an easy walk in the woods that is especially pleasant in spring when the nearby Middle Fork Tuolumne River roars, or in autumn when oaks glow with color. Watch for logging and railroad relics.

Around .9 mile from the picnic area, railroad ties lie scattered on either side of the grade. In places you'll need to step over or walk around downed trees. At 1.4 miles the grade ends, but a trail continues .2 mile to a point 100 feet above the river. Huge clumps of Indian rhubarb dot the banks and the water riffles over rocks into an inviting green pool, a lovely spot for lunch or some toe-wiggling in the stream. Return the way you came. Near the concrete foundation, you can continue along the railroad bed, which leads to the day-use entrance road.

To continue exploring, drive another mile on Evergreen Road to Peach Growers Tract to visit the company sawmill site and/or walk the Peach and Fig Growers mainline 2 miles to Camp Mather. Turn left at the row of mailboxes beside the Peach Growers Tract sign. Instead of driving into the tract, park near Evergreen Road and walk upslope behind the mailboxes. You'll soon see a grassy depression below, once the mill pond. Bear right and pick up the grade heading north to Mather. The concrete ruins of the sawmill and two wooden water tanks lie between the tract road and the millpond. You can follow the railroad grade about 2 miles to Camp Mather.

14
Rainbow Pool on the South Fork Tuolumne River
A Small Dot on the Map with a Big History

■ THE DETAILS

Getting There: From Groveland, take Highway 120 east 14 miles and turn right (south) off Highway 120 immediately before the bridge spanning the South Fork Tuolumne River to reach Rainbow Pool.

Nearest Campgrounds: Between Groveland and Rainbow Pool are two small Forest Service campgrounds, The Pines and Lost Claim. A mile above the pool is Sweetwater. Each has piped water.

Lodging: Groveland has the Hotel Charlotte 209-962-6455, Buck Meadows has Buck Meadows Lodge 209-253-9673.

Further Info: Groveland Ranger District, 24525 Highway 120, Groveland, CA 95321, 209-962-7825.

Hike Distance: 2 miles round trip to the confluence of the Middle and South Fork.

Facilities: Picnic tables and restrooms at Rainbow Pool.

Difficulty: Easy.

Best Time to Go: Late spring, summer, autumn.

Cautions: Stay on road—rushing waters are deadly.

Starting Elevation: 2800 feet. Hike has an elevation loss/gain of 400 feet.

Other Maps: Jawbone Ridge 7.5 minute topo, Tuolumne 15 minute topo, or Stanislaus National Forest map. If you use Jawbone Ridge map, be aware of two errors on it: Rainbow Pool is at the gaging station symbol, **not** where marked on the map, and there is **no** campground at the pool.

The Central Sierra Nevada is blessed with soul-stirring scenery, a broad spectrum of year-round recreational opportunities, and abundant historical sites. Located in the bosom of this diverse territory, Tuolumne County alone would require a lifetime to fully explore. For backpackers and day hikers, the options are virtually unlimited on its hundreds of miles of trails and seldom-used Forest Service roads.

If you enjoy combining a scenic hike with lively history, an exploration of Rainbow Pool on the South Fork Tuolumne River offers a rewarding experience. An easy, eye-pleasing hike nearby explores the heart of the Tuolumne River

Bill Foster (right) and friend from Sonora enjoy Rainbow Pool below Cliff House in 1936.

canyon. Tiny dots indicating small communities or historical sites pepper area maps. Rainbow Pool is one of these flyspecks. Nevertheless, it was the setting for significant events in the chronicles of the Sierra Nevada.

Just east of Buck Meadows on Highway 120, one of the finest vistas along this incredibly scenic stretch of road makes a sudden, dramatic appearance. At the turnout called *Rim of the World*, the profound canyons of the South and Middle Forks Tuolumne River magnetize one's attention. The shiny, silver ribbon of the Tuolumne River threads its way through a nearly vertical chasm more than 2000 feet below. Beyond this awesome abyss, forested ridges and other far-off gorges lead to snowy crags puncturing the skyline above High Country. To the right (east), the twin 100-foot falls of the Middle Fork appear as bright specks in the distance.

Shortly east of this dizzying viewpoint, Highway 120, the modern version of historic Big Oak Flat Road, plummets into the South Fork Tuolumne River canyon. A keen eye can spot the old road twisting back and forth across the newer route. A high bridge now completely bypasses Rainbow Pool where freight wagons, stagecoaches, pedestrians, and autos once crossed the river on a covered bridge.

By turning off the main highway before the new bridge, you follow a short, paved access road that leads to Rainbow Pool picnic area and an inviting swimming hole. Except for a foundation or two, shards of crockery, bits of broken glass, and a few puzzling feet of rusty rails, nothing remains to tell the tale of its moment in history. In January 1997, when an unprecedented volume of water rampaged through South Fork canyon, the old bridge buckled and collapsed. Torrential rainfall considerably remodeled the sandy beach and shoreline surrounding the pool.

Before the Big Oak Flat Road Company built a covered bridge at Rainbow Pool in 1870, the South Fork was simply spanned by logs. Big Oak Flat Road was a toll road until Tuolumne County bought it in 1915. Between 1895 and 1915, a salty, eccentric character named John Cox was the only tollkeeper. Before 1895 tolls were collected at Crane Flat within Yosemite Park.

The toll gate sat near the bridge's south entrance, and here Cox was master of all he surveyed for 20 years. The covered bridge, reminiscent of those in the East, was the handiwork of James Lumsden. Talented James and brother David built numerous bridges, flumes, and trails in the county, but they are most famous for carving a tunnel through "The Dead Giant" in Tuolumne Grove in 1878. Cox was in his sixties when he arrived at the South Fork. Before moving to the mountains, he was a reporter for a San Francisco newspaper. Why he chose to leave city life is unknown, but local legend says that a broken romance turned him into a loner. During the Civil War Cox was a bugler in the Confederate Army, and the plaintive sounds of his horn could be heard piercing the clear mountain air as travelers left his hermitage on the river.

Immediately below Lower Bridge, as it was called, a lovely, small waterfall tumbled into deep Rainbow Pool. Cox was so charmed by this beautiful place that he built his cabin on a large rock formation jutting out over the cascade. In spite of the vastness of the country surrounding his cabin, his arena was limited to a few hundred feet of the toll gate. He always had to be within hearing distance of the toll station. His year-round, solitary existence in such a narrow sphere would drive most people around the bend, but Cox, who was spellbound by this tiny spot on the South Fork, was a contented man. The teamsters regularly delivered to him all he needed—food, firewood, tobacco and medicine—and these freight men always found time to gossip, bringing news of the outside world.

Margaret Schlichtman, in her wonderfully informative book, **The Big Oak Flat Road**, relates that in spite of his gruff manner, Cox was really softhearted. One day a man showed up at the toll gate weighted down with a heavy pack. Tired and penniless, he asked if John might turn his head while he crossed the bridge. He had urgent business up the line, and the river was so dangerously high that he couldn't risk fording it. Cox took his job very seriously and could not allow such an impropriety. Instead he offered an alternative. "I'll tell you what; seeing that the rate is 25 cents for a man walking, suppose you run instead." John watched with his integrity intact as the weary pedestrian sprinted across the bridge.

After the turn of the century, the colorful and exciting stagecoach era gave way to the automobile age. The Holmes brothers of San Jose made history in 1900 when their Stanley Steamer arrived in Yosemite Valley via the Wawona Road. In 1901 two Locomobiles wheezed into Yosemite on the Big Oak Flat Road, causing great anxiety to tollkeeper Cox. An urgent letter to company headquarters asked, "What toll should I get from the new horseless vehicles that occasionally struggle by?" The reply was "50 cents for each passenger each way" and the definition of an automobile was "a vehicle not used with horses."

The advent of these "blunt-nosed beetles," as John Muir described the automobiles, stirred up such great controversy in the Park that they were refused entrance. Not until 1913 were autos cautiously allowed. Even then, some 65 stringent regulations and a $5 entry fee were imposed on early motorists. For better or worse, times had changed, and by 1915 octogenarian John Cox was out of work when his position was terminated after the Big Oak Flat Road became a free route.

Rainbow Pool, once home to a reclusive toll collector, became the busy location of a thriving inn for tourists. First known as Fall Inn, it was later renamed Cliff House. Nellie Bartlett and William Wilson, a brother and sister partnership, leased the property from Tuolumne County in 1924 and added rooms to Cox's cabin on the rock ledge overhanging the South Fork. The concrete foundations on the upstream side of the bridge are the remnants of a few cabins cantilevered over the river. With the refurbished old dwelling as the hub, a bustling resort complex survived for 34 years.

Besides national and foreign travelers, some of the engineers on the Hetch Hetchy project boarded there during the construction of O'Shaughnessy Dam between 1919 and 1923. The pool below the waterfall that had so captivated Cox, and into which he plunged for his daily bath, became a popular swimming hole for the inn's guests. After a destructive fire in 1939, the owners immediately rebuilt the resort, but in 1958 another disastrous fire razed Cliff House, and one more landmark on the Big Oak Flat Road was lost.

Two other important ventures further enrich the Rainbow Pool area's history. The Hetch Hetchy Railroad steamed through here during construction of San Francisco's colossal water project in Hetch Hetchy Valley to the northeast. Built

A churning waterfall tumbles into Rainbow Pool, site of rich Sierra history. Tollkeeper John Cox built his cabin atop the huge boulder, later to become the hub of Cliff House Resort.

between 1916 and 1917 mainly to haul cement to the dam site, HHRR also carried supplies and equipment to this enormous project. The line closed in the late 1930s after the dam was raised another 85 feet, and the tracks were removed for scrap in 1949. Below the pool a sharp eye can see tracks protruding from the earthen bank.

Another massive water project, the Golden Rock Ditch, ran along the mountainside above Rainbow Pool. Originating at Harden Flat a few miles up the road, the 100-mile-long ditch began carrying water in 1860 to supply mines, orchards and ranches between Coulterville and Big Oak Flat. Water from the Middle Fork Tuolumne River was dammed at Harden Flat before flowing through a complicated network of canals, flumes and reservoirs. At Buck Meadows you can see the remains of an inverted siphon pipe on the north side of Highway 120. The pipe replaced a 12-story-high flume which thundered to the ground in 1868 during a windstorm. A historical plaque commemorates the site of the Golden Rock Water Company's Big Gap Flume.

■ THE HIKE

Highly recommended, especially at spring run-off, a picturesque 2-mile round-trip walk near Rainbow Pool leads to the confluence of the South and Middle

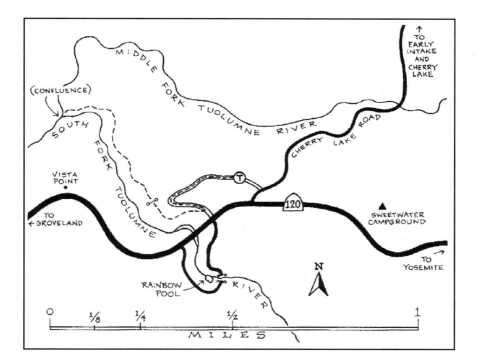

Forks. Seeing the powerful Tuolumne River roaring and leaping through a wild canyon provides a thrilling experience. To find the trail, return to Highway 120, drive east .25 mile over the high South Fork bridge and turn left on Cherry Lake Road, then immediately turn left again on another fragment of Old Big Oak Flat Road. Drive a short distance to a parking area near a gate.

Walk past the gate and follow the road downhill, and then turn right onto an unsigned dirt road heading down a narrow canyon, following the dancing South Fork waters downstream to their confluence with the Middle Fork. This long-abandoned road was once used by "tractor trains" pulling sled trailers on steel runners filled with men, materials, and supplies from the railroad to South Fork Tunnel Camp, one of Hetch Hetchy's major construction sites.

The tunnel camp buildings clung precariously to the steep mountainside, and the cookhouse actually spanned the waterfall where the two rivers merge. At the end of the road, a U-shaped tunnel under the streambed replaced an elevated 92-foot steel pipe, 225 feet long, that joined the tunnels on opposite sides of the canyon walls. A hiker today must search diligently to find the slightest trace of these engineering works. Leisurely retrace your steps back to your car, savoring the extraordinary watershow, rugged terrain, wildflowers, and seclusion in this river-carved gorge.

Although largely forgotten, a wealth of noteworthy history surrounds the dot on the map known as Rainbow Pool. It is well worth your time to explore this special niche in the Sierra. Even if you aren't a history buff, it offers a great spot for a picnic, and the deep pool below the fall remains just as alluring as it was to the crusty toll collector 100 years ago.

15
The Wonders of Bower Cave
Diana Pool via the North Fork Merced River Trail

■ THE DETAILS

Getting There: From Highway 49 in Coulterville, turn east on County Road J132 (Main Street). Beyond town, continue on paved, signed Greeley Hill Road. Go 6.5 miles to the town of Greeley Hill and continue 1.7 miles to a fork. Bear right on Greeley Hill Road and drive 4.2 miles to the unsigned North Fork Merced River bridge. Park on the left before crossing it. A stone historical monument is just across the bridge on your left, and the short walk to Bower Cave begins there.

Nearest Campground: The Pines, a Forest Service campground open year round just off Highway 120 west of Buck Meadows, has 12 sites with piped water (May through October only).

Lodging: Coulterville has Hotel Jeffery 209-878-3471. Groveland has Hotel Charlotte 209-962-6455. Buck Meadows has Buck Meadows Lodge 800-253-9673.

Further Info: To obtain an access permit for the cave area, contact Groveland Ranger District, 24525 Highway 120, Groveland, CA 95321, 209-962-7825.

Hike Distance: Short walk to Bower Cave, 2 miles round trip to Diana Pool on the North Fork Merced River Trail.

Difficulty: Easy.

Best Time to Go: Late spring, early summer, or autumn.

Cautions: Permit required to visit cave area. Do not attempt to descend into the cave. The access is very dangerous.

Starting Elevation: 2500 feet.

Other Maps: USGS Buckhorn Peak 7.5 minute topo, Stanislaus National Forest map.

Last spring while wandering a back road above Coulterville en route to Bower Cave, I recalled fond childhood memories of accompanying my parents on their Sunday drives. Most kids in my generation hated them more than lima beans, but not me. I lived for Sundays and the opportunity to investigate offbeat, unfrequented places.

Those outings instilled a life-long love of discovery and exploration, a passion for nature—the wilder the better—and a longing to have experienced the pioneer life. Nearing the cave, I thought how exciting to have arrived in a horse and buggy rather than in a four-wheel-drive truck.

Originally called Marble Springs Cave, Bower Cave lies near the North Fork Merced River, 13 miles northeast of Coulterville on the original Coulterville-Yosemite Road completed in 1874. A plaque embedded in a stone monument briefly tells the story of this first road into Yosemite. Three hundred yards up the slope and directly behind the marker, the distinctive, dove-gray rock formation holding the cave looms into view.

The landscape surrounding the cavern is characteristic foothill scenery: pines and hardwoods with a chaparral understory, squadrons of jays and woodpeckers, herds of squirrels, the river's pleasant monologue, hillsides starred with flowers and an air of gentle wildness. The cave is not the dark, sinister, bat-infested hole you may envision. Rather, it is sunshine-filled because it is open at the top. Swallows and hummingbirds dart in and out, and columbines, bleeding hearts, ferns and moss grow on the cave floor. Although several tall, big-leafed maples once grew inside the cave, maples now grow only around the rim of the opening.

Bower Cave is remarkable for its peculiar structure resembling a roofless grotto and for its lakelet at the bottom. Thought to have one of the West's largest underground lakes, most of the cave lies underwater. It is part of a lengthy limestone belt running as far north as El Dorado County. When the Sierra Nevada was birthing, molten matter rose to the surface, heating and recrystallizing the limestone to form marble. As acidic water trickled through the cracks and corroded it, the ceiling eventually collapsed, forming a large grotto.

A 1918 brochure describes the cave: "The cave is 1000 feet in circumference. The fresh water lake is 85 feet wide and 130 feet long. Four large bigleaf maples, two of them 7 feet in diameter at the base, grow in the cave and protrude from the mouth of the cave. The trees are heavily covered with sheets of thick moss from their base to their topmost branches, 280 feet from the ground. The entire south

This postcard from the 1920s shows three of the Wenger's ten children inside Bower Cave.

wall of the cave covering 400 feet from end to end is shrouded in moss a foot thick. The cave's other walls are covered with crystal and onyx formations in thousands of hues and shapes, including figures of animals, lions, bears, monkeys, as well as human forms and faces. Huge rugs of solid moss, fringed with onyx and crystal, hang from the walls and ceilings of numerous small tunnel-like caves off the walls of the main cave."

Besides the cavern's unusual geological features, the human history associated with it is ancient. Several thousand years of Native American tenancy bestow significant cultural and religious importance to the site. Miwok legend tells us that the cave, *Oo'-tin,* was home to the First People and a sacred site of wonder and awe. For at least 3500 years before white immigrants discovered it, Miwoks believed the cave was the center for the creation of the world and its inhabitants. Before taking his place in the heavens, Evening Star lived here with the many animals that later claimed the earth and sky. Miwoks today still believe the cavern is a sacred passageway, and after death their spirit returns to Mother Earth through the cave.

Exactly who the first white man was who saw it is not verified. Mariposa County records reveal that by 1856 miners Nicholas Arni and Frederick Schoebel had claimed the land surrounding a "strange and charming" cave where they established a ranch and quarried limestone. Of greater significance, they were the first to develop and promote the cave as a tourist attraction. At first, a windlass lowered people into the cave in a bathtub-size bucket. Later a steep stairway was constructed to the cave bottom where lively dances were held on the wooden dance floor. In October 1856 the **San Francisco Herald** touted its potential as a "fashionable resort."

Arni bought out Schoebel in 1858, but debt forced him to sell the 200-acre property to Henry Becker and James Torney in 1861. Soon after the deal closed, Becker bought out Torney and became the sole proprietor. Becker, credited with choosing the name Bower Cave, lived at this idyllic spot with his much younger wife and young daughters and provided simple lodging, meals and cave tours for visitors. Starting in the 1860s, thanks to **Hutchings' California Magazine** and Whitney's guidebooks, Bower Cave became a renowned attraction on the way to Yosemite.

On a winter's day in 1863 the peaceful atmosphere at Bower Cave was disrupted by three gunshots. According to neighbors, Becker was prone to drunkenness and spousal abuse. As a result of one of these whiskey-fueled rages, a terrified Marie shot her husband. An investigation concluded that, fearing for her life, she killed Becker in self-defense. After Becker was buried on the property, Marie continued to accommodate tourists. A few months later she married Louis Pechart and managed the inn and cave business for the next 30 years. Sightseers were given a cave tour on the lakelet in a small rowboat by Marie and later by her eldest daughter Caroline. Marie divorced Pechart in 1893, then sold him the property for $800 and moved to Oakland.

Bower Cave remained in the family for many decades. When Pechart died in 1898, Caroline, who had married Frederick Wenger in 1878, inherited 300 acres

*The "upper room" of Bower Cave housed the plat-
form on which the band played. The dance floor was
at the bottom of the grotto.*

of land, including Bower Cave, from her stepfather. Until the Wengers and their nine children moved to the cave in 1900, Pechart's son Emile worked the ranch and maintained the cave enterprise. Florence Wenger, last of the ten children, was born at Bower Cave.

Over the years, they made many improvements and additions at the cave site. A large dance floor, encircled by a railing, was built on the bottom of the grotto. The orchestra perched on another platform attached to a side wall above the lake. Steep, sturdy wooden stairs were installed to the floor 50 feet below and seats were fashioned on the mossy banks under the maple trees. Trout were planted in the lakelet but needed to be hand-fed because the water couldn't sustain life.

A new ranch house inn built in 1898 carried on the tradition of lodging and meals for travelers. As Yosemite's popularity increased, travelers by the thousands came to see its fabled sights, with many of them stopping overnight at Bower Cave to add to their adventure. Locals also frequented the cavern to enjoy the magical spot for family outings, birthday parties, camp outs, and dancing in the moonlight on soft summer nights.

Even after Bower Cave dwindled in popularity as quicker routes opened to Yosemite, there were brief sparks of rekindled interest. In February 1945, two years after Caroline's death at age 85, the Wenger heirs sold the property for $17,000 to J. L. Rice of Modesto. Rice's dream was to develop the area into a rehabilitation center for disabled veterans, giving them a place "to get well and enjoy themselves" free of charge. He was never able to raise sufficient funds to make his worthwhile dream a reality. A tragic event forced Rice to close the cave to the public when in the early 1950s a visitor plunged down the rotting staircase and was killed.

In 1953 at Rice's request, a young Stanford marine biology student named Jon Lindbergh, son of the famous aviator, became the first diver to explore the lake. In the mid-1960s state officials examined Bower Cave as a possible state park. They were highly enthusiastic about the site's potential as a scenic attraction of important historical significance. Unfortunately, the bond issue, which included the $1.35 million Bower Cave project, failed to pass. Finally in 1981, Rice's widow sold the property to the Linkletter family corporation.

In 1940 Modesto moviemakers J.N. Cavanaugh and Tom Satariano. Planed to produce six short films, the first of which was to be shot at Bower Cave. Cavanaugh, obviously enchanted, stated, "In my ten years' experience in and about Hollywood . . . I have never found any stage construction to fit a fairy story as do the natural formations of Bower Cave." In August 1940 an audition was advertised locally, but we don't know if the film was made.

Resting quietly out of the public's interest for many decades, Bower Cave has now returned to the limelight. The cave and 835 acres of private land owned by the Linkletter family were acquired by Stanislaus National Forest. The Trust for Public Land coordinated a complex land exchange to make this possible. The Bower Cave area may once again open for public use, but at present, access is only allowed to the rim of the entrance because of the potential hazard of the cave site. You must obtain a permit from the Groveland Ranger District before entering the area.

The Bower Cave environs today are much the same as they were 145 years ago before discovery by white men. They still drowse peacefully in a near natural state. An old foundation or two and a few ancient apple trees are virtually the only clues to a long history of habitation.

■ THE HIKE

For a more ambitious hike after examining the cavern area, take an easy walk downstream along the river on the North Fork Merced River Trail as far as you like. Find access to the pleasant alder-lined trail near the bridge behind a metal gate just off the road. You'll find beautiful pools carved in granite .5 mile from the gate and many inviting places to linger and have a picnic lunch. Indian rhubarb and water grasses dot the shoreline. If you continue downstream around one mile from the gate, Bean Creek flows down on your right. You can follow it upstream about 400 feet to a lovely cascade glissading over smooth rock into Diana Pool, as locals call it.

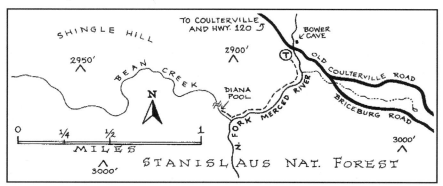

16
Muir's Mossy Boulder
Famous Footsteps on the Upper North Fork Merced River

■ THE DETAILS

Getting There: From Groveland, drive Highway 120 east for 7 miles, then turn right onto Smith Station Road (J20). Go 6 miles, then turn left on Greeley Hill Road. Follow it 4.2 miles to the North Fork Merced River bridge. Just beyond the bridge, turn left on old Yosemite-Coulterville Road (USFS Road 2S01). Proceed 4.5 miles and turn left at the sign for North Fork Merced River onto Road 2S62. Just before the North Fork, bear left into a small clearing and park.

Nearest Campground: See Chapter 15.

Lodging: See Chapter 15.

Further Info: Groveland Ranger District, Stanislaus Natl. Forest, 209-962-7825.

Hike Distance: About 1.5 mile round trip.

Difficulty: Easy.

Best Time to Go: Late spring or early autumn.

Cautions: Watch for rattlesnakes and poison oak.

Starting Elevation: 3200 feet.

Other Maps: USGS Lake Eleanor sw 7.5 minute topo, Stanislaus National Forest map.

Tucked away in a remote section of Stanislaus National Forest a few miles east of Groveland, the seldom-seen upper North Fork Merced River tumbles through a heavily forested, trailless landscape that is rarely visited, much less heard of. Not far from the old Coulterville-Yosemite Road, Muir enthusiasts will certainly enjoy the discovery of a huge flat-topped boulder upon which John-of-the-Mountains spent a night in June 1869.

This virtually unknown ramble in the foothills above Bower Cave (see Chapter 15) offers plenty of solitude and a taste of the things that fueled Muir's passion for the natural world. I daresay that not many of us today would so acutely feel the depth of emotion and spiritual intensity he experienced while studying this mass of stone lodged in the stream.

Nevertheless, Muir's altar rock provides an unusual and important piece of Muiriana because the accumulation of such firsthand observations led him to become the nation's foremost wilderness advocate, to pioneer the Western conservation movement, and to provide the driving force behind the creation of the national park system and the Sierra Club.

About two millennia ago a Roman philosopher observed that chance makes a plaything of one's life. Fortunately for us, by chance John Muir was unable to find a ship to take him from Cuba to explore the South American wilderness in 1867. Otherwise, he might have spent his life studying that continent instead of coming to California.

As soon as 29-year-old John Muir stepped off the steamer in San Francisco on March 27, 1868, he asked a tool-carrying carpenter for the quickest way out of town. "Where do you want to go?" the man inquired. "To any place that is wild," answered Muir. Startled by the odd reply and eager to get away from this intense young man, the carpenter promptly directed him to the Oakland ferry.

Thus began Muir's legendary journeys into the California wilderness when it was still wild. Not quite yet had sheep and cattle grazing, farming and lumbering blighted the virgin landscape. It was still pristine, "one sweet bee pasture" throughout its entire length and breadth.

Accompanied by a shipboard acquaintance named Chilwell, Muir started for Yosemite on April 1, carrying only his signature equipment: a blanket, tea, bread and a notebook. Walking south to Gilroy and then east to Pacheco Pass, they trekked through a "landscape so covered with flowers they seemed to be painted." From the summit Muir was even more stunned by the astonishing panorama below. Many years later he reminisced that of all he had seen in his explorations, the image of the flower-filled great Central Valley before him with the white-walled Sierra Nevada shining on the far horizon was the most memorable, the most overwhelming. As pictured by Muir, it was an enormous "lake of pure sunshine, 40 to 50 miles wide and 500 miles long . . . a vast flower garden level like a lake of gold."

By compass, the two men waded through this glorious sea of wildflowers to the Merced River, crossed it and followed it to Yosemite Valley. After eight days of exploring, sketching, collecting specimens and observing animal life, Muir was spellbound by Yosemite's Olympian grandeur and its rich biological and geological diversity. Unaware that he soon would be known as the "prophet of wilderness," Muir recognized that by going to the mountains he had come home.

Determined to return

The author perches on John Muir's mossy boulder in the North Fork Merced River.

to Yosemite for extensive field studies as soon as he earned money for provisions, Muir descended to the San Joaquin Valley and found work harvesting, shearing sheep and breaking mustangs. Chilwell drifted away, but Muir stayed on as a shepherd, which allowed him time to study the area's flora and fauna. Wondering how he could pack enough for a summer trip, Muir solved the problem in May 1869. Rancher Pat Delaney wanted a trustworthy man to supervise moving his 2500 sheep to high alpine meadows. He promised Muir that a herder and his dog would do the work, assuring him ample time to study rocks, plants and scenery.

By mid-June the wooly bundles had nibbled their way to a lovely meadow near the North Fork Merced River above Bower Cave. While encamped for a few days, Muir went roaming and had one of his numerous mini-adventures that revealed his passion and reverence for wild things and wild places.

Walking along the North Fork, Muir observed trees growing on flood deposits, evidence that more than a century had passed since a torrent of extraordinary proportions had swept downstream. Furthermore, he was intrigued by the way ordinary spring flood waters heaped small boulders into dams, creating cascades and flower-rimmed pool basins. Moreover, lodged firmly in the middle of one of these channels sat an eight-foot-tall cubical mass of granite carpeted with moss on top and down its sides. He concluded that nothing less than a "master flood" could have transported such a massive piece of granite there.

As he rested on its nearly level, altar-like top, Muir was enchanted by the cascade's refreshing gauzy spray, the green pool ringed with lilies and foam bells, and the dappled sunlight sifting through a canopy of alder and flowering dogwood. Soothed by the sylvan nook's gentle beauty and the water music of the little fall and river slip-sliding past the altar rock, he wrote, "the place seemed holy, where one might hope to see God." After dark, he returned to spend the night atop this woodland shrine and found it even more magical than by day. Deeply moved by the experience, he gave "thanks to God for this immortal gift."

His acquaintance with this mossy boulder teaches us that absolutely nothing escaped his keen sense of observation. Nothing was too insignificant or too commonplace for study and notation. Such devotion to details, concealed from an unpracticed eye, emphasized his awareness of the perfect harmony and interconnection of everything in the natural world. Through Muir's encounter with a large chunk of granite, we can almost feel the fire that burned within him. For Muir everything in nature was simultaneously a research laboratory and a temple for worship.

Bushwhacking in rough, trailless terrain one spring, I clambered over gigantic downed conifers, juked through a maze of poison oak, and tip-toed among acres of nodding, pink bleeding hearts hoping I'd find Muir's mossy boulder. Suddenly, unmistakably, it stood before me, standing firm and square and solitary as Muir had described it. Looking at the detritus of the January 1997 hundred-year watery rampage in the Sierra, I marveled at the force of the "master flood" that carried it here.

I knew I had to get on top of it and connect with Muir's appreciation of this special place. I too gave myself up to the same serene wildness that refreshed and nourished his soul 132 years ago.

■ THE HIKE

To find Muir's mossy boulder, from the parking area, walk a short distance on the remnant of an old road heading downstream. When you come to a large downed tree, look for a place to rock hop across the stream. This should be an easy ford because the infant North Fork is not far from its headwaters. Be advised there is no trail. It's a toss-up which side you choose to bushwhack your way downstream. Generally, across the river is a bit easier.

After crossing, you will spot a little rock cairn in front of a tall cedar. From here you'll be on a faint game trail that will disappear and reappear; don't rely on it. Pick your way through brush, lots of poison oak, and over and around downed trees, souvenirs of January 1997 storms. Staying about 100 feet above the North Fork is easier than walking at streamside.

As you continue downstream, be on the lookout for a clearing of sorts near the river. Cut downhill to find Muir's mossy rock sitting in the stream. On its upstream side, a small cascade feeds a pool. The rock itself, roughly an eight-foot cube, will be obvious. In late April and May, the gorgeous pink blooms of bleeding hearts carpet the forest floor. Above you, the creamy-white bracts of dogwood dance in the breeze. A jungle of sword ferns, some six feet tall, line the bank.

When you leave, you might offer thanks to John Muir, both for his lifelong battle to preserve our priceless natural heritage, and for his advice to "climb the mountains and get their good tidings."

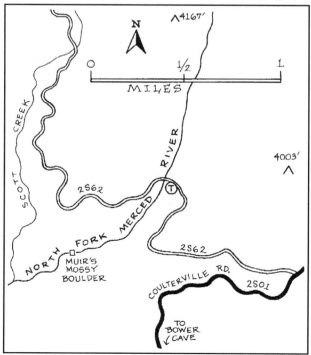

17
Hite's Cove on the South Fork Merced River Trail
Riches, Romance and Wildflowers

■ THE DETAILS

Getting There: From Mariposa, take Highway 140 east for 22 miles to Savage's Trading Post (also Sisochi Gallery) located at the confluence of the Merced River and its South Fork. The signed trailhead lies uphill to the left of Redbud Lodge.

Nearest Campgrounds: See Chapter 4.

Lodging: Redbud Lodge 800-272-2301 at the trailhead has rooms. Mariposa has several choices.

Further Info: Sierra National Forest, 5158 Highway 140, Mariposa, CA 95338, 209-966-2456. Redbud Lodge/Savage's Trading Post 209-379-2301.

Recommended reading: **Wildflowers of Hite's Cove**, available at Savage's Trading Post.

Hike Distance: 8.4 miles round trip.

Difficulty: Moderate.

Best Time to Go: Spring.

Cautions: No bikes allowed. Please don't pick the flowers and pack out all trash. Backpackers must have campfire permits. During summer the trail is closed due to high fire potential.

Starting Elevation: 1400 feet. Up to 600 feet gain.

Other Map: USGS El Portal 15 minute topo.

You can experience one of God's gifts to the planet in a canyon just west of Yosemite Park, definitely another of the Creator's masterpieces. En route to the park on Highway 140, more than a million visitors annually zip across the bridge where the South Fork Merced River joins its main stem. The vast majority of motorists haven't a clue that they've just passed one of the most historically significant spots in the Central Sierra, as well as the jumping off point for an outstanding spring jaunt and a dazzling, phenomenal wildflower pageant.

The undulating 4.2-mile trail leading to Hite's Cove, paralleling the South Fork Merced, is filled with flowers, rugged foothill beauty, inviting swimming and fishing holes, and mining relics. If you crave the joy of spending time in spring's embrace, it doesn't get any better than this. Sometimes high above the river, sometimes alongside it, the trail threads a slender, steep-sided gorge, offering an intimate acquaintance with quintessential canyon scenery. Here also began a shameful chapter in California history with the arrival of miners in an area inhabited by Native Americans. Equally important is the locale of a rich mining community between 1861 and 1881.

We have Dr. Ralph Mendershausen to thank for most of what we know about Hite's Cove. His fascinating book, *Treasures of the South Fork*, is the definitive work on this remarkable region. Wild and free, the South Fork Merced River begins its 41-mile course in the alpine realm of the Clark Range. Racing through narrow and precipitous gorges, it briefly becomes tamer as it tumbles through Wawona's gentle terrain. Beyond Wawona, the South Fork again accelerates on the final leg of its journey when it dives into the lower canyon, eventually merging with the main stem Merced at Savage's Trading Post on Highway 140. Each spring the lowermost 4 miles of the canyon between Savage's and Hite's Cove are a mecca for wildflower lovers who come to immerse themselves in one of the most spectacular displays in the Sierra Nevada.

The earliest inhabitants in the canyon were southern Miwoks who lived in harmony with their environment and one another. By 1848, however, trouble appeared in paradise, personified by James D. Savage. Savage initially came to California in 1846 to join John Fremont's battalion to fight the Mexican War. After that war and before the '49er Gold Rush, Savage discovered gold in the South Fork Merced canyon and built a trading post near its junction with the main river. Soon this White Chief of the Foothills had five wives and hundreds of Indians mining gold for him in exchange for white man's food and goods. Because he was mining the Merced before '49ers swarmed into the area and commanded a huge, cheap labor force, his profits were staggering. Reportedly, Savage's total revenue was $500,000, an enormous sum in that era.

In just two years, the native population was overwhelmed by miners and settlers, resulting in numerous skirmishes. Careless miners destroyed Indian food sources and usurped territory they had inhabited for centuries. Fearful for their own survival, they tried to expel the settlers from the mountains. Finally in 1850, the Indians attacked Savage's South Fork trading post, the first of several events igniting the so-called Mariposa Indian War.

After the raid, Governor McDougal deputized a posse called the Mariposa Battalion to hunt down the 350 miscreants led by Chief Tenaya. Savage, a major in the state militia, headed the posse. Ironically, a momentous sidebar to Savage's hounding Indians through the mountains was the Euro-American discovery of Yosemite Valley in March 1851. Unimpressed with the Valley's snow-mantled, rocky splendor, the Major's only comment was, "It's a hell of a place."

In the end, the clash between the two cultures was inevitable and the results predictable. The few remaining Indians were herded onto a reservation in the San Joaquin Valley. After Savage was murdered by a rival trader in 1852, most of the Indians fled the reservation and returned to the mountains. Nevertheless, their traditional way of life was sadly over.

A keen observation by author Kenneth Brower reveals that "the astonishing thing about Yosemite is the speed with which it went from prehistory to present. In 1851, the valley was Ahwahnee, a secret valley known only to Indians. By 1855, the Ahwahneechee were gone and the first tourist party had arrived." As a result of the Gold Rush, in only four years an ancient people who had called Yosemite home since 1400 B.C. had been virtually eliminated.

A few years later another white man figured prominently in the history of the South Fork canyon. In 1861 John Hite was guided by an Indian woman to an outcrop of gold above the cove that now bears his name. For this lucky man, the stuff that dreams are made of came in the form of a rich surface vein. Immediately, Hite hit the jackpot. Encouraged by the claim's early productivity, he soon upgraded from simple recovery techniques to large stamp mills. In 1862 Hite recorded his claim, and by 1864 a ten-stamp, water-powered mill was in place. Formidable amounts of labor and engineering skills were required to make the new 20-stamp mill operational in 1868. Among other things, a mile-long water ditch and diversion dam had to be dug, and massive equipment freighted from Stockton to Mariposa had to be delivered to the cove.

A gang of 40 Chinese accomplished this herculean task by manhandling tons of ponderous machinery down to the cove from the ridge 2500 feet above it.

The remote town of Hite's Cove in its prime around 1881. The hotel perches above the 40-stamp mill and footbridge at the lower end of the Cove.

Additionally, they were the earth movers who shoveled out the canal necessary to run the new mill. According to Dr. Mendershausen, the construction of Hite's Cove Road, connecting the canyon to Mariposa, was the crowning touch of their many labors. Today it remains an engineering marvel, zigzagging sharply five miles down to the South Fork. Requiring five years to complete, it was finished in 1870.

As mining operations at Hite's Cove expanded, so did the community. By 1881 when the mine reached its zenith, the population ranged between 75 and 150, including many Indians and Chinese. At its peak, the settlement boasted a dance hall, hotel, boarding house, storehouse, blacksmith shop, store, two saloons, two residences, a cluster of shacks, mine-related buildings, tramway, suspension bridges, 40-stamp mill, Chinatown, orchard, garden and alfalfa pasture.

The 40-stamp mill in use after 1875 was capable of crushing about 50 tons of ore per day. In a time when gold was valued at $20 per ounce, Hite became a millionaire. By all accounts, the earth gave up $3 million from her treasure chest during his 20-year tenure in the strikingly handsome South Fork canyon. For reasons that aren't clear, in 1881 Hite sold his mine for $600,000 to New York investors. Perhaps he knew the mine's output was declining or perhaps something personal motivated him to sell. We'll never know for certain, but he did remain a partner in the investment group.

The mine shut down within a year after the sale due to over-extension of capital for repairs and expansion plus a lawsuit against Hite. Hite was accused of selling a mine that had been plucked clean of profits. However, the case was thrown out of court, and Hite then sued the investors for a debt owed his sawmill. In the end, he regained full ownership before selling it to another investment group for $100,000 in 1895.

Hite's later years were marred by poor health, alcoholism and many troubling events. After marrying a white woman in 1897, he found himself ensnared in a famous, shocking and protracted divorce with his Indian wife, Lucy. Racial prejudice combined with a rare and highly unusual divorce case initiated by a non-citizen, non-white woman created sensational fodder for scandal-loving newspapers. In 1906 Hite, age 76, died in San Francisco, but ten years later legal wrangling over his will and complicated marital status lingered on. In the final analysis, lawyers received more of Hite's money than the litigants.

■ THE HIKE

Hikers today can see massive cone grinders, arrastras and a Pelton wheel just off the trail .5 mile before the cove proper. These ponderous relics and reworked tailings from Hite's mine are near what appears to be a sandy beach, which is actually pulverized mine tailings. At the entrance to the cove, cellar holes and ruins of a stone building remain in what was Chinatown. All that survived a fire in 1924 are a few black locust trees and the hotel foundation. Here and there

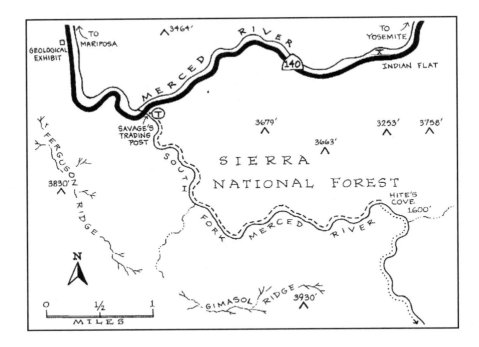

twisted cables and anchor bolts from the wagon and foot bridges at the lower and upper ends of the cove and fragments of rusted equipment lie scattered about. Hite Mine is easily recognizable up the steep slope behind the flat hotel site. Also extant is evidence of some mining work in recent years.

The remnants of mining days seem trivial in comparison to the more enduring and priceless natural features of the South Fork canyon. Its free-flowing river, wild beauty, heart-stopping wildflower show, and recreational opportunities by far eclipse any human intrusion. All of this is yours to behold by simply getting out of your car at Savage's Trading Post and walking all or any part of the 4.2-mile footpath to Hite's Cove. En route, particularly in the first 2 miles, it is possible to identify more than 50 species of wildflowers during peak bloom. Although the profusion varies with weather conditions, first blooms pop out in February and increase in numbers until April or May.

The South Fork Merced canyon offers something to suit many interests. The botanist, hiker, history buff, birdwatcher, fisherman and rockhound will all be amply rewarded. For most of us, just the simple pleasure of walking in such a remarkably beautiful setting on a warm spring day is enough. Whatever your focus, be thankful that this wild river corridor has been protected by Congress from any kind of development.

Note that if you can safely ford the South Fork at Hite's Cove, you can continue upstream on a trail along the river's west bank.

18
Yosemite Mountain-Sugar Pine Railroad
Narrow Gauge Steam Trains near Yosemite's South Entrance

■ THE DETAILS

Getting There: From Oakhurst, drive 15 miles north on Highway 41 toward Yosemite. Turn right at the sign for Narrow Gauge Inn & Yosemite Mountain Sugar Pine Railroad.

Nearest Campground: Lupine-Cedar Campground at Bass Lake, open year round, has 113 sites.

Lodging: In Fish Camp, Narrow Gauge Inn 888-644-9050, open April to October, has 25 rooms.

Further Info: For information about schedules, special events and summer moonlight rides, write the railroad at 56001 Yosemite Highway 41, Fish Camp, CA 95323, or call 559-683-7273.

Hike Distance: No hike, excursion train only. For a nearby hike, see Chapter 19.

Difficulty: Easy.

Best Time to Go: Weather permitting, trains operate from April through November.

Cautions: None.

Starting Elevation: 4240 feet.

Map: Sierra National Forest map.

Unknown to more than a sprinkling of travelers zipping over Highway 41 on their way to Yosemite, a piece of a vanished era has been kept alive in the small community of modern Sugar Pine. In the Sierra National Forest just below Fish Camp between Oakhurst and Yosemite, four miles of track run through what was prime timber country owned by Madera Sugar Pine Company (MSP) between 1899 and 1931. The three-foot-wide, narrow gauge railroad recreates an extremely important and fascinating era when eastern Madera County mountains were heavily networked with tracks, today carrying passengers over restored tracks into the woods, now dense with second-growth trees.

Supplying the muscle for this nostalgic journey in the woods is a relatively light, 167,000-pound engineering marvel known as a Shay locomotive built in 1928. These wood-burning locomotives were used to haul logs from the woods to the mountain mills. From their point of origin, they had to be dismantled, freighted by 16-mule teams and then reassembled in the mountains. These formidable engines, unique creations designed specifically for logging operations, have "each articulated wheel a driver, giving the engine many times the power of a normal locomotive." About 300 Shays were built, but by 1960, most had been dismantled for scrap metal, and only about 30 intact Shay locomotives exist today.

The tiny logging railroad we see today represented a dream come true for Swiss-born Rudy Stauffer who wanted to revive a part of the Sierra Nevada's colorful past. In the 1950s, the Stauffers bought land near Yosemite and became intrigued with the MSP's abandoned tracks running though their property. In time, Rudy and Luce Stauffer acquired locomotives (including the largest Shay ever built), tons of spare parts, and rolling stock from the defunct West Side Lumber Company in Tuolumne County. By August 1967, after equipment and track restoration, the Yosemite Mountain-Sugar Pine Railroad was ready for passengers. Max Stauffer, Rudy and Luce's son and the railroad's current owner, opened the Narrow Gauge Inn in 1967 along a portion of the MSP logging railroad that ran through his property.

Somehow it's a comfort to know that the haunting, lonesome call of the steam locomotive still echoes through the Sierra Nevada, reminding us of a rowdy and flamboyant time that is gone forever. In this automation age with dazzling sci-fi technology a part of our daily lives, we often overlook the astonishing accomplishments of the period from the Gold Rush to the early years of the 20th century. The Madera Sugar Pine Company was one of these vanguard operations, the granddaddy of all central Sierra logging ventures. The MSP, besides being the oldest, proved to be the most financially successful.

Gold, of course, played a star role in the drama of California's early settlement, but after the Civil War, the enormous forests of virgin timber drew the attention of eastern lumber barons. By 1900 logging was a major player in California's economy, and the Madera Sugar Pine Company was a dominant force in the industry.

It had its beginning among the early sawmill operations at work in the Central Sierra of the 1850s, the majority of which were small and short lived. As lumbering technology advanced and became better capitalized, larger ventures were bankrolled. The first significant logging enterprise in the Central Sierra was the California Lumber Company. In 1876 a brilliantly engineered and skillfully constructed 52-mile-long V-flume, then the longest in the world, floated rough cut lumber to the finishing mill site in the new town of Madera (Spanish for wood or lumber). The 40-acre complex included drying and retail yards and a box factory. From Madera the finished product was shipped by rail to various destinations. Three years later a severe drought devastated the local economy, and the company declared bankruptcy.

In 1880 the reorganized company began doing business as the Madera Flume and Trading Company (MFT), operating very successfully for several years and building a four-mile, narrow gauge logging railroad in 1899 to transport timber to the new mill at Soquel. A small, workhorse locomotive named *Betsy* furnished the muscle for this pioneer logging line. By the close of 1892, the Madera Flume and Trading Company faced a nationwide economic slump and the logging-off of most of their timber supply. By 1898 they had to shut down all facets of their business.

Nevertheless, a year later the firm was resurrected, underlining the basic soundness of large-scale logging in the Central Sierra. In 1899 two MFT executives combined forces with wealthy Michigan lumbermen who owned vast tracts of nearby timber lands to establish the Madera Sugar Pine Company. They built a large, upgraded sawmill and company town at Sugar Pine, very near the south entrance to Yosemite National Park. The great V-trough flume was extended two miles to the new mill site at Sugar Pine, and the original 52-mile-long flume was completely rebuilt.

By 1900 the MSP held 22,000 acres of timber in Mariposa and Madera counties. Over the next 30 years other tracts were leased or bought. Their timber requirements were staggering; each season's cut depleted 1000 acres, translating to 500 million board feet per year. In order to keep up, Madera Sugar Pine laid 140 miles of tracks, although not all of it was in use at the same time. Skillfully engineered wooden trestles spanned deep gorges, steep grades and treacherous curves. The logging railroads were extraordinary accomplishments in this rough and inaccessible terrain.

Of all the technological improvements in the logging industry utilized by MSP throughout its long history, the great V-flume remains to many its most innovative accomplishment, symbolizing Yankee ingenuity in the glory days of Sierra logging. The V-flume was an unorthodox and extraordinary means of transporting lumber, and it revolutionized logging in the Sierra. With the advent of flumes, the sawmill could be situated in the cutting area and only the usable, rough cut lumber floated to the finishing mill, eliminating the time-consuming and astronomical cost of conventional transportation.

J.W. Haines was believed to have built the first flume in 1859, a 12-mile trough bringing Eastern Sierra water to the Comstock Lode. The Madera Sugar Pine flume was 4½ times as long, 54 miles from Sugar Pine to Madera. It required constant surveillance and maintenance, but during winter a skeleton crew stayed on for extensive repairs to get ready for the next season. At the end of the cutting season in November, flume herders closed their stations and shipped all gear and personal belongings on flume boats to Madera. Repair crews and lumberjacks also used flume boats for rapid transit down the line. According to accounts of old-timers, the ride was wild and thrilling, surpassing anything devised by modern theme parks. The upper flume sections were steep and dangerous in places; on some grades the boats hurtled down the trough at 50 mph!

For the first 30 years of the 20th century, the flume floated 1.5 billion board feet of lumber down to the drying yards in Madera. From there, lumber was shipped by rail and freight wagons throughout the West. Madera Sugar Pine Company, with its largest mill at Sugar Pine, was the biggest, oldest and most profitable of all the Central Sierra lumber outfits. It was also a premiere player in the economic development of the San Joaquin Valley.

The 30-acre camp at Sugar Pine was in reality a small, bustling city. Facilities rivaled those of many small towns: barber shop, hospital, saloons, brothels, store, post office, dormitories and houses, company offices and shops, mess halls, community center, school, church, gambling and opium dens and a baseball field. Most of the bachelors lived in company dormitories, and married men and their families lived in small cabins. Well away from others in what can only be described as a ghetto, Chinese laborers, and later Mexicans who replaced them, had their own quarters. On September 9, 1922, a fire swept through Sugar Pine camp. Only 15 houses and the school survived. With phenomenal speed, bigger and better facilities were completed, and by April 1923, the camp reopened for business.

The Great Depression of the 1930s marked the end of the Madera Sugar Pine. The mill at Sugar Pine cut its last log in November 1931, and the huge camp permanently closed. When the economic climate showed no signs of improvement by 1933, the MSP management was forced to shut down all their facilities. The oldest, most profitable lumber company in the Central Sierra quietly disappeared. By 1937 the locomotives, mill equipment, railroad tracks, buildings, and all other properties had been disposed of. The marvelous and historic V-flume was cannibalized for scrap lumber, and what was left deteriorated and collapsed. A sad footnote is the fate of old *Betsy*. This spunky little engine that worked the woods for nearly 60 years was junked for $25.

A Forest Service historian stated that in April 1930, a year before the Sugar Pine Mill closed, the company deeded back to the United States all the thousands of acres the MSP had amassed during the 30-year life of the corporation except for the land at Sugar Pine Camp itself. After the mill closure in 1931, George Tolladay bought the property with plans to develop the area into a summer resort. Surprisingly little is left of the extensive settlement and mill complex at Sugar Pine Camp. The log pond is still visible, but only the remains of the concrete powerhouse exist nearby. Presently, many private residences stand where the MSP buildings once stood.

Though the "whistles blow no more" as in the early days when massive lumbering operations were in full swing, the recreated remnant of the historic railroad runs daily during summer and on a limited basis in April and May and September to November. Passengers may detrain at Slab Creek for a picnic, then catch the next train when they're ready to return. The little Yosemite Mountain-Sugar Pine Railroad that played such an important role in California's development offers a snapshot of a colorful and exciting bygone slice of western Americana.

For further reading, *Thunder in the Mountains* by Hank Johnston is a well-written and illustrated source book for a comprehensive study of MSP operations. For a detailed description of fluming, read Johnston's *The Whistle Blows No More*.

19
Lewis Creek National Scenic Trail
Flume, Flowers, Falls and Warm Springs

■ THE DETAILS

Getting There: Drive Highway 41 north from Fresno or Oakhurst, or south from Wawona or Yosemite to find the three trailheads. The south trailhead is off Cedar Valley Drive north of Yosemite Forks, the middle trailhead is just north of the 4000-foot elevation sign on Highway 41, and the north trailhead is off Sugar Pine Road near the community of Sugar Pine.

Nearest Campgrounds: Big Sandy has 18 primitive sites along Big Creek east of Fish Camp. Grey's Mountain has 26 primitive sites on North Fork Willow Creek east of Yosemite Forks. Both USFS camps are on Jackson Road (6S07).

Lodging: Oakhurst and Fish Camp have several choices.

Further Info: Mariposa/Minarets Ranger District, Sierra National Forest, Box 10, North Fork, CA 93643, 559-683-4665 or 559-877-2218. Write or stop in for a free trail description/map.

Hike Distance: Up to 7.4 miles round trip, or a 3.7-mile shuttle.

Difficulty: Moderate for downstream, moderately strenuous for upstream or round trip.

Best Time to Go: Spring, early summer, autumn.

Cautions: None.

Starting Elevation: 3360 feet at south trailhead, 4000 feet at middle trailhead, 4240 feet at north trailhead.

Other Maps: USGS Bass Lake 15 minute topo, free Lewis Creek Forest Service map.

Just north of Oakhurst, one of the most beautiful lower elevation trails in the Central Sierra begs for your boots. This could easily be called a designer hike, combining a variety of elements that are alluring to everyone who enjoys walking in the mountains: a broad sensory appeal, waterfalls, solitude, lively history, wildflowers and streamside walking through a peaceful forest setting. Add to that three trailhead options, from easy to moderately strenuous, and you'd be hard pressed to find a lovelier destination to celebrate springtime in the Sierra.

Lewis Creek Trail was added to the National Recreation Trails System in 1982 because of its outstanding combination of scenic and historic qualities. The trail is 3.7 miles long, and its middle access is only a short walk from Highway 41.

Located five miles from Yosemite's south entrance station, the path lies in Sierra National Forest. Hiking mainly takes place from late April through November with winter access when weather permits. The shaded trail meandering along Lewis Creek ranges in elevation from 4240 feet on the north end to 3360 feet on the south.

Characteristic of elevations around 4000 feet, you'll find a smorgasbord of vegetation here, affording an eye-pleasing and fragrant mix of sights and smells. Aromatic incense cedars, stately sugar and ponderosa pines, elegant white firs, sturdy oaks, graceful dogwoods, alders and wild filberts (California hazel) make up the dense forest canopy along the route. Among the ubiquitous manzanita, pungent bear clover (mountain misery) and the tropical scent of western azalea blooms add their spicy flavors on the forest floor.

During spring and summer, an impressive collection of wildflowers will keep you company along the way. Depending on weather conditions and the month, expect to see among others Clarkia, pennyroyal, exotic-looking tiger lilies, foxglove, wild ginger, Indian pinks and shooting stars. Closer to the tumbling creek, giant evergreen woodwardia (chain fern), spearmint, bracken and sword ferns add texture and brightness to the shrubbery.

Many tempting pools, Corlieu warm springs and two handsome cascades lend their watery charms to this delightful riparian environment. Although only dropping about 20 feet, Red Rock Falls is situated in a pretty niche where the waters of Lewis Creek slip-slide over a ledge of slick, reddish rock. Further downstream, 80-foot Corlieu Falls is Madera County's highest waterfall. Though not especially high, Corlieu Falls is exceptionally beautiful and multifaceted. Rather than a sheer drop, water descends in stages by finding several routes over rocky shelves and crevices. Lush foliage lining the stream banks completes this lovely waterscape.

An aura of historical events clings to the Lewis Creek environs, and relics of them can be spotted by an observant visitor. Most of the trail parallels the route of the old Madera Sugar Pine Lumber Company flume in service from 1900 to 1931. Extending 54 miles from Sugar Pine Lumber Mill to Madera in the San Joaquin Valley, the flume carried more than one billion board feet of lumber during its three decades of operation. See Chapter 18 for more about the flume.

Missouri-born Clifford Corlieu (pronounced Corlew) arrived in California in the 1870s. For many years he was a rancher and logger in Auberry Valley east of present-day Fresno. After his daughter married and moved to Sugar Pine upstream from the falls, he visited her periodically and became familiar with the area. Charmed by the picturesque cascade that now bears his name, he decided to build a cabin overlooking the falls and nearby warm spring. Corlieu piped the warm spring water into a large pothole, creating a natural hot tub. A personable and gentle man with a lifelong affection for nature, Corlieu lived here from 1910 until his death in 1929.

Few remnants of the Corlieu homestead remain except for three terraced flats reinforced by rock walls, an ancient apple tree, a portion of the water wheel assembly used to generate electricity and the "bathtub." Just off the trail near the homestead site, a sharp-eyed hiker can see his grave marker. Please do not remove any artifacts you may find along the Lewis Creek Trail.

According to Sierra National Forest literature, a resort was built near the trail at Corlieu Falls in the 1930s. The rustic resort and cabins were removed, however, by the Forest Service in the early 1940s because of various problems. Later, Corlieu's son-in-law opened a museum-restaurant on one of the trailheads near the site of the former resort. He filed 20 mining claims along the trail and unlawfully sold them to buyers who built homes and cabins on them. Finally in the late 1960s, the Forest Service removed the illegal dwellings and museum-restaurant, allowing the area to return to its natural condition.

Other than lending his name to a photogenic waterfall, Corlieu is perhaps best remembered for his poetry. Forest Service information states that "in his last years of peaceful retirement, Corlieu wrote a book of verse speaking of his love for God, his fellow man and the glories of nature." His poems were published in 1962 under the title *Sierra Sanctum, Written Reveries of a Cliff Man*.

■ THE HIKE

To experience the entire 3.7-mile route, either begin at the southern trail access off Cedar Valley Drive or to the north off Sugar Pine Road. The trail is downhill from north to south with an 800-foot elevation loss. If you don't choose to ramble 7.4 miles round-trip, place a shuttle car at one end.

The middle trailhead is ideal for those who only want to venture a short distance on this beautiful path. From here you can reach upper and lower Corlieu Falls with very little effort in .5 mile.

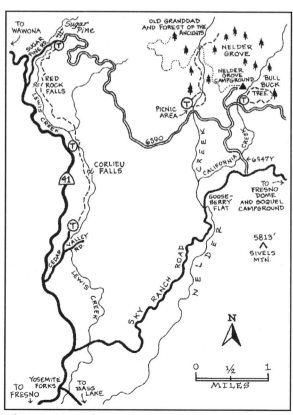

Chapters 19 and 20

20
Nelder Grove of Giant Sequoias
Big Trees Without Big Crowds

■ THE DETAILS

Getting There: From Oakhurst, drive 4.1 miles north on Highway 41 toward Yosemite. Just past Bass Lake Road, turn right on Sky Ranch Road (Road 632). Proceed almost 7 miles and turn left, then go one mile to the sign for Shadow of the Giants Trail and Nelder Campground. You reach Shadow of the Giants trailhead in .5 mile. For the Bull Buck Trail, drive to the end of the campground and park near the small picnic area by the creek. You'll spot a signpost indicating the way to Bull Buck.

Nearest Campground: Nelder Grove Camp, open May through September, has 7 primitive sites with no piped water.

Lodging: Oakhurst has several choices.

Further Info: Mariposa/Minarets Ranger District, Sierra National Forest, Box 10, North Fork, CA 93643, 559-683-4665 or 559-877-2218.

Hike Distance: Bull Buck Trail: one-mile loop, Shadow of the Giants Trail: 1.2-mile loop.

Difficulty: Easy.

Best Time to Go: Spring, summer, autumn.

Cautions: Snowfall closes access to the Nelder Grove area. Check at USFS Ranger Station on Highway 41 for road conditions and weather information.

Starting Elevation: 5400 feet.

Map: See Chapter 19, page 117.

Other Maps: USGS Bass Lake 7.5 minute topo, Sierra National Forest map

Nelder Grove, a fine stand of giant Sequoias, nestles within the Sierra National Forest in eastern Madera County just outside Yosemite National Park's southern boundary. This truly special region merits your investigation and appreciation for its restful, undeveloped atmosphere. The ambiance is cozy and intimate, the air spicy with a fragrance that can only be experienced in a dense coniferous forest. The peacefulness is all the more remarkable considering Nelder lies only a few miles south of a bustling, much-publicized stand of Big Trees. Most visitors, even if they've heard of it, passed by it for the renowned Mariposa Grove in Wawona.

Although remote, Nelder is easily accessible. You can find it 11 miles above Oakhurst by turning off Highway 41 onto Sky Ranch Road, Road 632. From there, follow the signs to a turnoff on your left indicating the way to Nelder Grove. Be advised that Nelder Grove is not accessible during winter.

Originally, Nelder was called Fresno Grove of Big Trees because it was within Fresno County before the creation of Madera County. Later, it was named in memory of John A. Nelder who in 1875 homesteaded 156 acres which included part of the grove. The grove is relatively small, encompassing 1540 acres with about 110 mature Big Trees which share living space in a thick forest of pine, white fir and incense cedar. It has long been home of one of the largest trees on earth. The grove's undisputed patriarch, the Bull Buck Tree, boasts of being thicker at the base (99 feet in circumference) than the world's largest tree, the General Sherman in Sequoia National Park, but is 27 feet shorter.

Upon entering Nelder Grove you'll notice how few people there are. It is not unusual on any given day, especially mid-week, for you to be the only person strolling through these woods. You will also not see any kind of commercial development, no paved roads, no shuttle buses, postcard racks, snack bars, and no Nelder Grove T-shirts for sale. In short, you can't spend a dime here. If you are attracted to the hubbub of mini-shopping centers and planned activities in a so-called wilderness setting, then Nelder Grove isn't for you. But if, like me, you enjoy the natural state of things with nothing to do except wander and absorb the silence and beauty of these stately forest sentinels on their own terms, then welcome to Nelder Grove.

Nelder Grove's Bull Buck Tree, 99 feet in circumference and 246 feet high, is one of the world's largest trees.

According to James Hutchings in his venerable classic **In the Heart of the Sierras** (1886), both coastal and Sierra redwoods were named in honor of Sequoyah, a Cherokee chief. Sequoyah (1770-1843) became famous as the creator of an 86-character alphabet for the purpose of supplying his tribe with a written language. Because his intelligence and inventiveness "exalted him as far above his people as the lofty redwoods of the Coast Range towered over other trees," the botanist Endlicher deemed it appropriate to "perpetuate his name through one of the most imposing productions of the vegetable kingdom."

John Muir's fascination with the giant Sequoia prompted him to write: "The Big Tree is nature's finest masterpiece . . . the greatest of living things. It belongs to an ancient stock . . . has the strange air of other days about it, a thoroughbred look inherited from the long ago." The last of Muir's solo trips in 1875 through the Sierra Nevada was to gather information about the history and distribution of the giant Sequoia. Beginning in Wawona, he walked 20 miles southeast to Fresno Grove, since named Nelder Grove, where he happened upon a congenial hermit named John Nelder. Nelder had been a '49er who, when health and gold disappeared, realized that real contentment and wealth were not measured by material things. He moved into the woods to spend his remaining years in the home he'd found at last amidst the majesty of the Big Trees. A reclusive and gentle man, Nelder lived among his beloved trees until he died when his cabin burned in 1889.

Lamentably, Nelder Grove was not always the tranquil place it is today. The first mention of the grove was in 1851 in a soldier's diary. His detachment of James Savage's Mariposa Battalion was encamped at Crane Valley (now Bass

Madera Flume and Trading Co. built a sawmill at Nelder Grove in 1881. This mile-long gravity tramway moved a rider and a load of lumber from the mill at Nelder to the flume at Soquel. Empty carts were hauled back by animal teams.

Lake), and on one of their forays in pursuit of Indians they discovered the grove. To local Native Americans, the Big Trees occupied hallowed ground. They believed it extremely bad luck to fell this sacred tree or to harm the owl who guarded it. When they encountered loggers and teamsters they would warn them of the bad fortune that would surely visit them.

However, their warnings fell on deaf ears. Profit not preservation ruled for many years in Nelder Grove, as it did in all 75 of California's groves. In the late 1870s loggers felled such a great number of the giants that many mammoth stumps remain as mute witnesses to the vandalism. The Sequoia's phenomenal resistance to decay made it desirable for fence posts, grape stakes and shingles, but the Big Trees really proved to be of little commercial value because the wood was so weak and brittle. To make the destruction more regrettable, very often a cut giant Sequoia would shatter when it thundered to the ground. Even intact downed trees were abandoned because they were too large and too expensive to handle.

After logging operations ceased in 1892 in Nelder Grove, serenity returned, and in 1928, it was added to Sierra National Forest. Now, only a few relics from logging operations and enormous Sequoia stubs remind us of an era before the words "ecology" and "environmentalism" became a part of our national consciousness. It is satisfying to know that after decades of strong public outcry and political wrangling, these Sierra Big Trees are protected for as long as they may stand, and they can stand for three millennia.

On one level, I have mixed feelings about spotlighting the Nelder Grove environs. If too many travelers learn of it, I fear that yet another secluded nook in the Sierra may fall prey to multitudes of people and possible development to accommodate them. Because I want to keep the "wild" in wilderness, I worry about its relative obscurity being compromised. On the other hand, I encourage you to experience Nelder Grove because I believe that only a well-informed public with firsthand knowledge of wild beauty can protect it and places like it from tour buses, trinkets, T-shirts and other forms of commercial exploitation.

■ THE HIKES

Particularly pleasant and informative is Shadow of the Giants Trail, a self-guided, 1.2-mile path meandering among these gentle giants along Nelder Creek. A special treat in late spring is the heady perfume of wild azaleas in bloom. The flowering of graceful dogwood trees provides an unforgettable springtime show. If you'd like to spend more time in this tranquil environment, a seven-site primitive campground nestles among enormous Sequoia stumps along California Creek. Huge motor homes are not appropriate. Near the campsites paths lead into the heart of the forest, with a one-mile loop trail to the 2700-year-old Bull Buck Tree. The volunteer ranger in residence during summer will gladly answer questions and suggest what to see in the grove.

21
Willow Creek Trail
Hiking to Angel Falls & Devil's Slide

Of all the factors that have shaped the fate of the destiny of the Sierra National Forest, few have generated more lasting change than that which came with the development of hydroelectricity.

~Gene Rose

■ THE DETAILS

Getting There: Drive north from Oakhurst on Highway 41 for 4 miles and turn right on Road 222, signed for Bass Lake. Go 4 miles and bear left on Road 274. Go one mile to trailhead parking on the left side of the road, on the west side of the bridge over Willow Creek.

Nearest Campground: Chilkoot Campground, open May through September, has 14 primitive sites and no piped water 4.5 miles up Beasore Road (FH7) from the town of Bass Lake.

Lodging: Several choices around Bass Lake.

Further Info: Mariposa/Minarets Ranger District, Sierra National Forest, Box 10, North Fork, CA 93643, 559-683-4665 or 559-877-2218.

Hike Distance: 4.6 miles round trip.

Difficulty: Moderate.

Best Time to Go: Spring, summer.

Cautions: Stay on the trail and away from Angel Falls and Devil's Slide where many have been killed or injured.

Starting Elevation: 3400 feet. 700 feet gain to Devil's Slide.

Other Maps: USGS Bass Lake 15 minute topo, Sierra National Forest map.

The lower mountains of the Central Sierra Nevada are laced with miles of un-crowded trails leading to off-the-beaten-path destinations. The region, just a few miles from Yosemite Park, abounds in choices for hikers of every description and ability. Awaiting explorers 8 miles northeast of Oakhurst, Willow Creek Trail offers a delightful streamside trek in Sierra National Forest above Bass Lake. Whether you are a tenderfoot or a seasoned strider, the moderate 2.3-mile hike alongside the leaping waters of Willow Creek provides a superb springtime jaunt.

Panoramic views, fast-moving cascades plunging into a myriad of deep rocky pools, charming Angel Falls and the slick granite spillway of Devil's Slide at trail's end guarantee a memorable outing.

A tributary of San Joaquin River, North Fork Willow Creek crashes into four-mile-long Bass Lake near the trailhead. Officially called Crane Valley Reservoir, the lake has a long, colorful past. Because it's near the San Joaquin Valley, only an hour north of Fresno via Highway 41, Bass Lake is the tourist hub of the southern Yosemite area. It has become a busy summer mecca for water enthusiasts, especially skiers who love the lake's 75 to 78 degree temperatures. If the growl of speedboats isn't music to your ears, avoid Bass Lake from Memorial Day to Labor Day.

You don't need to travel far from the bustle of Bass Lake to find places like Willow Creek. The peace and solitude of backcountry trails, out-of-the-way campgrounds, quiet streams, subalpine lakes and giant Sequoias lie within an hour's drive of the lake. For non-hikers, many miles of unpaved roads allow motorists and mountain bikers an opportunity to immerse themselves in Sierra National Forest's spectacular scenery.

At least 1200 years before Willow Creek waters created Bass Lake, the North Fork Mono people lived here. Below the lake lies a drowned meadow where ancient tools and utensils have been found. The North Fork Mono lived at the heart of an important lane between the Owens Valley Paiutes of the Eastern Sierra and the Chukchansi Yokuts and Ponoichi Miwoks of the Western Sierra. Though the Mono occasionally squabbled with other tribes, their lush meadow homeland surrounded by densely forested hills was a tranquil foothill niche.

Peaceful, that is, until it was discovered in 1851 by a detachment of the Mariposa Battalion during the so-called Indian War of 1850-51. Led by Major James Savage on one of their forays in punitive pursuit of Indians, the militia established a base camp in the meadow. As the soldiers approached the meadow, a huge flock of birds, incorrectly identified as cranes, took flight. Not surprisingly, the men named the place Crane Valley, foreshadowing irrevocable changes for the Mono's ancestral grounds.

The Indian safehold at Crane Valley disappeared very quickly. By the early 1850s, thanks to the Gold Rush, miners and settlers invaded the meadowland and hillsides. Though some Native Americans chose to move, most were forced to leave. A few stayed and mingled with the new culture. The valley hosted farmers, ranchers and large bands of sheep, but a severe drought and homesteader hostility in 1877 pressured shepherds to graze their "wooly bundles" elsewhere.

Before long, lumber barons coveted the vast timber stands around Crane Valley. Logging railroad tracks spread their tentacles through the woods, sawmills sprouted, and a great flume floated lumber 54 miles to Madera in the San Joaquin Valley. By the 1920s, Madera Sugar Pine Company employed hundreds and cut 100,000 trees annually. The first rangers of the four-million-acre Sierra Forest

Reserve, forerunner of Sierra National Forest, struggled to curtail abuse of public lands, such as cut-and-run logging, sheep and cattle pasturing, and mining.

The advent of hydroelectric power produced the most dramatic change in the Sierra National Forest, the results of which rippled far beyond tiny Crane Valley into the nation at large. The pioneering technology created to divert Willow Creek's waters through a penstock high above the valley to run a turbine 1400 feet below and transmit 11,200 volts of power to Fresno 36 miles distant was absolutely revolutionary. Except for a few small plants, electrical technology and long-distance transmission were still in embryonic stages of development.

Credit for this amazing breakthrough goes to John Eastwood, a brilliant and daring civil engineer from Fresno, who recognized the massive hydroelectric potential of the upper San Joaquin River. He and John Seymour of the Fresno Water Company organized the San Joaquin Electric Company, started selling stock and by 1896 had a small powerhouse in operation. Many unprecedented engineering problems had to be solved in harnessing such tremendous water pressure (600 pounds) generated by the 1400-foot drop.

Human difficulties also plagued the experimental project. A rival gas and electric outfit in Fresno bought land and water rights upstream of the hydroplant and deliberately diverted most of the stream's flow, causing the powerhouse to shut down frequently during the summer. Lack of a dependable water supply and two drought years forced the company into bankruptcy in 1899.

Undaunted, Seymour regrouped and formed the San Joaquin Power Company, bought out his rival's land and water rights above the powerhouse, and began damming up Crane Valley in 1901 to ensure a reliable level of water to generate electricity. Crane Valley Reservoir was enlarged to its present size, four miles long by one-half mile wide, in 1910.

The reservoir was renamed Bass Lake after one of the logging companies dumped industrial wastes into the lake and killed most of the native fish. The government ordered the company to make reparations, which it did by stocking the reservoir with bass. Since 1930, Pacific Gas and Electric has owned the Bass Lake system.

John Eastwood went on to even greater achievements in the new field of hydroelectricity. His genius put into reality a complicated network of tunnels and reservoirs into which the falling water would be shunted into one powerhouse after another as it dropped through San Joaquin River Canyon, thereby repeatedly utilizing the flow. His Big Creek Project was the largest hydroelectric facility of the era. Read Gene Rose's ***Sierra Centennial: 100 Years of Pioneering on the Sierra National Forest*** for more about this project.

Unless you know, and few people do, you'd never suspect that this beautiful riparian environment harbored such momentous, breakaway history. It was here at Willow Creek, which originally was known by the unwieldy name of North Fork of the North Fork of the San Joaquin River, that the dawning of the hydroelectric age took place.

■ THE HIKE

From the trailhead parking area, the path parallels Willow Creek's right bank on a moderate grade upstream through cozy oak-conifer forest, leading 2.3 miles to Devil's Slide. Angel Falls is a spectacular, wide cascade shaped like angel wings only .6 mile from your car. In years of at least average precipitation, Willow Creek is a rowdy, roaring stream careening downhill to its terminus at Bass Lake. Above the falls, it calms down somewhat as it slithers through the woods and slip-slides over water-polished granite.

Over the centuries, wild Willow Creek has carved numerous huge potholes in its rock-lined channel. You'll find much visual drama to enjoy and photograph in this 2-mile stretch. If you have the time and energy, continue past Angel Falls 1.5 miles to a Y-junction. Follow the spur on your left .2 mile to Devil's Slide. The main trail proceeds to its end at McLeod Flat Road in .8 mile. Not far from the trail split, you'll certainly hear the sound and fury of this stunning section of white water. Devil's Slide is a fantastic chute pocked with large, rounded cavities in the bed rock, a scenic place for a break and some trail snacks while you admire this dramatic aqueous location.

When you're ready, head back to the main trail and retrace your steps downhill. The return journey affords another perspective of Willow Creek, the cradle of hydroelectricity, as well as some excellent vistas of glittering Bass Lake in the distance.

Caution: Willow Creek's beauty can be fatal, especially near Angel Falls and Devil's Slide. More than a dozen people have died and many more have been injured. Some hikers have slipped on the wet, slick granite and been severely battered or drowned when tricky currents trapped them in potholes. The danger is real. Heed the posted warning signs. Stay on the trail!

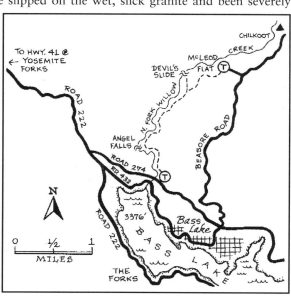

22
Jackass Lakes
Watery Gems in Ansel Adams Wilderness

■ DETAILS

Getting There: From Oakhurst, drive 4 miles north on Highway 41 and turn onto Road 222 toward Bass Lake. From the north end of the lake, go 5.8 miles and turn onto signed Beasore Road. Continue about 29 miles to signed "NORRIS CREEK TRAILHEAD-2 MILES." Turn left on the rough, unpaved entry road and park at the end near Norris Creek.

Nearest Campground: Upper Chiquito Camp 16 miles up Beasore Road has 20 sites and no piped water, open June through September.

Lodging: Several choices around Bass Lake.

Further Info: The required wilderness permit, current road and trail conditions and maps are available at Mariposa-Minarets Ranger District, Sierra National Forest, 57003 Road 225, Box 10, North Fork, CA 93643, call 559-683-4665, 559-877-2218.

Hike Distance: 4.6 miles round trip to Lower Jackass Lake, 6.6 miles round trip to Upper Jackass Lake.

Difficulty: Moderate.

Starting Elevation: 7600 feet. Elevation gain: 1000 feet to lower lake, 1700 feet to upper lake.

Other Maps: USGS Merced Peak 15 minute topo. The Sierra National Forest map is recommended for an overview and identifying peaks, roads, other trails, etc.

Local legend has it that this trinity of lakes in Sierra National Forest owes its name to a bygone era when the lakes were planted with trout carried in basket panniers strapped to the backs of jackasses. Located just 2 miles inside Ansel Adams Wilderness and a few miles outside Yosemite's southern edge, Jackass Lakes offer a highly scenic, off-the-beaten-path, moderate backpack or an easy day hike. If you opt not to tote a backpack, four Forest Service campgrounds are nearby.

The shortest way to lower Jackass Lake, elevation 8600 feet, from Norris Creek Trailhead offers a good choice for an early summer conditioner. Novice packers and youngsters will also find the 2.3-mile trail within their capabilities. A short, but steep, cross-country route to upper Jackass Lake is immeasurably

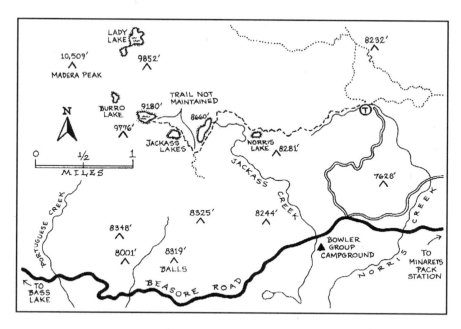

worth the extra mile and 700-foot elevation gain. With map in hand and by following occasional ducks or cairns(several stones stacked in an obvious, non-natural way to mark the route) to this pristine lake, you will understand why wilderness is so important to our souls. The 180-degree panorama of the Sierra Crest and the pine-studded, profound canyons of the Middle and South Forks of the San Joaquin River provide a jaw-dropping experience. Because of remote trail access in a lightly used neck of the woods, hikers, anglers, mountain climbers and all manner of nature enthusiasts can expect virtual solitude in a classic High Sierra setting.

Formerly known as Minarets Wilderness, Ansel Adams Wilderness covers 228,650 acres of sublime backcountry scenery. Named in honor of Ansel Adams, legendary photographer of the Sierra Nevada, it is renowned for spectacular alpine architecture, sparkling lakes, craggy peaks, steep rock-walled gorges, scores of polished granite domes, glacier-carved canyons and dense forests. It's one of five wilderness areas located within Sierra National Forest which comprise 43 percent of its total terrain. According to the Wilderness Act of 1964, these lands are "where earth and its community of life remain untrammeled, where man himself is a visitor who does not remain." With no improvements or developments other than trails, these unsullied areas of dramatic scenery offer outstanding hiking, backpacking and horseback riding.

■ THE HIKE

After parking your vehicle at the end of rough, unpaved, 2-mile-long Norris Creek access road, follow the trail along the stream, lush with wildflowers in early season. The hushed, cathedral-like atmosphere in a dense forest of red fir and lodgepole pine is occasionally punctuated by the muffled booming sounds of grouse, scoldings of Steller jays and excited chatter of red squirrels. Your upward trek leads to a wilderness boundary sign at one mile and reaches tiny, shallow Norris Lake at 1.5 miles. Take a breather here at 8300 feet elevation for a few minutes before continuing the 300-foot, .8-mile climb to lower Jackass Lake.

The trail flanks the right (north) side of Norris Lake and soon ascends a ridge with stunning southern and eastern views. The forest thins somewhat to reveal transcendent vistas of the sharp-spined Minarets, Mount Ritter and Banner Peak. As you pause on the ridgeline to drink in the sights, you might want to think about the observations of a High Country hiker many decades ago. "The value of the Sierra lies in its being what it is—a region of marvelous scenic beauty, moderately difficult of access. Let us remember that there will always be those who know that the most marvelous views are seen only after physical effort to obtain them, who prefer intimacy with the mountains to their own personal comfort, and who love the smoke of campfire in their eyes and the granite ground upon which they sleep. Let us save a place for them."

Proceed on the ducked route along the bedrock ridge (you're almost there!), and then briefly descend to large, lower Jackass Lake, a beautiful example of a backcountry lake. Except for wind playing in the pines, silence reigns. As you sense the absolute harmony and perfect order of nature, you feel soothed and comforted. From the granite cliff on one side, huge boulders have tumbled down to the shoreline. Ripples appear as brook and rainbow trout rise to snag insects. Water-loving flora and tall conifers ring the lake, their deep greens a striking contrast to the stark, gray granite. At the outlet stream, the chilly waters of Jackass Lake break into a series of cascades, eventually merging with the San Joaquin River far, far below. Reedy and shallow, the other end is a paradise for mosquitoes. Around the shore you'll find many inviting places to picnic and take a refreshing dip. A good campsite is at the south end near the outlet. Other sites on a rocky ridge above the lake have a view.

On the second day, if you find yourself longing to get higher and wilder, hike cross-country to middle and upper Jackass Lakes, about a mile each way. On the way you'll notice that middle Jackass is more like a tarn than a lake. While it's not far to the upper lake, it nevertheless is a steep and rocky 700-foot haul. No defined trail exists, though it does show on the topo map, so you will have to rely on infrequently placed stone ducks and a map to guide you there.

The duck-marked route starts at the lower lake's southwest end and climbs to a stream (possibly dry by late August) leading to a small box canyon. Stay on the left side of the stream running through it. Upper Jackass Lake lies on a bench just

Just inside Ansel Adams Wilderness, jewel-like and granite bound lower Jackass Lake will satisfy the longing for wild places.

above the canyon. As you catch your breath and your pulse slows, you'll be able to relate to the old-timers' advice that the best views are seen only after physical exertion to obtain them. As they say, it doesn't get any better than this.

Pick a lunch spot and plan to linger at least an hour or two to absorb the wild scene spreading before you for 100 miles along the Sierra Crest, with the faraway pale tops of the White Mountains jutting above the high desert of Owens Valley. With the aid of a map, you will be able to identify a bazaar of fantastic, jagged peaks and pinnacles on the horizon: Triple Divide, Mount Ritter, Mount Davis, Mammoth Mountain, Mount Ansel Adams, and Seven Gables among them.

Experienced, conditioned, off-trail trekkers will enjoy the challenge of scrambling another 400 feet beyond upper Jackass to petite Burro Lake near timberline at the foot of Madera Peak. For those wanting to bag a peak, the climb to its 10,509-foot summit is non-technical.

Back in camp, sitting around a cozy fire or perhaps perched on the ridge slightly above, you may be treated to the ethereal phenomenon of alpenglow. When atmospheric conditions are just right, as the sun slides below the horizon, the peaks flush with a surreal orange-red glow. Witnessing the day's last hurrah flaming across the sky-kissing summits is a religious experience for High Country zealots.

You can, of course, hike greater distances and to loftier destinations than Jackass Lakes, but the vistas will be no grander or more varied, nor the adamantine air more intoxicating and wild. You'll harbor the images of this trip in your mind's eye for a very long time.

23
Mono Hot Springs
Hike to Doris & Tule Lakes in the Surrounding Wilderness

■ THE DETAILS

Getting There: Take Highway 145 or 168 east from Highway 99 or 41. Highway 145 ends at the tiny community of Prather from which you climb into the mountains on Highway 168. Follow 168 past Shaver Lake to Huntington Lake, then turn east on Forest Highway 80, Kaiser Pass Road, and follow it 15 curvy and steep miles, then turn left and go 2 miles to Mono Hot Springs.

Nearest Campgrounds: Mono Hot Springs Campground, on the South Fork San Joaquin River near the hot springs, has 30 sites with piped water, open May to September. Tiny Bolsillo Camp 3 miles west has 3 sites and piped water, open June to September.

Lodging: Mono Hot Springs Resort 559-325-1710. Call Shaver Lake Chamber of Commerce 559-841-3350 for choices on the drive to Mono Hot Springs.

Further Info: For general information, High Sierra Ranger Station 559-877-7173. For reservations, information, or a brochure, call Mono Hot Springs Resort 559-325-1710 or write General Delivery, Mono Hot Springs, CA 93642.

Hike Distance: 1.5 miles round trip to Doris Lake, 3.2 miles round trip to Tule Lake.

Difficulty: Easy to Doris Lake. Moderate to Tule Lake.

Best Time to Go: Late May to September for hot springs, June or July to September for hikes.

Cautions: None.

Starting Elevation: 6560 feet at Mono Hot Springs, 6540 feet for hikes.

Elevation Gain: 300 feet for Doris Lake.

Other Maps: USGS Mt. Givens 7.5 minute topo, USFS Ansel Adams Wilderness map, Sierra National Forest map.

Sprinkled throughout the Sierra, many uncrowded and low-profile recreation areas beckon to outdoor lovers. One such secluded spot is Mono Hot Springs along the South Fork San Joaquin River deep in Sierra National Forest above Huntington Lake. Lacking the plush atmosphere of highly commercial resort or theme destinations that cater to the visitor's every need, real or imagined, Mono

Hot Springs remains relatively anonymous because it's simply not easily accessible.

Use of the hot springs predates its discovery by Euro-Americans by centuries. Most likely, Western Monos (Monache) and Mono Lake Paiutes were the original visitors. Although these tribes had other hot springs in the area, their Mono Hot Springs camp was the largest. Good fishing in the South Fork, plentiful game, ample shade and forage plus the soothing mineral waters made the location especially popular. It became a favorite summer meeting and trading center for these two groups from the eastern and western sides of the Sierra.

We have no record of the first white man to enter the region. Perhaps it was a trapper or hunter using the well-trodden Indian trail. One author, however, suggests it was probably "one of the many Basque shepherds who were known to use the region in the latter half of the 19th century." We do know that the Brewer Party of Whitney's California Geological Survey in 1864 passed "several miles upstream but made no mention of the springs or the name Mono." When Theodore Solomons visited the region 30 years later while routing a High Sierra trail, the name was in use.

By 1918 when engineer and dam builder David Redinger of the Edison Company's Big Creek Project visited the area, the springs were well known. He wrote that "located on the South Fork San Joaquin River about 3 miles below Vermillion Valley (now Lake Edison), Mono Hot Springs was a favorite stopover to break a hot and dusty trip . . . the U.S. Forest Service had installed a large concrete tub at the principal spring, sheltered by a roughly constructed shake cabin . . . the old tub was enjoyed by many passersby."

After completion of the Big Creek Project, the Edison Company turned over its web of construction roads in the woods to the Forest Service for public use in 1929. Circa 1934 at Mono Hot Springs the Civilian Conservation Corps (CCC) built a campground and a bath house long enough to accommodate 18 tubs. From the very beginning, despite the financial hard times during the Great Depression, Mono Hot Springs was a popular destination for enthusiasts of remote mountain hideaways.

About the same time, San Joaquin Valley entrepreneur Walter Hill approached Sierra National Forest officials about opening a resort at the springs. Skeptical that a business could succeed in such an isolated place with difficult access and a short season, the Forest Service was reluctant to issue a special use permit. Finally, Hill's persistence was rewarded with the necessary paperwork for a 99-year lease on the property.

Using his own money, Hill began building in 1936. Because of the great distances and expense involved in transporting construction materials from the valley, he utilized native materials, especially river rock from the nearby South Fork San Joaquin. Mortared rock was used for the foundations and walls of 22 cabins, a general store and a restaurant all of which still stand today. In summer 1937 Mono Hot Springs officially opened for business. The original tiny bath

Doris Lake in Ansel Adams Wilderness with John Muir Wilderness peaks behind it.

houses are gone, but visitors still use the concrete tubs.

Hill and his two daughters and sons-in-law ran the resort for 26 years. One daughter, Eula Hill Miles, who served as postmaster, related, "For many years before and after World War II, Japanese Americans from the valley used it extensively. Whole families moved in and remained for the season." Business was lean during the war years due primarily to gas rationing and the shameful internment of all U. S. citizens of Japanese ancestry. Eula recalled so "many wonderful times up there" and that her "dad stopped building after he had used up all the nearby river rocks."

In 1963 Hill sold the property to the Frank Winslow family who has operated Mono Hot Springs to this day. The resort retains a laidback, unsophisticated charm despite a number of improvements during the last 38 years. Almost immediately after the purchase, Winslow removed the timeworn and ramshackle bath houses and redirected the hot spring flow to a new A-frame bath house closer to the cabins on the north side of the river. In 1985 the A-frame was replaced by an upgraded structure with showers and a Jacuzzi.

The season at Mono Hot Springs, weather depending, runs from late May to the end of September. The general store is well-stocked with brand-name staples, veggies, meat, beer and wine, fishing supplies, backpacking food, souvenirs, clothing and magazines. The restaurant offers a complete menu of home-cooked fare. It and the post office are open everyday, and a pack station providing day rides and pack trips is within 6 miles of the resort. The original cabins, the majority made of native stone, range from a very simple, basic bachelor to a large two-bedroom. Most are equipped for housekeeping. Regardless of size, all the cabins are rustic and without TV or phone. A Forest Service campground sits across from the resort along the river.

In an outdoor mineral pool, you can soak and take in the breathtaking sight of 12,349-foot Mount Hooper all at the same time. The new bath house has individual therapeutic hot tub rooms with a bench for a blanket wrap if desired.

Showers and Swedish-style massages are also available. Fees for all facilities are reasonable. Thrifty campers and foot-sore hikers still enjoy the original 67-year-old concrete tubs today.

Next to soaking up the therapeutic mineral waters, fishing is the most popular activity. Numerous lakes and streams in the surrounding area provide excellent sport for anglers. The South Fork San Joaquin is stocked with trout every two weeks. Additionally, large Edison and Florence Lakes are only a few miles away.

Spectacular wilderness surrounds Mono Hot Springs on three sides, with the 228,600-acre Ansel Adams Wilderness to the north and the vast John Muir Wilderness, the Sierra's third largest at 580,600 acres, to the east and south. You pass the relatively small Kaiser Wilderness, 22,700 acres, around Kaiser Pass on the way to Mono Hot Springs. Naturally hikes abound in the area. Our described hike heads north to little Doris and Tule Lakes via a trail that begins at Mono Hot Springs. Hikers will enjoy the resort or campground as a base from which to explore an assortment of trails from easy to challenging. Ask at the High Sierra Ranger Station about other nearby trails.

Should you decide to see what the magnificent mountain scenery in and around Mono Hot Springs is all about, be advised that you will do it slowly! Although well worth it, the trip involves a considerable time investment because of the sidewinder twisting and turning of Kaiser Pass Road. The steep, one-lane route beyond beautiful Huntington Lake creeps over Kaiser Pass, elevation 9300 feet, and crawls down exposed cliffsides with heart-stopping scenery, tough to appreciate if you're driving.

Then it gets worse. The road's surface before you reach Mono Hot Springs junction is often pot-holed and unpaved. A stop at High Sierra Ranger Station not far before the Mono Springs junction is highly recommended for a well-deserved break away from the car and an opportunity to take in the stunning vistas. Bottom line, if you are a hurry-up-and-get-there-and-back-motorist, stay home. You'll be more satisfied just reading about Mono Hot Springs. For the adventurous lover of mountain byways, however, this is a truly great expedition.

Before going, check out the Sierra National Forest map for an overview of the area. It's never wise to travel in remote areas without a map.

■ THE HIKE

Mono Hot Springs offers a fine base camp for further exploration of the rugged mountain country near the end of infamous Kaiser Pass Road. To get started, try the trails to nearby Doris Lake and/or Tule Lake. Both provide beautiful scenery for only a modest investment of energy. Because the hike to each of them is short, you can visit both on the same outing. Your reward for hiking these rather mundane trails will be evident at these lovely little lakes.

From the entrance to the lower campground, walk north on dirt Forest Road 7S10 past the signed "Mono Tourist Pasture." At a fork take either branch (they soon merge) to a parking-turnaround area. Head left (north) and pick up the trail in the granite outcrops. Shortly you'll enter Ansel Adams Wilderness Area and come to a signed junction for Doris and Tule Lakes.

If you plan on visiting both lakes today, go to Doris Lake first. After you climb to Doris, take the short trail that winds around a rocky outcrop, then ascends to its top. You are treated with terrific views of the handsome cliff-bound lake and High Country peaks to the east.

When you've had your fill, return to the Tule Lake junction. To visit Tule Lake, turn right to begin the easy 1.25-mile climb to Tule. Just before reaching it, you'll pass a huge "forest" of tules. The shimmering little lake is ringed with reeds and dotted with lily pads. Perch on some rocks at the lake's north end before returning to Mono Hot Springs.

From the hot springs, short drives lead to more challenging hiking in Ansel Adams, John Muir and Kaiser Wilderness areas. For a highly scenic drive, follow the sinuous road north to the vast reservoir called Lake Edison. In summer you can take a taxi boat to reach the Mono Creek Trail at the east end of the lake in John Muir Wilderness. With an early start, you'll have time to hike the trail up dramatic Mono Creek to explore the vast glacier-carved canyon. Mono Creek Trail meets the John Muir Trail about 2 miles from the boat landing. Don't miss the last boat back or you'll have an extra 4 miles to hike!

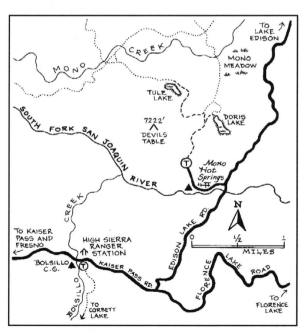

III
The Incomparable Valley
🐻 VISITING YOSEMITE VALLEY 🐻

WITHIN YOSEMITE VALLEY'S SEVEN SQUARE MILES, less than one-half of one percent of the Park's total area, Mother Nature has concentrated an unrivaled, spectacular display of natural wonders and geologic features. Despite the crowds, one must not shun the Valley. That would be akin to visiting the Louvre and skipping the Mona Lisa, as one writer put it. John Muir, bewitched by Yosemite's spell for nearly 50 years, called it "the incomparable valley . . . as if to this one mountain mansion Nature has gathered her choicest treasures."

The crowds do come, more than four million visitors a year and growing. The question to ask is, "When can we plan a visit to encounter fewer people?" It all depends on what you want to do and see. Certain attractions, like the hike to the top of Half Dome (Chapter 29), are only possible because of weather from mid-May through about mid-October. The enthralling and towering waterfalls of the Valley reach their prime in April and May, in turn bringing their own influx of visitors. If you visit during these peak seasons, try to avoid weekends, holidays, and, most of all, holiday weekends. Even during peak season, Valley visitation ebbs a bit from Tuesday to Thursday (barring those holidays).

Another wise tactic is to avoid the biggest attractions during the busiest times. The hikes in this section, with the exception of Half Dome and Mirror Lake, are chosen because they are somewhat less well known. You can also rise early and head right for the waterfalls or, second best, visit them during the quieter dinnertime and long summer evening hours before sunset. Another suggestion is to plan your Valley visit before Memorial Day Weekend or after Labor Day.

Autumn and winter are distinctly enchanting, tranquil seasons to visit Yosemite Valley. The tumultuous waterfalls and rambunctious Merced River of spring fame are vastly diminished, but so are the crowds that jam the Valley between Memorial Day and Labor Day. By comparison, it appears nearly deserted, and it often seems you have the world class scenery all to yourself.

You can almost hear the landscape breathe a sigh of relief as it settles in for a few months of rest and rejuvenation, free at last from the masses of humanity who come to marvel at its peerless beauty. The Valley, home to a wonderful concentration of broad-leafed trees, puts on a flashy show in October and November. Oak, dogwood and big leaf maple flaunt themselves shamelessly in a

Adventuresome Kitty Tatch and a friend kick up their heels on Overhanging Rock at Glacier Point with the Valley far below. The rock is off-limits to modern visitors.

burst of glittering hues. Also touched by the ancient sorcery of autumn, meadow grasses and ferns are lambent with mellow amber tones. Although the days are sunny, Jack Frost is decidedly in the air.

Winter brings dramatic changes to Yosemite Valley. Muted shades of gray, brown and green replace fall's vivid palette. The ambiance is contemplative and hushed, the diamond air fragrant with forest spices. When the sun peeks out after snowfall or a rainstorm, the scene becomes a Japanese watercolor. Purling fog creates a moody effect and softens the severity of bold granite forms. Shrouded in mist, soaring rock walls, domes and peaks are all the more majestic.

■ A CAPSULE HISTORY OF YOSEMITE PARK

Although we think of Yosemite's commercial development as recent, it began within a decade of Euro-Americans discovering it. Because Yosemite Valley in the 1850s was public domain, land was available to homesteaders. Soon the Valley's pristine quality yielded to private homes, businesses, orchards, sawmills, gardens and pastures, rutted roads, fences and gates, water pollution, extinction of wildlife, and obstruction of views by buildings. One only has to look at old photos to see how cluttered and developed the Valley was.

Not only the Valley was being ruined, but also the surrounding country was besieged by loggers, miners, cattlemen, and, most destructive, sheepherders. Vast flocks of grazing sheep denuded the greenery and trampled fragile areas for countless square miles. The herders burned the brush, and often the forest with it, to improve pastures and open pathways for herd movement.

Publicity about Yosemite started with James Hutchings who traveled extensively throughout California from 1853 to 1855 in search of "scenes of wonder
and curiosity" for his monthly *California Magazine*. In July 1855, Hutchings
came to Mariposa pursuing rumors of a waterfall six times the height of Niagara
Falls and incredible granite formations in a remote place called Yosemite Valley.
With him was the young artist Thomas Ayres, hired to sketch the fabulous sights.

Hutchings, Ayres and two companions constituted the first tourists in Yosemite
Valley, spending five days in "luxurious scenic banqueting," exploring and sketching. When they returned to Mariposa, Hutchings wrote the very first printed
description of this incomparable Valley for the *Mariposa Gazette*. Starting with
the *San Francisco Chronicle*, newspapers across the nation reprinted his article.
More than anyone else, Hutchings spread the gospel of Yosemite to the world at
large. For 47 years until his death in 1902, he was profoundly committed to promoting Yosemite and deeply involved in its growth. He never envisioned that his
efforts would lead to over four million visitors in 1996 from a mere 41 in 1855.

By 1856 a more permanent human intrusion was evident when Yosemite
Valley was surveyed for a reservoir and canal to bring water from the Merced
River to John Fremont's mines near Mariposa. By the end of that year, two rough
horse trails were built to convey the travelers who would surely come to this
wondrous place. In 1857 the first primitive hotels opened for business.

Fortunately, a few visionaries happened to be in the right place at the right time.
Reverend Thomas Starr King, pastor of San Francisco's Unitarian Church, was a
famous and influential lecturer and writer. After visiting the Valley in 1860, he saw
how the binge of commercialism and homesteading were taking a heavy toll on the
natural resources. He was the first of many to push for Yosemite becoming a park.
Frederick Law Olmsted, the nation's premiere landscape architect and then manager of Fremont's Mariposa land grant, toured Yosemite in 1863. He too observed
the ruination of the Valley and Mariposa Grove of Big Trees. Using his considerable influence, he convinced California Senator John Conness to introduce a bill in
Congress to establish a park around Yosemite Valley and Mariposa Grove.

Finally, the Yosemite Grant, signed into law by President Lincoln on June 20,
1864, gave Yosemite Valley and Mariposa Grove to California for "public use,
resort, and recreation, and to be inalienable for all time." This vital legislation
became a benchmark for future preservation of lands too precious to use for
economic gain. It made homesteading, farming, logging, trespassing and other
activities unlawful, but it took two years to become reality. Even when a Board
of Commissioners was created in 1866, the Yosemite Grant lacked teeth to remove homesteaders, which ultimately required 11 years of legal battling. Moreover, the Valley continued to deteriorate because the Commissioners vacillated
between their roles as protectors and developers, and because the Grant made no
mention of how its regulations were to be enforced.

John Muir played an extremely pivotal role in preparing the way for Yosemite
to become a national park. He first arrived in the Valley in 1868, losing his heart

and soul to the "sublime granite cathedral." Soon his work as explorer, researcher, interpreter and defender clearly placed him atop the list of Yosemite spokesmen.

In the early 1870s, Muir began writing for various publications about Yosemite's appalling condition, but even then the special interest groups were powerful, and he had to wait nearly 20 years for his message to find a stronghold. Finally in 1889, Muir found an ally in Robert Underwood Johnson, editor of the popular and respected *Century Magazine*. After a camping trip with Muir in the High Country seeing the damage first hand, he pressured his influential eastern friends to make Yosemite a national park.

At last, the Yosemite Act of October 1890 set aside 1500 square miles of "reserved forest lands surrounding, but not including, Yosemite Valley." While the Valley had been a state park since 1864, this unwieldy park within a park situation lasted until 1906 when California turned over their park to the federal government.

Following the precedent set at Yellowstone in 1886, Interior Secretary John Noble ordered the U. S. Cavalry to protect the new Yosemite Park. Captain A. E. Wood was the first military commander and superintendent. Accompanied by creaking supply wagons and strings of braying pack mules, he led Company I of the Fourth Cavalry into Wawona on May 19,1891 to take charge of the Park. Having no authority in Yosemite Valley, Wood established headquarters near the Wawona Hotel. Inheriting command of an unmapped and vaguely defined wilderness, the Cavalry spent three years learning the lay of the land before they could face the two major headaches—trespassing sheepherders and landowners' rights in and bordering the Park.

The Cavalry developed an extensive network of trails, blazing them with a large "T" on conifers along the way, aiding their pursuit of illegal sheep and cattle herders. The soldiers made detailed maps, settled property disputes and began the tradition of planting trout in the lakes. Their 16- to 20-hour days found them surveying and marking boundaries, building bridges, fighting fires, nabbing poachers, creating interpretive displays, patrolling Tioga Road, and rescuing hikers.

Improvising for his lack of legal power to arrest herders, Captain Wood devised a clever strategy to rid the Park of all the "woolie bundles" that annually munched the mountains bare. Troopers drove sheep to one Park boundary while other soldiers marched the herders on an arduous five-day journey to the opposite boundary, ejecting them from the Park. After a few seasons of lost profits as the sheep scattered to the four winds, mixed with other herds, or were lost to the elements and predators, owners ordered their shepherds to find grazing outside the Park.

It took almost four years to eradicate illegal hunting. Animal and bird populations were nearing extinction before the Cavalry educated the public that the slaughter of native wildlife couldn't be tolerated. For years raw sewage from five large campgrounds had seriously polluted the Merced River, and concessionaires bitterly resisted the Army's rigid sanitary procedures.

By 1895, Yosemite Valley was experiencing serious problems, but the Army was not sanctioned to address them. John Muir summarized conditions in the Valley in a letter to *Century Magazine* editor Johnson. "It looks ten times worse now than when you saw it seven years ago." Saloons, warehouses, barns, homes, pigpens and chicken coops littered the once pristine Valley. Most of the trees had been cut for lumber or firewood. Muir concluded, "As long as the management is in the hands of eight politicians appointed by the ever-changing governor of California, there is but little hope." The situation continued to deteriorate for ten more years.

Finally in 1906, thanks again to Muir's unflagging efforts, California ceded Yosemite Valley and Mariposa Grove to the federal government. That year the Army moved their headquarters to the present site of Yosemite Lodge in the Valley. Military presence in the popular Valley soon became the source of increasing tension and conflict. The Cavalry had inherited a 40-year history of weak, inconsistent management. Soldiers now had to become diplomats, contending with tourists, residents and park concessionaires constantly pushing for more development.

Nevertheless, the Cavalry had come to the rescue, being instrumental in stabilizing and unifying the infant Park. The Horse Soldiers distinguished themselves by their dedication in guiding Yosemite National Park through its early and critical years. Many places in Yosemite bear the names of men of the Cavalry because of their exemplary service over the 24 years of Army presence.

With only a brief interruption during the Spanish-American War, the Army guardianship lasted until 1914 when the nation's involvement in World War I led to their withdrawal from civilian duties. Their influence in Yosemite's history was considerable, and they left behind an impressive legacy of achievement. To quote Muir, "Blessings on Uncle Sam's soldiers. They have done their job well." A colorful chapter closed in 1914 with the appointment of Mark Daniels, the first civilian superintendent.

24
Artist Point & Artist Thomas Hill
Through the Artist's Eye

■ DETAILS

Getting There: The hike starts at the Bridalveil Falls parking area on Southside
   Drive. You'll find it 1.8 miles east of the junction of Highways 120 and 140, or,
   if coming from Wawona, 1.5 miles after leaving the Wawona Tunnel.

Nearest Campground: Sunnyside Walk-In Campground, just west of Yosemite
   Lodge, has 35 tent sites available on a first-come, first-served basis. For
   reservations for other park campgrounds, call 800-436-7275.

Lodging: Yosemite Lodge 559-252-4848 has 245 rooms.

Further Info: Yosemite National Park recorded info line 209-372-0200.

Hike Distance: 3.6 miles round trip to Artist Point. Also .5 mile round trip to base
   of Bridalveil Falls.

Difficulty: Moderate.

Best Time to Go: Spring or autumn.

Cautions: None.

Starting Elevation: 3940 feet. 700 feet elevation gain.

Other Maps: Earthwalk Press **Yosemite Valley** map, USGS Yosemite 15 minute topo.

Yosemite Valley's grandeur and uniqueness so captivated several renowned landscape artists in the late 1880s that they came and lingered for months or even
years. Thomas Hill, creator of the powerful painting that graces our book's cover,
was   one of these prestigious 19th century artists who strove to capture the
essence of this incomparable place. Hill first visited the Valley in 1863, but from
1884 until his death in 1908 Yosemite Park was his home. Born in England in
1829, 11-year-old Hill emigrated with his parents to Massachusetts. He began
his career painting coaches. Later he decided to become an artist and studied at
the Philadelphia Academy of Fine Arts.

In 1861 and in poor health, Hill moved to San Francisco. He established a
studio and for the next few years made frequent sketching trips to Yosemite.
Favorable recognition of his work prompted Hill in 1868 to study for six months
in Paris with Paul Meyerheim, a well-known figure painter. His mentor was so
impressed with Hill's painting of a French forest scene he urged him to concen-

trate on landscapes, rather than pursue his ambition as a portrait artist.

Hill returned to the United States and took up residence in Boston. It was there, from a previous sketch, that he painted "*Yosemite Valley*" which earned him great acclaim as a landscape artist. Also, his canvas of Yosemite was one of the earliest portrayals offered to the eastern art circles of the sublime Valley in the Sierra Nevada.

Once again in frail health due to a chronic respiratory condition, Thomas Hill returned to San Francisco in 1871 and became associated with the San Francisco Art Association. A gargantuan painting (10 feet by 6 feet), titled "*Great Canyon of the Sierras*," revealed a stunning view of Yosemite as seen from Artist Point. Judge Crocker of Sacramento purchased it for $10,000, an enormous sum of money in those years. By now Hill had joined the ranks of prominent landscape painters such as Albert Bierstadt, William Keith, Chris Jorgensen, Lady Constance Gordon-Cummings and Thomas Moran.

From his base in San Francisco, Hill continued to make frequent forays into Yosemite. Hill was a prolific worker, often returning to the studio with as many as 100 sketches. He worked furiously to keep up with the rush of orders and commissions throughout the United States and Europe. At the Philadelphia Centennial Exposition in 1876, Hill's "*Yosemite Valley*" and "*Donner Lake*" paintings garnered the top awards for landscape painting. This honor assured his reputation as one of the premier artists of the era.

One of Hill's most famous works had nothing to do with the Sierra. Governor Leland Stanford commissioned him to paint a picture commemorating the meeting of the Union and Central Pacific Railroads on May 10, 1869. Titled "*The Last Spike*," it depicted the driving of the final golden spike and the silver hammer that struck it, along with the Governor and other distinguished dignitaries. However, much to Hill's great disappointment, the Governor refused to accept the finished canvas. It is believed that because Hill painted Stanford so conspicuously in the large group witnessing the ceremony, other influential colleagues were offended by the lesser attention paid to them. Curiously, the painting was purchased after Hill's death because of its historical significance. It now resides in the Crocker Art Museum in Sacramento.

By 1883 Hill could be found in residence at his studio in Yosemite Valley. After gale force winds swept his workshop off its foundation in 1884, Hill moved to the charming and stately Wawona Hotel, 25 miles south of the Valley, where he occupied rooms 10 and 11. During the winter months he hung his hat in the much warmer foothill climate of Raymond in eastern Madera County. The Washburns, owners and concessionaire of the extensive Wawona complex, considered his presence an important cultural asset and attraction for their enterprise. Besides, one of Hill's nine children, Estella, was engaged to hotelkeeper John Washburn.

The Washburns built a three-room studio for Hill in 1886 only a few yards from the main hotel building. It was a cozy, frame cottage with a screen porch that Hill, for some reason, had painted pink. In addition to his landscapes, Hill

Yosemite Valley still appears uninhabited from the breathtaking vantage point at Artist Point along the abandoned Wawona Road.

filled the studio's interior with curiosities. Various animal pelts, wasp nests, huge dead rattlesnakes, dried flowers, Indian baskets and war implements, deer antlers, mounted animals and other natural artifacts attracted nearly as much interest as his paintings.

Even when he was at work, guests were always welcome in his studio. Genial, hospitable, short and slight in stature, never without a cigar in one hand and a paintbrush in the other, Hill was capable of chatting, chewing his cigar and creating simultaneously. With the possible exception of his pink studio, he possessed none of the Bohemian traits usually associated with his calling. Hill was also a devoted father to his several sons and daughters. He earned several small fortunes during his lifetime with his paintings of Yosemite and other Sierra landscapes, but he was not a shrewd investor. As a consequence, he suffered the loss of almost as much money as he made. Long-ailing, 79-year-old Thomas Hill died on June 30, 1908 in Raymond, California.

Hill and other prestigious artists of the period were influential contributors to the recognition, popularity and, ultimately, the protection of Yosemite as a national park. His magnificent landscapes were viewed by countless admirers nationally and internationally. People who had never seen this great national treasure called Yosemite could visualize it through his work and realize the importance of its preservation.

You can see some of Hill's paintings at the Yosemite Museum, and several enormous landscapes are on display in the Oakland Museum and Sacramento's Crocker Museum. His studio, no longer pink, was remodeled after this death and used as a soda fountain, employee recreation hall and for storage. Currently it's a wilderness permit and information center.

■ THE HIKE

For a unique way of connecting with Thomas Hill's vision, take an easy walk up the old Wawona Road to Artist Point. It offers a secluded, hidden Yosemite away from summertime crowds. At Artist Point the modern visitor can experience what Hill found more than 100 years ago, a view of Yosemite Valley unmarred by roads, vehicles, structures and people.

From the Bridalveil Falls parking lot, walk carefully west on the left side of the road leading to Glacier Point and Wawona for .3 mile, then bear left onto an unmarked boulder-blocked dirt road. Climb gently uphill through deep forest cover along this cool and shaded route, which is mostly viewless until it reaches Artist Point at 1.8 miles.

Even if you're not a good judge of distance, the breathtaking vista will be very obvious. Pause here for awhile where Artist Creek tumbles down the mountainside and take in the overwhelming scenery that has inspired so many talented artists. Should you feel like a longer jaunt before retracing your steps, continue up the historic road to meet the Pohono Trail at 2.4 miles, which continues up to Inspiration Point described in the next chapter. When you return to the parking area, you might also consider taking the popular, short and easy paved hike to the base of Bridalveil Falls, .5 mile round trip.

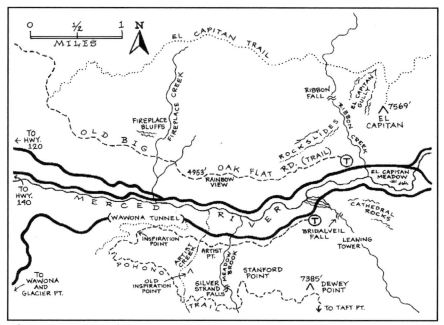

Chapters 24, 25 and 26

25
Inspiration Point & Artist Thomas Ayres
Virgin Views of Yosemite Valley

There are some moments, some experiences that come to us untranslatable in any human speech, and this was one . . . how long we might have stood there, we cannot say.

~Susie Clark, 1890

■ THE DETAILS

Getting There: Head for Yosemite Valley via Highways 140, 41 or 120. Leave your car at Bridalveil Falls parking area on Wawona Road (Highway 41) 120 yards west of its intersection with Southside Drive on the Valley floor.

Nearest Campground: Sunnyside Walk-In Campground, just west of Yosemite Lodge, has 35 tent sites available on a first-come, first-served basis. To reserve other park camps, call 800-436-7275.

Lodging: Yosemite Lodge 559-252-4848 has 245 rooms.

Further Info: Yosemite National Park recorded information line 209-372-0200.

Hike Distance: 5.2 miles round trip. 1.3 miles to Meadow Brook Creek, 1.8 miles to Artist Creek/Point, 2.4 miles to Pohono Trail junction, 2.6 miles to (New) Inspiration Point.

Difficulty: Moderate.

Best Time to Go: Spring or autumn.

Cautions: None.

Starting Elevation: 3940 feet. 1460 feet elevation gain to Inspiration Point.

Map: See Chapter 24, page 143.

Other Maps: USGS El Capitan 7.5 minute topo, Yosemite Association's *Map & Guide to Yosemite Valley.*

Along the original Wawona Road is a sharp bend known as Inspiration Point (elevation 5391 feet) where a commanding, almost surreal vista of Yosemite Valley is freeze-framed. With shocking suddenness, as if the earth had fallen away from beneath your feet, the deep chasm and vast army of domes, peaks, spires and pinnacles is unexpectedly exposed.

The history surrounding Inspiration Point is as impressive as the view. The Wawona

This image of Yosemite Falls, sketched in pencil by Thomas Ayres in 1855, was the first artistic representation of Yosemite to reach the public.

route had been one of three primary Indian trails into and out of Yosemite Valley for centuries before being traveled by equestrians and pack animals, then stagecoaches and automobiles. This popular stagecoach route constructed in 1875 was abandoned in 1933 with the completion of road realignment and the lengthy Wawona Tunnel.

Today, the little-known and seldom-used, long-forsaken road offers solitude during any season. Even during Yosemite Valley's peak summer months, you're not likely to encounter anyone on your walk along this historic road. The grade is moderate through a mixed forest canopy of oak, pine and cedar. Ceanothus and manzanita dominate the understory. If conditions permit in winter, exchange your hiking boots for snowshoes to trek the 2.6 miles to Inspiration Point.

At the rocky promontory along this ancient pathway that became Inspiration Point, two signal events occurred in Yosemite's human history that forever sealed its future. As a result of these events, a tremendous influx of miners and settlers flooded the foothills surrounding the Valley, and Yosemite's pristine landscape became a casualty of publicity and the Gold Rush.

The first incident commenced on the brink of this isolated and mysterious mountain when Major James Savage's Mariposa Battalion paused on March 27, 1851 as the surpassingly beautiful Valley burst into full view. A few hours later they would become the first non-natives to enter its peaceful, grand setting, and in two days its timeless tranquility would be irreversibly altered. The militia was on a punitive mission to round up a band of "marauding, naughty aborigines" and force march them to a reservation on the Fresno River. Savage's only re-corded comment about the Valley was, "It's a hell of a place."

Frustrated at finding only deserted bark lodges and angered that the Ahwahneechees had fled the Valley, Savage ordered his men to burn the Indians' food caches, acorn granaries and villages. Satisfied at the sight of black smoke clouds rolling through the Valley, Savage vowed that if he couldn't capture them, then he would starve them into submission. Ultimately, the Yosemite natives were either expelled from their homeland and exiled to live among other tribes in the Eastern Sierra, herded onto reservations or killed.

The recorded history of Yosemite opened tragically on "a discordant note of misery and violence." By mid-1853, Native Americans no longer prevailed in the Yosemite region. A culture that had survived in harmony with one another and their environment since at least 1000 B.C. was gone, never to reunite as a distinct, cohesive group.

Except for a handful of prospectors and hunters, the general public remained unaware of the new-found Valley, even after the three shameful Indian campaigns were over. A few reports of the expeditions appeared in San Francisco papers, but they focused more on military tactics than scenery. Nevertheless, miner-turned-journalist James Hutchings was lured to Yosemite by the notation in one article of a 1000-foot waterfall and formidable granite formations.

Seeking "scenes of wonder and curiosity" for his monthly illustrated magazine about California, Hutchings arrived in Mariposa in 1855. Accompanying him was the young artist Thomas Ayres, hired to sketch the fabulous sights of their odyssey in wild and remote locations. After many dead ends in finding any local who knew the trail, Hutchings engaged two Ahwahneechees as guides. Thus began the second signal event.

On June 27, 1855, this group with vastly different motives and objectives than the Mariposa Battalion also paused at Inspiration Point to feast their eyes on the resplendent scene. By the end of the day, Hutchings, Ayres and two companions made history as the inaugural tourist party to enter Yosemite Valley where they spent five days exploring and sketching. The second assault began as secrets of the Valley's wondrous sights were soon broadcasted. Inevitably, discovery led to publicity.

Upon return to Mariposa, Hutchings wrote the first printed description of Yosemite for the fledgling *Mariposa Gazette*. Soon afterward, journalists throughout the state reprinted his article. His glowing and heartfelt praise of Yosemite's spectacular landscape raced like wildfire across the country and to Europe. The feature story in *Hutchings' California Magazine* the following year detailed his Yosemite journey and included sketches by Ayres. Not only sightseers but potential businessmen were now attracted to this virgin real estate.

More than anyone else, it was Hutchings who spread the gospel of Yosemite. He was profoundly committed to its promotion and development for 47 years until his death in 1902. Just four years after Yosemite's discovery by James

Savage, tourists started to trickle in, from a mere 42 in 1855 to a flood tide of 4.3 million in 1997. Beginning in 1856 with the first crude hotel, Yosemite Valley's transformation was underway.

The untimely death of Thomas Ayres reveals an interesting historical sidebar. The young artist was lost at sea en route from San Pedro to San Francisco in April 1858. Sometime between 1856 and 1860, U.S. Navy Commander James Alden purchased ten of Ayres' original Yosemite sketches in San Francisco. Many years later the heirs to these priceless drawings brought them home to the Yosemite Museum near the very spot where some of them were created.

Although Ayres was the front-runner of many distinguished non-Native American artists of national and international fame, he was by no means the first artist in Yosemite. Thousands of years before his sketches made in 1855, Native Americans created pictographs (rock paintings) using primarily white, gray, orange and red pigments. Because of their antiquity and inestimable cultural and historical significance, the location of the pictographs is not publicized.

Today, the view from Inspiration Point can only be witnessed by hikers. The former stage and automobile route has come full circle by reverting to the trail it used to be in pre-discovery days when the Valley was still an Indian safehold. The view is precious because man-made intrusions are neither visible nor audible. With the passage of time, the growth of cedars, pines and oaks has somewhat obstructed the vista. Nevertheless, the overview of the Valley and the High Sierra above it is as enthralling now as when previous generations looked down on the same incomparable landscape.

■ THE HIKE

Walk cautiously west on the left side of the road leading to Glacier Point and Wawona for .3 mile. Turn left onto the broad unsigned track, Old Wawona Road. A journey up this abandoned track offers a secluded Yosemite Valley experience and a unique way to connect with significant Sierra history. Winding gently uphill, the abandoned road bed is sheltered by deep forest cover and is essentially viewless until it reaches Artist Point, 1.8 miles from the Bridalveil Falls parking area. Even if you're not a good judge of distance, the breathtaking snapshot will be obvious. Pause here for awhile where Artist Creek tumbles down the mountainside and take in the splendid scenery. From this vantage point, the Valley appears uninhabited.

Since 1855, many renowned landscape painters have captured the vista from Artist Point. It was at this spot that one of Yosemite's resident artists, Thomas Hill, painted his famous *"Great Canyon of the Sierras."* His huge six-foot by ten-foot canvas portrays a stunning view of Yosemite.

Continue up the historic road which meets the Pohono Trail to Glacier Point at 2.4 miles, .6 mile past Artist Creek. At the trail junction, bear left on the Pohono Trail and follow it .2 mile to Inspiration Point. When you have had your fill of the view, either return the way you came, or, if you're not yet ready to turn back, wander up the Pohono Trail a bit farther.

For purists of Yosemite lore, it should be noted that there have been several Inspiration Points. The original Inspiration Point (elevation 6603 feet), from which the 1855 pioneering tourist party had their initial sighting of this great chasm, was along an ancient Indian trail at a jutting promontory they dubbed Mount Beatitude. By the close of the 1800s, Mount Beatitude was dropped from maps and renamed Inspiration Point, later known as "Old" Inspiration Point. From this location Thomas Ayres sketched the first picture of Yosemite on June 27, 1855. At "New" Inspiration Point (destination of this hike), 1200 feet below, travelers on the Wawona Road between 1875 and 1933 got their first, thrilling glimpse of Yosemite. Another "New" Inspiration Point, more commonly called Rainbow View, appeared on the opposite side of the Valley at a stunning vista along Big Oak Flat Road (see Chapter 26). All these Inspiration Points are still accessible—and inspiring—to hikers willing to seek them out.

26
Hiking Old Big Oak Flat Road to Rainbow View
Seeing a Hidden Yosemite

■ THE DETAILS

Getting There: From Highway 140, pass through Yosemite National Park entrance station and continue east as the highway becomes one way at Pohono Bridge. This road circumnavigates Yosemite Valley. Drive around the loop to its western end until you spot marker V 9 on your right. Turn right onto a dirt maintenance road and bear right. Either park there or drive a short distance to a small parking area surrounded by piles of logs.

Nearest Campground: Sunnyside Walk-in Campground, 3 miles east, has 35 sites available on a first-come, first-served basis. To make reservations for other Yosemite Valley campgrounds, call 800-436-7275 (Destinet).

Lodging: For all lodging in Yosemite, call 209-252-4848. For reservations in El Portal/Mariposa, call 800-321-5261.

Further Info: Yosemite National Park General Information 209-372-0200.

Hike Distance: 2 miles round trip to first viewpoint, 4 miles round trip to Rainbow View, 8 miles round trip to junction with El Capitan Trail.

Difficulty: Easy to moderate (some boulder scrambling necessary to reach Rainbow View).

Best Time to Go: Spring or autumn.

Cautions: None.

Starting Elevation: 4000 feet. 360 feet elevation gain to first viewpoint, 950 feet to Rainbow View, 1800 feet to El Capitan junction.

Map: See Chapter 24, page 143.

Other Maps: A free map of the park is available at the entrance stations. For more detail, get the USGS Yosemite 15 minute topo or Earthwalk Press **Yosemite Valley** map.

This is one of the beautiful walks from the Valley floor, one not found in most guidebooks. It offers seclusion during peak tourist months and stunning post-card views of the magnificent landscape. This hike beginning at V 9 awaits those willing to abandon the automobile and experience a hidden Yosemite. Meaningless unless you have a copy of **Yosemite Road Guide** in hand, V 9 is one of the

Valley's 27 road markers. The numbers are keyed to paragraphs in the Park booklet which identify and explain important features.

V 9 denotes an interesting geological formation near the base of El Capitan, one of the Valley's most famous landmarks. What the book doesn't tell you is that V 9 marks the spot where the historic Big Oak Flat Road entered the Valley in 1874 or that the old road ascends to an unbelievably stunning vista. One of the best ways to appreciate the colossal forces that sculpted the gorge's fabled grandeur is to get above it. From a viewpoint not far up this pioneer roadbed, you can

A stagecoach negotiates the steep grade into Yosemite Valley on Big Oak Flat Road, with Bridalveil Falls in the background.

envision a pre-discovery Yosemite—no vehicles, no structures, no roads, and no people are visible. As you take in the astonishing scenery and solitude, you can easily pretend you're the only person in the Park. As a bonus, one rarely encounters hikers on this little-known route.

While the abandoned road you will be walking may seem primitive by modern standards, it represented a quantum transportation leap for early Yosemite visitors. Today, we really have no conception of the former inconveniences and hardships inherent in a trip to experience this sublime environment. For 23 years after discovery by Major Savage's Mariposa Battalion, Yosemite was only accessible by crude horse trails. Pioneer tourists found themselves involved in a long and exhausting odyssey requiring great measures of stamina, patience, time and money.

Nevertheless, in spite of the arduous journey, visitation increased slowly but steadily during the 1860s. Not surprisingly, it didn't take long for businessmen along the approach routes and in the Valley itself to recognize the profit potential and need for comfortable lodging and appetizing meals. First, these entrepreneurs had to get the tourists out of the saddle and into the relative luxury of a stagecoach, and of course this could only be accomplished by constructing wagon roads. Bear in mind that although it was a great improvement, a stagecoach ride was still a fatiguing, bone jarring, costly expedition over narrow washboard roads.

The advent of the stagecoach was as revolutionary as the automobile would be a few decades later. The gateway communities of Coulterville, Big Oak Flat and Mariposa were well aware of the importance of being the first to complete a toll road into Yosemite, because it was believed that the winner would capture the lion's share of the tourist trade. Competition between the Big Oak Flat and Coulterville companies was an especially keen and sometimes bitter rivalry.

Big Oak Flat (BOF) Road was the second of three turnpikes completed in the mid-1870s that made Yosemite Valley accessible to wheeled vehicles. Preceded by Coulterville Road in June 1874 and followed a year later by Wawona Road in 1875, BOF Road opened to traffic on July 17, 1874. In the final analysis, while Coulterville was first (by one month), it was not the most successful. By 1879, BOF and Wawona Roads were transporting more visitors.

Technically originating at the loading levees in Stockton where river boats dropped their cargo and passengers, BOF Road proper began in Chinese Camp, a few miles south of Jamestown along present-day Highway 49. Its name derives from the mining settlement of Big Oak Flat some ten miles north of Coulterville. Eventually, the modernized version of the historic roadway that wormed through the hills of southern Tuolumne County became Highway 120.

In 1857, local resident Tom McGee cleared and blazed a saddle trail over the 33-mile western portion of the ancient Mono Indian trail between the settlement and Tamarack Flat near the northwestern rim of Yosemite Valley. After subsequent widening and improvements, the trail was called Big Oak Flat Road. By the summer of 1874, the turnpike company made use of an extant horse trail and completed the remaining 15 miles to the Valley floor.

By far the most difficult segment of construction was from Gentry's Station (hostelry) on the brink of towering cliffs to the Valley 2500 feet below. Known as the infamous Zigzags, it amounted to only three miles, but the 16 percent pitch was terrifyingly steep over unstable terrain. At a cost of $16,000, a crew of talented Italian stone masons completed the seemingly impossible, switchbacking route in just five months. Rocks were cut and hand fitted, without mortar, to crib up the steep walled sides of the serpentine roadbed.

Finally, on July 17, 1874, a gala procession of 52 vehicles began the precipitous descent from Gentry's. At the foot of El Capitan, the jubilant caravan of 512 participants was greeted by a wildly cheering crowd of campers and Valley residents, followed by a rowdy celebration that nearly depleted "the local supply of libations and restoratives."

■ THE HIKE

To get your boots on this old road, find marker V 9 near El Capitan. Turn onto the dirt service road, bear right, and drive a short distance to its end. Usually, a large number of logs are piled up around a small parking area. The trail begins here at the Valley terminus of BOF Road.

Follow the route west heading gently uphill through an interesting mix of vegetation: pines, cedars, oaks, bay trees, the uncommon California *torreya* (nutmeg), and colorful clumps of wildflowers in spring. Note that the blacktopped surface is still intact in many places. Less than a mile brings you to the first major rock slide. The roadway was obliterated in 1942, but an obvious trail skirts the edge of a gully where you will have to scramble over some boulders. On the other side of the gully, the narrow road resumes. Somewhere along here, perch on a chunk of granite and take some time to let the grand vista fill your senses.

Directly across the Valley, a dramatic view of Bridalveil Fall captures your attention as it plummets 620 feet down sheer cliffs before wending its way to the Merced River. The native people called it Pohono, "the fall of puffing winds," because at low volume, its water gets pushed around by gusts of wind. The meadow across the road from the fall is where John Muir and Teddy Roosevelt camped in 1903 while Muir urged the president to work for wilderness protection.

The picture of Yosemite Valley is framed by El Capitan on the north and Cathedral Rocks on the south. This perspective offers an up close and personal acquaintance with El Capitan, one of the largest exposed granite blocks in the world, rising 3200 feet above the Valley floor. At the far eastern end of the canyon, the unmistakable shape of Half Dome dominates the horizon. The free map available at entrance stations can help identify other prominent features.

Retrace your steps, or, if you are reluctant to leave and feel energetic, continue up BOF Road. About another mile farther, and after some cautious clambering over a boulder field caused by rock slides in the 1940s, brings you to the metal railings of Rainbow View, so named for the rainbow dancing in Bridalveil Fall during summer afternoons. This vista gave travelers their first unexpected, breathtaking glimpse of the stupendous gorge they were about to drop into. Early stage drivers dubbed it "Oh, My!" Point because of their passengers' startled exclamations at the view and shocking steepness of the cliff they had to descend. Later it was renamed New Inspiration Point.

Though certainly a boon for travelers and entrepreneurs, the three roadways boosted the influx of visitors, underlining the end of Yosemite Valley's innocence and irrevocably altering its environment. BOF Road was used by buggies, stagecoaches and freight wagons for 40 years until 1913 when autos were permitted to enter the park. Eventually, traffic increased to the point that a control system was imposed restricting uphill and downhill traffic to alternating hours. By 1940, a new highway between Crane Flat and Merced River Canyon replaced the intimidating Zigzags. By then, the old route was infrequently used, but it was maintained for downhill traffic until 1942 when the monstrous rock slide rendered it impassable.

Walking along a portion of the Big Oak Flat Zigzags offers a superb sensory appeal. However, perhaps the most rewarding aspect of the journey is a sense of moving, literally, through a significant stretch of Sierra Nevada history. Co-mingling your footsteps with many thousands of others who have traveled this old track provides a satisfying connection and continuity with our heritage that is too often neglected in our hurried culture.

27
Grandeur of the Ahwahnee Hotel
A Hike from the Ahwahnee to Mirror Lake

On March 25, 1851, the party went into camp near Bridalveil Fall. That night around the campfire a suitable name for the remarkable valley was discussed. Lafayette H. Bunnell...urged that it be named Yosemite after the natives who had been driven out. Although the whites knew the name of the tribe, they were apparently unaware that the Indians had another name, Ahwahnee, for their Deep Grassy Valley.

~**One Hundred Years in Yosemite**, Carl P. Russell

■ THE DETAILS

Getting There: The Ahwahnee is on the north side of the Valley, just east of Yosemite Village. You might find parking there, or you can take a free shuttle bus from other Valley locations.

Nearest Campgrounds: Lower Pines and North Pines Campgrounds are near the hotel. For reservations for Yosemite Valley campgrounds, call 800-436-7275.

Lodging: For all lodging in Yosemite Valley, call 209-252-4848.

Further Info: Yosemite National Park General Information 209-372-0200.

Hike Distance: 2.4 miles round trip or 2.8-mile loop.

Difficulty: Easy.

Facilities: Restrooms and water at the Ahwahnee Hotel.

Best Time to Go: Late spring and early summer for wildflowers and waterfalls, October and November for autumn color.

Cautions: None.

Starting Elevation: 3900 feet. 200 feet gain to Mirror Lake.

Other Map: USGS Yosemite Valley 7.5 minute topo.

With the exception of Half Dome, the Ahwahnee Hotel is Yosemite Valley's most well known landmark to millions of visitors from around the world. In a woodland setting of stately pines, graceful dogwoods and majestic oaks dramatically back-dropped by sheer granite walls, this venerable hostelry was designated a national historic structure in 1977.

Completed in 1927, the luxurious hotel was specifically designed to blend into the natural scene. Employing a style known as rustic or environmental architecture, the massive and elegant structure was built on a scale to match the towering cliffs surrounding it. Faced with granite blocks and concrete beams stained and molded to resemble cedar, the Ahwahnee Hotel seems to have "grown" out of the formations for which Yosemite is famous.

In 1925, the directors of the newly formed Yosemite Park and Curry Company (chief concessionaire) awarded the project design to architect Gilbert Stanley Underwood of Los Angeles with the mandate "for a hotel that fits the environment." James McLaughlin, a San Francisco contractor, was selected to build the hotel. When work began in spring 1926, McLaughlin promised it would be done by December 15, 1926. The guaranteed price tag was set at $500,000 plus his fee.

From day one, the project was fraught with heated arguments, delays, divergent ideas and numerous plan changes. Building costs soared to over a million dollars and the opening delayed by seven months. The primary fault lay with the temperamental, stubborn architect, his absences and incomplete plans. Differences of opinions among Curry Company directors and McLaughlin's idea that such a complex, immense building could be finished so quickly also contributed.

Nevertheless, after months of disputes and revisions, ground was broken in April 1926. The hotel was named Ahwahnee, the Indian word for Yosemite Valley, believed to translate to "deep grassy valley." The building site for this unique structure was an historic site in its own right. Once called Kenneyville, it held a bustling tourist business. In 1885, Coffman and Kenney began an extensive livery stable there. That cluster of about 15 buildings was torn down to make room for the new hotel.

Dating even farther back than Kenneyville, Mr. A. Harris opened a public campground near the Ahwahnee site in 1878. To be independent of hostelries, many visitors were bringing their own camping equipment into Yosemite. The Harris Camp Ground, the first of its kind, sold provisions, rented equipment, and offered stable facilities. Harris even grew fodder there for the animals. This campground also was removed to build the Ahwahnee.

Everything about the Ahwahnee is massive, appearing to have been built to accommodate a race of giants. The great exterior columns of native rock, rising six stories high, bring to mind an ancient European castle. A tall child can easily stand upright in the cavernous stone fireplaces. In the dining room, enormous sugar pine trees, stripped of their bark and waxed, provide structural support as well as rugged visual appeal. The dimensions of this vast room, capable of seating 425, are staggering: 150 feet long, 51 feet wide and 34 feet high.

To the delight of diners, the grandeur of Yosemite Valley's incomparable beauty rushes inside through ten cathedral-like, floor-to-ceiling windows. Equally impressive, though somewhat smaller, the Great Lounge also brings the drama of Yosemite indoors through its ten mammoth windows, crowned with brilliantly colored stained glass panels of California Indian design. Light filtering through these bold geometric patterns is stunning. The solarium, a peaceful spot for guests to relax, captures views and light from three directions.

Originally, 14 public rooms comprised the first and mezzanine floors. The dominant interior decorating theme was California Indian in flavor, although other striking influences were incorporated. Among them, priceless Persian and Basque rugs and wall hangings, wrought-iron fixtures and chandeliers, Art Deco touches and an early California motif ran through the decor. The Ahwahnee is a shadow from the past, grand testimony to the period when only wealthy Americans could afford to visit national parks. Its elegance is legendary and even today dress codes are outlined. Once, even U.S. Secretary of Commerce Herbert Hoover was stopped at the entrance because he was clad in his fishing togs.

The grounds then included tennis and badminton courts, swimming pool, golf course, croquet and archery areas, amenities now gone. In a shady pine grove nearby, private cottages, each with its own wildflower garden and outdoor furniture, housed guests who preferred more seclusion. Prices on opening day, July 14, 1927, ranged from $10 to $50 including meals, nearly twice the cost for lodging at Camp Curry across the Valley.

The Ahwahnee had gained such prestige that in 1927 a Christmas dinner and pageant based on Washington Irving's description of an 1819 holiday banquet at the manor of Squire Bracebridge was initiated. The famous Bracebridge Dinner became an instant tradition; the extremely popular feast and theatrical presentation still thrives today.

As integral to the history of Yosemite National Park as the Ahwahnee Hotel is, the concept behind it is equally remarkable. Today, one might wonder why top government officials allowed, in fact pushed for, building the Ahwahnee. The question rose as to whether Yosemite Valley should remain completely natural or become "enough urbanized." Evidently for the fledgling National Park Service (NPS), headed by millionaire Stephen Mather, such hotels were quite acceptable.

Bear in mind that in the 1920s the infant NPS sincerely believed their success was measured by the sheer numbers of visitors. Mather's dream was to attract huge numbers of tourists to the nation's parks. He envisioned this being accomplished by building comfortable, modern lodging, more roads, trails, campgrounds and expanding services. With increased visitation and public support, Congressional monies would follow. Obviously, concessionaires delighted in this kind of thinking. Because Yosemite was openly the apple of his eye within the system, Mather was determined that his pet park would have a first-class luxury hotel.

A peek behind the scenes prior to the Ahwahnee's gala opening in July 1927 offers a perspective of the currents of change as they sparked through the atmosphere in Yosemite. The national economy was in a major boom cycle after World War I. The Roaring Twenties era was a time of affluence, free-wheeling entrepreneurs, lavish hotels, high style and high living. The phenomenal increase in automobile usage resulted in an explosion of tourism. People were on the move, and Mather wanted to steer them into the parks. National parks were on their way to becoming resort destinations, attracting a different type of visitor than campers and hikers.

As a consequence, an alliance of the NPS and the concessionaire evolved quickly into a mutually satisfactory but contradictory bond—one supposedly dedicated to protecting the natural environment and the other dedicated to making money by creating structures and services in a wilderness setting. In fact, both the NPS and the concessionaire were guilty of short-sighted goals. The "get 'em in and keep 'em happy" philosophy reigned, which in the long run has not best served to preserve Yosemite's fragile ecology.

The 74-year-old hotel has seen many changes since opening day. (For a full history, read Shirley Sargent's book, *The Ahwahnee Hotel*.) It has survived economic slumps, gas rationing, large corporations buying in and out, droughts, floods, fires, the automobile age, wars, interior and exterior facelifts and renovations, conflicts between environmentalists and recreationists, numerous park superintendents, the Hippie invasion of the 1960s and '70s, and television and movie makers.

In years to come, the Ahwahnee will face other changes and probably will survive them, too. Whether we agree or not with the presence of an elegant hotel in a national park is a moot point. The grand old Ahwahnee is an extraordinary repository, almost a museum, of artifacts, paintings, architecture, decorations, and design themes. It is staged against a unique location, one of the most scenic on earth. The Ahwahnee will endure, prompting untold numbers of visitors to make their reservations a year in advance for the privilege of saying "I was there."

The hotel's 99 rooms and 23 cottages rent for $320 per night, and the Queen's Room on the sixth floor goes for $900. Meal prices are comparable to a five-star San Francisco restaurant. For a seat at Bracebridge Dinner, participants are selected by lottery months before the event.

Fortunately, visitors are most welcome to wander through the public rooms and absorb the elegance and grandeur of a bygone era in this historic and very special hotel. The Ahwahnee is indeed a striking monument to our past, a monolith embraced by Yosemite's grandeur.

■ THE HIKE

Begin your walk on the edge of the hotel's valet parking area at the foot of Yosemite Valley's towering north wall. A trail sign near a flat rock containing several grinding holes points the way to Mirror Lake/Meadow.

Though it's not wilderness, Yosemite Valley is a splendid place to walk. Despite its summertime popularity, it's certainly possible to find solitude by getting your feet on a trail—especially if you're out and about early. You can flee the crowds at popular roadside attractions and the village center to experience the Valley's incomparable scenery in ways only hikers know.

The short jaunt to Mirror Meadow runs along the base of the talus slopes

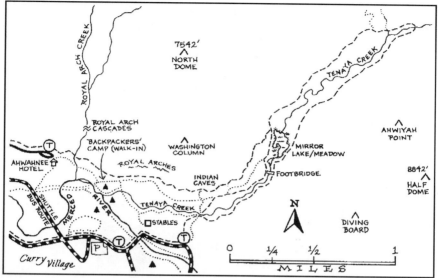

Chapters 27 and 28

beneath Royal Arches and Washington Column through a fine forest of pine, fir, cedar, laurel, oak and dogwood. Soon you cross a creek originating from Royal Arches 1000 feet above. The so-called arches were sculpted by the exfoliation, or leafing away, of layers of granite which created enormous stone arcs. To some, they look like rocky rainbows.

At .4 mile you meet a junction where a path forks right for the stables, but you continue straight. Your trail closely parallels a paved bike path to around .8 mile, then veers closer to the base of the cliff. Scores of huge rockfall boulders spalled from Washington Column litter the ground. Watch for impressive views of Half Dome across the Valley.

At .9 mile, on a flat forested stretch, you enter the Indian Caves area. The Ahwahneechees used the caves for storage and occasionally for shelter during severe weather. The caves are actually spaces created by fallen stacks of talus boulders. Near the trail's north side is a low, squat slab of granite pocked with mortar cups where acorns were pounded into meal.

Continue below Washington Column, pass the old Mirror Lake parking lot, and walk through a boulder strewn field to reach the western edge of Mirror Meadow/Lake at 1.2 miles. Interpretive signs help visitors understand the constantly changing natural world. For many decades the NPS dredged sand from Mirror Lake to preserve its popular reflective quality. Finally, in 1971, they wisely decided to let Mother Nature do her own work. Since then the natural transformation from lake to meadow to forest has been in progress. See the next chapter for more about Mirror Lake's history.

From the small wooden bridge, pause to gaze at Mount Watkins, Half Dome and Cloud's Rest. From here you can retrace your steps, continue eastward to circumnavigate the lake (described in Chapter 28), or take a slightly different route back to the hotel.

For the latter option, cross the little bridge. In .6 mile the trail splits. Stay to the right toward Yosemite Village and briefly walk on the bike path. When you come to the Group Camp on your left at 1.2 miles, turn right to leave the bike path at a sign indicating El Capitan and Yosemite Falls and follow the trail you started out on back to the Ahwahnee Hotel.

Mount Watkins looms behind four smiling visitors, illustrating the once superb reflective qualities of Mirror Lake.

28
Mirror Lake-Mirror Meadow
A Lake in Natural Transition

■ THE DETAILS

Getting There: Drive to the upper end of Yosemite Valley and park in the Curry Village lot. Take the free shuttle bus to the trailhead at the Mirror Lake Junction (stop 17), or to the Lower Pines (stop 19) in winter.

Nearest Campground: Backpackers' Walk-In Campground, east of the Ahwahnee Hotel, has 25 tent sites, 2 night maximum, available on a first-come, first-served basis. For reservations for other park campgrounds, call 800-436-7275.

Lodging: Yosemite Lodge 559-252-4848 has 245 rooms.

Further Info: Yosemite National Park recorded info line 209-372-0200.

Hike Distance: 2 miles round trip or loop to Mirror Lake. 4.5 miles round trip or 5-mile loop to Snow Creek's confluence with Tenaya Creek.

Difficulty: Easy.

Best Time to Go: Late spring, early summer for lake reflections, autumn for color.

Cautions: No bike riding allowed past .5 mile. In winter, shuttle bus does not stop at Mirror Lake Junction or other upper loop stops. Then you must walk from Lower Pines Campground entrance, adding .6 mile round trip to trail mileage.

Starting Elevation: 3990 feet.

Elevation Gain: 120 feet to Mirror Lake, 200 feet for long loop.

Map: See Chapter 27, page 157.

Other Map: USGS Yosemite Valley 7.5 minute topo.

Mirror Lake, nestled in the shadow of colossal Half Dome at the eastern end of Yosemite Valley, is vanishing. Each year the lake shrinks as silt and sediments carried down the canyon cut by Tenaya Creek gradually displace the water. Eventually, it will be reduced to a pond and, ultimately, replaced by a meadow. What we see today, part lake and part meadow, is the result of natural processes at work in the Yosemite environment.

Even though Mirror Lake slowly diminishes in size and depth with every passing year, its woodsy setting continues to lure countless visitors. Since the incomparable Yosemite Valley was first discovered by Euro-Americans in 1851, the lake's calm, glassy surface has stimulated the creative juices of painters, poets and photographers. Truly magnificent scenery surrounds the lake. Early morning reflections of the soaring cliffs in its unruffled waters are enchanting, making it a popular destination. Some of the most renowned photographs of Yosemite Valley depict stunning mirror images of Half Dome and Mount Watkins seeming to rise out of Mirror Lake's waters.

Many park visitors, especially old-timers, mourn the loss of this placid oasis and express disappointment that Mirror Lake is slowly disappearing. Similar to the contrived spectacle of the Firefall, the public was conditioned to accept the unnatural as natural. At the time of discovery, Mirror Lake was not the deep, serene jewel that people became accustomed to. Most visitors have not been aware that the lake was merely a shallow, boulder-blocked pond until 1884.

At that time, it was dammed by hotel owner and journalist James Hutchings who moved huge chunks of granite across the outlet stream to augment its reflective qualities, increasing the area of the lake by nearly six times. Between 1914 and 1971, after the lake dried up in autumn, the National Park Service maintained its artificial size by excavating tons of sand and gravel to spread on icy or snow-covered roads. A decision was made in 1971 to allow the lake to return to its natural condition and dredging was discontinued.

Known as "Sleeping Water" by Native Americans, the tranquil and beautiful setting that inspired artists and charmed all manner of people was also the scene of commercial development. Mirror Lake House, an unpretentious wood struc-ture, was built by Gordon and Whorton in 1870. Essentially, it was a tavern providing wine, liquor and rowboats. In 1874, due to some infraction of their lease agreement with the Yosemite Commissioners, they were evicted from the premises. William Howard, ex-Mariposa County Sheriff, leased the property and turned it into a profitable enterprise. Howard expanded the business by building a toll carriage road to the tavern, renting rowboats, and constructing a 40 by 60 foot platform over the water for dining and dancing. After the state bought out his toll road and made it a free route in 1879, the Commissioners shut down the business, dismantled Mirror Lake House and its dancing plat-form, and eliminated all the rubbish and debris.

The enterprising Washburn brothers who owned the Wawona Hotel complex and Yosemite Stage and Turnpike Company get credit for developing an ice industry in the Yosemite region. Besides their ice cutting and storage building at tiny Stella Lake in Wawona (see Chapter 41), the Washburns used frozen Mirror Lake as a source of natural ice production. About 1890 they built an ice house on the western end of the lake to supply Valley hotels, camps and businesses. After completion of the Cascade Power Plant in 1918, ice cutting at Mirror Lake was abandoned. Later, the ice house was removed.

Even though it's now in a natural transition from lake to meadow, you can see a scaled-down version of its former reflective fame during spring snow melt. To a lesser degree than when it was artificially maintained, its surface still mirrors the surrounding granite domes and peaks. However, by mid-summer the lake is usually dry. During the dry months, the area looks more like a gravelly lake bottom than a meadow. If the old man-made dam were removed, the water table would likely drop enough for trees to invade the meadow, ultimately obscuring all views.

■ THE HIKE

An easy, mostly flat walk to Mirror Lake/Meadow still offers an enjoyable Yosemite Valley excursion. While the lake is slipping into history, the formidable and dramatic rock formations encircling it are still very much with us. Since shuttle buses disgorging huge numbers of people no longer visit the lake, the setting is definitely quieter. Even bicyclists must leave their wheels in a parking area away from the lake.

A shuttle bus stops about one mile from the lake/meadow, at stop 17. You can either hike or ride the paved bike path or walk the footpath not far to the east. At .2 mile both paths approach Tenaya Creek. The bike trail crosses it on Tenaya Bridge while the footpath veers east to follow the base of the canyon wall below Half Dome. No bike riding is allowed beyond .5 mile. Work has been in progress to rehabilitate the area, removing 800 tons of old roadbeds, obliterating a network of unsightly trails and installing interpretive signs. Visitors can now stroll through history along the former carriage road and see the locations of the ice house, man-made dam and Mirror Lake House and platform.

Both paths reach Mirror Lake around one mile. Once you absorb the scenes at the lake/meadow, consider extending your walk up canyon through the diverse and colorful forest surrounding Mirror Lake/Meadow by continuing around it to the left (north), following signs to Snow Creek. Since most folks choose to walk only to the lake rather than around it, you'll find fewer people and more solitude. In May the lovely, creamy white blossoms of dogwood trees light up the forest. Views of Half Dome, Mount Watkins, Basket Dome and deeply glaciated Tenaya Canyon are superb. If you think you're hearing voices from above, you probably are. At times, rock climbers can be heard, if not seen, inching their way up Washington Column.

Late spring and very early summer are perhaps the best times for a stroll to and around Mirror Lake and up the canyon beyond it. A particularly pleasant site is at the easternmost end of the canyon floor 1.25 miles beyond the lake. Immediately before the footbridge spanning Tenaya Creek, walk off trail to your left (east) for a few hundred feet. You'll soon see chortling Snow Creek racing to merge with Tenaya Creek. Along this woodsy stretch, find a spot for a rest and a trail snack and enjoy the sound of tumbling water all around you. From here, either return the way you came, or continue past the footbridge and follow the loop trail back down canyon past the lake, then follow either footpath or bike trail to the shuttle bus stop.

29

Half Dome

Yosemite's Grand Gray Dome

The eye is compelled as if by force of physical attraction to return to this extraordinary mountain, which one can never tire of contemplating.

~J. Smeaton Chase, **Yosemite Trails**

■ THE DETAILS

Getting There: Drive to the upper end of Yosemite Valley and park in the Curry Village parking lot. Take the free shuttle bus to the trailhead at Happy Isles (stop 16).

Nearest Campground: Backpackers' Walk-In Campground, east of the Ahwahnee Hotel, has 25 tent sites, 2 night maximum, available on a first-come, first-served basis. For reservations for other park campgrounds, call 800-436-7275.

Lodging: Yosemite Lodge 559-252-4848 has 245 rooms.

Further Info: Yosemite National Park recorded info line 209-372-0200.

Hike Distance: 16.5 miles round trip.

Difficulty: Very strenuous.

Best Time to Go: Late May or early June, or after Labor Day.

Cautions: This is the most challenging and strenuous hike in this book, recommended only for fit hikers who can cope with dizzying heights and drop-offs. Do not attempt to reach the summit during thunderstorm activity. In that case, turn back! A wilderness permit is required to camp overnight along the trail, 209-372-0740. Trail closed mid-October through mid-May.

Starting Elevation: 4020 feet. Elevation gain of 4800 feet.

Other Maps: USGS Yosemite Falls, Half Dome 7.5 minute topos.

Of all Yosemite's unique geological formations, Half Dome is the star attraction, considered by most visitors to be unrivaled in its grandeur. The music of the waterfalls is certainly the anthem of Yosemite, but colossal Half Dome symbolizes this great national treasure more than any other landmark. Half Dome, simply put, overwhelms the emotions of Park visitors. Its commanding summit 4,748 feet above the Valley floor and its unusual, pleasing shape is unmistakable from many Valley and rim vantage points.

Long before Euro-Americans discovered Yosemite, Half Dome and other fabulous rock formations were explained in Native American legends. The Ahwahneechees, a subtribe of the southern Miwoks, who were living in Yosemite by 1000 B.C., called Half Dome "Tis-a-sack." According to legend, one day Great Spirit became so infuriated with the disrespectful, disobedient and angry behavior of a man, Nan-gas, and his wife, Tis-as-ack, that he turned them both into stone. Tis-as-ack became Half Dome, and her tears can still be seen as black streaks staining the great mass of rock. Nan-gas was changed into North Dome across the Valley, forever silent and forever separated from his wife.

Numerous Sierra features were named by Dr. Lafayette Bunnell and other members of the Mariposa Battalion, the initial white men to explore Yosemite Valley in 1851. It was Private Spencer who dubbed the split mountain Half Dome. Originally, it was called Rock of Ages by William Penn Abrams who saw it from afar two years earlier while bear hunting in the uplands. To Abrams and his companion, "it looked as though it had been sliced with a knife as one would slice a loaf of bread." This enormous granite monolith and other natural features changed names over the years. For a time it was called South Dome. Finally in 1865, Half Dome became its permanent label, indicated as such on maps.

Visitors frequently ask Park Service personnel, "What happened to the other half of Half Dome?" Well, don't bother looking for it at the bottom of Tenaya Canyon because it isn't there. Seeing isn't always believing. Contrary to what your eyes tell you, Half Dome never had another half. In fact, about 80% of its imposing body remains in place. Nor was it overridden by glaciers. Sitting like an island above a frozen sea, its summit was 500 to 600 feet above the glacial ice.

After many decades of controversy, lively debates and exhaustive studies, geologists concluded that Half Dome's remarkable shape was due to exfoliation, the leafing away of layers of granite much as layers of onion peel away from the center. The dome's dramatically sheer front resulted from the exfoliation of internal vertical fractures, or joints, in the bedrock. Glacial action relentlessly and ever-so-slowly bulldozed vast slabs of rock along massive, widely spaced fracture lines and moved them miles away. The smooth back side was sculptured by millions of years of "sheet or shell" fracturing, the cracking of rock along curved surfaces parallel to the surface. As the concentric shells weathered and disintegrated, a rounded dome formed.

With the help of binoculars, you can see ant-sized people atop the dome's 8,842-foot high point. From the Valley you can't see how large the summit is, about the equivalent of 17 football fields. The famous cable stairway leading to Half Dome's top also hides from Valley views.

Half Dome has been a magnet for hikers for 138 years. The first recorded effort to scale its heights occurred in summer 1863 by members of the California State Geological Survey. After a failed attempt, chief geologist Josiah Whitney emphatically commented that Half Dome was "perfectly inaccessible . . . it will never be trodden by human foot."

In 1934 a Civilian Conservation Corps crew stands on Half Dome's beak (the Visor) with a canine companion. The CCC replaced the Sierra Club's cable stairway that year.

Challenged by Whitney's declaration, in 1869 James Mason Hutchings and two friends decided to climb Half Dome, but they also failed. Two years later Yosemite's foremost trail builder, John Conway, and his nimble young sons tried and failed. Although Conway made it 200 feet farther than Hutchings, he was also thwarted by the sharp 45° angle of the dome's exfoliated granite slope. It seemed that Whitney might be right—Half Dome would remain terra incognita.

However, six years later, another Yosemite Valley resident achieved the impossible. Scottish born George Anderson, former sailor, ex-miner, trail builder and blacksmith, made his mark in Sierra history as the first known white man to stand on Half Dome's summit at 3 p.m. on October 12, 1875. Utilizing his blacksmithing skills, Anderson fabricated eye bolts on a forge at a cabin he built near a spring about a mile below the dome. An account of his feat by John Muir gives us a snapshot of his pluck and determination: "Anderson began with Conway's old rope, which has been left in place, and resolutely drilled his way to the top, inserting eye bolts every five or six feet apart, and making his rope fast to each succession, resting his feet on the last bolt while he drilled a hole for the next above . . . and thus the whole was accomplished in less than a week."

As a curious footnote to Anderson's daring exploit, he abandoned his boots because of difficulty in getting purchase on the smooth granite and iron eye bolts. He wrapped his feet and legs in cloth and slathered them with pine pitch but realized that only with great effort and loss of balance could he unstick his feet. Finally, he discarded the sacking and reached the top barefoot.

Even for a strong man, climbing Half Dome was a daunting, physically and mentally challenging test of endurance and courage. Amazingly, a few days after Anderson's triumph, a young woman who worked in a photographic studio in the Valley became the first female to witness the stunning 360° panorama from Half Dome. Sally Dutcher made history for womankind by pulling herself up the rope to the top of this gargantuan rock formation, a scary 900 feet from the base of the dome portion to the crest.

In spite of the difficulty and danger, climbing Half Dome became an increasingly popular goal for Yosemite's early tourists. Enterprising George Anderson anticipated making a lot of money from this growing interest. His ambitious schemes included a toll trail from the Valley floor, a hotel situated on the shoulder of rock at the base of the dome, and a sturdy wooden stairway to the top. As fate would have it, his plans were never realized. While gathering materials for the project in 1884, he sickened and died from pneumonia.

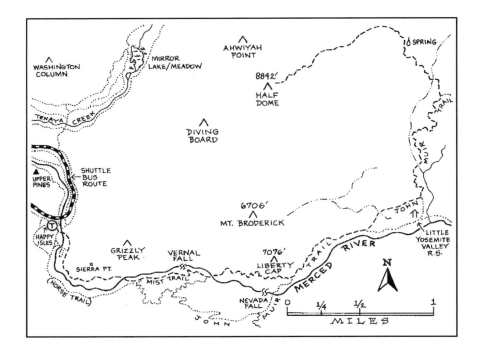

■ THE HIKE

The fascination and allure of reaching Half Dome's crest has not at all declined in the last 138 years. Even though it still involves a strenuous 8.25-mile hike from Valley to summit, an elevation gain of nearly 5000 feet, a sweat-popping 300-yard haul up the cables and then the process in reverse to get back down, it is still an extremely tantalizing destination.

The world as seen from the top is worth every ounce of effort it takes to get there, and it is indeed an effort. Frankly, other mountain tops in the park, some a bit lower and some even higher, are easier to summit for equally impressive views, but it is Half Dome, the world famous and legendary symbol of Yosemite, that captures the imagination and kindles the spirit of all manner of people to set foot on its broad top. For some it is akin to a pilgrimage. It has a mystique that resonates to a yearning many of us have for contact with high, wild places.

The shortest and most popular route to Half Dome's summit follows the Mist Trail on a steep ascent for 3.5 miles from Happy Isles Trailhead, passing Vernal Falls and Nevada Falls. Where the Mist Trail ends, you pick up the famous John Muir Trail, following it east on a gradual ascent to 4.5 miles, entering Little Yosemite Valley where overnighters are allowed to camp (permit required). Then follow the Muir Trail north on a steep ascent to meet the Half Dome spur Trail around 6 miles, having gained an elevation of 6980 feet. From there it's slightly more than 2 miles to the summit.

The 900-foot cable stairway up the dome section closely follows the original route, but it has been modified and improved upon. This final pitch to the top is made possible by two waist-high cables about three feet apart which are supported by upright pipes imbedded in the rock. Attached to the base of the pipes are two-foot long by four-inch wide cross steps. Nevertheless, the cables remain an intimidating, but thrilling, aspect of the journey. The potentially fatal drop-offs demand caution and a focused attention span. Hikers also need to be mindful of the weather. The sky-kissing dome acts as a lightning rod, and the push to the crest should be avoided, or aborted en route, if storm clouds gather. Be that as it may, thousands of hikers of all ages, sizes and shapes make it safely to the top each year between mid-May and mid-October when the cables are in place.

Other than the fact they survived the 8.25-mile trek and cable climb, most "Half-Domers" are first impressed with the size of the summit, an area encompassing about 13 acres. The next indelible impression is the view, and here words are meager substitutes for the sublime panorama extending to every horizon. In all directions, near and far, are vast stretches of forest, deep gorges, waterfalls, shimmering lakes, and a bazaar of mountains, peaks and domes. Below, Yosemite Valley is a study in miniature where absolutely every thing is dwarfed into insignificance from this perspective. Sharing the summit with you are squirrels, birds, wildflowers and the rare lungless salamander. Occasionally, acrobatic squirrels race up and down the cables, hoping to cadge a bit of your trail lunch.

■ OTHER CHOICES

Climbing Half Dome is not something most readers will choose to do, but hiking up to it is only one way to experience this renowned Yosemite landmark. If you don't climb Half Dome, you'll find many superb viewing places along Tioga Road, at Glacier Point and within the Valley to enjoy some quality time contemplating its varied moods at different times of day and in different seasons. Even hikers will admit that you can't see the dome when you're on top of it.

Unless snowfall has closed the road, treat yourself to an excursion to Glacier Point. An unbelievably scenic turn-out at nearby Washburn Point offers one of the most eloquent and intimate pictures of Half Dome in the Park, rivaled only by those at Glacier Point. Any hour of the day is powerful, but try to time your visit just before sunset when Half Dome catches and holds the last, rosy light of day. When atmospheric conditions are just right, the ethereal phenomenon of alpenglow fires its massive face with a surreal orange-red glow.

Witnessing the day's last hurrah spread across this mountain of solid granite underlines John Muir's description. "Never have I beheld so great and so gentle and so divine a piece of ornamental work as this grand gray dome."

IV
A Wealth of Glorious Terrain
🐻 YOSEMITE PARK OUTSIDE THE VALLEY 🐻

H ERE WE EXPLORE the vast and diverse 1183 square miles of Yosemite Park
not located in Yosemite Valley proper, a land area that covers 99.5 percent
of the Park. The hikes in these 14 chapters range from 3800 feet in elevation to
more than 13,000 feet and feature even more varied terrain than the hikes in the
previous section. While they together explore just a tiny fraction of the Park's
area and its more than 800 miles of trails, they nevertheless provide a represen-
tative sampling of the glorious terrain the Park offers.

About 90 percent of the Park's lands are preserved forever in their natural
state as Yosemite National Park Wilderness Area. Added to the wilderness system by Congress in 1984, this vast wilderness, the Sierra's second largest covers
681,150 acres. Eleven of the 14 hikes in this section enter the Park wilderness,
which is in turn surrounded on three sides by other wilderness areas.

In this section's 14 chapters, eight hikes start between 3800 and 5400 feet,
elevations close to elevations in the Valley itself. You'll find waterfalls and forests
in abundance here as well as ample uncrowded choices for three season hiking if
you're visiting the Park in spring, summer or autumn. The waterfalls reached by
these lower trails are little known but still gorgeous cataracts that are not generally
crowded, unlike the very popular falls of the Valley. The most spectacular waterfall in this section is 1400-foot Wapama Falls in Chapter 31. That chapter also
explores the controversial history of now flooded Hetch Hetchy Valley. The lower
elevation chapters explore local history: an early area resort and how its lands
became part of the Park, the three original roads into Yosemite Valley and how
they were built, a utopian development scheme at Foresta and what remains there
today, Galen Clark—"Mr. Yosemite"—and the Park's southern gateway at Wawona.
These chapters also explore the Park's three stands of giant Sequoia trees—Merced
Grove, Tuolumne Grove and Mariposa Grove, the latter near Wawona.

The other six hikes described in this section are truly High Country explorations. With starting elevations ranging between 7240 and 9945 feet, they are
best approached in summer or early autumn. Of course in summer they offer the
perfect escape when the crowds in the Valley start getting to you. As with all
High Country trails, these hikes need to be approached at a slower pace unless

your body has already adjusted to high elevation. The higher the hike the more adjustment required.

This section's High Country hikes include two peak climbs. Mount Hoffman, a favorite of both John Muir and the author, has both a rich history and provides one of the more accessible views of Yosemite's vast and dramatic wilderness. The other peak, Mount Dana, is the Park's second highest, offering a climb that's truly one of the ultimate High Country experiences. Another High Country choice ascends to dramatic Mono Pass on the Sierra Crest where 19th century miners' cabins still stand nearby. The High Country chapters also explore the Snow Creek Trail and a little known cabin that was important in the history of ski touring in the West. A sidebar accompanying the Mount Hoffman chapter describes the High Sierra Camps and how you can spend the night in the Park's backcountry without carrying a heavy pack.

Also in the section's High Country choices are two hikes in the Glacier Point area. Chapter 38 about the historic Four-Mile Trail explores one of Yosemite's earliest and most spectacular trails, which descends from Glacier Point to Yosemite Valley. Chapter 39 describes a wonderful moderate loop hike from Glacier Point Road that tours the top of Sentinel Dome, the apex of Sentinel Falls—the Valley's second tallest at 2000 feet—and Taft Point for a panoramic tour de force.

Whether you spend much time in Yosemite Valley or not, you owe it to yourself to explore the wealth of glorious terrain in the Park's vast primeval forests of immense trees, wildflower-dappled meadows and breathtaking granite High Country.

30
Carlon Falls
A River Hike near Yosemite's Western Gate

Come to the woods, for here is rest.

~John Muir

■ THE DETAILS

Getting There: From Groveland drive east on Highway 120 for 25 miles to Evergreen Road, signed for Hetch Hetchy. The turnoff is one mile before Yosemite's Big Oak Flat entrance station. Follow Evergreen Road for one mile to the far side of the South Fork Tuolumne River bridge immediately past Carlon Day Use Area. Park on the right side of the road. Begin walking upstream on the abandoned road heading away from the tiny parking area.

Nearest Campgrounds: Sweetwater Campground, 7 miles west of Evergreen Road on the north side of Highway 120, has 13 sites. Dimond "O" Campground, 5 miles up Evergreen Road from the trailhead, has 38 sites. Both are open April through October and have piped water.

Lodging: Groveland has the Hotel Charlotte 209-962-6455, Buck Meadows has Buck Meadows Lodge 209-253-9673 and Sugar Pine Ranch 209-962-7823.

Further Info: Stanislaus National Forest, Groveland Ranger District, 24545 Highway 120, Groveland, CA 95321, call 209-962-7825.

Hike Distance: 2.8 miles round trip.

Difficulty: Easy.

Best Time to Go: Late spring for falls, autumn for color.

Cautions: Use caution around the falls and the chilly river.

Starting Elevation: 4320 feet. Gain to falls is 110 feet.

Other Maps: USGS Ackerson Mtn. 7.5 minute topo, Stanislaus National Forest map.

Barely inside Yosemite Park's western border, a little known two-tiered cascade, Carlon Falls, tumbles 60 feet over broad granite benches into a deep green pool. A gentle trail beside the South Fork Tuolumne River offers a surefire way to savor late spring in the mountains. Hikers will find themselves dwarfed by towering conifers and hardwoods in an enchanting, densely forested landscape. Some of the largest Douglas firs you'll ever see grace this quiet, woodsy setting. The narrow, river-cut valley also harbors Pacific dogwood, lovely and showy in both spring and fall. By June the sweet, heady scent of wild azalea and pungent bear clover, also called mountain misery, joins the spicy fragrance of incense cedars and pines. At the base of lofty sugar pines, the ground is littered with cones the size of a loaf of bread. In summer, millions of lady bugs blanket the red-brown bark of cedar trees. Factor in a dancing waterway punctuated with deep holes, lively riffles, an exuberant waterfall, and you have the ingredients for a wonderful outing. Don't forget the camera!

Besides providing a delightful walk, the Carlon Falls neck of the woods features engaging Sierra history. Between 1916 and 1938, it was the locale of Carl Inn. Although the popular resort was never within Park boundaries during its 22-year lifespan, it nevertheless can claim a legitimate place in Yosemite lore. Today, however, only a few foundations hint at any human activity.

In 1916 Dan and Donna Carlon established Carl Inn resort in a grassy flat adjacent to the South Fork Tuolumne River. The young couple picked a great location. In addition to the site's abundant natural charm, the Tioga, Hetch Hetchy-Mather and Big Oak Flat Roads, all important Central Sierra routes, passed right by Carl Inn, virtually guaranteeing its success accommodating mountain vacationers and Yosemite-bound travelers.

From a modest beginning, Carl Inn quickly evolved into a substantial complex capable of lodging 100 guests plus a large staff. Except for employee tents, a few guest cabins and a swimming pool on the north (left) side of the river, the compound's many buildings and facilities were concentrated around the small meadow on the south side of the stream.

The business grew and prospered in this superb location until disaster struck in

Before 1939, Carl Inn, next to the South Fork Tuolumne River, was a very popular resort because of its location at the hub of three major Central Sierra travel routes.

1920 when a fire razed most of the structures. That same year, the Carlons divorced. Donna kept the leased Carl Inn property owned by White and Friant Lumber Company. She quickly rebuilt, becoming a very successful innkeeper. Over the years, she instituted many costly improvements and remodels, elevating Carl Inn from a rustic outpost to a full service resort. Then in 1927, a kitchen fire destroyed the main building. Again, the plucky owner rebuilt, bigger and better than ever.

During the early 1930s, changes were afoot in the South Fork Tuolumne River valley which would shatter Carl Inn's future. A major realignment of Big Oak Flat and Tioga Roads was in the works. Eventually, the resort would no longer be on the route of these important travel lanes. Additionally, Yosemite Sugar Pine Lumber Company was running out of trees in the mountains high above the Merced River, and they began casting about for cutting areas in lower elevations.

They struck a deal with White and Friant Lumber Company, owners of the 7200-acre Carl Inn Tract, for timber rights. Destructive clear-cut logging practices, miles of roads and noisy, polluting trucks and equipment would sully the resort's pristine environment. About the same time, the federal government was on a mission to acquire 15,570 acres of private holdings inside Yosemite, as well as to add other desirable, critical buffer lands surrounding the Park.

The National Park Service began a concerted effort to purchase old growth timber areas along the western border and make them protected Park property. In the meantime, as the wheels of government moved slowly in that direction, the Great Depression had put a temporary halt to logging operations near Yosemite. American philanthropist John D. Rockefeller, Jr., ultimately made the monumental purchase possible, contributing half the $3.3 million price.

The balance came from a congressional fund created to acquire private lands in national parks. As a result, 12,000 acres of virgin timber straddling Big Oak Flat Road were added to Yosemite National Park in 1937. In 1939, thanks to private donations and matching government monies, the magnificent sugar pine forest comprising the Carl Inn Tract was purchased for $1.2 million and added to Yosemite acreage.

On the heels of the purchase, the National Park Service revoked all leases on their recently acquired property. Now that the resort was inside Yosemite, the federal government demolished all of the Carl Inn structures that had been built within the new boundary. Only two cabins, no longer standing, outside the line in Stanislaus National Forest were left intact. For years they housed employees of a state road maintenance crew.

In 1938 Carlon Campground was established in Stanislaus National Forest adjacent to the Carl Inn site. At first it amounted to only a few picnic tables and tent spaces. In 1964 it was enlarged to 18 sites. By 1995 the streamside environment was tired and deteriorated from decades of heavy use. Wisely, the Forest Service permanently closed the area to camping. The grounds were cleaned up and converted to a picnic site. Today, Carlon Day Use Area is steadily recovering from its former overuse.

■ THE HIKE

To get in motion toward the falls, park on the far (north) side of the South Fork bridge just beyond Carlon Day Use Area on the right side of Evergreen Road. Follow the wide trail, actually an old road used by Carl Inn guests to access some cabins, on the north side of the river. Very shortly you'll spot the foundation of the resort's swimming pool as you head upstream on the 1.4-mile hike to Carlon Falls.

Beyond the pool ruins, the wide track narrows as it penetrates deeper into the woods. It may not seem like you're in Yosemite National Park, but remember that you are. Dogs, horses and mountain bikes are not permitted on this trail. You can't help but notice the immensity of the trees in this splendid forest. It's obvious that wildfire hasn't raced through these woods in a very long time. Here

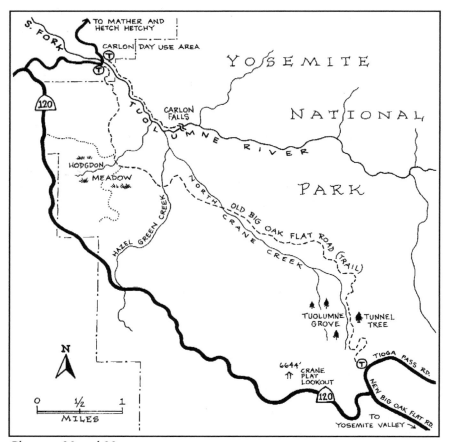

Chapters 30 and 33

and there, a few toppled giants have blocked the trail, and you'll need to either clamber over them or scoot around them.

The gentle path and the river parallel each other, sometimes closely, sometimes farther apart. Many places by the stream invite you to linger awhile, perhaps to wriggle your toes in the chilly water. Near the banks, huge clumps of Indian rhubarb (umbrella plant) grow four to five feet tall. Around one mile, a sizable washout forces you to detour briefly uphill around it.

Nearing the falls, which you'll hear before seeing, two gigantic deadfalls lay across the trail, one after the other. It's much easier to detour around than to hoist yourself up and over. For safety sake, proceed toward the uphill end of the trees. Just below the cascade, pick one of the spur trails down to the water.

Carlon Falls is a stunner as it crashes over a granite ledge and meanders through a boulder-choked stretch before bouncing over a series of five benches into a large, deep pool. Explorers will find much visual interest to enjoy at this watery niche in the Sierra. The river sloshes and swirls in sitz bath-sized potholes carved in the granite. Out of one flourishes Indian rhubarb; lodged in another is a hefty boulder.

Carefully pick your way on a faint path through flood boulders tossed up on the bank to the top of Carlon Falls. You'll find several rocky perches above and below the falls to sit and take delight in this gorgeous riparian setting. Only serious bushwhackers will want to continue beyond the top of the falls. When it's time to leave, return to the trailhead the way you came.

A bonus feature of Carlon Falls is that it runs all year long, assuming normal precipitation. Though with a lesser volume than during snow melt, the waterfall is also charming in autumn when oaks, dogwoods and other deciduous trees sport their brilliant fall finery. We can be thankful that this impressive old growth forest was spared from clear cutting in the 1930s.

As Abraham Lincoln said, "A country with no regard for its past will have little worth remembering in the future." If you agree with Lincoln's thought, you might wonder why the National Park Service or Forest Service did not place an interpretive sign at the site of Carl Inn to mark its novel place in Yosemite-Sierra Nevada history.

31
Exploring Hetch Hetchy
Visiting Waterfalls at Yosemite Valley's Flooded Twin

■ THE DETAILS

Getting There: Take Highway 120 east from Groveland for 25 miles. One mile west of Yosemite's Big Oak Flat entrance station, turn left and follow Evergreen Road 7.5 miles to its junction with Hetch Hetchy Road at Camp Mather. Turn right and go 9 miles to O'Shaughnessy Dam. The ranger at the Hetch Hetchy entrance gate will give you a park map and answer questions.

Nearest Campground: Hetch Hetchy has a campground for backpackers only, wilderness permit required. See Chapter 30 for other nearby camping.

Lodging: Evergreen Lodge 209-379-2606, 10 miles before reaching the dam on Evergreen Road, has food and rustic lodging. Also see Chapter 30.

Further Info: Yosemite National Park recorded info line 209-372-0200.

Hike Distance: 5 miles round trip to Wapama Falls. More strenuous hikes (one way distances): 6.5 miles to Rancheria Falls, 8 miles to Laurel Lake, and 12 miles to Lake Vernon.

Facilities: Toilets at trailhead.

Difficulty: Easy.

Best Time to Go: May and June.

Cautions: No pets are allowed on any park trails. Hetch Hetchy has no services of any kind. In spring the force and volume of Wapama Falls may prevent further progress.

Starting Elevation: 3800 feet. Gain for round trip to Wapama Falls is 460 feet.

Other Map: USGS Hetch Hetchy Reservoir 15 minute topo.

Dammed and inundated in the early 1920s to create a water supply for San Francisco, the Hetch Hetchy Valley was the scene of one of the stormiest conservation fights in history.

This Sierra valley, the victim of man's thirst for water, still offers scenic vistas. Although the once-beautiful valley is a paradise lost, one can still appreciate many of its spectacular features. May and June are ideal months to explore this rugged, uncrowded corner of the Sierra. Although the elevation is nearly the same as Yosemite Valley, temperatures can be uncomfortably warm in midsummer. Located in northwestern Yosemite Park, Hetch Hetchy remains markedly less visited primarily because the peaceful and sensational landscape exists without commercial distractions or facilities.

Before the waters of the Tuolumne River were captured by O'Shaughnessy Dam in 1923 to supply water and power for San Francisco, the Hetch Hetchy Valley bore a remarkable resemblance to Yosemite Valley. Although smaller and more compact, it shared the same rugged splendor. As one writer put it, "It is still a phenomenon that Nature, with her magnificent carelessness, should have chosen two designs so nearly alike." Indeed, the similarities between Hetch Hetchy and Yosemite were striking: glacially sculptured cliffs, towering waterfalls, polished granite domes, a deep valley dominated by a meandering river, nearly the same elevation above sea level, a lush meadow floor liberally sprinkled with oak, pine, cedar and wildflowers, and formed by the same geological forces.

Ample evidence indicates that for centuries Paiute and Ahwahneechee Indians made yearly visits here to gather acorns and grind them in bedrock mortars, but historians cannot agree on the first white man to see Hetch Hetchy Valley. It was either Nate or Joe Screech, on a bear hunting trip in the late 1840s, who first saw the valley from the cliffs above. Some time later, one of the brothers asked an elderly chief, who claimed the land in the area, about this wondrous place. The chief feigned ignorance of such a valley but said that if Screech could find one, it would be his. In 1850 Nate Screech managed to get down into the valley and found the same chief and his wives. Understandably surprised, the chief kept his

Hetch Hetchy Valley as it appeared prior to inundation in 1923.

word and left the valley to Screech as promised.

Brother Joe Screech blazed the first trail into the valley from Big Oak Flat, some 38 miles away. For many years sheepherders and cattlemen grazed their stock in the fertile, flat-bottomed valley, and Indians continued to harvest acorns. The name Hetch Hetchy is a corruption of the Indian word "hatchatchie," designating a variety of grass with edible seeds.

This gorgeous valley, which once rivaled Yosemite Valley, is gone forever, drowned under 400 feet of water. The complete story of how it came to be covered by water is long, fascinating and complicated with murky political shenanigans beyond the scope of this book. However, as early as 1870, the same year John Muir first explored the Hetch Hetchy Valley, San Francisco engineers were prowling the Sierra for reliable sources of drinking water to meet the needs of a rapidly expanding population. After studying 14 possible Sierra water sources, they chose the Tuolumne River in 1901.

Muir, the Sierra Club and many other preservationists across the country fought a desperate campaign to prevent Hetch Hetchy from being dammed and flooded. A raging, nationwide conservation battle ensued for the next 12 years. Bear in mind that Yosemite was already protected and designated a national park in 1890. Dedicated people waged a pitched battle to save the Hetch Hetchy portion of the national park lands from the outrageous intrusion. Nevertheless, San Francisco's persistence was successful. The city was granted water rights on the Tuolumne River with the passage of the Raker Act, signed into law by President Woodrow Wilson on December 19, 1913.

According to President Wilson, "It seemed to serve the pressing public needs of the region concerned better than they could be served in any other way, and yet did not impair the usefulness or materially detract from the beauty of the public domain." Interesting thoughts from someone who had never seen the valley in question.

Like it or not, for better or worse, Hetch Hetchy Valley became history when the Tuolumne River was imprisoned by the O'Shaughnessy Dam. Whether it made sense to tame an untouched wilderness to supply water to a growing city 150 miles away or to violate a public domain, supposedly protected by federal law, is purely academic now. Hetch Hetchy is a done deal and has been for 80 years.

O'Shaughnessy Dam, named for the project's chief engineer, was built between 1919 and 1923 to create the eight-mile-long Hetch Hetchy Reservoir. It was designed to collect and store run-off from 459 square miles of watershed, translating to 420,000 acres.

Despite the controversy surrounding its existence, the entire Hetch Hetchy Water Project was a thoroughly brilliant engineering masterpiece spanning nearly 20 years. The project brought Sierra water by gravity flow to San Francisco through an extraordinarily vast and complex system of reservoirs, canals, dams, flumes, tunnels, pipes, penstocks and aqueducts. Even a railroad was created to service its unimaginable construction needs and huge workers' camps.

This mammoth construction enterprise was the largest ever attempted in the West at that time. Just the surveying took many years, and building O'Shaughnessy Dam alone required almost four years, 24 hours a day in all seasons, to pour concrete hauled in by the Hetch Hetchy Railroad. Between 1935 and 1938, the dam was raised 85 feet to its present height of 430 feet above bedrock, increasing the storage capacity to 306,000 acre-feet of water. The original project cost, up until 1934 when water first reached San Francisco, was $100 million. The design of the entire project was so fine-tuned and ingeniously planned that it could be altered as needed without changing the original design.

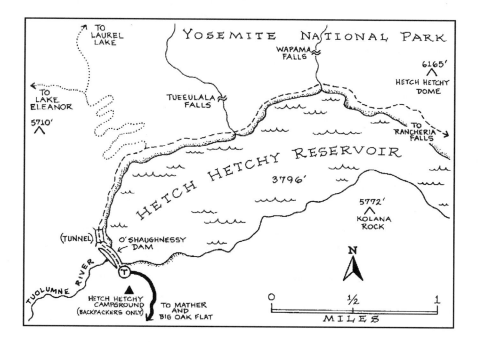

▪ THE HIKE

Today, just driving to Hetch Hetchy provides a wonderful experience. Once you leave Highway 120 you'll be intimately surrounded by the beauty of the Sierra Nevada mountains. Upon arrival, pause on the dam for a few minutes to absorb the feeling of this special place, still glorious despite the mountain of concrete you stand on. Gaze up the canyon and try to visualize the wild grandeur of the valley before the Tuolumne River was dammed. You might also want to think about all the timber removed from the valley plus the additional 6+ million board feet of lumber cut from inside Yosemite National Park for building the dam.

The two prominent granite features are Kolana Rock to the right and tiered Hetch Hetchy Dome on the left. In spring, robust 1400-foot Wapama Falls thunders down, and Tueeulala Falls is a lesser, but lovely, cataract. The chalet to the right is for the use of City of San Francisco Water and Power high muckamucks.

After crossing the dam, walk through the 500-foot lighted tunnel. You're following the old road to Lake Eleanor (see Chapter 12). Past the tunnel, your trail ascends gently, skirting the reservoir on the abandoned road, passing many wildflowers in late spring.

At the junction at .9 mile, the old road to Eleanor veers left to climb 1200 feet to the canyon rim, also the way to Laurel Lake and Lake Vernon. Our hike turns right following a trail that continues alongside the reservoir, climbing, dipping and curving in and out of drainages. Pass seasonal Tueeulala Falls around 1.5 miles, then continue on the meandering path above the shore before making a rather steep descent to thundering Wapama Falls at 2.5 miles, a great stopping place for a trail lunch. Near its base the fall splits into several streams which the trail crosses on five steel bridges. The run-off at Wapama may be so heavy that you can't get past it. **Do not attempt to cross if the bridges are more than shin-deep in water.** After a break you can return the way you came, or if the water level and your energy allow, you can follow the path east to Rancheria Falls at 6.5 miles, a moderately strenuous trek.

At some point on your journey, you can decide for yourself whether you agree with President Wilson's statement when he sealed Hetch Hetchy's fate in 1913 or the belief of the San Francisco Water and Power Department that, if their water project had failed, Hetch Hetchy very possibly could have become a twin of Yosemite Valley in yet another way—thousands of daily visitors, smog, noisy restaurants and bars, curio shops and hotels. Important lessons were learned from losing the battle over Hetch Hetchy. Conservation forces grew stronger after the defeat. It's unlikely that such an invasion of National Park lands will ever be repeated, especially with the heightened awareness of the American people to preserve the wild, beautiful places of this earth.

32
Merced Grove of Big Trees
John McLean and the Coulterville Road

■ THE DETAILS

Getting There: From Big Oak Flat entrance station, follow Highway 120 southeast for 4.5 miles to a road sign and post marked B 10 (3.5 miles west of Crane Flat Campground) and park.

Nearest Campgrounds: Hodgdon Meadow Campground, near Big Oak Flat entrance station, has 105 sites open year round, while Crane Flat Campground 3.5 miles east of the trailhead has 166 sites open May through October. Both require reservations (800-436-7275) from May through October.

Lodging: For nearest choices outside the park, see Chapter 30. For lodging in Yosemite Valley call 209-252-4848.

Further Info: Yosemite National Park General Park & Road Info 209-372-0200.

Hike Distance: 3 miles round trip.

Difficulty: Easy.

Best Time to Go: Spring for dogwood blooms, autumn for color.

Cautions: None.

Starting Elevation: 5400 feet. Gain for round trip to Merced Grove is about 100 feet.

Other Maps: USGS El Portal & Lake Eleanor 15 minute topos.

In summer 1867 one of those chance events that can alter history took place. Transplanted easterners Dr. and Mrs. John McLean and their son decided to vacation in Yosemite, a place of wonders they'd heard so much about. Arriving in Coulterville by stagecoach, they then rode 50 tough miles on horseback to the Valley. The rigorous trip made Mary McLean so ill that she was bedridden for a week after reaching their hotel. Regrettably, she was unable to enjoy the scenery she'd come so far to see. The family returned to San Francisco, retracing the same exhausting itinerary. A disappointed Dr. McLean concluded that surely Yosemite merited easier access.

By June 1872, when he realized that none of the three competing turnpike companies would soon complete a road into the park, he jumped into the business of road building. For the next 30 years until his death in 1902, he would follow his dream of building the Coulterville Road, depleting his entire personal fortune and entangling him in a prolonged nightmare of political red tape. Today, only the most ardent Sierra history devotees have even heard of Dr. McLean, who died a pauper and without tribute for his enormous achievement. Because of him, visitors were able to travel in a wheeled vehicle the entire distance to Yosemite Valley. Sadly, no monument, no plaque and no place name in Yosemite bears the name of this pioneer road builder who, because of a vacation, reshaped the course of travel in the Central Sierra Nevada.

It's a tremendous understatement to say that a visit to Yosemite in the early days was not easy. For 23 years after its discovery by white men in 1851, Yosemite was accessible only by crude horse trails. The journey was a time-consuming, arduous and involved undertaking. Beginning in San Francisco, travelers boarded a ship for a 12-hour boat ride to Stockton via the San Joaquin River. They then piled into a stagecoach for a dirty, bone-jarring ride on rudimentary wagon roads to one of three end-of-the-line towns: Coulterville, Mariposa or Big Oak Flat.

Next came two or three more days of a bun-busting, jolting horseback ride on incredibly steep trails just to reach the rim of the Valley. The worst was yet to come, a terrifying, precipitous trail nearly straight down to the Valley floor. The rider needed to muster extraordinary faith in the sturdy mountain pony's instinct for survival. Furthermore, it was very costly. Tourists had to pay dearly for all facets of the trip, which included ship and stage fares, fees for the horses, packers, guides and all meals and lodging.

To add to their misery, only primitive hotels, often just shacks, were available both along the route and in the Valley itself. California pioneers regarded horseback travel as an ordinary experience and the crudeness of trails commonplace. As stories of Yosemite's grandeur spread quickly to the East and across the Atlantic, many more travelers braved the hardships. To eastern and European travelers, however, not at all accustomed to the hardships of saddle travel California-style, it was a fatiguing, frightening and seemingly endless journey.

It didn't take long for the businessmen along the approach routes and in the Valley to recognize the need and profit potential for providing more appetizing meals and comfortable accommodations. The top priority was to get people out of the saddle and into the relative luxury of a stagecoach. Of course, this could only be accomplished by constructing wagon roads.

In spite of the arduous journey, visitation to Yosemite continued a slow but steady growth during the 1860s. However, for it to increase on a grand scale businessmen from Coulterville, Big Oak Flat and Mariposa began organizing turnpike (toll road) companies to build better roads. Each community was well aware of the importance of being the first to reach the Valley; the winner would capture the lion's share of the tourist trade. Rivalry was especially keen between the Big Oak Flat and Coulterville groups.

In September 1868 some businessmen from Big Oak Flat organized the Yosemite Turnpike Company for a road beginning in Chinese Camp and ending beyond Tamarack Flat at the very brink of the Valley. They were granted an exclusive 50-year franchise by the State of California on February 20, 1869. In September 1869, the Yosemite Board of Commissioners gave them exclusive permission to build a road into the Park on the north side, but with the important stipulation that it be completed by July 1, 1871. Unfortunately, the Big Oak Flat company ran out of money and time with their road only completed as far as the rim. Consequently, they forfeited their exclusivity.

Meanwhile, the Coulterville community realized that to remain competitive they also needed a wagon road into the Park. The Coulterville Road Company was organized in February 1870, and within three months, a labor gang was pushing ahead a new road from the end of an existing road at Bower Cave. Because the Big Oak Flat group lost their exclusive right for a northside entrance, the Yosemite Commissioners awarded the exclusive right to Coulterville, providing that they have the road work done within the year 1873.

It was a new ball game. The Coulterville group would collect the tolls and become an important overnight tourist stop. With the Big Oak Flat Road ending on the edge of a cliff, it seemed doubtful that visitors would choose that route because it would still involve a scary horseback ride down to the Valley. Furthermore, the Mariposa (Wawona) Road outfit on the south side was in big financial trouble and forced to sell out to their creditors.

In 1872 when the road project was lagging, Dr. McLean became President of the Coulterville and Yosemite Turnpike Company. The road had only reached Crane Flat, and due to dwindling funds, just a few men were on the job. McLean thrust his whole-hearted attention as well as his bank account into revitalizing the Coulterville Road venture. The push for completion began in earnest under his capable management, including a scenic but costly detour through the Merced Grove of Big Trees. The project proved significantly more expensive than McLean estimated due to the extreme difficulty of some of the terrain, especially the last 2500 yards down to the Valley floor. The unusually severe winter of 1872-73 also impeded progress for six months.

Immense Sequoias dwarf a hiker in Merced Grove.

The Big Oak Flat company fired up again as they saw their rival nearing completion. Finally, after three failures to get the Yosemite Commissioners to allow them to continue their road into the park, they appealed to the State Legislature to repeal the decision. Their arguments were convincing. In 1874 the State ruled that the Commissioners "had made an error in granting exclusive rights to any company and that both thoroughfares might enter the Valley on equal terms." This decision was a devastating blow to Dr. McLean. Later, even the Commissioners agreed that he had been treated very unfairly. Now the race was really on. Coulterville had been granted a time extension, and Big Oak Flat was back in the game.

The contest ended on June 17, 1874, when McLean and his supporters drove the first wheeled vehicle into the Valley. What a triumphant moment this was for him. Even the legislature couldn't take this historic moment away from him. Despite the damaging decision dealt him by State lawmakers, the Coulterville Road entered the history books as the pioneer stage road into Yosemite. However, their monopoly on stage travel lasted only one month. On July 17, 1874,

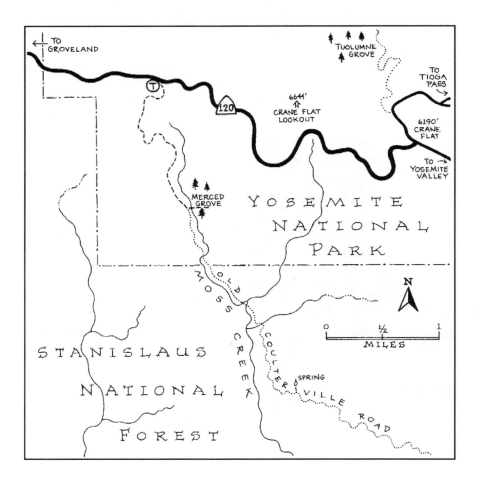

the Big Oak Flat Road was completed.

Even though the Coulterville Road was the first, it was by no means the most successful, thanks mainly to the fateful decision by the State. By 1879 the Big Oak Flat and Wawona routes were transporting more passengers than the Coulterville route. McLean was justifiably a "bitter and disheartened" man when he stated that he wouldn't have invested a dime had he known that another road on the same side of the Valley would have been allowed entrance. Other factors worked to his disadvantage. The nation was sliding into a depression in 1874, and the Park Commissioners decreed that tolls had to be collected outside Yosemite. Ultimately, the federal government declared that all toll roads into the Park would be made free to the public.

So it went for this generous, competent man who had earned a legitimate place in Central Sierra history, the unwitting victim of political maneuvers which left him $60,000 in debt by the time he died. He wasted many years in expensive, futile litigation with the government in trying to recoup his losses. In subsequent years, the Coulterville Road fell into disrepair and was little used, especially after completion of the Yosemite Valley Railroad in 1907 and the opening of Highway 140 in 1926. In 1920 the road became public domain after its 50-year franchise expired.

Today the 37-mile long old road is rough and passable only in sections to high clearance, four-wheel-drive vehicles and is difficult to follow in places because of the network of logging roads in the area. About all that remains as evidence of its existence is a dotted line on a map. Lonely and abandoned, it seems amazing that it was such a history-maker or that someone would have spent a fortune on this deserted track.

■ THE HIKE

You can experience the most accessible segment of the original Coulterville Road by taking an easy walk to Merced Grove of Big Trees. The old road leads to Yosemite's smallest stand of giant Sequoias, about 20 mature trees, which was probably discovered by the Joseph Walker Party in 1833. During May, hundreds of dogwood trees grace the forest with their lovely, creamy-white flowers. In autumn their scarlet foliage is equally stunning.

The trailhead is marked by a road sign and a post labeled B 10 on Highway 120. Follow the dirt track for one mile and then bear left at the fork down into the grove. Be on the lookout for the long-abandoned Merced Grove cabin built as a retreat for the Park Superintendent. After you explore the grove, return the same way.

Read *Yosemite's Yesterdays, Volume Two* by Hank Johnston for a detailed history of the Coulterville Road.

33
Old Big Oak Flat Road
Hiking to the Big Trees of Tuolumne Grove

■ THE DETAILS

Getting There: For Tuolumne Grove (eastern) trailhead: From Crane Flat on Highway 120, follow Tioga Road less than one mile to Tuolumne Grove parking area on your left.

For Carlon (western) trailhead: Drive one mile west from Big Oak Flat entrance station on Highway 120. Turn right (east) on Evergreen Road and go one mile. Turn right into Carlon Day Use Area before the bridge. The hike follows Old Big Oak Flat Road behind the locked gate.

Nearest Campgrounds: See Chapter 32.

Lodging: For nearest choices outside the Park, see Chapter 30. For Yosemite Valley lodging, call 559-252-4848.

Further Info: Yosemite National Park general info (recorded) 209-372-0200.

Hike Distance: 12 miles round trip or 6-mile one way hike with car shuttle. To Tuolumne Grove: 2 miles round trip from Highway 120 trailhead, or 11 miles round trip from Carlon.

Difficulty: Easy to moderately strenuous.

Best Time to Go: Anytime.

Starting Elevation: Carlon 4320 feet, Highway 120 trailhead 6200 feet. Elevation change to Tuolumne Grove: 500 feet from east, 1560 feet from west.

Map: See Chapter 30, page 174.

Other Maps: USGS Ackerson Mtn. 7.5 minute topo or Lake Eleanor 15 minute topo and/or free Yosemite Park map available at entrance stations.

The lower elevations of the Sierra Nevada supply a bounty of hiking opportunities during late fall and winter that are often snubbed when more spectacular High Country trails are open. When the High Country is snowbound, hikers need only set their sights lower down the mountain to find trailheads suitable for the season. If you store your boots in mothballs at the end of summer, you'll forfeit many rewarding journeys.

Tuolumne Grove of Giant Sequoias near Yosemite's western boundary is an excellent place to spend a day in nature's woodsy embrace. It is, indeed, a hike

Owners of the original Big Oak Flat Road detoured their route through Tuolumne Grove en route to Yosemite Valley, cutting a 12-foot-tall by ten-foot-wide tunnel through the Dead Giant to draw visitors attention to its immense size.

for all seasons. Depending on weather and your level of conditioning, you can cover distances ranging between 2 and 12 miles on foot, snowshoes or cross-country skis.

A choice of starting points expands your options. Either begin at Crane Flat inside the park or in Stanislaus National Forest at Carlon Day Use Area alongside the South Fork Tuolumne River. Whether you opt for 12 miles round trip or 6 miles one way with a car shuttle, or any distance in between, your ticket to this peaceful setting is the original Big Oak Flat Road.

Don't expect forever views from widow-maker drop-offs, waterfalls, or shimmering lakes. This outing is all about trees—oak, pine, cedar, hemlock, fir, dogwood—and close encounters with the king of all 450 species of conifers, the majestic *Sequoiadendron giganteum*. Chances are good that no one will notice if you want to give one a hug. If you take pleasure in being tucked into the cozy environment of a fragrant forest, this hike's for you.

Big Oak Flat Road earned a spot in Sierra chronicles in 1874 for being the second road completed into Yosemite Valley, losing the race with the Coulterville

Road by only one month. Its name derived from the early mining camp of Big Oak Flat, home to a colossal oak, 30 miles west of Yosemite. The settlement in turn shared its name with the road passing through it.

At Tamarack Flat, a few miles above Crane Flat, the historic route plunged into Yosemite Valley along a series of marvelously engineered switchbacks. The narrow, serpentine road could be driven until 1942 when two massive rock slides obliterated the switchbacks to all but hikers. Until about 1990, a 6-mile section of the original road through Tuolumne Grove was drivable in the downhill direction.

At that time, with the welfare of the Big Trees a priority, the route between the grove and Hodgdon Meadow became accessible to pedestrians only. The magnificent colony's health and serenity are no longer tainted by swarms of automobiles buzzing through the woods. The grove is also much less visited because many people simply do not want to walk 2 miles round trip.

■ THE HIKE

Requiring a shuttle, the 6-mile-long hike described in this article heads out from Carlon Day Use Area and ends at Tuolumne Grove trailhead parking on Highway 120 one mile east of Crane Flat. Reverse the starting point for a downhill trek. Park on the right (east) side of Evergreen Road and walk around a locked gate, behind which is Yosemite National Park. The abandoned road quickly bends south and ascends 400 feet in slightly less than 1.5 miles to Hodgdon Meadow.

In 1865 at Hodgdon Meadow, the Jeremiah Hodgdon family grazed cattle on the lush homesteaded clearing and housed horseback travelers in their crude, summer cow camp. After the opening of Big Oak Flat Road into Yosemite Valley, Hodgdon built an inn of sorts, still rough but capable of lodging 60 people.

Should you decide to wander in the rolling meadowland, be on the lookout for a heap of boulders to the north near the crest. If you are lucky, you will find a couple of smooth, flat-surfaced granite boulders pocked with grinding holes. Nearly 100 mortar cups imply that this was once the heart of a sizable Native American community.

In the meadow, two roads intersect the historic Big Oak Flat route. Bear left at each of them. Prior to crossing Hazel Green Creek, note a sewage treatment system on the left. As the road snakes uphill through stands of lofty conifers and lacy dogwood, you will get a taste of what early travel was like. In the era before macadam, imagine choking on dust a foot thick while enduring a bone-rattling stagecoach ride over this deeply rutted track.

North Crane Creek, about 3 miles from the trailhead, offers a reasonable stopping point for less conditioned walkers. You will come to an obvious parking day-use area, a memento from the past when vehicles were allowed to intrude upon this handsome, tranquil forest. After a rest and snack break, either turn around here or continue steeply uphill to Tuolumne Grove and eastern trailhead parking off Highway 120.

For most High Country aficionados, aspens represent the color standard against which all other trees must pass muster in the fall, but here in lower elevations dogwood steals the show. As you approach the grove and linger in it, watch for them among the tall conifers. Displaying lovely chaste-white flowers in spring, a dogwood becomes a flashy hussy in autumn tricked out in deep scarlet leaves. Seen through openings in the forest, these graceful beauties are stunning.

Before long, the "Dead Giant" looms into view beyond a picnic area. This immense tree is said to have measured more than 120 feet in circumference in its prime. It was already a 200-foot-tall snag when a tunnel was cut into it in 1878. Owners of Big Oak Flat Road believed the novelty of being able to ride through a Big Tree would entice visitors to use their road and give them a greater appreciation of a Sequoia's enormity.

Near the tunnel tree, a short interpretive trail loops among the Sequoias. Interpretive signs offer fascinating information about their natural history and character. A wealth of astounding statistics, such as how big and how old and how fast they grow or that its seeds are so tiny that it takes 91,000 of them to make a pound, will fly right out of your ears when you behold these forest masterpieces. Impressive as statistics are, they are soon forgotten in the overwhelming presence of a giant Sequoia. Both their size and age simply boggle the mind. No language has enough superlatives to describe them. Everything about this ancient race of trees is heroic in scale and cannot be absorbed in a single glance. You must spend quality time among them to assimilate their majesty and extravagant proportions.

Much of their charisma and allure is heightened by not congregating in pure stands. Because they are dispersed among lesser trees, their appearance is all the more startling and unexpected, and most visitors feel humbled and reverent by the towering display of nature's abundance.

Tuolumne Grove is one of three groves within Yosemite. By no means as large as popular Mariposa Grove near Wawona, some two dozen mature Big Trees and hundreds of their younger kin dwell among companion species in the 25-acre preserve. Relics of 40 species that flourished 100 million years ago in the northern hemisphere, they are among America's rarest trees.

Presently, they are confined to 75 isolated islands between 5000 and 7500 feet elevation in scattered groves along the western slope of the Sierra from Placer to Tulare County. Their greatest concentration, however, is in the southern one-third of the range. Although Sequoias are among the last of their kind, they are reproducing sufficiently to continue in existence until the next Ice Age, assuming, of course, that mankind leaves them standing.

Trapper and explorer Joseph Walker and his expedition were the first Euro-Americans to look into Yosemite Valley from its north rim in 1833. Walker and his men also have the distinction of being the discoverers of giant Sequoias. A published account by Zenas Leonard stated, "We have found some trees of the redwood species, incredibly large—some of which measure 16-18 fathoms (96-108 feet) around the trunk at the height of a man's head from the ground."

Whether they saw the colossal specimens in Tuolumne Grove or nearby Merced Grove, or both, we may never know with certainty. Nevertheless, Leonard's succinct description gives us an unmistakable snapshot of the largest trees on earth. His narrative stands as the earliest historical document about Yosemite and also establishes the Walker party as the first to behold *Sequoiadendron giganteum*.

To complete the 6-mile journey along Old Big Oak Flat Road to your shuttle vehicle or driver, walk another mile, gaining 500 feet in elevation to the parking area along Highway 120. If you are on a round trip 10-mile hike, the grove makes a good turnaround point. An alternative is taking an abbreviated outing to the Big Trees by walking a little over a mile downhill from the Highway 120 parking lot.

Sequoias are awe-inspiring any time of year, but they are especially magnificent when crowned with snow. Fortunately, the highway to the trailhead is kept open during winter so you may negotiate the closed road into the grove on snowshoes or cross-country skis. Evergreen Road to the Carlon trailhead is also open except in the most severe conditions.

In whichever season you choose to commune with these "ambassadors from another time," you will surely agree with John Muir's thoughts: "The Big Tree is nature's finest masterpiece, the greatest of living things. It has the strange air of other days about it, a thoroughbred look inherited from the long ago."

34
Foresta Forever
Ramble to Little Nellie Falls

■ THE DETAILS

Getting There: Take New Big Oak Flat Road (Highway 120), either north from its junction with Highway 140 in Yosemite Valley for 3.2 miles to the first road (signed Foresta) after the long lighted tunnel, or east from Crane Flat junction for 7 miles. Head south and west on paved Foresta (Old Coulterville) Road for 1.7 miles and park across from Big Meadow near a wooden bulletin board.

Nearest Campgrounds: Hodgdon Meadow Campground near Big Oak Flat entrance station has 105 sites open year round, reservations required May through September. Crane Flat Campground has 166 sites open June through September, call 800-436-7275 for required reservations.

Lodging: Try Cedar Lodge in El Portal, 209-379-2612. For lodging in Yosemite Valley call 209-252-4848.

Further Info: Yosemite National Park recorded information 209-372-0200. Stanislaus National Forest, Groveland Ranger District 209-962-7825.

Hike Distance: 6 miles round trip.

Difficulty: Easy.

Best Time to Go: Spring.

Cautions: Be careful around the falls.

Starting Elevation: 4300 feet. 500 feet elevation gain to falls.

Other Map: USGS El Portal 15 minute topo.

Few people are aware of Foresta's existence even though it is a mere ten miles from Yosemite Valley where millions of sightseers visit each year. Foresta is a historic 200-acre tract on the extreme western edge of Yosemite National Park. While an occasional visitor can be seen snapping a quick photo of lovely Big Meadow with its ancient barns, Foresta is certainly not a tourist destination. Virtually unknown are its miles of secluded hiking, beautiful waterfalls, spring wildflowers and rich and lively history.

If you recognize the name Foresta at all, it may recall the 24,000-acre conflagration that raged through Yosemite in summer 1990, devastating the small community. After the fire in a controversial plan, Foresta was considered as a site for relocating National Park Service and concessionaire offices and employee housing out of overdeveloped Yosemite Valley. Or, Foresta may be remembered as the site of a government land grab in the 1960s when NPS officials decided that the private inholding was "incompatible with the purposes of the park and an intrusion to the natural area."

The heavily timbered land known since the early 1900s as Foresta has an even older history filled with colorful and stirring events. To Native Americans, the region was called *O'Pim*, and for more than 2000 years, Miwok Indians lived in the Big Meadow area. According to estimates by the Yosemite Park archaeologist, at least 50 archaeological sites dot the environs, nearly two dozen of which have been studied and documented.

Foresta's centuries of relative anonymity ended with the completion of Coulterville Road in June 1874. This very first stage road into Yosemite Valley passed through the Miwok safehold a few miles below the Merced Grove of Big Trees.

Big Meadow's lush soil, abundant grass and water, and vast forests caught the interest of early ranchers. German-born John Meyer and Peter Mieson were Big Meadow's first pioneers. They began improving the land in 1873, finding Big Meadow ideal for raising crops and grazing cattle. Soon John Meyer's brother George acquired his holdings, continuing the partnership with Mieson. After becoming U.S. citizens, each man homesteaded 160 adjoining acres around Big Meadow. Enterprising and hard-working, the young men collected tolls for Coulterville Road, provided meals for travelers, tended horses, and raised vegetables for an eager Yosemite market.

The old house just beyond the barns in Big Meadow, now occupied by Yosemite Institute employees, was the Meyer ranch house. The original structure burned years ago. In 1874 Meyer and Mieson permitted an independent, maverick Scotsman named George Anderson to build a cabin on the property in exchange for carpentry work. Anderson became well known in Yosemite for his trail-building skills, climaxed by establishing a route up the supposedly inaccessible heights of Half Dome. Anderson is best remembered for his triumph as the first Euro-American to stand atop 8,842-foot Half Dome in October 1875.

In 1878 the fourth pioneer to reside at *O'Pim* was Thomas Rutherford who homesteaded 160 acres along the southern boundary of Big Meadow. Rutherford built a blacksmith shop and sawmill near Crane Creek; his mill sold most of its products to Yosemite Valley residents. The ditch from Crane Creek, used to power his mill, is still visible 123 years later. The mill was across the road from the old Meyer ranch house on the edge of the meadow.

Rutherford lived only six years after establishing his homestead. Upon his death in 1884, Rutherford was the first to be interred in Big Meadow Cemetery, the only non-native burial ground in the area. Between 1886 and 1911 four other men were buried beside him. Plain chunks of granite were used as markers which, over the years, became obscured by brush and pine needles. In 1957 the tiny pioneer graveyard was cleared, and natural granite tombstones once again denoted the deceased.

Old Coulterville Road passes Big Meadow and barns built by pioneer settlers Meyer and Mieson in 1873.

To come upon these tall granite stones is a moving experience, almost like stumbling across an ancient Druid ruin.

In 1887 James McCauley bought Rutherford's homestead at public auction for $100. His nearby 40 acres combined with Rutherford's 160 acres comprised the area that became the Foresta subdivision. McCauley was no Johnny-come-lately to the area. Arriving in Yosemite in 1870, he was one of its earliest settlers. This pioneer entrepreneur's accomplishments include originating the famous Yosemite Firefall display in 1871, building the Four-Mile Trail between Yosemite Valley and Glacier Point, and being owner-operator of the popular Mountain House hostelry atop Glacier Point.

After the government made a major overhaul of boundary lines in 1905, the Meyer and McCauley ranches became private enclaves within Yosemite Park. As legal owners of private property within and surrounded by U.S. government lands, they had to comply with strict federal rules and regulations, as would all future owners of Foresta property.

Following McCauley's death in 1911, his family sold 40 acres of the original homestead to Charles Snell and Veranus Lathrop for $5500. Snell and Lathrop were promoters and real estate developers who wanted to subdivide the property. Their expansive plans included many conveniences for future residents and visitors and a road between the subdivision and El Portal in Merced River canyon below. They chose Foresta as its name "to designate it as a forest tract." Expenses were much higher than expected, and lot sales were disappointingly low. In spite of this, the promoters bought 160 more acres from the McCauleys to bring their inholding to 200 acres.

By summer 1913, Snell was in financial trouble and had to forfeit his Foresta dream. Costs of building the road to El Portal far exceeded estimates. The seven-mile road, needed to connect Foresta with the Yosemite Valley Railroad station in El Portal, was a critical link in Snell's plan to create a community where educators and philosophers could hold cultural programs. From the depot, buses would transport people to Foresta and on to Yosemite.

Replacing Snell was Alfred Davis. He first completed the all-important route to El Portal. Davis then continued the scenic byway north to meet Big Oak Flat Road at Crane Flat, allowing visitors to travel through Tuolumne Grove en route to Yosemite. Davis spent considerable money advertising and promoting Foresta's 1230 lots and the Summer Assembly with "seminar discussions under the peacefully thought provoking surroundings of the primeval forests of Yosemite."

Like Snell, Davis had great optimism for the future of Foresta. However, most of his grandiose plans never materialized and lot sales provided little income. Designed to appeal to people of culture and education, the Chautauqua-like Foresta Summer Assembly featured programs presented by prominent intellectuals. Instead of the hundreds expected to attend, often only 20 or 30 came. Davis was broke by autumn 1918 and out of the picture by 1919. Other developers tried unsuccessfully to turn Foresta into a profitable venture. On paper at least, Foresta was a good idea, but the timing was wrong. Transportation difficulties, under-capitalization, World War I and the Great Depression all contributed to the failure of this grand scheme.

Troubles, human-caused and natural, have plagued Foresta's history from the beginning. After various real estate projects collapsed, Foresta was nearly forgotten for years. During the Depression and World War II, many property owners lost their lots because they were unable to make payments or pay taxes. Until 1950 only a few cabins had been built, but when electricity arrived in 1951, 74 cabins were constructed during the next ten years. The National Park Service had been wanting Foresta's private land since 1929. Finally, in 1962, the U.S. government began condemning unimproved lots and launching an aggressive program to acquire the rest.

The area has suffered many fires throughout its existence, but the monstrous inferno that roared through Yosemite in 1990 was the worst in 100 years. By some

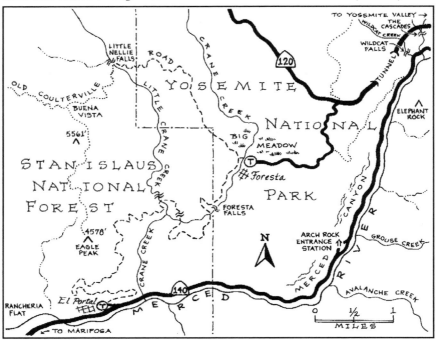

Chapters 34 and 35

miracle, 17 of the 80 cabins were left standing. More than half of Big Meadow burned, but by another miracle the historic Meyer barns and ranch house were untouched.

Travelers looking down on Big Meadow and Foresta from Big Oak Flat Road right after the fire witnessed a grim scene. Except for startling patches of green here and there, blackened tree skeletons speared the sky for miles around. The exposed earth looked ruined and sterile. However, like the mythical Phoenix rising from the ashes, Foresta was reborn. Just three weeks after the firestorm, green shoots of plants and trees began emerging from the nutrient-rich ash. The next spring brought a spectacular wildflower display, all the more dramatic in contrast to the dark scorched earth. Rebirth was also evident on the human level as some property owners rebuilt their dwellings. Today many thousands of re-seeded young pines carpet the forest floor. Eventually, the burned area will flourish with a vigorous and amazing diversity of flora created by the same forces that destroyed it.

Not long after the conflagration, a resident was seen wearing a T-shirt with a touching, life-affirming message. White pine trees and lettering on a bright green background proclaimed "Foresta Forever." As one park ranger advises, "Don't look up at the blackened trees. Look down at the life that's coming back." It's true—Foresta is forever.

■ THE HIKE

Hiking to Little Nellie Falls provides a delightful early season ramble. Seekers of obscure waterfalls will want to add this one to their list. Besides Little Nellie Falls, Foresta has other off-the-beaten path destinations. A peaceful walk around trailless Big Meadow is an enjoyable experience. Please respect the antiquity of the venerable barns and any Native American objects you may find. Chapter 35 features a longer hike down the old road to El Portal with more waterfalls and grand vistas.

To reach Little Nellie Falls, begin your walk on dirt Coulterville Road heading northwest from Big Meadow. As you gain elevation, Half Dome and El Capitan pop into view east of the meadow. After topping a low ridge beyond the second side road on your left, you leave the burned zone. Follow Coulterville Road for 3 miles to this picturesque cascade. About 2 miles from Big Meadow, where the road forks, bear left to the falls. The road straight ahead, closed to auto traffic by a locked gate, was the road to Crane Flat built by Davis in 1914. About .3 mile before the falls, pass through a gate marking the boundary between Yosemite Park and Stanislaus National Forest.

The area around Little Nellie Falls was mostly untouched by the 1990 fire. Formed by Little Crane Creek, Little Nellie gracefully tumbles 30 feet into deep granite pools. Colorful, fragrant wildflowers add charm and visual appeal to this oasis set in a shady canyon. The road beyond the falls leads 6 miles to the Merced Grove of Big Trees.

For a comprehensive and definitive study, *Foresta and Big Meadow* by renowned Yosemite historian Shirley Sargent is recommended reading.

35
Old Foresta Road
Historic Route Past Waterfalls to El Portal

People ought to saunter in the mountains, not hike. . .these mountains are our Holy Land.

~John Muir

■ THE DETAILS

Getting There: Take New Big Oak Flat Road (Highway 120), either north from its junction with Highway 140 in Yosemite Valley for 3.2 miles to the first road, signed Foresta, after the long lighted tunnel, or east from Crane Flat junction for 7 miles. Head south and west on paved Coulterville Road for 1.7 miles and park across from Big Meadow near a wooden bulletin board. If you park or have someone drop you at the bulletin board, the walk through Foresta adds 30 minutes and a mile to your outing. Otherwise, drive through the tiny community to the end of the blacktop and park off the road. To do a shuttle, leave the second vehicle at the El Portal post office just off Highway 140.

Nearest Campground: See Chapter 34.

Lodging: See Chapter 34.

Further Info: Yosemite National Park recorded information 209-372-0200. Stanislaus National Forest, Groveland Ranger District 209-962-7825.

Hike Distance: 6 miles one way to El Portal, or one mile round trip to Foresta Falls from end of blacktop. If you start at the bulletin board, add one mile for one way or 2 miles for round trip.

Difficulty: Moderate.

Best Time to Go: Spring.

Cautions: Be careful around rushing streams and waterfalls.

Starting Elevation: 4200 feet. Descent to El Portal loses 2200 feet elevation.

Map: See Chapter 34, page 194.

Other Map: USGS El Portal 15 minute topo.

Terra incognita except to locals, this abandoned dirt track on the extreme western edge of Yosemite represents a bit of heaven on earth for early season hikers. Foresta Road snakes across a steep ridge between the wee community of Foresta just inside park lands and El Portal along the Merced River. Six miles of hairpin turns and 2200 feet of elevation separate the two points. In between, ample rewards await explorers craving wildflowers, waterfalls and solitude.

The road corkscrewing through a scenic setting high above Merced River canyon dates back to 1912. The newly incorporated Foresta Land Company bought 200 acres of patented land from the estate of James McCauley who had homesteaded the property long before it became part of Yosemite National Park. "To designate it as a forest tract," the company chose the name Foresta.

The goal for this heavily-timbered acreage about 12 miles from Yosemite Valley was to create a summer resort similar to eastern Chautauqua assemblies. Designed to appeal to refined, educated and cultured people, the Foresta Summer Assembly planned to feature programs presented by prominent intellectuals and expected to attract hundreds of people.

Foresta Land Company staked, numbered, and blocked out 1230 lots measuring 50 feet by 100 feet and sold them for $100 each as vacation lots for summertime camping in what they hoped would become a permanent community. Expansive plans included many conveniences for future residents and visitors, as well as a wagon road connecting Foresta to the Yosemite Valley Railroad terminus in El Portal.

Although great enthusiasm and optimism abounded in charting Foresta's future, most of the grandiose plans never materialized. In spite of costly advertising campaigns and classy brochures, lot sales were disappointingly low, and expenses were

Solitude and seldom seen waterfalls await hikers along abandoned Foresta Road.

much higher than anticipated. For more about Foresta's history, see Chapter 34.

Despite the scheme's failure, by 1990 Foresta had 80 cabins used by full-time residents and vacationers. Then in August of that year, a monstrous conflagration destroyed 24,000 acres in Yosemite. Foresta virtually burned to a crisp, with only 17 cabins, two historic barns and a ranch house surviving the lightning-caused holocaust.

Today many thousands of saplings are thriving, but for years to come, manzanita and other fire-loving shrubs will dominate the slopes. Ironically though, plant life has regenerated vigorously and abundantly. Tree seedlings and plants have flourished in the nutrient-rich ash, making spring wildflower displays spectacular since 1991. Especially eye-catching, masses of lupine with fragrant purple blooms grace the hillsides around Foresta. In recent years, some of the property owners have rebuilt their dwellings.

■ THE HIKE

If you would like to experience Old Foresta Road and its quiet, lovely landscape, you have a few options to consider. You can hike uphill and back from El Portal, or hike downhill and back from Foresta. Either way, you would gain 2200 feet elevation in 12 miles round trip. Alternately, you may choose to invoke John Muir's wisdom and "saunter in these mountains." You can accomplish this with a car shuttle. A vehicle in place at El Portal will allow you a leisurely downhill ramble with ample time and energy to appreciate the wildflowers and waterfalls in this seldom visited location.

For a 7-mile hike, you can start at the wooden bulletin board at the road fork at Big Meadow, adding 30 minutes to your outing. Otherwise, drive through the tiny community to the end of the blacktop and park off the road. As you walk the road beyond the blacktop, Crane Creek is on your left. In early season, it roars on its downhill plunge to merge with Little Crane Creek before joining the Merced River in the canyon far below.

Before long, you pass lush pasture lands sometimes inhabited by a large herd of horses. This beautiful, pastoral setting is the site of the historic McCauley ranch whose ancient buildings burned during the 1990 fire. Soon you hear booming Foresta Falls about .5 mile past the gate. When the remarkably photogenic cascade is in full career, you'll need to snap pictures before or after the bridge because of the mist swirling about. Beyond wide, noisy Foresta Falls, you exit Yosemite Park and enter Stanislaus National Forest.

Heavy tree cover segues to more characteristic chaparral growth and full sun along the exposed ridge. From this point, big vistas of rugged Merced Canyon and its steep-sided hills will mesmerize. Many species of wildflowers accompany you along the way to El Portal. Around 1.5 miles, cross a bridge made necessary by a second Crane Creek waterfall. Before long you'll see in the distance the third and final cataract created by Little Crane Creek sliding over slick granite.

Although eclipsed by Yosemite Valley's famous waterfalls, the less renowned cascades along Foresta Road are nonetheless gorgeous specimens.

The third and smallest of Foresta waterfalls approximately marks the halfway point, a good place for a lunch break. Just before the bridge, scramble uphill on a short spur road that leads to a derelict mining camp. Beyond the carcass of a rusting bus, clumps of white saxifrage and delicate seep-spring buttercups brighten the banks and wet, rocky niches. Water-loving, long-stemmed western tofieldia grow right out of the stream.

Rushing and leaping downhill for hundreds of feet, the silvery ribbon of Crane Creek remains in sight nearly the rest of the way. All too soon the route becomes black-topped as you reach the uppermost edge of El Portal. A quaint hamlet just a mile west of the park line on Highway 140, El Portal is a small, tightly-knit community populated mainly by park service employees and their families. A picturesque collection of dwellings, ranging from rustic cabins to more upscale cottages and homes, hug the hillside above the Merced River. At the bottom of the slope, the post office comes into view where your shuttle vehicle or driver is parked.

36
May Lake & Mount Hoffman
Climbing One of John Muir's Favorite Yosemite Peaks

■ THE DETAILS

Getting There: From Crane Flat drive 28 miles east on Highway 120. Turn left onto a section of Old Tioga Road, signed May Lake, and drive 1.8 miles to trailhead parking area.

Nearest Campground: Porcupine Flat Campground, on the north side of Highway 120 about 3 miles west of the turnoff that leads to the trailhead, has 52 sites and no piped water.

Lodging: Tioga Road (Highway 120) has two summers-only hostelries: White Wolf Lodge to the west and Tuolumne Meadows Lodge to the east. Call 559-252-4848 for all park lodging.

Further Info: Yosemite National Park recorded info 209-372-0200. Overnight wilderness permits 209-372-0740.

Hike Distance: 6 miles round trip to summit, 2.4 miles to May Lake, 3.6 miles from lake to summit (all round trip).

Difficulty: Strenuous to Mount Hoffman, moderate to May Lake.

Facilities: May Lake has both a High Sierra Camp, reservations required, and a backpackers' camp.

Best Time to Go: Summer, autumn.

Cautions: No swimming at May Lake. Abandon plans to summit if thunderstorms approach.

Starting Elevation: 8847 feet. Elevation gain to May Lake: 480 feet, to summit: 2003 feet.

Other Maps: USGS Tenaya Lake & Yosemite Falls 7.5 minute topos or Wilderness Press' **Hetch Hetchy Reservoir** 15 minute topo.

John Muir advised that one of the best ways to spend time in Yosemite was to go straight to Mount Hoffman. A century later, his recommendation still rings true. The 3-mile trek to Mount Hoffman's 10,850-foot summit provides the most definitive, comprehensive views of this great Park's diverse landscape. Requiring no technical climbing or mountaineering skills, Mount Hoffman, in the geographic center of Yosemite's 1200-square miles, offers unrestricted visual access to a wilderness of mountains, peaks and domes in every quadrant.

Cradled at the foot of Mount Hoffman, deep-blue May Lake (elevation 9270 feet) is 1.2 miles from the trailhead and makes a great base camp for those who opt to linger in this striking, subalpine environment. In addition to one of the park's five backcountry High Sierra Camps (advance reservations only), a back-packers' camp sits just above the lake's south shore. Although the route to the top is short, it is nevertheless strenuous. For hikers unaccustomed to high elevation rambles, a stopover at May Lake will help you to acclimatize before ascending the remaining 1.8 miles to Hoffman the next day.

As far as we know, members of the California State Geological Survey, led by Josiah Whitney, were the first non-native Americans to reach Hoffman's summit on June 24, 1863. The peak was named for Charles Hoffman, survey topographer and cartographer. Born and schooled in Germany, the young engineer came to California in 1858 and stayed with Whitney's Survey throughout its existence between 1860 and 1874. He remained in the United States and later pioneered the American school of cartography. Hoffman named May Lake in honor of his sweetheart, Lucy Mayotta Browne, whom he married in 1870.

From the meticulous and detailed journal of William Brewer, geologist and Whitney's second in command, we can read about the first recorded ascent of Mount Hoffman. On June 23, 1863, after six days of examining Yosemite Valley, the men "bade adieu to the valley" via the terribly steep Indian Canyon trail and followed the ancient Miwok-Mono Indian trail eastward to the uplands. That night they camped at Porcupine Flat where the sight of jagged, snow-mantled Sierra peaks stirred their souls. Sleep was difficult in the presence of "a group of mountains so high of which absolutely nothing is known."

The next day Whitney, Hoffman and Brewer "climbed a peak over 11,000 feet (later corrected to 10,850 feet) in height about 5 miles from camp . . . it commanded a sublime view. Perhaps over 50 peaks are in sight . . . many of them mere pinnacles of granite, streaked with snow, abounding in enormous precipices." Though lacking the "picturesque beauty of the Swiss Alps," the High Sierra in Brewer's estimation was "sublimely grand . . . its desolation its greatest feature."

Although similar, John Muir's experience on Mount Hoffman during his first summer in the Sierra as a shepherd was more complex and multileveled than Brewer's. Muir was indeed gifted in being able to witness the beauty and minutiae of nature with the heart and soul of a poet and the clinical eye of a scientific observer. Fortunately, he was also able to eloquently, passionately record his discoveries and adventures for us to share in his love for Yosemite, which to him represented one of the most important places on Earth.

Muir found exactly what he wanted in the mountains—wildness. The higher he journeyed into the Sierra the more his rapture increased, the more at home he felt. Never did Muir feel Yosemite wilderness was desolate or savage, nor did he ever feel alone. Always in the company of "brother creatures and plant people"

In this 1863 photo, Charles Hoffman, topographer and cartographer for the California State Geological Survey, takes measurements just below Mount Hoffman's western summit.

and the myriad sights and sounds of the natural world, he was never lonely.

On July 26, 1869, Muir reached Hoffman's broad summit, the highest elevation he had yet attained. Without doubt he was overwhelmed by the vast congregation of mountains surrounding him, but his attention was also riveted by nature's boundless manifestations at ground level. At first sight, the summit appeared dull and lifeless, but he noticed its surface was rich with plant life and studded with crystals of quartz, mica, feldspar, hornblende and tourmaline whose colors dazzled when struck by sunbeams.

Looking more closely at the flashing display, he discovered a multitude of tiny alpine wildflowers all but hidden among the sparkling radiance. Muir's poetic soul was so moved by the scene that he remarked, "You saunter among the crystals and flowers as if you were walking among stars." Until sunset he explored, studied the flora and fauna and reveled in the incredible rendezvous of granite formations, forests, meadows and lakes spreading in every direction.

Beholding Mount Hoffman's classic High Sierra scenery is an experience you'll remember for a lifetime. At this point in the heart of the Park, the quintessence of Yosemite is revealed to you. It's one of those places so special and spectacular that it's worth visiting annually. Worth a thousand words, the summit panorama exposes an unequivocal picture of the titanic power of glacial action in Yosemite's dim past. Hulking, tri-crested Mount Hoffman is also historically significant because it was the first known peak in the region to be climbed by Euro-Americans in 1863, and it was here that young John Muir began formulating his revolutionary glacier theory to explain Yosemite's origins.

On another level, forget about academics and indulge yourself in the million-dollar vista. Don't be surprised if all you can articulate is "WOW!" For most people this is the most common and oft-repeated utterance as they drink in the sights. You'll surely agree with Muir's observation that on no other Yosemite mountain are you more likely to linger. Because nothing approximates Hoffman's elevation for miles, the view is wide-open. Aided by a park map, you can identify nearly every peak in your line of sight.

■ THE HIKE

The 1.2-mile trail to the lake winds moderately uphill through a mixed conifer forest and over slabs of granite. Fine views of High Country peaks puncture the skyline as you switchback up a short, steep slope just before the lake.

Dramatically backdropped by Hoffman's massive eastern face, May Lake's lovely setting can be a destination in itself or a rest stop before continuing up the mountain. Abandon your ascent if a thunderstorm is imminent; lightning can be

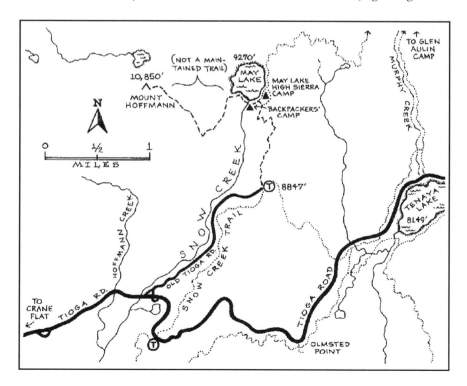

fatal. Not officially maintained, the 1.8-mile unsigned route to Mount Hoffman skirts the backpackers' camp on the lake's south shore. Proceed across a large outcropping of rocks and continue through a small gap leading up to a flowery, linear meadow about 400 feet long.

At the south end of the meadow, near a saddle, the trail passes among some

hike continues on page 206

■ THE HIGH SIERRA CAMPS

Even if your idea of camping in Yosemite is a suite at the Ahwahnee Hotel, most people find something tempting and primeval about visiting the wilderness. If the truth were known, lots of people fantasize about "getting out there" to remote areas of the Sierra. Unfortunately, most never get beyond the dreaming stage because they don't know how to go about it, or they erroneously believe backcountry trekking is the exclusive realm of strapping youngsters and fitness freaks. Granted, backpacking may not be for everyone, but you can experience the spectacular grandeur of Yosemite's High Country in relative luxury with only a day pack on your shoulders.

Unique to Yosemite National Park are the High Sierra Camps, designed to accommodate backcountry travelers who, for various reasons, choose not to carry everything needed on their backs. Originally called "Hikers Camps," the High Sierra Camps were conceived in 1916 by the new National Park Service to coax visitors into Yosemite's isolated regions.

The original Hikers Camps were simple, rustic affairs with separate dormitory-style tents for men and women, a kitchen and dining tent and employee quarters. Before long, people on horseback as well as hikers were attracted to the convenient facilities, and the name changed to High Sierra Camps. Since 1916 there have been eight different camps, but the present number of six has been in place for many years.

Because of their lofty elevations ranging from 7150 to 10,300 feet, the camps have a brief season, generally late June to Labor Day. Except for Tuolumne Meadows, which you can drive to, the other five are accessible only by trail. Glen Aulin, May Lake, Sunrise, Merced Lake and Vogelsang camps still rely on pack mule trains to bring in all supplies and to take out used linen, towels and refuse. Placed roughly in a circular pattern, it's about an 8-mile hike between camps.

Today's camps are still rustic and unadorned, offering wood stove-heated tent cabins which sleep either four or six, comfortable beds with linens, adjacent showers and toilet facilities, hearty family-style breakfasts and dinners, and box lunches on request. A very small store in each camp sells film, candy, insect repellent and the like. Camp sizes vary, but most sleep about 50 people.

Because of the short season and the tremendous popularity, you must make reservations well in advance. For information write the High Sierra Desk, 5410 E. Home Ave., Fresno, CA 93727 or call 559-454-2022.

You can use the High Sierra Camps several ways. Many love the seven-day guided loop trip. Led by a ranger/naturalist, up to 15 hikers spend a night at each of the six camps. Participants learn about the terrain and history, have time to view the diversity of the backcountry and develop camaraderie with fellow hikers. If joining a group isn't your style, you can do it on your own as most do. Choose one camp and stay as many days as you wish, or travel to as many camps as you'd like. Many hikers prefer staying a night at each of several camps with an extra day at one camp to rest and explore the area before moving on. Equestrians continue to enjoy the camps, too. Each site also has a backpackers' camp nearby, and it's even possible for these non-camp hikers to buy a meal in the dining tent. However, you need to make advance reservations for meals or check at the camp desk upon arrival.

High Sierra Camp life is an enjoyable and rewarding experience. The food is good quality and plentiful. The employees are generally enthusiastic, helpful, friendly college students who love their jobs. These young people do it all, cook, split wood for your stove, wait tables, change beds, clean cabins and do dishes. Guests have many options: hike, fish, climb peaks, swim, stroll to nearby areas of interest, study geology, birds or wildflowers, sit in the sun, read or sleep. Your day can be as stimulating or as restful as you want. After dinner the nightly campfire is a tradition, and bedtime is usually early for most folks.

The reservations office will send you details and information on what to bring. You really don't need two-thirds of what you think you do! Backpackers are right—every ounce counts. Toiletries, personal gear and a change of clothing are all you really need. Don't let the thought of an 8-mile hike between camps intimidate you. Most of us in good health and in reasonable physical condition can readily walk that far. In fact, many High Sierra Camp visitors are senior citizens. The trick to walking in altitude is to go slowly, especially at first. Taking rest stops allows your body time to adjust and to give you the opportunity to absorb the world class scenery.

High Sierra Camps can be a transitional step into true backpacking, or they can be an end unto themselves. Maybe it's time you stopped being an armchair High Country visitor and find out what you're missing.

If you're a doubting Thomas and need to see for yourself what a High Sierra Camp looks like before signing up, a short 1.2-mile hike to May Lake makes a great sampler. The rather steep path is loaded with astonishing, panoramic vistas of the Sierra Crest. Inspect this High Sierra Camp, stroll around, have a trail lunch at the lake, and spend time admiring this breathtaking setting. As the old saying goes, one picture is worth a thousand words.

trees and then climbs northwest (right) steeply up a ridge. Don't make the mistake of walking past the meadow. Continue ever upward toward your goal, the westernmost and highest summit topped by a small radio transmitter. At the base of this rocky eminence, your final effort will be to boulder-scramble about 100 yards to the summit.

After catching your breath from the 1530-foot ascent from May Lake, break out the trail snacks and settle in for a, well earned rest. Don't let sassy marmots con you into a handout! Before leaving, explore the nearly flat summit plateau. Far below the north rim, a litter of turquoise lakes glitter in the sun. From the east rim, you'll delight in a stunning view of May Lake. Return the way you came; other routes can be dangerous.

Looking south from Hoffman's summit past The Thumb to Half Dome and Cloud's Rest.

One year I rambled to Mount Hoffman twice, once in mid-July and again in late September. In July I left the warmth of my sleeping bag at May Lake backpackers' camp to get a pre-dawn start up Hoffman's slope to experience sunrise from the summit. In early morning air as crisp and dry as a vintage Chardonnay, I arrived in time to witness the sun come up like thunder over the Sierra Crest. Even after more than a dozen pilgrimages to this mountain top over the years, "WOW!" was still the most fitting exclamation. On this morning, only four marmots and I shared sunrise gilding a stony wilderness of peaks.

In September I car camped at Porcupine Flat west of May Lake junction. I headed up the trail to Mount Hoffman in late afternoon so that I'd be on top by sundown. Except for three hikers on their way back, I had the mountain all to myself. Not long after I had poured a cup of tea from my thermos and munched a bagel, a violent sunset ignited the sky with gaudy carnelian and vermillion hues and flushed the peaks with an unearthly glow.

Each journey was fit for the gods. Any time of day, however, is a good time to trek to Hoffman, but I lean toward Muir's assessment: "Best of all are the dawn and sunrise . . . no mountain top could be better placed for this most glorious view. In the midst of such beauty, who wouldn't be a mountaineer?"

37
Snow Creek Trail
A Scenic Descent into Tenaya Canyon

■ THE DETAILS

Getting There: Take Highway 120 (Tioga Road) to road marker T 22, .6 mile east of May Lake turnoff, 3 miles west of Tenaya Lake. The trailhead lies west of an abandoned road. For a shuttle hike, have your driver or a car meet you at Curry Village parking area at Yosemite Valley's east end.

Nearest Campground: Porcupine Flat Campground, on the north side of Highway 120 about 3.6 miles west of the trailhead, has 52 first-come, first-served sites and no piped water.

Lodging: Tioga Road (Highway 120) has two summers-only hostelries: White Wolf Lodge to the west and Tuolumne Meadows Lodge to the east. Call 559-252-4848 for all park lodging.

Further Info: Yosemite Information Office, Box 577, Yosemite, CA 95289, 209-372-0200.

Hike Distance: 9.3 miles for one-way shuttle hike or 5 miles round trip to cabin junction. Add .75 mile for side trip to Snow Creek Cabin.

Difficulty: Strenuous for one-way hike. Moderate for 5-mile hike.

Best Time to Go: Summer or early autumn.

Cautions: Take it easy if you make the very steep and long descent. If you have bad knees, find another trail.

Starting Elevation: 8530 feet. One-way hike has 4430 feet elevation loss while shorter hike loses and gains 930 feet.

Other Map: USGS Yosemite Falls 7.5 minute topo.

Restless and eager for the opening of Sierra High Country roads and trails, I began the preseason ritual of rummaging through a slew of topos to plan summer and fall outings. From a smorgasbord of tempting destinations, I finally decided to kick off the year hiking the 9.3-mile Snow Creek Trail, which requires a car shuttle. Because I had not hiked it in awhile, I studied the map to recall the route from Highway 120 down to Mirror Lake in Yosemite Valley.

What can change on a map in three years? Actually very little. Certainly neither the location of Tioga Road, Yosemite Valley nor the serpentine trail linking them had disappeared, but that's not the point. Kindred souls with a passion for maps will understand that poring over contour squiggles and taking imaginary hikes provide a most satisfying exercise. Place names such as Devils Dance Floor, Unicorn Peak, Silver Apron and Whizz Dome are like jewels in my mouth, and I say them out loud to hear their fanciful sounds as I trace black-lined trails in the wilderness.

While scrutinizing my Yosemite Falls topo, I was intrigued by a dot indicating "Snow Creek Ranger Cabin," .3 mile east of the trail. Somewhere from the caverns of memory, a thought surfaced that this might be the structure built on Mount Watkins' shoulder in 1929 by Yosemite Park and Curry Company to pioneer hut-to-hut cross-country ski touring in the Sierra. A bit of sleuthing eventually validated my memory. Besides eye-popping scenery, a hike with an intriguing historical component always adds to the adventure.

Casual walkers should not attempt Snow Creek Trail. Except for a short climb over a lateral moraine at the start, it's a long, steep downhill journey. Even stalwart hikers will feel the effects of the 4430-foot descent in their knees and thighs. The route becomes increasingly abrupt as it dips into Snow Creek Canyon and then plunges into Tenaya Canyon. Local old-timers sometimes call the lower trail's notorious nine dozen switchbacks the Tenaya Zigzags.

■ THE HIKE

From a small trailhead parking area by a gated road leading to an old quarry, the path heads west to briefly climb a moraine, then bends south on top of it. Enjoy the next .5 mile walking on the crest, the last level terrain you'll tread until Yosemite Valley. Note old license plates tacked to red firs and western white pines above you to mark the way for cross-country skiers between Tioga Pass and the Valley. A colossal boulder, or erratic, dumped by a retreating glacier, offers a Kodak moment as does part of the jagged Cathedral Range to the east.

Just past the erratic, our route begins a sinuous, 1000-foot decline for 2 miles to a junction with a trail from Tenaya Lake to the east. As you near the trail fork, the upper portion of Half Dome's massive face looms large, hinting at views yet to come. To experience a piece of important Sierra history, turn left (east) here for a detour to Snow Creek Cabin. The Snow Creek Trail bears right, continuing toward Yosemite Valley. For the cabin, walk .3 mile and look for a trailside drainage channel on your right. If you come to a smooth granite slope on your left, you've gone too far. Turn right at the shallow ditch, cross a damp thicket, and hop over a creeklet.

About the same distance beyond the Snow Creek tributary, look for the cabin in a small clearing. Although only 300 yards or so from the trail, it is hard to see because of its weathered, shingled exterior and forest setting. Now used only occasionally by Yosemite backcountry rangers and expert trans-Sierra skiers (permission required), you'd never suspect this deteriorating building was the birthplace

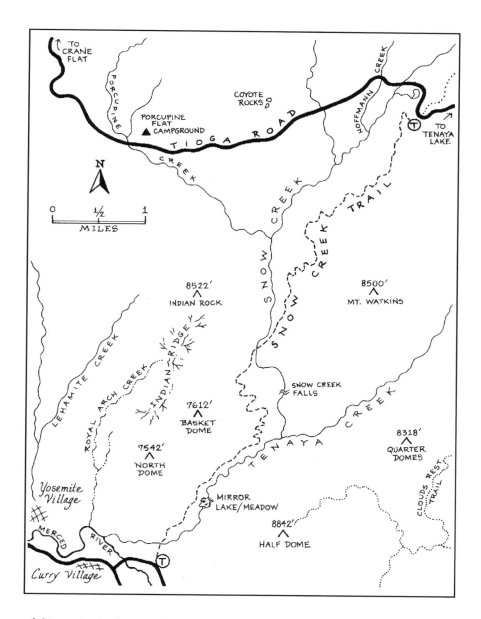

of ski-touring in the United States. Nor would you guess it was designed by one of the architects of the stately Ahwahnee Hotel complex in Yosemite Valley.

In 1929 the Yosemite Park and Curry Company asked Ted Spencer to design a rustic shelter reminiscent of Swiss mountain huts to serve as the first in a network of cabins for High Country ski tours. Snug but basic, the hut slept 16 people. From the Valley far below, hardy visitors arrived on foot, snowshoes or horseback carrying their skis. Two-day tours cost $37, or $65 for a six-day grand tour including a cook and guide.

Up close and personal views of Half Dome accompany hikers throughout the steep descent into Tenaya Canyon.

Impressed by the immense popularity of ski-mountaineering in the Alps, Yosemite Park and Curry Company owners believed High Sierra ski tours would significantly expand the scope of winter activities in the park, increasing tourism during their lean season. However, it was an idea whose time had not yet come. Though Yosemite pioneered in providing cross-country ski trips and a European-style hut-to-hut system, American skiers were then neither numerous, experienced enough nor adventurous enough to make it successful. The concept didn't catch fire as expected because the 1930s saw an exploding interest in downhill skiing, shifting the focus away from touring. Young American skiers were more fascinated with downhill velocity than with the often strenuous, mountaineering style of skiing. After only five seasons, Snow Creek Cabin closed in 1934 for lack of clientele.

Retrace your steps to the junction after investigating the small compound. For the shorter outing, head back uphill to the trailhead. One-way hikers should brace themselves for the 3500-foot, view-packed descent to Mirror Meadow. Switchbacks drop you into Snow Creek Canyon in one mile, 500 feet below the junction. Stop along Snow Creek for a break before the final, most taxing leg of the journey.

Just beyond the footbridge over the stream, our trail joins with another coming down from Porcupine Flat .25 mile south of Highway 120. Shortly, you begin 108 switchbacks down, down, down to the floor of Tenaya Canyon. Stop frequently to rest your legs and absorb the sights in this severely glaciated gorge. Though the trail is very steep, the majesty of the enduring granite landscape provides ample distractions from gravity's inconveniences.

Cloud's Rest and Half Dome completely rule the scenery. These grand, gray behemoths bring to life an observation by explorer and nature writer Smeaton Chase in 1911. "Great is granite, and Yosemite is its prophet." At elevations of 9962 feet and 8842 feet respectively, they are two of Yosemite's most recognized and scenic formations. Cloud's Rest looks like a vast granite wave, its sheer 4500-foot-high face the largest expanse of bare rock in the park. Enormous piled-up slabs of granite make up the narrow summit ridge line where clouds often linger.

Just west of it is the unmistakable and eye-compelling hemispherical mountain known around the globe, Half Dome. The star attraction of all Yosemite's unique geological features, it's unrivaled in its grandeur. Music of the waterfalls is certainly Yosemite's anthem, but mighty Half Dome symbolizes Yosemite more than any other landmark. Brooding and mysterious, the monolith appears as a polished granite helmet, so close you can almost reach out and touch it.

Gaze up Tenaya Canyon during one of your pauses en route to Mirror Meadow. A sharp eye can see that it is not configured like Yosemite Valley. Note that it's clearly V-shaped, not U-shaped as ice-carved canyons are supposed to be. Because Tenaya Canyon lacks major vertical joint planes, linear parallel fractures in the bedrock, a U-shaped valley didn't develop.

Although it's difficult to take your eyes off the commanding and intimate presence of Half Dome, a wealth of visual drama awaits in this magnificent chasm where granite is king. A park map will aid you in identifying other formations. If you have never understood or witnessed the power of moving rivers of ice, this is the place to "get it." No geology course or text could hope to explain it more graphically, more eloquently, than this stony panorama before you.

To the east, Pywiack Cascade is an elegant ribbon of water created by Tenaya Creek's dive over the massive canyon wall, plummeting 600 feet to enter Yosemite Valley. Much closer to you on the north side of the gorge is Snow Creek Falls. That long, lean cataract leaps 2000 feet down the canyon wall in a deeply recessed cleft. It can't be seen as a whole from any one location, but one of the best view points is along Snow Creek Trail.

Cloud's Rest and Half Dome continue as the reigning landmarks in your view. As you pound the switchbacks, you might tip your hat to those pioneer cross-country skiers who climbed to Snow Creek Cabin from Yosemite Valley. Near the bottom, the trail passes by a cliff before entering a forest dominated by oaks. Near Tenaya Creek on the canyon floor, the trail intersects Tenaya Canyon Loop Trail.

At this junction, turn right (west) and walk a nearly level mile along Mirror Meadow to its end. From here, walk a gently sloping .5-mile on an abandoned paved road to a shuttle bus stop. Ride the free shuttle to where your car or driver is waiting at Curry Village parking area.

Some hikers consider this a long, punishing, hard-on-the-knees hike. While that's true, everyone who loves the granite architecture of Yosemite should take this journey at least once in a lifetime. Said Elmo Robinson in 1930, "Let us remember that there will always be those who know that the most marvelous views are seen only after physical effort to obtain them, who prefer intimacy with the mountains to their own physical comfort."

38
Four-Mile Trail between Glacier Point & Yosemite Valley
Where the Firefall Once Fell

■ THE DETAILS

Getting There: For the Glacier Point (upper) Trailhead, turn east off the Wawona Road (Highway 41) onto Glacier Point Road and drive 16 miles to its end. For the Valley trailhead, drive into Yosemite Valley and park at the Sentinel View parking area near road marker V 18.

Nearest Campground: In the Glacier Point area, Bridalveil Creek Campground, open June through September, has 110 units at 7200 feet elevation, available first-come, first-served.

Lodging: For Yosemite Valley, call the central reservation number 559-252-4848. Outside Yosemite, for El Portal try Cedar Lodge 209-379-2612. For Mariposa, try Mariposa Lodge 209-966-3607 or Mother Lode Lodge 209-237-7277.

Further Info: Yosemite National Park 209-372-0200.

Hike Distance: 4.6 miles one way, 9.2 miles round trip.

Difficulty: Strenuous, especially for uphill or round trip.

Best Time to Go: Late spring through early autumn.

Cautions: The trail is closed during winter.

Starting Elevations: Glacier Point Trailhead: 7240 feet. Lower (Valley) Trailhead: 3980 feet.

Elevation Gain: 3260 feet from the Valley to Glacier Point. Comparable elevation loss for one-way descent.

Other Maps: USGS Yosemite 15 minute topo, Wilderness Press' **Yosemite National Park** map.

Undoubtedly some readers remember the unique, thrilling presentation of Yosemite's Firefall and fondly cherish the memory of seeing it. On the flip side of the coin, many considered it an unnatural, commercialized exhibition and are relieved it no longer occurs. Certainly many readers have neither seen it nor have any notion of what it was. Whatever your position, the Firefall was an integral part of the Yosemite experience for 90 years. Good or bad, right or wrong, it was a distinctive, internationally known event witnessed by millions between 1872 and 1968.

It is widely accepted that the first Firefall from Glacier Point was the brain-child of James McCauley in either 1871 or 1872. Exactly what inspired the man to push a mound of fire over the cliff is a mystery. It may have been a flair for the dramatic or just pure accident when some of the sparks from a campfire blew over the cliff in a gust of wind. Whatever the origin, the spectacle captured the imagination of those who spotted it from the Yosemite Valley floor 3200 feet below Glacier Point, encouraging McCauley to build larger fires. Before long, the Firefall became a nightly tradition during summer months.

Requests for the Firefall became so frequent and numerous that McCauley decided to charge $1.50 per person for hotel guests and campers in Yosemite Valley as compensation for his efforts. His success with the Firefall seemed to have uncovered a talent for theatrics. Flaming gunny sacks, fireworks and even crude bombs were incorporated into the show.

James McCauley was one of Yosemite's earliest settlers. Before arriving in Yosemite Valley in 1870 he worked in the mines around Mariposa for several years. Yosemite was then a state park, and it was an important priority of the park commissioners to improve old Indian paths so visitors could reach the Valley rim and the High Sierra beyond it. Because no money was available to achieve this goal, a few responsible men were granted trail-building privileges and allowed to charge tolls to offset the cost.

In 1871 McCauley hired John Conway, who later became superintendent on the famous Zigzags portion of the Big Oak Flat Road, to begin construction on the Four-Mile Trail from the foot of Sentinel Rock in Yosemite Valley up to Glacier Point. This historic trail, designed for horse and foot traffic, cost $3000, a hefty sum in those days, and required 11 months to complete. The toll was $1, considered reasonably priced. The steep trail, switchbacking 4 miles up the 3200 foot cliff to Glacier Point, was indeed a masterpiece. Not until 1929 did more skilled engineers modify and improve the trail's grades.

The McCauley family lived in the toll house at the base of the trail near a colossal boulder. The house is long gone, but the boulder hasn't moved an inch. Apparently, this and other enormous chunks of granite split off Sentinel Rock during the violent Inyo County earthquake of March 1872. For some reason, McCauley chose to build his house among these massive hunks of granite. In addition to making his mark in history books for the Firefall and Four-Mile Trail, he built the Mountain House atop Glacier Point, which provided meals and lodging. In 1897 the McCauleys left Glacier Point, and the cliff was dark for a few years. Mountain House was a landmark until it and the Glacier Point Hotel were destroyed by fire on August 9, 1969.

After David and Jenny Curry appeared in Yosemite in 1899, they revolutionized hostelry operations in Yosemite and other national parks. They were both teachers in Palo Alto who spent their summer vacations managing camping tours in such places as Yellowstone. In 1899 they started with seven tents, one paid cook and several college students who worked for room and board. They called it Camp Curry, and from this very modest beginning evolved the giant Yosemite Park and Curry Company.

David Curry was entertaining, charismatic and imaginative, a born showman who quickly revived the Firefall for his guests. At first it was done to honor prominent clients and to celebrate special holidays, but within a few years it again became a popular nightly feature.

Curry went a step beyond McCauley's Firefall, ritualizing the event by turning it into a pageant with a traditional procedure. The bonfire itself required a considerable amount of skill and preparation to be effective. One employee was in charge of setting up the bonfire, lighting it at 7 p.m. and pushing it over the edge at 9 p.m.

Contrary to what you might think, the quantity of fuel for the fire was quite small. The bark fragments, gathered from fallen red fir trees around Glacier Point, amounted to about the equivalent of a cord of wood and were piled in a three-foot-high circle. It took two hours for the fire to burn down to a mass of glowing coals about the size of walnuts. The "Firefall Man" used a long-handled pusher equipped with a metal heat shield. This man determined the character of the Firefall, and precise timing was essential for an even flow of falling embers.

Just before 9 p.m. all lights in the Camp Curry vicinity were doused, and a hushed expectancy settled over the crowd awaiting the famous call. David Curry would bellow, "Hello, Glacier!" Seconds later the faraway response, "Hello, Camp Curry!" could be heard through the absolute silence.

"Let the fire fall!" Curry boomed, and the stream of fire was slowly pushed over the cliff. At times the red-hot mass plummeted straight down the sheer wall, lazily spreading out like a fan as it neared the ledge below. Other times a river of fire waved back and forth like an incandescent waterfall. It would continue for a few minutes until finally the last of the cascading embers flared briefly and then gradually faded away. The night was dark again. The entranced on-lookers were utterly still for some moments until the spell was shattered by the intrusion of the Camp Curry lights piercing the velvety blackness.

A pre-1920 postcard depicts the famous Firefall ceremony, a popular event spanning 90 years.

Many spectators believed that the

Firefall should be seen twice, first from the Yosemite Valley floor and then from Glacier Point. It was their opinion that watching the fire mound being pushed over the cliff somehow gave them a sense of participation in the show. Only once was the Firefall presented from the north side of the Valley, causing a fire that burned for days. At least one time the Firefall was staged from the heights of Half Dome. The potential danger of starting a forest fire below Glacier Point was negligible because the embers landed on a wide, rocky ledge and little vegetation existed on the granite walls to ignite. Occasionally, Firefalls were arranged during autumn and winter. To prepare for these times, large quantities of red fir bark were hauled to Glacier Point well in advance and then covered for protection from rain and snow.

The Firefall continued for many years after David Curry's death in 1917. Untold numbers of Yosemite lovers were saddened to learn that the final Firefall would be held on January 15, 1968. Times had changed, and National Park Service officials responded to increased criticism of such an unnatural spectacle and the damage done by throngs of onlookers trampling fragile meadows. The litter, congestion, pollution and other problems caused by hordes of people jammed into a small area proved far more damaging than the Firefall ever was. That January night a long-beloved tradition became part of this great Park's diverse, fascinating history. Today's Yosemite visitor can still see evidence of the Firefall by looking up the cliff to Glacier Point. Just below the overhanging rock the granite has been blackened by nearly a century of hot ashes falling down it.

The Four-Mile Trail is still a popular route for hikers, although one should be in good condition to attempt it. The trail closes during winter. The easiest way to experience the Four-Mile Trail is to arrange a car shuttle or take the bus to Glacier Point and hike down to the Valley floor. The Four-Mile Trail is really 4.6 miles in length with a 3200-foot elevation change. When the route was upgraded and slightly realigned in 1929, an additional .5 mile was built in to lessen the steepness, with other improvements over time accounting for the other .1 mile.

The cozy, sheltered magic of deep forest cover punctuated with startling glimpses of Yosemite Valley and the High Sierra offer superb sensory appeal. Perhaps the most rewarding aspect of the journey, however, is the sense of moving, literally, through a stretch of history. Commingling our footprints with the thousands of others who have trod this path for 130 years provides a much-needed link with our past, a sense of connection and continuity that is all too often abandoned in the hurry-scurry pace of our future-oriented culture.

■ THE HIKE

For adventuresome and well conditioned hikers, in Yosemite Valley park at the trailhead of the Four-Mile Trail, a strenuous and steep route ascending to Glacier Point. Remember, what goes up must come down. The return trip to the Valley is equally steep. On the left, 250 yards from the sign, you'll have no trouble spotting the condo-sized boulder near which James McCauley built his toll house. You may even find some square nails and shards of crockery and glass. Look, but leave them there. Unless you're a veteran hiker, you may only want to allow yourself 20 to 30 minutes on the trail to get a feel for it.

If you prefer a one-way downhill hike, and are prepared for it, a one-way hikers' bus will transport you to Glacier Point and drop you off so that you can hike back down to the Valley on the Four-Mile Trail. Call Yosemite Lodge, 209-372-1274, for ticket price and time schedule. At Glacier Point, the trail starts near the gift shop. The historic Mountain House and Glacier Point Hotel were located close to the rim here. If you're going the distance, be sure to take water and a lunch, and wear sturdy hiking boots.

Whether you hike or not, an excursion to Glacier Point is highly recommended. It is world famous as one of the most stunning overlooks on this planet. From the railings at the brink, you'll have an eagle's view of the 3214 feet of air space separating you from Yosemite Valley. The panorama combining mountains, canyons, waterfalls, valleys and skyscraping peaks is unlike anything else in the American West and provides an absolutely unforgettable experience.

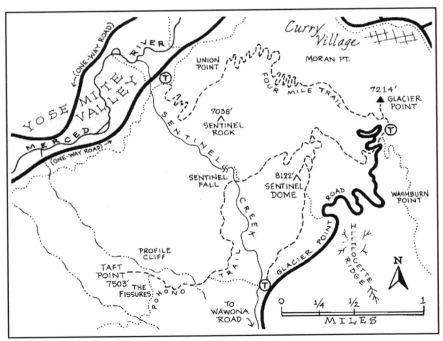

Chapters 38 and 39

39
Sentinel Dome-Taft Point Loop
Breathtaking Vistas from Yosemite Valley's South Rim

■ THE DETAILS

Getting There: From Yosemite Valley, take Wawona Road, signed "HIGHWAY 41, FRESNO." Go 9.2 miles, then turn left onto Glacier Point Road. Go 13.4 miles to signed Taft Point/Sentinel Dome trailhead parking.

Nearest Campground: Bridalveil Creek Campground on Glacier Point Road, open June through September, has 110 sites with piped water, available first-come, first-served.

Lodging: Yosemite West Cottages 209-372-4567 are just outside the park, 6 miles west of Badger Pass. For Park lodging call 559-252-4848.

Further Info: Yosemite National Park 209-372-0200.

Hike Distance: 5.5-mile loop, or 2.2 miles round trip to Sentinel Dome, 2.4 miles round trip to Taft Point.

Difficulty: Moderate.

Best Time to Go: Late June to October.

Cautions: Because of potentially lethal drop-offs at Taft Point, Sentinel Dome and Sentinel Falls, children must be under strict control at all times.

Starting Elevation: 7720 feet.

Elevation Gain: 480 feet to Sentinel Dome, 1060 feet for loop.

Map: See Chapter 38, page 216.

Other Maps: USGS Yosemite 15 minute topo or Half Dome 7.5 minute topo.

Looking at Sentinel Dome's steep, bald top from the trailhead definitely makes you wonder about its accessibility for nonclimbers. However, its back side is vastly less intimidating, amounting to only a short sloping walk to the top. Both Taft Point and Sentinel Dome thrill hikers with sensational vistas of Yosemite Valley, waterfalls and the vast waves of High Country peaks. By combining them into one trip, you're in for a truly unforgettable visual experience.

Consider a jaunt to Sentinel Dome on the evening of a full moon. Pack a trail dinner and plan to be on top early in the evening, or at least before dark. Witnessing sunset and moonrise from this vantage point is something you won't soon forget. Even though the moon is bright, bring a flashlight for the return journey.

■ THE HIKE

At the trailhead, a trail sign indicates left for Taft Point and right for Sentinel Dome. If you are doing the loop, bear right. Alternating between forest and granite slabs, the trail ascends gradually with Sentinel Dome in view most of the way. At .75 mile, the path merges with an abandoned road that leads to the dome's northeast side. As you near the dome's base, look for a spur trail on your right leading eventually to Glacier Point and Yosemite Valley. For the loop, you will later take this route to reach Taft Point. Though there is no trail up the dome's bedrock, the way is obvious. Just zigzag up the slope about 60 yards to the large summit.

It's hard to imagine that you can gain such sublime, far-flung views with so little effort. Sentinel Dome is the second highest point on the Valley rim. Only Half Dome's 8842-foot crest is higher. An uninterrupted 360-degree panorama awaits you at the broad, rounded summit.

Near a dead Jeffrey pine, an inscribed compass rose identifies many features in your line of sight. The subject of millions of photos, the gnarly old tree finally succumbed in the late 1970s after years of vandalism. Stately even in death, the pine makes a dramatic frame for photographers shooting the distant mountains. After a stroll around the top, pull up a boulder and savor one of Yosemite's most stupendous views.

When it's time to leave, carefully descend on a course comfortable for you, returning to the remnant of the old road at the base. Soon, turn left on the signed trail you spotted on the way up. Follow it rather steeply downhill to a small radio facility. You will catch close-up glimpses of Half Dome on the way. At the building, bear left in front of it. Shortly, you will come to another junction. Again, stay left (southwest) on the Pohono Trail heading for Taft Point.

Continue on a downward traverse beneath Sentinel Dome, enjoying wonderful peeks of Yosemite Valley through the foliage. Directly across the canyon, you're treated to the entire 2400-foot plunge of Yosemite Falls. About a mile past the little radio facility, cross Sentinel Creek which soon leaps over the rim to become Sentinel Falls. Take a detour on a use trail along the creek to a wide overlook at the brink of the falls. Be careful. You will no doubt want to linger here awhile and savor the magic as you stand at the top of one of Yosemite's waterfalls.

Beyond the creek, the Pohono Trail briefly parallels the rim and then angles into a magnificent red fir forest. In contrast to the dark, rich color of the bark, bright chartreuse lichen decorates many of the trees. A moderate climb of nearly a mile brings you to a trail fork. Turn right (west) and begin a half-mile descent to Taft Point.

In addition to many wildflower species blooming on the sunny, gravelly slopes, an impressive variety of moisture-loving plants inhabit tiny damp meadows en route to the Point. As you emerge from the forest, the path drops steeply to an

The Fissures, Yosemite Valley, California.

Victorian-era visitors marvel at the vista from Taft Point, 3500 feet above Yosemite Valley.

exposed, rocky shelf. Take your pick of the many use trails that fan out toward the rim.

You'll quickly realize that you've hit another scenic jackpot. Watch your step because it's easy to become distracted at this awesome overlook. The five Taft Point fissures are deep, vertical cracks that cut through a rocky apron overhanging the Valley's south rim. These narrow crevices were formed by millennia of erosion removing the granite along joint planes in the bedrock. From El Capitan to North Dome, all the central portion of Yosemite Valley is before you in an unbroken sweep.

This viewpoint was named to commemorate President William Taft who visited Yosemite in 1909. From the railing at Taft Point proper, you can stare into the dizzying depths of the Valley 3500 feet below. To the left are clumps of granite to rest against as you drink in the amazing scenery.

Return the way you came to the trail fork. There you stay to the right, leaving the Pohono Trail on your left that you hiked from Sentinel Dome. Walk .5 mile east to your trailhead.

40
Wawona & the Meadow Loop
Exploring the History and Splendor of Wawona

■ THE DETAILS

Getting There: Take Highway 41 (Wawona Road) to Wawona in the southern corner of Yosemite Park.

Nearest Campground: Wawona Campground has 100 first-come, first-served sites open year round one mile north of Wawona Hotel.

Lodging: Try historic Wawona Hotel 559-252-4848 or the modern Redwoods Guest Cottages 209-375-6666. Tenaya Lodge 800-635-5807 is in Fish Camp, about 10 miles south.

Further Info: Yosemite National Park 209-372-0200.

Hike Distance: 3.5-mile loop.

Difficulty: Easy.

Facilities: Wawona has grocery stores, gas, golf, stables, gift shops and meals.

Best Time to Go: Nicest in spring, but also pleasant in summer and autumn. In winter you can exchange hiking boots for snowshoes or cross-country skis.

Cautions: Please don't trample the meadow.

Starting Elevation: 4000 feet. Loop has 200 feet gain.

Other Maps: USGS Wawona 7.5 minute topo, Wilderness Press *Yosemite Park & Vicinity* map.

Wawona sits on a beautiful meadow along the South Fork Merced River 27 miles south of Yosemite Valley. What we today call Wawona was called *Pallahchun,* "a good place to stop," by the Nuchu people. For centuries the peaceable Nuchus inhabited this secluded forest paradise. Its beauty is of a restful and mellow nature, quietly wooing one's heart rather than demanding attention. Plentiful game, lush meadows heavy with waving grasses and wildflowers, massive granite formations, vast stands of pine and oak, the sacred Big Trees of staggering dimensions and a tumbling, boisterous river provided idyllic living in this gentle wilderness. Located about midway between Yosemite Valley and the foothills, it was indeed a good place to stop. Galen Clark, a discouraged and dying miner, thought so too.

Lured to California for reasons of health and the siren call of gold, Galen Clark arrived in Mariposa in 1854. He tried his hand at mining but barely made enough to feed himself. While the climate agreed with him, constant exposure and the strenuous work of mining intensified a chronic respiratory condition. By 1855 he was a penniless and disgusted gold-seeker and hired on as a surveyor for John C. Fremont's Ditch Company. Colonel Fremont's ambition was to bring water from the South Fork Merced River to the mines in his Las Mariposas Land Grant. However, as luck would have it, a life-changing event presented itself to Clark in summer 1855.

In August 1855, a sightseeing trip to Yosemite Valley irrevocably altered the course of his life. Galen was among 17 miners who came to see its treasures. On horseback they followed the Mariposa Trail, the oldest route into Yosemite, which passed over Chowchilla Mountain. They camped near the South Fork in present-day Wawona and then rode the remaining, rugged 25 miles to the Valley. Clark was so utterly impressed and emotionally awed by the grandeur of this "vast mountain temple" that he spent the rest of his life deeply involved in it.

Early in 1856 a Mariposa physician cautioned Clark that death from tuberculosis was looming on the horizon, but just might be stalled by a mountain climate. Choosing to pass the remainder of his days in a place that had captured his heart, Clark homesteaded 160 acres at Pallahchun, believing it to be, literally, a good place to stop. After a year of leisurely exploring his surroundings, he built a 16 feet by 20 feet cabin. Known as Clark's Station, it provided rustic overnight accommodations for visitors en route to Yosemite. Never could Clark have imagined that this humble lodging would be the forerunner of the world famous Wawona Hotel.

The pure Sierra environment proved to be a powerful elixir. Clark lived 55 more years, dying in 1910 just shy of his 96th birthday! This fascinating pioneer had a profound influence on Yosemite. Among his many accomplishments in the half century he devoted to this much-beloved place are: pioneer developer of the South Fork region, exploration and naming of the Mariposa Grove of Big Trees, appointment in 1866 as the first Yosemite Guardian (a position held for 21 years), acclaim for his thorough knowledge of the Yosemite region, and author of books about the Park. His grave in the Yosemite Cemetery lies beneath a giant Sequoia he planted himself, graced by a self-chiseled granite marker. Galen Clark was "Mr. Yosemite," a legend in his own time.

Superintending the new Yosemite State Park, which included the Big Trees, was so time-consuming that Clark couldn't satisfactorily perform his duties as innkeeper and Guardian. Because he was a poor businessman and sank considerable money into improving his property and trying to complete the Mariposa Stage Road to his hotel, Clark was forced to take in Edwin Moore as a full partner in 1870. Clark eventually moved to the Valley in 1865 to dedicate all his energy to the Olympian task of managing the Yosemite Grant. Even with a partner, debts mounted until the entire property, including 1160 acres of land, hotel and furnishings, sawmill, blacksmith shop, water supply, buildings, the toll road and a bridge across the South Fork was sold to 39-year-old Albert Henry Washburn for a pittance and cancellation of a $20,000 debt.

By 1867 Washburn was in the livery business and keenly aware of Mariposa's significance as a half-way stop and outfitting center for the rapidly growing Yosemite traffic. He rented every type of conveyance that could be pulled by a horse or mule and all manner of gear and guides for saddle parties. Washburn was on his way to becoming known as the "transportation king of the Sierra." In May 1871 Washburn began operating a stage line from Mariposa to Clark and Moore's Station. Washburn was a frequent visitor at the station and knew both men well. He was also familiar with their growing debts and inability to complete a road between their station and the Valley. He realized that with the road in place and new buildings, he could transform Clark and Moore's primitive hotel into a popular resort.

The take-over by Washburn officially occurred on December 26, 1874, but before the ink was dry the toll road had been pushed four miles beyond the South Fork Station. Rather than innkeeping, the top priority was to complete the road and compete with the Coulterville and Big Oak Flat routes. Nonetheless, the hotel remained open that winter, renamed Big Tree Station.

On July 22, 1875, a huge celebration marked the road's entrance to the Valley near the base of Bridalveil Falls. Although Washburn received the honors, it was pioneer Galen Clark's vision and reputation that culminated in Washburn's success. Even though Wawona Road was not the first to reach the Valley, it was more popular and prosperous because of access to the Big Trees and Glacier Point.

Albert Henry Washburn was the key figure in the hotel and transportation business in the Yosemite area between 1875 and his death in 1902. Washburn's Yosemite Stage and Turnpike Company evolved into a large-scale enterprise. Besides the Big Tree Station, he owned large hotels in Raymond and Ahwahnee, the Sentinel Hotel in the Valley and the Mountain House at Glacier Point. Additionally, his stage line carrying passengers from the train depots in Raymond and Merced was very profitable.

A disastrous fire in November 1878 razed the motley pioneer buildings. Out of the ashes grew the distinctive look of Wawona, with its decidedly New England flavor. Within a week, construction began on the 140 feet by 32 feet two-story structure with covered porches upstairs and down. Praised as the "grandest hotel in the mountains of California," Washburn and his brothers opened its doors on April 1, 1879. This venerable hostelry remains in use 122 years later. Over the years they added other buildings, cottages and improvements, and Big Tree Station grew to a bustling village. Vegetables, fruit and livestock were raised in the meadow. Jean Washburn, Henry's wife, felt that Wawona would be a more appropriate name because it was the native's word for the giant Sequoias they held sacred. The years rolled prosperously by, and the Wawona complex became famous under Washburn family leadership.

The Great Depression caused tourist travel to decline dramatically in the Yosemite area as it did everywhere. Business was so diminished with visitors only coming in dribs and drabs that, rather than face bankruptcy, the Washburns chose to sell the Wawona complex in 1932. There was no cash to meet the large payroll, stock dividends and loan payments on extensive improvements. The U.S. government bought the 2665 acres of land, and Yosemite Park and Curry Company purchased all 50 buildings and their furnishings. As chief concessionaire in Yosemite, the Curry Company took charge of operations in Wawona immediately. Exit the Washburns and the gracious, long tradition of the

The venerable Wawona Hotel complex near Mariposa Grove was considered the "Sleepy Hollow of the West" because of its idyllic setting.

family-owned and operated resort. Enter the U.S. government, the Curry Company, red tape and impersonal management. Sadly, an era was over.

■ THE HIKE

You may be pleasantly surprised to have the loop around Wawona Meadow virtually to yourself despite its partial use as a golf course. To the delight of wildflower enthusiasts, some unusual and rare species bloom in spring. White star tulips, ladyslipper orchids, coral root, fragrant wild azaleas and several kinds of lilies are among the flowery treats in and around the mile-long meadow.

To begin your ramble, start at the golf course across from Wawona Hotel. A road cutting through the course leads to a parking area and interpretive sign. You will quickly leave behind the manicured lawn and enter the meadow on an abandoned dirt road that skirts the picturesque rail-fenced grassland.

Stay out of the center of the fragile meadow, especially when it's damp and boggy. If you must leave the trail to enter the meadow at all, please walk with extreme care. You will almost certainly see mule-tailed deer grazing on the lush golf course or meadow. Please don't feed or approach them. At 3.2 miles you reach a closed gate, beyond which you must cautiously cross Highway 41. Your path continues to the hotel where it recrosses the road, returning to the golf course and trailhead.

The sight of the golf course rankles many Yosemite visitors who consider it intrusive and inappropriate in a national park. Opened in 1918, it was the first golf course in the Sierra Nevada. Before it opened, the lush, verdant meadow was farmed to raise crops and vegetables for the Wawona Hotel. Not long after James Savage's Mariposa Battalion entered Wawona in March 1851, the Nuchu peoples' pristine meadowland was tamed and commercialized. Nevertheless, Wawona Meadow is one of Yosemite's lovely overlooked spots, particularly for wildflower buffs.

■ OTHER SUGGESTIONS

A wealth of scenery and activities abounds in the Wawona Basin. You can be active and hike your socks off on the many trails (Chilnualna Falls rivals any cascade in the Valley, see Chapter 41 for directions) or just sit on the hotel's covered porch and watch the pine trees grow. You can even play golf on the meadow that once raised crops. A free park map or an informational guidebook available in Wawona shops offers many ideas on how to enjoy the area.

You can step back in time at the Pioneer History Center, a collection of historic buildings, ride in a horse-drawn carriage, enjoy guided horseback rides, or choose from a variety of hikes.

Many explore the majestic Mariposa Grove of Big Trees. If you do, I suggest you ride the open-air tram to the top of the grove, get off at the Tunnel Tree, and walk back a short distance to the Galen Clark Tree. The tram driver will direct you. You'll be on the old road to Wawona Point, .5 mile ahead, where sweeping views of the entire Wawona Basin allow you to glimpse what the region looked like 100+ years ago. Either walk back and reboard the tram, or better yet, walk the easy 2.5 miles down through the grove to get better acquainted with these magnificent, gentle giants, the world's largest living things.

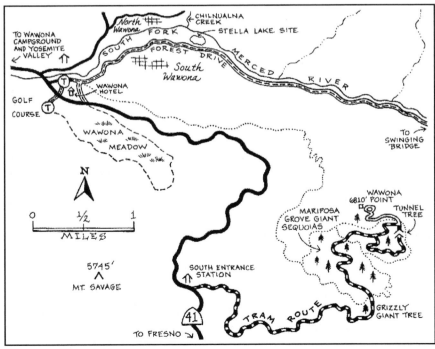

Chapters 40 and 41

41
Stella Lake
A Renounced Remnant Of Yosemite's Past

■ THE DETAILS

Getting There: Take Highway 41(Wawona Road) to the little community of Wawona just inside Yosemite Park's south boundary. A few hundred feet north of Wawona Hotel, turn east on Forest Drive and park near the post office.

Nearest Campground: See Chapter 40.

Lodging: See Chapter 40.

Further Info: Pick up a Wawona and Mariposa Grove Guide/Map at the gift shop or store. It is much more specific than a topo map. Yosemite Park Wawona Ranger Station 209-375-9520. Yosemite Park general info 209-372-0200.

Hike Distance: One mile round trip to Stella Lake site, 4 miles round trip to the swinging bridge.

Difficulty: Easy.

Best Time to Go: Spring, autumn.

Cautions: None.

Starting Elevation: Stella Lake is at 4000 feet, negligible gain.

Map: See Chapter 40, page 224.

Other Maps: Wawona/Mariposa Grove Guide/Map, USGS Wawona 7.5 minute topo.

There is something wondrously therapeutic about water. Although subtle, something powerfully restorative and rejuvenating happens when a human being is near a body of water. In the Sierra Nevada we're blessed with hundreds of lakes. Depending on whether we want to be soothed or stimulated, we can easily find a lakeside destination to suit us. From remote alpine gems to lakes that are beehives of activity, Californians can find a choice not far from home.

Indeed, even the names of lakes conjure up moods and activities. Lake Shasta attracts houseboaters who enjoy its warm foothill elevation. Backpackers find the alpenglow spreading fiery color over the Minarets above Shadow Lake worth the hike in. Active watersports at busy resorts like Bass Lake please some, while city-weary campers seek out quieter places like Cherry Lake to satisfy their water yearnings.

What picture comes to mind at the mention of Stella Lake? What happened at this quite famous Sierra lake? Unless you're a Sierra old-timer or have a keen interest in Yosemite lore, most likely the picture will be blank. To begin the tale of this historic lake, I must state that it no longer exists. You can find the remains of Stella Lake along Forest Drive about .5 mile behind the grand old Wawona Hotel. Very little has survived except for a large depression bordered by earthen dikes. No more than an abandoned pit, the old lake site requires a bit of imagination to visualize its former beauty and unusual usage.

In a vanished, gentle era, Stella Lake provided Wawona residents and tourists a serene setting for swimming, boating and picnics during warm months. However, it was not created for that purpose. Besides providing an idyllic spot in the deep woods, the lake was used mainly for natural ice production, something the modern visitor takes for granted. Ice was an extremely important item in the days before electricity came to the mountains.

To understand how Stella Lake and the ice operation came about, we need to look back to 1874 when the three Washburn brothers purchased Galen Clark's rather crude lodging house, soon developing it into the Wawona Hotel we see today. Besides the hotel, these savvy businessmen built the Wawona Road to Yosemite Valley and operated the Yosemite Stage and Turnpike Company, thereby controlling key factors in the growing Yosemite tourist trade. Two of their lesser known but historically significant accomplishments were Stella Lake and the

Ice harvesting at Stella Lake.

Washburn Ditch, each a clever, far-sighted element in their plans.

Two-mile-long Washburn Ditch rerouted water from the South Fork Merced River and channeled it to irrigate the extensive farming area across from the hotel. By 1908 the ditch also supplied water to generate electricity for the hotel buildings. Because the water needed to flow at a specific level to keep the 500 lights working, "a system of headgates with removable boards, floats and signal lights evolved." The operation required an electrician at the plant and a ditch keeper to walk the length of the ditch daily checking for cave-ins and obstructions. Over the years the peaceful stroll along its banks became known as the Brook Walk and was a popular activity for Wawona residents and visitors. You can still walk a portion of it beyond Stella Lake today.

The perceptive Washburns saw the potential advantages of refrigeration in catering to a numerous and growing clientele. In 1886 they excavated the artificial reservoir that became Stella Lake to produce ice for cold storage at Wawona. They created Stella Lake from scratch rather than by enlarging a natural feature, such as an existing basin or pond that only had to be deepened. The rocks and dirt removed were used to build the dam, retaining walls, and earthworks around the lake. Diverted water from small streams and drainages filled the reservoir.

During the coldest winter months the Washburns hired a few local men to cut ice from frozen Stella Lake and store it in the ice house next to the pond. When the ice became five to ten inches thick, they sawed it into long strips. Then they herded the ice strips onto a horse-powered conveyor belt that took them directly into the ice house. They stacked the ice in layers and covered it all with sawdust. The last ice house, built in 1897, was stout and sturdy, an 18 feet by 38 feet wooden building with a gabled, shingled roof. The double interior walls were at least eight inches thick and packed with sawdust for insulation.

In 1890 the enterprising Washburns also built an ice house at Mirror Lake in Yosemite Valley to supply local hotels. Although the ice plants at Stella Lake and Mirror Lake weren't the only ice-making facilities in the Sierra, the Washburns get credit for pioneering them. You can still see a fine example of an ice house near the Ranger Station at Lake Eleanor (Chapter 12), built by the city of San Francisco during the gigantic Hetch Hetchy Project in the 1920s.

The completion of the Yosemite Valley Railroad in 1907 resulted in sharply increased tourism. Automobiles were allowed entry to Yosemite in 1913, and subsequent years saw the numbers of visitors increase significantly. Concessionaires, including the Washburns in Wawona, quickly realized the need to expand accommodations and recreational facilities to meet the demand. Even tiny Stella Lake was not overlooked. In 1916 a dock, boat house, new rowboat, bath house and diving board were added for the enjoyment of guests.

Stella Lake was named for Estella Hill Washburn, daughter of famous Yosemite landscape artist and Wawona resident Thomas Hill. She married John Washburn in 1885. When the lake was finished the following year, he named it in her honor. Evidently the path around the lake was a favorite walk for romantic young couples on moonlit nights. Thomas Hill handcrafted two rowboats, *Honest John* and *Maid of the Mist*, to use on the lake.

Two events contributed to the demise of Stella Lake, a change in technology and Mother Nature both playing a role. The Wawona Hotel installed modern refrigeration equipment in 1935, utilizing electrical power supplied by a penstock and pelton wheel. Ice cutting continued as backup. When power lines were installed in 1946, ice from Stella Lake was still cut as a precaution against glitches in the new system. The last year of natural ice production at Stella Lake was 1949.

The tempestuous winters of 1950 and 1955 ultimately wrote Stella Lake's obituary. Raging floodwaters in both years caused major damage to earthen dikes, opening a gaping hole that was never repaired. The enchanting and popular Brook Walk along the Washburn Ditch was also seriously impaired when high water roared through it. Finally, in 1956 the Park Service removed the 70-year-old ice house as part of their clean-up campaign. The Brook Walk, too, was never restored because the Park Service "felt its use would be a possible hazard, difficult and expensive to maintain." Some local men made some repairs so that water would run through it, but the Park Service put a stop to that in 1962. When the Wawona Hotel complex was added to the National Register of Historic Places in 1975, the Stella Lake site should have been included.

■ THE HIKE

By taking an easy wooded walk, you can view the deep depression of the former lake, the dam and inflow channels, and a part of the dike along the South Fork Merced River. To reach the Stella Lake site (you can also drive to it), begin your walk on Forest Drive, which shortly becomes dirt. Follow the unpaved track for .5 mile. Then look for the Stella Lake site just north of the road where you can see a rather shallow but large depression, the rock dam and inflow channels of the former lake. At the site's west end below the dam sat the ice house. The horse-powered conveyor machinery was on the level landing in front of the dam.

To continue your history journey, walk another 1.5 miles to the swinging bridge and cross the South Fork Merced River. Bear right and follow the fishermen's trail upstream as far as you would like. In .3 mile you can spot a small dammed pool across the river used for Wawona's domestic water supply. The stonework there is part of the old Brook Walk along Washburn Ditch. One can follow it for a short distance before the route becomes obscure. (The lower ditch turns away from the river to run along the mountainside before reaching the hotel complex.)

■ OTHER SUGGESTION

By bearing left at the fork just past the swinging bridge, you can hike to fine Chilnualna Falls in 5 miles (14 miles round trip from the post office, elevation gain 2500 feet).

Sources: *Yosemite's Historic Wawona* by Shirley Sargent and "Stella Lake" by Robert Pavlik, *Yosemite Association Journal*, Vol. 54, No. 1, 1992.

42
Mono Pass & Bloody Canyon
Following 9600 Years of Human Footsteps

■ THE DETAILS

Getting There: Drive Tioga Road (Highway 120) into the High Country. Mono Pass Trailhead is at road marker T 37, 5.5 miles east of Tuolumne Meadows Campground, 1.5 miles west of Tioga Pass entrance station.

Nearest Campgrounds: Tuolumne Meadows Campground, 5.5 miles west of the trailhead, has 314 sites, open June through mid-September, half first-come, first-served. To reserve a site call 800-436-7275. Tioga Lake Campground, about 2.5 miles east of the trailhead, has 13 first-come, first-served sites in Inyo National Forest, open June through September.

Lodging: Tuolumne Meadows Lodge has tent cabins in summer. Call 559-252-4848 for tent cabin availability and all park lodging.

Further Info: Yosemite National Park 209-372-0200.

Hike Distance: 8 miles round trip.

Difficulty: Moderately strenuous.

Best Time to Go: Summer, early autumn.

Cautions: Please do not remove any historic artifacts.

Starting Elevation: 9700 feet. Gain to Mono Pass: 905 feet.

Other Maps: USGS Tuolumne Meadows and Mono Craters 15 minute topos.

After Highway 120 over Tioga Pass opens for the summer season, it's time to head for the High Country. Some of the most glorious scenery in California awaits you in the Tuolumne Meadows-Tioga Pass region of Yosemite National Park. As well as beautiful scenery, the area has a rich history. Countless world travelers, particularly mountain enthusiasts, rightly proclaim it to be without equal or comparison. If you are a hiker, miles and miles of trails from easy to strenuous will lead you into the heart of its wildness. Tuolumne Meadows, elevation 8600 feet, is just a short drive from Tioga Pass, the eastern entrance to the Park on Highway 120. Once you have seen its grandeur, you'll want to visit again and again.

By no means do you have to hike to enjoy this endless landscape of immense granite domes, clusters of jagged peaks, sparkling lakes, snow-clad mountain tops, tumbling streams and virgin forests. However, hitting the trail certainly allows you to experience it more intimately and to taste "the tonic of the wilderness." In whatever way you choose to view this wonderland, you'll realize that no words can adequately describe it; you simply have to see to believe.

As unsurpassingly gorgeous and commanding of our senses as this spot is, its history merits our attention, too. Archaeologists have learned from prehistoric living sites that on the western and eastern side of the Sierra Crest, trade goods were exchanged back and forth over the mountains for about 9600 years. In spite of a succession of ice ages, this transmontane "highway" never completely disappeared. Until the late 1800s a lively trade took place through Tuolumne Meadows along a route known as the Mono Trail, between the Miwoks of Yosemite and the foothills and the Northern Paiutes in Mono Basin. Their trade alliances lasted for many centuries, even though their cultures and languages were very different. From the east side, via Bloody Canyon, came such commodities as pine nuts, salt, baskets, tobacco, rabbit and buffalo robes and the highly prized obsidian from the Mono Craters volcanic area. From the west flowed acorns, paint ingredients, bear skins, beads, baskets, arrows and shell ornaments, the latter from trade with coastal tribes.

The Yosemite and Mono peoples met each year in Tuolumne Meadows during a late summer celebration to trade their goods, renew friendships, exchange ideas and occasionally arrange marriages. Sadly, by 1900 these annual meetings ended because so few Yosemites were left to pack their wares to the rendezvous, and the remaining survivors had little need for obsidian. Until the 1920s the Mono still used acorns but had to make the long trek to Yosemite Valley themselves for the harvesting. In time, this yearly practice fell away, and 96 centuries of trade between east and west came to a close.

In a much different fashion, miners were instrumental in the history of Mono Pass. Following the killing of two prospectors in Yosemite Valley in May 1852, Lieutenant Tredwell Moore of the Mariposa Battalion was dispatched on a punitive mission to capture Chief Tenaya and his braves who had fled to the Mono Pass area. Lieutenant Moore was also on the lookout for signs of mineral deposits. He returned to Mariposa without Tenaya but with some promising ore samples, sparking a major movement of prospectors to the Sierra Crest. James Hutchings, famous for promoting Yosemite tourism, printed in his *California Magazine* the news of a gold discovery in the High Country and stirred up great interest among prospectors and tourists. After hearing the news, Tom McGee cleared a rough horse trail from Big Oak Flat to Cascade Creek on the western side of Yosemite Valley, through Tuolumne Meadows and up to Bloody Canyon on the Sierra Crest. This roughly followed the course of the ancient Mono Trail used by the Indians, the forerunner of the present-day Tioga Road.

By 1857 hordes of miners were swarming over the slopes east and west of the crest. By 1876 the Tioga Mining District encompassed a huge area from the base of Bloody Canyon on the east, over Mono Pass and down to Tuolumne Meadows on the west. The furious activity generated 350 mining locations in the District. The boom days lasted, as they did most everywhere, only a few years. By 1884 the vast majority of miners disappeared as the precious metal either eluded them or petered out. Of the numerous camps strewn throughout these high, isolated and windswept places, only a handful exist today as reminders of those exciting days.

■ THE HIKE

Should you be moved to see the remains of one of these camps, grab your boots and get on the Mono Pass Trail. This hike is not for couch potatoes. It is 8 miles round trip, reaching an elevation of 10,600 feet at Mono Pass. Even if you were unaware of its historical significance, the scenery is spectacular. The views constantly improve as you approach the crest. On the way you'll pass two spur trails, about a mile apart, on your right. Ignore them and stay left heading for the pass on the boundary between Yosemite Park and Ansel Adams Wilderness. At Mono Pass the vista down Bloody Canyon toward Mono Lake and the high desert of the east side is stunning.

When you stop at the pass for a rest and lunch, think about the naming of this canyon. The widely accepted story is that it derived from the blood of pack animals cut by sharp rocks as they struggled desperately through this treacherously narrow and steep gash in the earth. Now look to your right (southeast) to a sandy bench dotted with whitebark pines. You'll spot a trail leading from Summit Lake to the remains of four log cabins about 300 yards away that were made from whitebark pines, once the homes of workers at the nearby Golden Crown and Ella Bloss mines. It's worth the five-minute walk to inspect them at close range and imagine what their lives might have been like.

It seems curious that most miners paid so little attention to the fantastic beauty of their surroundings. Historical documents from those days make scant reference to the area aside from their narrow focus on mineral deposits. As you gaze out one of the cabin's window openings, remember that the route you've driven and walked today keeps alive 9600 years of human traffic in this remote location. Perhaps the echoes in the wind will allow you to see Indians walking by, hauling trade goods in colorful baskets, or hear the rowdy shouts of the miners or smell the sweat and leather from pack animals laboring through Bloody Canyon. You might even find obsidian pieces along the trail. For a few moments, Mono Pass' faded history might come alive for you.

For the best views, don't turn back when you reach the Mono Pass sign. Continue a few minutes past the summit for vistas of Mono Lake and the surrounding desert. If you really feel energetic, hike .75 mile down to gorgeous Upper Sardine Lake.

We're fortunate to have an area of such outstanding scenery where we can still experience first-hand the remnants of the old days that are all around us in the Sierra Nevada Mountains. At Mono Pass, as everywhere else you visit, please make sure the only things you take are memories and all you leave behind are your footprints, and even then, walk softly.

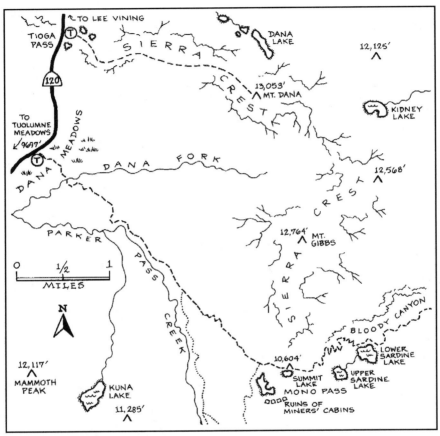

Chapters 42 and 43

43
The Mount Dana Experience
Ascending to Heaven's Gate on the Sierra Crest

■ THE DETAILS

Getting There: Drive Highway 120, Tioga Road, to Tioga Pass and park near the entrance station.

Nearest Campgrounds: Tioga Lake Campground, one mile east, has 13 sites, while Ellery Lake 2 miles east has 14 sites, both open June through September. If those are full, you'll find 200 more sites in several campgrounds in the 11 miles east toward Lee Vining down on Highway 395. All these campgrounds operate on a first-come, first-served basis.

Lodging: Tuolumne Meadows Lodge has tent cabins in summer. Call 559-252-4848 for tent cabin availability and all Yosemite Park lodging.

Further Info: Yosemite National Park 209-372-0200. Mono Basin Ranger Station, Inyo National Forest, Box 429, Lee Vining, CA 93541, 760-647-3000.

Hike Distance: 5.8 miles round trip.

Difficulty: Very strenuous.

Facilities: Restrooms are nearby.

Best Time to Go: Summer, early autumn.

Cautions: Abandon plans to summit if thunderstorms approach.

Starting Elevation: 9945 feet. Gain to summit: 3110 feet.

Map: See Chapter 42, page 232.

Other Maps: USGS Tioga Pass and Mount Dana 7.5 minute topos.

Trekking to the top of Mount Dana is more than just another High Country hike. It's a formidable journey with enormous contrasts, offering unlimited Western and Eastern Sierra views beyond description, while closer to earth, resplendent masses of wildflowers provide a crash course in alpine flora. Scraping the sky immediately east of Tioga Pass, Mount Dana, elevation 13,053 feet, is the second highest peak in Yosemite National Park. Only Mount Lyell, a mere 60 feet higher, surpasses Dana's cone-shaped, reddish brown summit in height. Dana offers a superb opportunity to bag a peak without requiring any technical mountaineering skills.

The south face of Mount Dana, Yosemite's second highest peak at 13,053 feet.

Going the distance to Mount Dana's summit is definitely not for uncondi-tioned walkers. The trail gains a whopping 3110 feet in slightly less than 3 miles. Fortunately, you needn't reach the summit to receive rich rewards from this hike. No matter where you stop, you will have experienced some of the most awesome beauty in the West. With each step upward, the vistas increase and expand, almost to the point of sensory overload. From the top, the 360-degree panorama embraces the entire Mono Basin, Wheeler Crest 40 miles to the southeast, the mystical White Mountains, Saddlebag Lake hinterlands with sawtooth crags rim-ming them, Tuolumne Meadows, the Cathedral Range and Mount Lyell.

The rarefied air and steep trail encourage us to proceed slowly. A leisurely pace allows time to marvel at an incredible world of diminutive alpine flowers blooming their hearts out at our feet. In the Mount Dana environs, nearly 170 species of wildflowers, grasses, and sedges thrive in this seemingly sterile, stark and rocky landscape. Between mid-July and September, the flower pageant above timberline rivals any in the Sierra Nevada.

Centuries before the footprints of explorers, scientists, shepherds, miners, mountaineers and hikers marked this region, Native American hunters scaled Yosemite's peaks in search of bear and bighorn sheep. Others sought spiritual enlightenment through vision quests, and shamans believed their powers were strengthened by spending time on mountain tops.

The first recorded ascent of Dana occurred on June 28, 1863, by two members of the California State Geological Survey headed by Josiah Whitney. Geologist William Brewer, Whitney's right-hand man, and Charles Hoffman, topographer and artist, named the peak in honor of James Dwight Dana, foremost geologist of the era. Brewer's trip diary indicates that they "were up very early . . . and made the summit in 4 hours. So up by 10 a.m. and stayed nearly 4 hours" taking bearings and barometric readings. At the time, Dana was believed to be the highest mountain in California. Brewer was impressed by the forever views and "scenes of wildest mountain desolation and Mono Lake at our feet. It is not often that a man has the opportunity of attaining that height or of beholding such a scene." The following day he climbed Dana again, this time accompanied by Whitney, who exclaimed that the vista was the "grandest ever beheld" of all his worldly travels.

Six years later John Muir came to wander the wild, alpine realm of the Sierra. He began his exploration of every nook and cranny in the High Country, formulating his own ideas about glacial erosion and Yosemite's distant origin. Pompous Josiah Whitney, threatened by Muir's glacier theory, publicly denounced him as an "ignoramus . . . a mere shepherd." Finally in 1930, after decades of heated debates and exhaustive studies, Dr. Francois Matthes, eminent geologist and cartographer, validated the "ignorant shepherd's" theory.

In summer 1869 Muir climbed Mount Dana to trace the course of the Dana Glacier to where it converged with the Lyell Glacier and gouged out Tuolumne Meadows. While in the meadows on August 26, 1869, he witnessed the ethereal phenomenon of alpenglow spreading its rosy fire over Mount Dana. It was here that Muir gave the Sierra Nevada its other name: "Well may the Sierra be named, not the Snowy Range, but The Range of Light."

Mount Dana, along with other peaks in the vicinity, swarmed with miners for a few hectic years between 1877 and 1890. By 1878 the Tioga Mining District, boasting 350 claims, covered an area extending eight miles north and south along the crest, down into Bloody Canyon, and along the Dana Fork of the Tuolumne River. Although virtually nothing remains to tell the tale of these scattered, isolated mining camps on the slopes of Dana, Kuna Peak, Gibbs, and White Mountain, because of their remoteness it is indeed startling and unexpected to come upon a few weathered boards, a tailings dump near a partially collapsed tunnel, rusty square nails, or a rock foundation. Particularly puzzling to the unknowing hiker are the quite tall stumps of whitebark pines, sawed when the snowpack was deep. Should you find any artifacts, look but let them remain.

■ THE HIKE

Unsigned Mount Dana trail begins directly across from the Tioga Pass entrance gate on the south side of the road. Don't attempt this hike if the weather looks ominous. Severe thunderstorms at this elevation occur frequently in summer. If you're en route and the sky appears threatening, turn back immediately.

Before setting out, check with the ranger on duty for the current weather report and trail conditions. Mid-July to early October are the best months for the trek to Dana. Be sure to bring a map to identify the dozens of mountains and jewel-like lakes. Start early in the day, and plan to be off the mountain by mid-afternoon. Depending on the amount of snowpack, be aware that the trail may have snowy or icy stretches well into summer.

The trail is one of use and not officially maintained by the Park Service. Please stay on the path. Although it may not seem so, this is a very sensitive environment. The route was laid out many years ago by Dr. Carl Sharsmith. Dr. Sharsmith was a celebrated ranger-naturalist in Yosemite's High Country for 63 years, as well as a renowned alpine botanist. The path over the final, rocky mile below the summit is rather ill-defined. However, Dr. Sharsmith cleverly and subtly marked the way by painting orange-yellow splotches on the rocks to resemble lichens.

The trail starts out deceivingly gentle, meandering by two small lakes in a park-like setting and passing through riots of wildflowers in Dana Meadows. During years of plentiful moisture, the rich blue lupine and royal purple larkspur often stand six feet tall. Other species, too, attain almost unbelievable heights in this lush, wet arena. Not far beyond the ponds, the footpath begins to hint of the steepness ahead, and within .5 mile of the trailhead the gradient increases sharply. The landscape teems with brilliant wildflowers, and sparkling creeks tumble merrily through grassy meadows. As you start up a moraine, watch on your left for a carving of a female figure facing upslope on a lodgepole pine trunk. More than a century ago some lonely Basque shepherd created the artwork, reminding us of a time when alpine grasslands were thick with sheep.

The view-packed ascent becomes more demanding as you reach timberline near 11,000 feet. Rocky, arid slopes replace the lusher, subalpine environment. Keep your pace slow and steady, pausing when you need to catch your breath. Note a three-foot tall rock cairn when you arrive at a broad plateau. Here, the more or less defined trail ends. Be alert for the orange paint splotches here and there on the rocks, pointing the way to the summit.

The plateau offers a good place for a longer break to take in the ever-widening panorama. The luxuriant flower growth on the lower slopes gives way to Lilliputian-like alpine gravel gardens. These cheerful miniature flowers, many a mere inch high, bloom briefly in this harsh land. Their low profile enables them to survive extreme winter conditions and brutal, high-elevation winds. Be careful where you walk. Some of these tenacious little plants have waited 20 years to blossom. Your hiking boots could easily end their glorious moment in the sun.

From the plateau, a tough 1000 feet below the summit, you'll spot a few paths angling east (left) toward a ridge. Follow the most conspicuous one to a saddle around 12,150 feet. When you gain the saddle, ascend along a rocky ridge to Dana's summit. Somewhere along the jagged upthrust, take a well-deserved breather to gaze at Glacier Canyon and the milky, turquoise waters of Dana Lake 2000 feet below. The glacier remnant hugging the sheer north wall dates back to the Little Ice Age which ended about 1800 A.D.

Unless the weather is deteriorating, spend ample time on the peak absorbing the incomparable vistas. Dana's final flowery gift to those who summit is the sky pilot (*Polemonium eximium*), named for a slang term meaning one who leads others to heaven. Aptly named, the rather large, lavender blue blossoms are found only on or near the tops of the highest mountains.

Although the hike down is easier on the cardiovascular system, don't be in a rush. The return trip will take its toll on your knees and thighs. With so much to see, an unhurried pace has great advantages. After a journey to Dana's lofty heights, you'll most certainly relate to a passionately held sentiment of John Muir: "In God's wildness lies the hope of the world—the great fresh, unblighted, unredeemed wilderness. The galling harness of civilization drops off, and the wounds heal before we are aware."

V
Birthed in Fire, Sculpted by Ice
🐻 THE EASTERN SIERRA 🐻

THE EASTERN SIERRA NEVADA is a vast land of extreme contrasts and dramatic, stunning scenery. The landscape is birthed in fire and sculpted by ice, with few places like it on this earth. Fascinated by its violent, volcanic origin and stark splendor, John Muir described it as, "Hot deserts bounded by snow-laden mountains, cinders and ashes scattered on glacier polished pavements, frost and fire working together in the making of beauty."

The Eastern Sierra, of course, encompasses the sunrise side of the entire 400-mile length of the Sierra Nevada, but the eastern quintessence of this "Range of Light" lies in the 125-mile stretch between Yosemite Park and Mount Whitney. Compared to the gentle upward rise on the western slope, the eastern escarpments are abruptly steep; only a few thousand feet separate crest from valley.

The seaward side receives more rain, is dense with vegetation and blessed with large rivers. In contrast, its eastern counterpart captures little moisture, has few and scattered forests with scanty undergrowth and small streams. The sparseness of vegetation allows the eye endless and unrestricted horizons. Truly, on a clear day you can see forever.

Stunning canyons carved by water and ice deeply gash the massive ramparts of the Eastern Sierra. Driving Highway 395, which follows the entire base of the Eastern Sierra, one can hardly imagine the lushness of these profound glacial troughs, home to sparkling streams, flowery meadows, chains of lakes, pine and aspen forests and a wide variety of animal life. Such exquisite alpine scenery in this highest and wildest part of the range is startling in comparison to the subtle tones and austere mood of the high desert environment along Highway 395.

The Eastern Sierra Nevada features a powerful, extraordinary landscape, one you're not likely to forget and certainly one you'll want to return to. One trip just isn't enough to absorb its many facets.

Donald Peattie gives a vivid snapshot of this vast and timeless land in *A Natural History of Western Trees*. "The eastern face of this range . . . forms, in places, one of the steepest, swiftest descents—almost a downward plunge—of the planet's surface. It faces the desert, and its slopes are arid. At first this side of the Sierra appears much less hospitable and charming, and it is certainly less accessible. But in time one comes to have a special affection for its dramatic scenery, for its pure, cold lakes so secretively concealed, for the bracing dryness of its air, for its greater wildness and lack of milling throngs of our fellow humans."

44
Bennettville & the History of Tioga Road
The Road to Broken Dreams

■ THE DETAILS

Getting There: Head for Tioga Pass on Highway 120 via the east from Highway 395 at Lee Vining or from the west through Yosemite National Park. The Bennettville area lies just outside the park boundary .9 mile east of the Tioga Pass entrance station. The signed trailhead on the left can be identified by a rusty piece of mining equipment. Park near the boulder-blocked old road.

Nearest Campgrounds: See Chapter 43.

Lodging: The closest services are at Tioga Pass Resort, 2 miles east of the entrance station on Highway 120. Housekeeping cabins, a store, a good restaurant and gas are available. Phone 209-372-4471 or write Post Office Box 7, Lee Vining, CA 93541. Lee Vining, 12 miles east of the entrance station, is a full service small town with several motels.

Further Info: Mono Basin Ranger Station, Inyo National Forest, Box 429, Lee Vining, CA 93541, 760-647-3044.

Hike Distance: 2.2 miles round trip to Bennettville, 4.2 to Fantail Lake.

Difficulty: Easy.

Best Time to Go: Summer, autumn.

Cautions: Stay out of the dangerous mine tunnel. Leave all artifacts where you find them.

Starting Elevation: 9550 feet. Gain to Bennettville: 250 feet.

Other Map: USGS Tioga Pass 7.5 minute topo.

The Road to Broken Dreams. That's what someone once called the Great Sierra Wagon Road, now the portion of Highway 120 over Tioga Pass in Yosemite's High Country, and what a sweet dream it was. However, like most dreams of men hell-bent in pursuit of precious metals, it was short-lived.

The road pierced like a dagger through the heart of this untouched wilderness, terminating on the western side at Crocker's Station east of Groveland. From there the road ran east to Bennettville east of Tioga Pass. The Great Sierra Wagon Road, an epic example of road construction in the West, was built solely to reach the mining camps in the alpine region of Tioga Hill. It had nothing to do

Bennettville in 1898, 14 years after its abandonment when the Sheepherder Mine failed to yield any silver.

with opening the High Country for the convenience of travelers or promoting its unrivaled scenic beauty. Sheer economics prompted the Great Sierra Consolidated Silver Company to punch a road through incredibly rugged terrain to service its mining operations and transport ore to market.

The Great Sierra Wagon Road was built in the phenomenally short time of 130 days without accidents or loss of life. Between April 17 and September 4, 1883, 160 Chinese and white laborers, using only hand tools and dynamite, completed the 56.5-mile project. Elevations ranged between 4200 feet at Crocker's Station and nearly 10,000 feet at Tioga Pass. If you have driven Highway 120 to the crest, surely you'll be impressed that such a feat was accomplished so rapidly, especially 118 years ago without modern equipment.

Just ten months after the road was finished, the Great Sierra Consolidated Silver Company ran out of cash, and the stockholders refused them more money. The company spent $300,000, then a king's ransom, for road building and mine development, but no silver was ever extracted. On July 3, 1884, the mine superintendent received orders to shut down all operations at Bennettville and nearby Dana City. Unemployed miners wandered off to other strikes, and by 1888, all properties, including the road, were sold at public auction.

What happened to these men with such great expectations and staunch belief in the mother lode of silver at Tioga? How did they happen to find this remote and unexplored location on the Sierra Crest? Why did their dreams melt away like spring snow?

By no means does the tale of Tioga Pass begin with the miners. Centuries before white men arrived in this wilderness, Native Americans from the eastern and western sides of the Sierra exchanged trade goods. For 9600 years the Mono and Yosemite Indians used a transmontane route between the Mono Lake environs and Yosemite Valley. Present-day Tioga Road, formerly the Great Sierra Wagon Road, roughly follows that ancient Mono Trail. In 1833 explorer Joseph Walker became the first white man to travel the Mono Trail. We have no accounts of other white men in the region until 19 years later.

In 1852 Lieutenant Tredwell Moore of the Mariposa Battalion used the trail in pursuit of a band of Indians who supposedly killed two prospectors in Yosemite Valley. Moore didn't find them, but he returned to Mariposa with some rich-looking ore samples. His specimens kindled much interest, but no immediate rush followed. By the late 1850s when the easy pickings in the western foothills petered out, miners began prospecting in the higher, more isolated places.

In 1860 a group of five men set out to poke around for gold in the Tioga Pass area before heading east to the latest boomtown, Aurora, Nevada. They found no gold, but one of the characters, Doc Chase, had a feeling that there was a "thundering big ledge of silver" on Tioga Hill. In a lather to get to the hot strikes at Aurora, he scratched out a claim on a tin can, stuffed it between two rocks and lit out for their planned destination. Why he never returned is a mystery.

Fifteen years later a young shepherd, William Brusky, found the rusty tin can. Believing he had found the "lost" mine, he took some ore samples to his father who told him to forget the worthless rocks and stick to herding sheep. However, Brusky persevered, and the following year had the samples assayed. The results proved that the ore was indeed thundering rich in silver. Not surprisingly, the word spread like greased lightning, and miners stampeded to the scene. By 1878 the Tioga Mining District was humming with the activity of over 300 claims on record.

On the other side of Tioga Hill, parallel to Brusky's Sheepherder Claim, another ledge of silver called the Great Sierra was discovered. Financed by $8 million worth of shares in 1878, the Sheepherder, Great Sierra and many smaller claims were purchased and combined by the Great Sierra Consolidated Silver Company. Mining experts agreed that a tunnel had to be drilled into Tioga Hill from the Sheepherder lode at Bennettville. Simultaneously, men over the hill at Dana City were to sink a vertical shaft which was to meet the tunnel. The theory was that the tunnel would hit the two lodes at right angles, thus enlarging the layers of greatest richness.

Two rough-and-ready settlements sprouted at the mining sites. A post office at the "city" of Dana was established in 1880 and then another at Bennettville in 1882. Bennettville was company headquarters and connected to civilization by the world's highest telephone line, as it was touted, to the town of Lundy ten miles north.

Actual work began in February 1882 with three shifts of miners working around the clock. Very soon it became obvious that hand-drilling methods were impotent against the unusual hardness of rock they encountered. Heavy drilling machinery and air compressors were needed to penetrate. At that time the mines were only accessible by trails from Lundy and Mono Pass. As you can imagine, hauling tons of supplies and equipment on the backs of men and animals at elevations of 10,000 feet and higher was punishing, grueling labor. Avalanches, 100 mile per hour winds, months of brutally cold weather and precipitous trails caused great suffering and loss of life. A road had to be built immediately to get supplies and equipment in and to get ore out. An eastern engineer, Charles Barney, headed the task, assisted by William Priest, engineer of the famous Priest's Grade on the Old Big Oak Flat Road. What an amazing job they did—56.5 miles in 130 days.

By summer 1884 almost 1800 feet of tunnel had been bored into the mountain at Bennettville and 100 feet driven vertically from Dana City, but not a speck of silver was brought out. The stockholders were getting jittery. Drilling progressed at a snail's pace. Only 23 feet per week was achieved in this ultra-dense rock. Highly competent mining experts were convinced that in another 200 feet they would strike the lodes. Time, just a little more time, was all they needed, but the clock had run out. For Thomas Bennett, Joseph Parker and the Swift brothers, who were the prime movers of this monumental venture, the project had become a nightmare. The company went belly-up, suspending work on July 3, 1884.

Within three months Bennettville and Dana City joined the ranks of mining camp ghost towns. As a consequence, the Great Sierra Wagon Road was abandoned and fell into serious disrepair until Stephen Mather, first director of the National Park Service, purchased it in 1915 for $15,500 and deeded it to Yosemite National Park. With the additional 11 miles completed to Lee Vining on the shore of Mono Lake, an unimaginably scenic, trans-Sierra route opened to travelers. Over the years the Tioga Road was extensively rehabilitated, realigned and paved to its current course and condition.

■ THE HIKE

Many motorists have driven the Tioga Road unaware of the human drama involved in its construction. Still more are unaware that you can actually walk a segment of the original track, "the road to broken dreams." On a short and easy walk you can see for yourself the mine and the town that started it all. To do so, find the dirt road across from Tioga Lake that's blocked by boulders. A piece of mining equipment and a wooden sign point the way. Bring your camera—the region is remarkably photogenic. Park your car by the boulders and walk up the obvious dirt road about one mile to Bennettville. Of the dozen or so buildings, only the assay office and two-story barn/stable remain. Carefully cross the lively, shallow stream to investigate the buildings. The wood has weathered to a lovely cinnamon brown color. While you're wandering around, a little imagination will reveal where other buildings once stood. Sparkling Mine Creek lends a special charm as it chatters and rushes by.

The Sheepherder Mine area above the ghost town is worth exploring, but you

At the Bennettville site today, only two buildings remain as a reminder of an exciting moment in Central Sierra history.

should NOT enter the tunnel because of unhealthy gas and other lurking dangers. As you overlook the ruins of Bennettville, thank your Higher Power that it never reached its projected population of 50,000! Had silver been discovered, the requirements for firewood and lumber for mine shafts and buildings would have been the death knell for the virgin forest you see spreading before you and as far away as Tuolumne Meadows. At this lofty elevation, Mother Nature's healing occurs slowly; tracks of the Great Sierra Wagon Road are still visible through the meadow. However, except for the tunnel site, the landscape is much the same as it was before the miners came. The abundance of wildflowers and other living things owe their lives to the absence of those multitudes.

If you want to extend your hike, follow Mine Creek upstream for .4 mile to pretty Shell Lake. You can continue up the trailless creek to a small unnamed lake around .7 mile or to Fantail Lake, the largest of the three, at one mile, about 100 feet higher in elevation than Bennettville. Note that you can also hike to Bennettville via a trail from site #1 at Junction Campground.

Bennett, Parker and Swift went to their graves bitter and disappointed, believing to their last breath in a vast fortune locked away in Tioga. Although never fully utilized for its intended purpose, the Great Sierra Wagon Road amounted to an extraordinary and priceless legacy for future generations. Financially, the "road to broken dreams" was a disaster. However, if wealth can be measured in terms of exquisite alpine scenery, solitude and sweeping panoramas, then the road succeeded by making it possible for all of us to share in the treasures of Tioga Pass.

The Tioga Road provides access to some of the most stunning vistas in the western United States. Whether you drive through it or, better yet, get your feet on its trails, spending some time in Yosemite's High Country will satisfy a deep longing most of us have for contact with wild places. After a day in this timberline atmosphere perhaps you'll relate to the sentiments of Thoreau: "There's something in the mountain air that feeds the spirit and inspires."

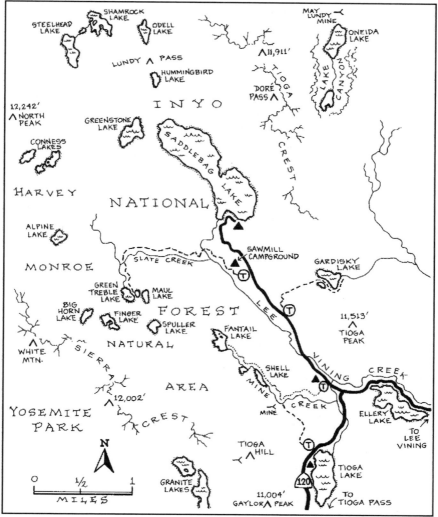

Chapters 44, 45 and 46

45
Gardisky Lake & Tioga Crest
A Timberline Trek

■ THE DETAILS

Getting There: Drive Highway 120 for 2 miles east from Tioga Pass entrance station, or 11 miles west from Lee Vining, then turn north on Saddlebag Lake Road and go almost 1.1 miles to trailhead on right.

Nearest Campgrounds: Saddlebag Lake Campground one mile up the road has 20 sites with piped water, open July through September. Junction Campground near the Highway 120 junction has 13 sites open June to October.

Lodging: Tioga Pass Resort, on Highway 120 near Saddlebag Lake Road, has housekeeping cabins, a store, a good restaurant and gas available. Phone 209-372-4471 or write Post Office Box 7, Lee Vining, CA 93541. Lee Vining, 12 miles east of the entrance station, has several motels.

Further Info: Inyo National Forest Mono Lake Ranger District 760-647-3044.

Hike Distance: 2 miles round trip to Gardisky Lake. Add .5 mile to Eastern Sierra vista, 1.2 miles to Tioga Peak, one mile to Tioga Crest saddle, or 4.9 miles to Doré Pass, all mileages round trip.

Difficulty: Steep and strenuous.

Best Time to Go: Summer.

Cautions: None.

Starting Elevation: 9720 feet. Gain to Gardisky Lake: 760 feet, to Tioga Peak: 1810 feet.

Map: See Chapter 44, page 245.

Other Maps: USGS Tioga Pass and Mount Dana 7.5 minute topos.

Speaking about the High Sierra, Mark Twain remarked, "The air up there is very fine and pure, bracing and delicious. And why shouldn't it be? It's the air that angels breathe." As I paused on the steep path to Gardisky Lake and gazed westward toward the Sierra Crest, Twain's observations rang so very true. I gazed at an incredibly spectacular view, one guaranteed to stop you in your tracks be it your first or fiftieth visit.

Back-dropped by sky the color of sapphires, enormous flocks of snow-white clouds hovered above a canopy of craggy peaks. Sprawled below, offering 3883 acres of lightly used wilderness, lay the majestic setting of Hall Natural Area (see Chapter 46). The air itself felt alive and breathing, and it wasn't much of a stretch to believe that I walked in the realm of angels.

Located just beneath Tioga Crest in Inyo National Forest between Hall Natural Area and Hoover Wilderness, Gardisky Lake nestles in a large, flower-filled meadow. Before Yosemite Park's reduction in size in 1906, the lake was near the Park's eastern boundary between 1890 and 1905. Despite its high elevation niche, the broad ridgetop basin hosts an astonishing wildflower display in late July and August. In hues ranging from delicate pink to magenta to lavender, baby elephant heads, heather, wild onions and irises grow profusely in this bouldery, alpine meadow.

■ THE HIKE

Though not far from civilization, casual hikers don't frequent Gardisky because of the stiff though short climb up to it. The trail starts along Saddlebag Lake Road at 9720 feet and ascends unmercifully to the pristine lake at 10,483 feet. Thanks in part to strenuous and/or lengthy access routes, much of this High Country remains out of reach to most mountain visitors.

You may need to stop a few times along the precipitous trail in this oxygen-scarce environment. Besides catching your breath, you'll have repeated opportunities to marvel at the sky-kissing peaks of the Sierra Crest soaring above Lee Vining Creek. The higher you climb, the better the vistas. Prominent on the skyline are White Mountain (12,057 feet) and Mount Conness (12,590 feet). Mount Conness, named for Senator John Conness who introduced legislation in 1864 that preserved Yosemite Valley and Mariposa Grove of Big Trees as a State Park, has one of the largest of the few remaining glaciers in the Sierra Nevada.

Near timberline the gradient eases considerably. Past a clutch of stunted whitebark pines lining a flowery meadow, the trail flattens out. Take a few minutes to examine the small, shallow ponds below the lake. Their bottoms are comprised of polygon-shaped rocks seldom encountered in high-elevation metamorphic terrain. The trail peters out as you near Gardisky Lake, named for a Russian immigrant who settled at Tioga Pass circa 1914. Stay slightly to the left of the tarns to reach the lake in about 200 yards.

For a rare, eye-popping sight, circle the lake's treeless landscape to its eastern outlet on a path made by the occasional angler in search of brook trout. You'll have to bushwhack a bit around a thicket of willows to get there, but you'll be glad you did. From this virtually unknown vantage point, where the stream dives over the edge, you have a dizzying glimpse straight down the cliff to Tioga Road (Highway 120), the huge V-shaped trough of Lee Vining Canyon, Mono Lake Basin, and the faraway White Mountains shimmering on the horizon. If you crave big views, big silences, and little human presence, it doesn't get much better than this. Find a spot on the brink of this high tundra meadow and break out the trail snacks.

You can retrace your steps to the trailhead after a rest at the lake, but if you're game to explore more such heavenly scenery, consider some wonderful options to extend your visit. If you'd like to bag a peak, with absolutely no technical skills required, a moderate ascent to the obvious summit of nearby Tioga Peak (11,513 feet) .4 mile south of Gardisky Lake provides more world class vistas. Whoever climbs Sierra summits will understand why shamans and prophets have always sought mountaintops to commune with their gods.

Another intoxicating High Country excursion from Gardisky is a cross country jaunt north to Tioga Crest, also .4 mile from the lake. To visit it, ascend due north toward the saddle above Gardisky Lake. Wildflower enthusiasts will find some rare plant species thriving in these windswept habitats. From the saddle you can easily follow Tioga Crest west and north toward Doré Pass, 2.25 miles from Gardisky Lake. If you do, be on the lookout for the inch tall alpine (snow) willow near Doré Pass, named for Paul Gustave Doré, a famous French artist. The United States Geological Survey in 1882 also named Doré Cliff, a formidable rock wall more than 1000 feet high north of the pass, in his honor.

Best left to another outing unless you're a very vigorous High Country hiker and have a shuttle vehicle in Lundy Canyon to the north, a view-packed sojourn over Doré Pass leads steeply down to Lake Canyon and the ruins of the rich May Lundy Mine and its tiny community. Eight tons of machinery were hauled over this 11,320-foot pass by sled from Lundy Canyon (see Chapter 47) up through Lake Canyon to the Tioga Mine (aka "The Sheepherder" or "Great Sierra") at Bennettville (see Chapter 44) during the fierce winter of 1882.

Most likely, though, after reaching the austere, rocky environs of Dore Pass you'll opt to retrace your steps to the trailhead via Gardisky Lake. Well-conditioned walkers might consider descending southwest toward large (340 acres) Saddlebag Lake, a trailless descent basically following the line of least resistance back to the car on Saddlebag Lake Road.

While hiking in the mountains, High Country in particular, I invariably mourn the lack of blank spaces on a map, longing for the surprise of primeval landscapes and the mystery of unnamed rivers and passes. When in this mood, I admit to whining that the only unexplored region in the Sierra Nevada seems to be the space between my ears.

I eventually take heart in knowing that I can pretend to be the first person to leave footprints where none have ever been. In a real sense, I am a pioneer voyager simply because the experience is new to me. Perhaps John Muir's eloquent language best describes the heady views from Tioga Crest and my sense of place in the Sierra Nevada, my spiritual home. "In the midst of such scenery, the day seems endless, the sun stands still."

In the final analysis, it's really unimportant that others have witnessed these wondrous sights before me. What matters is that today, at this very moment in time, I own them because they're virgin vistas to me.

46
Green Treble Lake & Hall Natural Area
Satisfaction in Wilderness Preserved

■ THE DETAILS

Getting There: From Highway 120, 2.1 miles east of Tioga Pass entrance station (11 miles west of Lee Vining), turn north onto signed Saddlebag Lake Road. Drive 1.5 miles to a sign indicating Sawmill Walk-ln Campground and park.

Nearest Campgrounds: Sawmill Walk-In Campground has 12 sites. Junction Campground near Highway 120 junction has 13 sites. Saddlebag Lake Campground has 20 sites with piped water. All are first-come, first-served.

Lodging: Tioga Pass Resort, on Highway 120 near the junction with Saddlebag Lake Road, has housekeeping cabins, store, good restaurant and gas available. Phone 209-372-4471 or write P.O. Box 7, Lee Vining, CA 93541. Lee Vining 11 miles east has several motels.

Further Info: Inyo National Forest, Mono Lake Ranger Station, Box 429, Lee Vining, CA 93541, 760-647-3044.

Hike Distance: 4.6 miles round trip to Green Treble Lake from parking area, 4 miles from Sawmill Camp. About 5.2 miles to Alpine Lake.

Difficulty: Moderate.

Best Time to Go: Mid-summer, autumn.

Cautions: No camping or fires allowed in Hall RNA.

Starting Elevation: 9780 feet at Sawmill Camp parking area, 9720 at camp. Gain to Green Treble and Maul lakes: 500 feet. Gain to Alpine Lake: 1330 feet.

Map: See Chapter 44 page 245.

Other Maps: USGS Tioga Pass 7.5 minute topo Wilderness Press *Tuolumne Meadows* 15 minute topo.

Tucked between Yosemite National Park and Hoover Wilderness, Harvey Monroe Hall Research Natural Area embraces 3883 acres of rugged subalpine and alpine territory lying completely within the steep eastern escarpment below the Sierra Crest. Elevations range from 9800 feet at Slate Creek to the 12,590-foot summit of Mount Conness. With 15 crystalline lakes, three active glaciers on the north faces of White Mountain, North Peak and Mount Conness, 350 species of flowering plants and ferns, heavenly timberline scenery, boisterous streams, a variety of animal life, solitude and important history, HNA is a must for High Country hikers.

Research natural areas were designed "to preserve natural conditions virtually free from disturbances excepting those necessary in the prosecution of scientific research." Essentially, these areas may be used only for study, observation, monitoring, and on-site educational activities. Under certain restrictions, they also serve the general public, as does Hall Natural Area (HNA).

Surprisingly, few people roam this alpine wonderland adjacent to Yosemite. Personnel for Inyo National Forest, managers of HNA, state that despite easy public access and great scenery, visitor use is light. Especially unfrequented is Slate Creek Valley in the east-central region. You won't find Slate Creek named on any map, but its headwaters are in the Green Treble Lake area. You'll find this pristine preserve only 1.5 miles from Highway 120 via Saddlebag Lake Road.

Besides lack of publicity, another reason for the absence of crowds is that Hall Natural Area has no officially maintained trails. The indistinct paths are few and far between and not indicated on topographic or Forest Service maps. Cross-country rambling in HNA, although easy, seems to discourage the majority of casual visitors. Penetrating a wilderness without the supposed security of a signed, obvious route can be a daunting experience to a novice hiker. Moreover, backpacking is not allowed. The area is for day use only, and no fires are permitted.

Credit for the protection of nearly 4000 acres of sublime, Eastern Sierra backcountry goes to Dr. Harvey Monroe Hall, a distinguished botanist at the University of California, Berkeley, and Carnegie Institute's Department of Biology at Stanford University. Of all his far-sighted and pioneering projects, perhaps the most significant was the establishment of "natural reservations," areas permanently set aside for the preservation of plant and animal life.

For 30 years, Hall observed with increasing alarm human encroachment upon the most pristine, remote mountain sanctuaries. He concluded that some parts of the American wilderness must be conserved in their natural states for future scientific study while some portions of these living laboratories should be available, if possible, to the public for low-impact recreation.

Dr. Hall's principal interests were improving methods of plant classification and their environmental adaptability. As early as 1902, he began exploratory excursions in the Tuolumne Meadows region of Yosemite Park searching for a locale to conduct experiments in alpine and subalpine life zones. His forays eventually led him to the Slate Creek drainage outside of Yosemite several miles northeast of Tioga Pass.

Impressed by Slate Creek Valley's rich biodiversity and varied geology and topography, Hall found this locale unexcelled for studying the effect of extreme climate on native flora. Ultimately, in 1933, because of his pioneer heredity and environmental studies in the region and his international reputation, the U.S. Forest Service designated this vast tract of land as a research natural area in perpetuity. Named in his honor the year following his death, Hall Natural Area was one of the first established in the United States. Today, there are more than 300 research natural areas nationwide.

Still standing and being considered for listing on the National Register of Historic Places is Timberline Station, established 1929. On 26.7 acres near Slate Creek at the eastern boundary of HNA, the experimental field station had two transplant gardens, a cabin, outhouse and a garage-storage shed. A one-mile spur road connected it to Saddlebag Lake Road. Timberline Station coordinated botanical research with sister stations at Mather (near Hetch Hetchy) and Stanford to study the heredity and environmental mechanisms of wild plants at different elevations. Several smaller transplant plots were between Snow Flat and Tioga Pass in Yosemite Park.

After Hall's death in 1932, Clausen, Keck and Hiesey of Carnegie Institute carried on his work. The combined work of the four researchers still stands as "the basic reference on the effect of varied environments on western North American plants."

Although Timberline Station's most active period was in the 1930s, Carnegie Institute conducted research there until 1971. Carnegie hasn't used the facility since then, but maintains it and makes it available to other scientists and institutions. The transplant gardens have been abandoned, and the garage has been removed. Under a new agreement, the Forest Service no longer permits soil manipulation and exercises complete control over policy, research and access to HNA. A special-use permit allows Carnegie Institute continued use of Timberline and vehicle access on the spur road to maintain the property. HNA has been closed to all wheeled vehicles, including bicycles, since 1966. Should the facility be granted historic status, it will not be restored to its original condition. Rather, it will be managed with a "benign neglect" policy.

■ THE HIKES

To explore HNA, begin at Sawmill Walk-In Campground, .3 mile from Saddlebag Lake Road. (If you begin at the campground's parking area, add .6 mile to the total distance.) The camp's setting offers a spectacular overview of the natural area. Historically, it was the site of Martin's Sawmill between 1882 and 1884, which supplied lumber to the Great Sierra Mine at Bennettville. Sawmill Camp provides an ideal base for day hikes in HNA.

Walk through the camp on a closed road and follow it to Timberline Station near Slate Creek at one mile. Take note of but do not disturb the buildings and transplant gardens. From the station, choose where to ramble by studying the map. I suggest you hike upstream through the heart of Slate Creek Valley, veering left up the south fork to Green Treble Lake at the headwaters. Remember that neither the creek nor the valley is named on maps other than the one in this book.

Take care to ford the creek at the easiest and safest point. About .5 mile from Timberline, you'll find the confluence of two forks of the stream. The north fork comes down from below Alpine Lake. For Green Treble Lake, bear left (south) and ascend along the south fork .5 mile to reach Green Treble, elevation 10,217 feet. Nearby Maul Lake lies just a short walk to the east, a few minutes away. All of the lakes in HNA were named by Al Gardisky, pioneer settler and innkeeper at Tioga Pass in 1919. He built the existing store and restaurant there in 1920.

Filled with superb views of the Eastern Sierra ramparts, this moderate cross-country trek makes a beautiful journey. Forests of juniper, hemlock, white bark and lodgepole pine soften the starkness of bare granite and metamorphic rock. Despite the elevation, an astonishing profusion of wildflowers and plants thrives in moist niches near stream banks, rocky crevices and in many narrow meadows. Before retracing your steps, enjoy a trail lunch at one of the isolated cirque lakes.

If you have more than one day, a hike up the north fork of Slate Creek to remote Alpine Lake is a memorable experience. From Timberline Station, a vague path, generally on the north side of Slate Creek, leads to it.

Prior to the Euro-American invasion of the region surrounding HNA, the effects of 10,000 years of human activity weren't noticeable. Magnetized by the discovery of gold in Mono Lake Basin beginning in the 1860s, a torrent of miners and settlers rather quickly destroyed native culture and irrevocably altered the landscape.

That any wilderness remains is a miracle. If miners, road-builders, sheep and cattle ranchers, logging companies, hydroelectric developers and real estate speculators had had free rein, wild places might have vanished. Today's threat, ironically, comes from those who love it most: hikers, campers, backpackers and sports enthusiasts. Because wild beauty is a fragile thing and never completely safe, we must all learn to monitor our actions and be stewards of the earth.

Fortunately, individuals with great wisdom and vision recognized the danger signals and understood why wilderness must be preserved for reasons beyond beauty and recreation. Muir once said, "We all travel the Milky Way together." Our survival on the planet may hinge on our ability to co-exist with every other life form. Research natural areas contribute invaluable information about plants and animals of which we have only limited knowledge and whose long-range significance we have yet to discover.

Special thanks to Wally Woolfsenden, archeologist for Inyo National Forest, for the use of his HNA Management Policy report and comprehensive knowledge of the area.

47
The Allure of Lundy Canyon
Ore and Aspens Beneath the Sierra Crest

■ THE DETAILS

Getting There: From the junction of Highway 395 and Highway 167, 7 miles
north of Lee Vining, turn west onto signed, paved Lundy Lake Road and drive 5
miles into the mountains. To find the Lake Canyon trailhead, turn left on a spur
road just below the lake's outlet and drive .3 mile to the locked gate and
trailhead. To reach the upper Lundy Canyon trailhead, drive about 2 miles
farther up the main road to its end beyond the resort.

Nearest Campgrounds: Lundy Lake Resort has 35 sites with piped water open
April through October, while Lundy Creek Campground about 2 miles down
canyon has 54 sites and no water, open May through October.

Lodging: Lundy Lake Resort, Box 550, Lee Vining, CA 93541 (no phone) has
basic housekeeping cabins. In Lee Vining, try Best Western Lake View Lodge
760-647-6543 or Murphey's Motel 760-647-6316.

Further Info: Stop at the visitor information center in Lee Vining or at the Mono
Basin Visitor Center 760-647-3044 one mile north of town for maps, books,
displays and specific information.

Hike Distance: (all round trip) For Lake Canyon: 3 miles to canyon, 7 miles to
May Lundy Mine. For Lundy Canyon: 1.2 miles to Lower Lundy Falls, 3 miles
to cabin, 5 miles to base of Upper Lundy Falls.

Difficulty: Moderate to strenuous.

Best Time to Go: Summer for wildflowers, autumn for color.

Cautions: Leave mining relics and other historical artifacts where you find them.

Starting Elevation: 7800 feet for Lake Canyon Trail, 8200 for Lundy Canyon Trail.

Elevation Gain: 1900 feet to Oneida Lake, 100 feet to Lower Lundy Falls, 600 to
upper falls.

Other Maps: Inyo National Forest map, USGS Lundy, Mount Dana 7.5 minute
topos.

Cruising along Highway 395 below the abrupt, bony spine of the Eastern Sierra,
most travelers are so enchanted by the striking vista across Mono Lake Basin
that they pass by unaware of Lundy Canyon, one of the region's most stunning

settings. Follow the sign pointing up Lundy Canyon for a highly scenic side road. Pretty in any season, in late September and early October when autumn paints the landscape with startling shades, this glacially-sculpted canyon is unrivaled.

This is a place not to be rushed. The more time you spend in this tranquil, secluded gorge, the more you'll be rewarded. Stay a few days to fully explore the Lundy environs. Before reaching Lundy Lake, elevation 7700 feet, you'll find a public campground along aspen- and willow-lined Mill Creek. Above the lake is a tiny rustic resort with a store and campground.

At this idyllic mountain get-away, you won't find the usual hustle of more commercial resorts where throngs of people mill around looking to be entertained. Instead Lundy radiates a peaceful, unsophisticated and low key charisma. The big attraction is simply the landscape. You'll find all the entertainment you need hooking a huge trout, hiking up the forks of the canyon past shimmering lakes and roaring waterfalls, watching a hawk ride a thermal, feeling the cool caress of night breezes, and smelling the spicy scent of Jeffrey pines.

Two lovely trails through this remarkably photogenic landscape beg for your boots. They offer riots of wildflowers in summer and especially dazzle in autumn when aspens sport intense orange and lemon hues. The farther up you proceed, the more dramatic the pageant becomes. You'll be surrounded by the aspens' glorious display, intensified by the deep green pines and the red-walled cliffs. Rivers of quaking gold tumble down the canyon walls for hundreds of feet.

Part of Lundy's appeal, besides its rugged beauty, is its rich history, dating back more than 120 years to the exciting days of pioneers and boisterous mining activity. Not much of the old town survives, but relics from the past are everywhere. Rusting tramways, tunnels, old trails, mining paraphernalia, collapsed buildings and decaying mills lie scattered throughout the area.

About 1878 William Lundy started a sawmill in the canyon to feed the hungry appetite of nearby Bodie (see Chapter 49), a booming gold town northeast of here. In 1879, a year of intense activity for both Bodie and Mammoth Lakes, William Wasson discovered veins of ore in Mill Creek, now Lundy Canyon. That same year Lundy and his two partners established claims, among them the famous May Lundy Mine, named after one of his four daughters.

The May Lundy Mine, located on a stark, sheer slope at 10,000 feet in Lake Canyon 3.5 miles south of Lundy, was worked continuously from 1878 to 1898. During its heyday Lundy's population reached 500, with the town bursting into existence by May 1880. According to its newspaper, the **Homer Mining Index**, "During that month upward of 30 frame houses, nearly all for business purposes were built, besides a number of log houses, two merchandise stores, seven saloons, two lodging houses, several boarding houses, two bakeries, a hotel, blacksmith shop, livery stable, assay office, butcher shop, post office, express office, sawmill and newspaper." Not bad for a newborn town. A telegraph line to Bodie, and later to Bennettville, connected Lundy to the world.

The Lundy Mining Company built a large store with several bedrooms upstairs. The first stamp mill was across from the store, and ore was laboriously toted down from the May Lundy by mules and horses. When a toll road was established in 1881 connecting Lundy to the mine in Lake Canyon, the mill was moved up to the ore site. The difficulty in negotiating the steep road from the mine stimulated development of "three

May Lundy Mine in 1895. Precariously perched on a talus slope high above Lundy Lake, an aerial tramway connected mine and mill.

saloons, a laundry and two boarding houses." Business was brisk as men from Bennettville nine miles south also used Lundy's conveniences.

Strike from your mind the romantic image of a gold seeker lazily swishing gravel around in a gold pan! Life was a tough, dangerous grind for hard-rock miners in this oxygen-scarce, rugged terrain. During long, brutally cold winters, the crude living quarters offered little comfort or protection from the months of raging winds and tremendous piles of snow. Like most mining camps, Lundy had plenty of colorful characters and murders, robberies and kidnappings. On top of daily hardships, whiskey and boredom often combined to shorten tempers and cloud judgments.

An important, but brief, relationship between Lundy and Bennettville mining camps provides an astonishing example of the courage, tenacity and ingenuity of hard-rock miners. Among the many extraordinary feats attempted or accomplished by these men, the following story illustrates one such mind-boggling venture in their quest for precious metals.

Before the Great Sierra Wagon Road (forerunner of Tioga Road, see Chapter 44) was built, only the treacherous Bloody Canyon-Mono Pass Trail (see Chapter 42) afforded access to Bennettville, headquarters for the Tioga Mining District. In 1881, an even steeper trail was constructed from Lake Canyon to Bennettville over the Sierra Crest by owners of the Great Sierra Silver Mine. Its purpose was to transport heavy-duty machinery necessary to drive a tunnel 1000 feet long through granite so hard "it took several shifts of miners to hand drill a single blast hole."

Arriving at Lundy from San Francisco via Reno, the lighter equipment was packed on mules and sent to Bennettville on the Bloody Canyon Trail. However, the more ponderous cargo consisting of an engine, boiler, air compressor, iron pipe and drills far exceeded the animals' capabilities. Instead, 16,000 pounds of machinery were hauled over the new trail by, if you can imagine, sleds in the dead of winter 1882!

After loading six huge hardwood sleds built at Lundy, 12 men began the Herculean labor of dragging eight tons of equipment 4000 feet up to the summit, and then down to Bennettville. The heaviest load was 4200 pounds. Two mule-powered bobsleds carried supplies. Aided only by nearly a mile of manila rope and blocks and tackle snubbed to nearby trees or steel bars pounded into rocks, a dozen men snaked the gear over cliffs, frozen lakes and icy talus slopes. Costing one man his life, the task required two months to drag the huge load a distance of nine miles. In a classic understatement, company manager J. C. Kemp remarked at the end of the journey: "It's no wonder that men grow old." The trail continued to be used by pedestrians and pack trains carrying dynamite and supplies until the mining operations closed. Today, hardy, High Country hikers enjoy the seldom-traveled route in search of solitude and magnificent scenery.

Weather was always a critical factor in the story of Lundy. Then as now, winters were severe. Avalanches posed a constant threat and resulted in much devastation and loss of life throughout the years. When the miners first built their cabins, they didn't realize the potential disaster of building the town at the base of barren, towering mountains. The winter of 1882 was particularly vicious. After days of monumental snowfall, three avalanches thundered down Mount Scowden, buried most of the town and killed several people. The dead were laid to rest in a little cemetery below the lake, scarcely visible since the fences around the graves have weathered away.

Besides mining activity, Lundy had several farms below the lake irrigated by diverting water from Mill Creek. The farms' produce found an eager market in Lundy and the Mono Basin. The town also had at least three sawmills along the

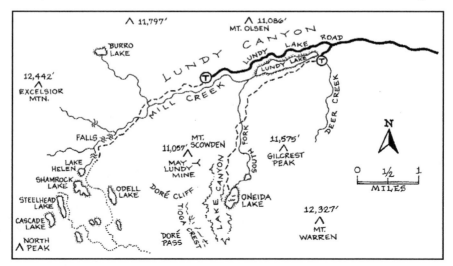

creek. These mills virtually denuded the area of trees in supplying timber for the mines and firewood for Bodie.

By the turn of the century, the glory years were nearly over, even though Lundy hung on for awhile longer. The May Lundy Mine was a major producer in the district, reportedly taking out $2 million in gold during its 20 years of production. Harsh winters, economic upheavals, fires, avalanches and the depletion of gold veins led to the demise of this once-thriving community. Although intermittent mining has continued on a small scale, very little success is evident. Production costs are simply too great to make it a truly profitable enterprise.

■ THE HIKES

Today's visitor doesn't have to leave the car—or stray far from it—to enjoy Lundy's gifts, but the best way to immerse yourself in this glorious landscape is to take a walk on one or both of two choice trails.

The highly scenic and historic hike to May Lundy Mine requires a very steep 3.5-mile climb up Lake Canyon. The signed trailhead is at the lower end of Lundy Lake near the dammed outlet. Rich with mining relics and rugged beauty, the route traces the old mining toll road and passes three lakes. The trail reaches Lake Canyon around 1.5 miles, bending south to follow South Fork Mill Creek upstream. Stay alert for remnant poles of the 120-year-old telegraph line.

The trail climbs via the historic sled route, eventually reaching Blue Lake, then Crystal Lake. The May Lundy Mine area around Crystal Lake abounds in artifacts and ancient equipment. Be extremely cautious if you explore the steep hillside above the lake. Just beyond the mining community site is Oneida Lake, your turn-around point. Its outlet was dammed and diverted to run a stamp mill.

The journey through the main stem of Lundy Canyon is much less taxing. Lower Lundy Falls is an easy .6 mile walk, offering a stunning sample of the canyon's wild beauty, tempting you to go farther. Though not very high or wide, this rowdy cataract looks textured as it races over a rough, rocky surface. The water takes on an unusual, gleaming whiteness due to the darkness of the underlying metamorphic rock. A short spur trail to the base of the falls gives another perspective of this gleaming cascade.

For more scenery that will leave you slack-jawed, continue to 1.5 miles where the path meanders through an extensive stand of huge aspens, complete with the remains of a log cabin. Wildflowers are splendid along this stretch. Beyond the cabin, you'll marvel at the nameless cascades streaming down the sheer canyon walls. Look for stair-stepping Upper Lundy Falls plunging through a slot in the canyon's headwall 2.5 miles from the trailhead. When you must, retrace your steps.

However you choose to experience Lundy, the canyon's real gold remains available to all of us. The treasures of majestic mountains, cascading streams, vibrant wildflowers, sparkling lakes, aspen groves, placid beaver ponds, numerous waterfalls and astonishing autumn color await your discovery.

48
Green Creek Canyon to East Lake

Dynamo Pond Sent Power to Bodie

■ THE DETAILS

Getting There: Turn west off Highway 395 onto Green Lakes Road, 4 miles south of Bridgeport, about 3 miles north of State Route 270. Follow Green Lakes Road 7 miles to its end and trailhead parking.

Nearest Campground: Green Creek Campground near the trailhead has 11 sites with piped water, open May through October.

Lodging: See Chapter 49.

Further Info: Bridgeport Ranger District, Toiyabe National Forest 760-932-7070.

Hike Distance: 4.8 miles round trip to Green Lake, 7.6 miles round trip to East Lake.

Difficulty: Moderate.

Best Time to Go: July, early August for wildflowers, September or October for fall color.

Cautions: Use caution at stream fords, possibly impassable at high water. Leave mining artifacts in place.

Starting Elevation: 8160 feet. Gain to Green Lake: 800 feet. Gain to East Lake: 1300 feet.

Other Map: USGS Matterhorn Peak 15 minute topo.

Veteran hikers and backpackers know that seven-mile-long Green Lakes Road provides entry to several sparkling High Country lakes in lightly traveled Hoover Wilderness and access to Yosemite Park's northeastern backcountry. After the dirt road passes a lakelet around 3 miles in, it cleaves the narrow canyon cut by Green Creek. During July and early August the landscape is vibrant with wildflowers, while thick stands of aspens produce brilliant color displays in autumn.

As well as a tranquil, lovely subalpine setting, the picturesque lakelet at the slender valley's entrance harbors a piece of revolutionary history whose significance rippled far beyond this tiny Sierra side road. Dynamo Pond's log-cribbed outlet and a few ruins are all that remain of a hydroelectric plant constructed in 1892 to supply power to the mines at Bodie.

Big, bad Bodie was one of the wildest, wickedest, richest and largest gold camps in the West. At its peak between 1877 and 1882, Bodie claimed 10,000 residents. Its mines yielded $35 million in gold and silver. Although the boom was ephemeral and most of the mines closed permanently by 1890, the Standard Company continued as Bodie's main producer until 1942.

Prior to 1892, energy for the mills was derived from steam generated by wood-fired boilers. A single mining company could consume 24 cords of wood per day. Over the years, Bodie's insatiable appetite for lumber, mine timbers, and cordwood for heating and machine operations resulted in a critical shortage. Tremendous quantities of wood were needed to simply survive long and nasty winters. For example in late 1878, more than 18,000 cords of piñon pine were stockpiled awaiting the first cold snap. In 1882, five million board feet of lumber and 27,000 cords of firewood were hauled to Bodie.

As wood fuel became increasingly scarce and more costly, the Standard Company's chief engineer and superintendent, Tom Legget, proposed that electricity could be transmitted by wires to any distance. This was then a radical concept because electricity had only been used where it was generated. After many meetings with company stockholders, he was granted permission to construct a power plant. Green Creek Canyon, eight miles south of Bridgeport, was selected as the nearest site with a reliable water source.

The Standard Company created Dynamo Pond by building a log-cribbed dam to capture Green Creek's flow, providing water to generate electricity in the plant below it. Capable of developing 6600 volts and 130 horsepower, Dynamo Pond was ready for a test in November 1892. Skeptics dubbed the project "Legget's Folly," and many stockholders believed the Company was wasting money on project construction, new equipment to replace steam-powered machinery, and the mill's closure to retrofit for electrical operation.

Meanwhile, the company ordered surveyors to install power poles in a perfectly straight line because it was feared that electricity could not turn corners and would "fall off the line and fly into space." A telephone line was built parallel to the power line. In spite of the scoffing from skeptics, the experimental 13-mile power line from Dynamo Pond to Bodie successfully carried the first long-distance transmission of electricity in history.

The unprecedented achievement at Bodie revolutionized the use of electricity in industry. News of the engineering breakthrough quickly spread around the world. Tom Legget soon became a famous man, in demand to build similar hydroelectric plants in the United States and as far away as Rhodesia and Australia. Ironically, residents of Bodie did not enjoy the benefits of electricity until 1910 when the population had dwindled to a few hundred.

■ THE HIKE

Don't be fooled by the rather desolate, uninviting entrance to Green Creek Canyon. Three miles up the road at historic Dynamo Pond, the barren hillsides give way to a moist, beautifully vegetated gorge that invites lingering. Campers can stay at the small Forest Service campground near the end of the road. You'll find the trailhead on the road's other spur nearby.

The trail follows the wooded canyon floor, passing a spring that flows down from the right. Your gentle track steepens after .5 mile, ascending over a rocky ridge, then up steady switchbacks to follow West Fork Green Creek. Enter Hoover Wilderness around one mile and draw near the noisy creek, revealing glimpses of volcanic Gabbro Peak ahead and granitic Monument Ridge on your right. Note the work of busy aspen-gnawing beavers along here.

Another moderate climb reveals a view on your right of the stream tumbling down from West Lake. More switchbacks bring you to a junction just below Green Lake by 2.3 miles. Our described hike takes the left fork, but consider a break for a side trip to Green Lake, a stunning emerald jewel only .1 mile from the junction. The right fork skirts the north shore of Green Lake past campsites, revealing vistas of Glines Canyon rising toward Virginia Pass on the Sierra Crest. Green Lake, rimmed with forest and wildflowers, provides a great location for a snack break before tackling more switchbacks. Another trail heads north from a lakeshore junction gaining 900 feet in elevation to reach West Lake at 3.8 miles.

From the junction below Green Lake, take the left fork to dip across the lake's outlet

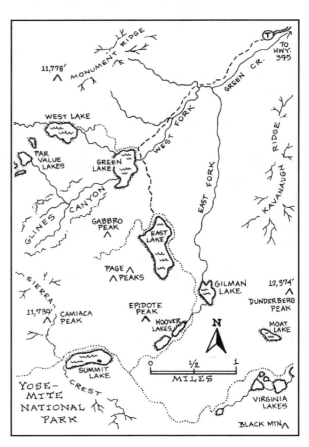

stream, where the ford may be difficult or impassable during high water runoff. Beyond the ford, follow the trail as it climbs steeply south heading for East Lake. Part way up you veer east to ford East Lake's outlet stream, then loop away from the creek before returning to it for two more fords.

When you enter the wildflower-filled meadow below East Lake's outlet, you're almost there. Top a rise around 3.8 miles to find 75-acre East Lake glistening beneath multi-hued Epidote, Page and Gabbro peaks, a fine spot to lunch while you soak up the magnificent scenery. You might notice the small flood-control dam at the lake's outlet, another legacy of Bodie's power works. Return the way you came.

Evening shadows creep over the spectacular terrain around Green Creek Canyon's West Lake.

49
The Blustery Rise & Fall of Bodie
High Desert Ghost Town Survives

■ THE DETAILS

Getting There: From Highway 395 7 miles south of Bridgeport, turn east on paved State Route 270 and go 13 miles to Bodie. The pavement ends 3 miles before Bodie, becoming a dusty, corduroy track giving one the idea of what it might have been like to arrive here a century ago.

Nearest Campgrounds: Virginia Creek Settlement 760-932-7780, on Highway 395 about .5 mile north of the Bodie turnoff, has several sites. Willow Creek Resort not far up the highway has 25 RV sites open May through September. Also see Chapter 47.

Lodging: Virginia Creek Settlement 760-932-7780 has several rustic rooms in an old west mining camp setting. Bridgeport has Best Western Ruby Inn 760-932-7241, Cain House 760-932-7040, Silver Maple Inn 760-932-7383, Walker River Lodge 760-932-7021. Also see Chapter 47.

Further Info: The park is open all year, weather permitting, 9 a.m. to 7 p.m. in summer, until 4 p.m. the rest of the year, or as posted due to road and weather conditions. Contact Bodie State Historic Park, P.O. Box 515, Bridgeport. CA 93517, 760-647-6445.

Hike Distance: It's up to you.

Difficulty: Easy.

Facilities: Restrooms, drinking water and picnic area but no services.

Best Time to Go: Summer and early autumn are ideal.

Cautions: No smoking, fires or camping. Stay out of old mines and other posted closed areas.

Starting Elevation: 8369 feet.

Maps: Excellent state park map, USGS Bodie 7.5 minute topo.

Slumbering peacefully in a state of arrested decay in the high desert hills east of the Sierra, the remains of Bodie endure just as time, weather and fire have left them. A state historic park since 1962, Bodie provides a classic example of what life was like in the last years of the rip-roaring mining camps.

Today, only about five percent of the buildings have survived, but what's left is

Five percent of Bodie's structures have survived for visitors to experience in the desolate, high desert terrain north of Mono Lake.

astonishing. Bodie is a genuine ghost town, not a restored tourist trap. Scores of residences and commercial structures line the streets. Bottles on the bar, caskets in the morgue, open books on schoolroom desks, clothes hanging on wall pegs and fresh flowers on a grave give one an eerie feeling that the town is waiting for life to resume. Although the huge Standard Mine complex on the bluff above town is closed, rangers lead tours Saturdays and Sundays at 11 a.m. and 2 p.m.

Bodie, "the land that God forgot," occupies a vast, starkly beautiful landscape. A sea of sagebrush extends to every horizon, and fretful winds stalk the barren hills. Bitterly cold in winter, blistering in summer, the isolated, remote town produced $30 million in gold and a million dollars in silver. It was a wild and wicked place with gunfights, murders and brawls the rule rather than the exception. The common question, "Have we a man for breakfast?" referred to the lethal, early morning shoot-outs.

Sixty-five saloons open round-the-clock fueled the fires of lusty, rowdy men in search of instant riches in this lawless environment. Gamblers, whores, hustlers, speculators and con artists also found Bodie the lodestone in which to ply their trades. Perhaps afraid that the Almighty was unfamiliar with her destination, a young girl from Truckee about to arrive in this turbulent society said a prayer, "Good-bye, God! I'm going to Bodie!" An editor of one of Bodie's newspapers reported that what she really meant was "Good! By God, I'm going to Bodie!" Bodie was either a sinful pit at the end of the earth or an exciting, free-wheeling arena of opportunity.

No territory in the Sierra Nevada was so remote that men bitten by the gold bug didn't find it sooner or later. Bodie was later. This fabulously rich area didn't even reach its peak until 30 years after the Gold Rush began. Located northeast of Lee Vining, Bodie is part of the arid and sun-baked 700-square mile Mono Basin surrounding Mono Lake. The Basin attracted prospectors after the Mother Lode placers became overrun and depleted.

Even though forbidden by Brigham Young to search for gold and threatened with fire and brimstone if they did, a group of Mormon miners in 1857 began the first mining venture in a promising area along Dog Creek, a few miles northwest of Mono Lake. Considerable excitement over the Dogtown deposits sparked a rush to the virtually unexplored Eastern Sierra. By 1859 much richer deposits were unearthed at Monoville, and the fickle miners abandoned Dogtown for the new diggings. Monoville ore was rich and extensive, but the lack of water to operate rockers and sluices caused many men to quit their claims and wander the desert like Bedouins in search of new locations. Such was the choice of William S. Body.

In 1848 Bill Body jettisoned a wife and six children in New York to join the horde of men who fled hearth and home "to see the elephant" in California. After 11 years in the Mother Lode, Body and three companions crossed the Sierra Crest via the Sonora Pass Trail to try their luck in Mono Basin. When they arrived in Monoville in 1859 they found every square foot of ground swarming with miners.

Body and his friends decided to move eastward to the desolate, rolling land later known as the Bodie Hills. There they staked claims and began laying in supplies from Monoville to carry them through the winter. In March 1860 Body and Black Taylor were caught in a severe blizzard and became separated. Taylor survived, but Body froze to death less than a mile from their cabin.

Haunted by Body's death, Taylor left their claim and drifted south to Benton where he was killed by hostile Paiute Indians. Tragically, neither man lived to see the spectacular results of their discovery. By 1862 the camp and mining district were named Bodie in honor of Bill Body. The change in spelling, according to some, came about by a sign painter's mistake. More likely, the change occurred to insure correct pronunciation.

The Bodie mines were worked in the early 1860s but were overshadowed by the extraordinary silver strike in Aurora 12 miles northeast. In 1863 only a handful of stubborn miners were struggling along while Aurora's population soared to 4000. Aurora funneled off the much-needed outside capital for exploration and development by the millions.

Bodie's ultimate boom and rise to prominence as the major producer in Mono Basin was slow and fraught with disappointment. Between 1863 and 1868 Bodie miners attracted the attention of two companies, which failed primarily because of undercapitalization and unrealistic expectations for quick return. Also factored in was the critical need for gargantuan quantities of lumber and firewood, as well as the shortage of food and supplies due to the camp's isolation.

After the last company folded, individual miners continued to work their claims, and Bodie seemed headed for oblivion. However in 1874, 15 years after Body's discovery, a cave-in exposed an incredibly rich body of ore in the old Bunker Hill Mine. The two owners turned a nice profit before selling it in 1876 to mining speculators in San Francisco. Renamed the Standard Company, in 1877 the mine paid for itself, met all expenses and declared dividends to its stockholders.

Responding to the Standard's phenomenal success, money and miners poured into town. The rush was on! Besides the Standard, 30 to 40 other companies were furiously exploring Bodie Bluff. The Bodie Company on land next to the Standard Company struck the continuation of the rich vein into its own property. In one month alone, the Bodie milled $600,000 in gold and silver bullion. Shares catapulted from 25 cents to $55 in just a few weeks.

By 1878 the rush to Bodie became a stampede, and by 1880 the town burgeoned to 10,000 inhabitants and 2000 structures. In the throes of gold fever it's curious how quickly forgotten are such things as the brutal climate, lack of medical care, inadequate housing, exorbitant living expenses, and lack of food, fuel and all the other conveniences and necessities of life that seemed so important in the "real" world.

Bodie had an insatiable appetite for wood. As sawmills at Bridgeport failed to keep pace with Bodie's growth, lumber was hauled in from as far away as Carson City, Nevada. Besides wood products for buildings and roofing, thick timbers were needed to support mine tunnels. Firewood was voraciously consumed to generate steam for the mine equipment and to heat buildings during the long, glacially-cold winter. The narrow gauge Bodie Railway and Lumber Company was established in 1881 to haul cordwood and lumber to Bodie. Originating in a pine forest at Mono Mills seven miles south of Mono Lake, the 37.5-mile line operated until 1917.

As they say, it was fun while it lasted. By 1879 no new rich strikes were made, and by the end of the year it was obvious there weren't going to be any. By 1881 the big party was essentially over, and the long, slow decline from glory years to ghost town began. Only the Standard and Bodie mines were destined to be the star producers. Peak output lasted only four years until the stock market collapsed in 1881. Within two years all the smaller mines began closing down, and by 1888 the population had dwindled to 1500.

The enormously successful Bodie and Standard operations consolidated in 1877 and carried on profitably, if not spectacularly, for 20 more years. The huge, wood-framed Standard Mill burned in 1899, but it was immediately rebuilt with the addition of a cyanide reduction plant. The new gold recovery process stimulated a resurgence of mining activity for another decade. As of 1910 only the Standard Mine was working.

The results of a radical experiment during Bodie's post boom days were felt around the world. In 1892 the town became the site of the nation's first electrical power transmission for industrial purposes. Although electricity had been developed, it had only been used where it was generated. In a canyon at the foot of the

Eastern Sierra, the Green Creek hydroelectric plant transmitted 6600 volts to the Standard Mine 13 miles away.

Because long distance power transmission was untested, engineers insisted that the poles be set in a perfectly straight line. It was their belief that electricity could not travel around curves or sharp angles and would "fly off into space." While revolutionizing electricity for industry, it took another 18 years before the citizens of Bodie enjoyed electrical power.

Gradually, all activity slowed to a snail's pace and then ceased altogether. By 1882 Bodie's boom had passed; miners deserted this town for new silver strikes in Arizona and Colorado. After mining stocks crashed in 1883, the town faded quickly. Less than a hundred people were living in Bodie during the 1930s. Ranchers dismantled some of the derelict buildings for their lumber or moved the buildings to other sites.

Then one day in 1932, little Billy Godward touched off a holocaust that razed the remaining buildings except for those visible today. Billy was spanked and sent home from a birthday party because, angry at being served gelatin instead of ice cream, he kicked over the table. Finding himself home alone, he grabbed a box of matches and set fire to a mattress. By day's end most of the town was in ashes.

Limited mining continued at Bodie until the Standard Company's cyanide plant burned in 1947, ultimately shutting down in the mid 1950s. A sole watchman was left to guard the deserted town against vandalism until Bodie was designated a state park in 1962.

Bill Body rests in the hillside cemetery overlooking the town named for him. Now only visitors wander the streets in search of the spirit of the wildest, biggest, most notorious mining camp in California. If you would like to escape the present for a few hours and step back into one of the most colorful and important chapters of life in frontier America, then by God, go to Bodie!

■ THE HIKE

The best way to get acquainted with Bodie is to pick up a walking guide booklet at the entrance station which profiles the history and location of the surviving buildings. You can easily spend a half day exploring the town, and the fenced town cemetery where decent folk were buried and Boot Hill for the bad guys also merit a look.

50

June Lakes Basin & Parker Lake

Lakes, Resorts and a Village Beneath Towering Peaks

. . . for everybody needs beauty as well as bread, places to play in and pray in where Nature may heal and cheer and give strength to body and soul alike.

~John Muir

■ THE DETAILS

Getting There: From Lee Vining, drive 5 miles south on U.S. Highway 395, then turn right onto State Highway 158. Go 1.5 miles, then turn right onto Parker Lake Road which heads directly toward the mountains for 2.5 miles to end at the Parker Lake Trailhead.

Since Highway 158 is a loop road, you can turn west onto either end. The scenic byway skirts four lakes and passes through June Lake village on its 16-mile loop before returning to Highway 395. Snowfall closes the loop's northern section in winter, but the southern end generally stays open.

Nearest Campgrounds: June Lakes Loop has seven campgrounds, mostly on the south end. Close to the hike is Silver Lake Campground with 65 sites and piped water, open May through September.

Lodging: Silver Lake Resort 760-648-7525 has housekeeping cabins. Boulder Lodge 760-648-7533 has cabins and motel units. If you plan to stay overnight, make reservations well in advance. An alternative is to stay in Lee Vining (see Chapter 47).

Further Info: June Lake Chamber of Commerce, June Lake, CA 93529, 760-648-7584.

Hike Distance: 4.7 miles round trip.

Difficulty: Moderate.

Best Time to Go: Summer, autumn.

Cautions: None.

Starting Elevation: 7950 feet. Gain to lake: 450 feet.

Other Maps: AAA Eastern Sierra map or Inyo National Forest map provides a helpful overview while USGS Koip Peak 7.5 minute topo has detail.

June Lakes Basin snuggles hidden from Highway 395 like a precious jewel. One of the numerous surprisingly luxuriant canyons in an arid and seemingly inhospitable landscape, this canyon drained by Rush Creek reveals itself quickly once you turn onto Highway 158. This good wide side road threads the heart of the Basin on a 16-mile loop, winding spectacularly past Grant, Silver, Gull and June lakes, ranging in elevation from 7130 feet to 7621 feet, before rejoining Highway 395.

Although it features an all-year resort concentrated around June Lake, the Basin's ambiance is tranquil and low key. Nestled against the bases of towering June Mountain (10,135 feet) and Carson Peak (10,909 feet), the resort area of June Lake has a cozy, European charm. Attractive inns, motels and restaurants cater to a wide variety of tastes and budgets.

The loop is well known for its outstanding outdoor opportunities. In winter the June Mountain ski area is a popular destination for alpine skiers of all ability levels. Miles of Nordic skiing delight those who prefer the skinny boards. The chalet atop June Mountain provides superb views of the Sierra and Mono Basin. In summer and autumn the June Lakes Loop is a recreation paradise. Hiking,

---

■ EXPLORE MONO LAKE

June Lakes Basin can be a destination itself or, if you have the time and inclination, it can provide a wonderful base from which to explore more of the incomparable Eastern Sierra hinterlands and its abundant scenic, historic and recreational resources. A host of touring possibilities lie within a few miles.

Sapphire-blue Mono Lake is but a shadow of its former self. It has been around for at least 700,000 years and was three to four times larger and 600 feet deeper during the last Ice Age 10,000 years ago. Since 1941 the lake volume has been drastically reduced by the diversion of four major feeder streams to supply water and power to the Los Angeles area. In the early 1990s, after a protracted battle to save Mono Lake, the State Water Resources Control Board placed permanent restrictions on diversion, allowing the streams to flow once again into the lake.

The old-as-Methuselah inland sea supports millions of nesting and migrating birds each year. Lining Mono's shores are eerie tufa towers, fantastic formations created as underground mineral springs mix with the lake's alkaline waters. Nearby Mono Craters' 12 dormant volcanoes and the lake's two islands testify to the region's fiery genesis.

A stop at either the Mono Lake Committee Visitor Center in Lee Vining or the handsome new Visitor Center near the shoreline will help you understand this unusual area recognized as a treasure of geology, wildlife and natural beauty.

camping, fishing, sailing, water skiing, horseback riding, bicycling, photography and botanizing lure outdoor enthusiasts to this dramatic setting. Because the wilderness soars all around you, hiking trails into the backcountry are steep.

Perhaps with the Sierra in mind, a poet once said, "Autumn is a gypsy with jewels in her hair." Fall in the mountains is indeed a bewitching time of year. For a few glorious weeks before the big sleep of winter settles in, the foliage shimmers with dazzling hues. During autumn the June Lakes Basin is especially colorful. Quaking aspen groves splash the mountainsides with brilliant gold, burnished orange and scarlet, providing one of the most vivid fall pageants on the eastern slopes. Being in the midst of these fluttering, flamboyant trees is an unforgettable experience. Autumn here can be as fleeting as a gypsy because it's subject to the whims of weather. Generally, you can expect to see color in late September or early October. Besides the garish aspen display, willows and cottonwoods lend their mellow, golden light to the show.

Most visitors to June Lakes Basin don't know about its unusual geological features. The Basin doesn't fit the characteristic pattern of glacially scoured canyons. Rather than a vertical gouge from mountain top to valley floor, the canyon curves like a horseshoe. In fact, a U.S. government surveyor in 1866-1867 named it Horseshoe Canyon. A million years ago the Rush Creek Glacier was the architect of this unique, sensational terrain. The 24-square-mile river of ice took a peculiar, curved course, unlike the straightness of other glacier-cut canyons in the range.

The loop's other singular aspect is the direction of Reversed Creek, aptly named

Parker Lake's lovely setting at the base of rugged Sierra peaks offers a fine example of Eastern Sierra scenery.

because June Lake's outlet stream runs toward the mountains, flowing through the horseshoe-shaped canyon to Grant Lake and then on toward Mono Lake. Glacial action also scooped out the depressions for what later became June, Gull, Silver and Grant lakes. You can witness the tremendous power of glacial movement near Boulder Lodge. Balanced Rock, a 100-ton chunk of granite, was deposited by a melting glacier atop another boulder.

Human history in the June Lakes territory is centuries old. Long before the advent of miners and settlers, the Numu people (also called Paiutes) inhabited the area. Before Euro-Americans destroyed the Numu's ages-old lifestyle, good hunting grounds and fishing provided them an excellent homeland. In autumn, they gathered nuts from piñon pines to supplement their diet during the long, cold winters. Mining activity in the Basin amounted to only a flash in the pan.

From the very beginning of its occupation by non-natives, the loop seemed destined to become a lodestar for fishing and other recreational pursuits. Trouble in paradise surfaced early in the 20th century when another of its natural resources became a focal point. Its waters caught the attention of developers in southern California.

By 1917 two historic projects were under way. The Rush Creek Powerhouse near Silver Lake, first in a long, complicated series of water exploitations, was completed to supply a thirsty and growing Los Angeles population. Workmen hauled materials over a rough dirt road from Highway 395. The heavy powerhouse equipment came by rail to Hawthorne, Nevada, and was then hauled on trucks via Bodie to June Lakes Basin. Nevada-California Electric Edison Company funded the original construction. It's still in the same site today. Interestingly, during the same era, San Francisco began their huge Hetch Hetchy Project to capture Western Sierra water.

In the same year Roy Carson, a carpenter at the Rush Creek plant, camped at Silver Lake while on a fishing trip. Enchanted by the scenery, he decided to build Carson Camp and become a full-time resident. After he finished the first cabin in 1920, another soon followed. Lumber for all the buildings came from a sawmill at Mammoth Lakes a few miles south. The new cabin housed a small store and living quarters. On an ancient wood stove from Bodie, Mrs. Carson turned out hearty loaves of bread and sold them to campers.

In 1921 the Carson's built a much larger building at Carson Camp, still used today as the resort's store and restaurant. "Carson's Camp—Where the Fishing is Always Good" changed to "Silver Lake—Gem of the Sierra" in 1940. Today, housekeeping cabins continue to offer guests comfortable lodging at gentle rates. To honor these pioneers, Carson Peak bears their name.

By 1924 the Forest Service put in a rough, dirt road from the highway at the southern end of the loop, and fishermen and power company employees completed the section between Silver Lake and June Lake. For the first time, the entire loop was accessible to automobiles. With the new road, civilization and development rushed in. First came Silver Lake Pines Tract, a subdivision incorporating two 80-acre parcels. The increase of full-time residents created a need for a post office, established in October 1927. For many years a dog sled team delivered the mail in winter.

As the loop attracted more tourists and permanent residents, private summer cabins, businesses and other resorts sprouted between June and Silver lakes. In 1933 several road improvements were made, although snow still closed the road during winter. Before the arrival of snowplows in 1937, the community moved about either on snowshoes or dog sleds in winter. Meanwhile, accompanying the development of June Lake was Hollywood's discovery of Silver Lake as a picturesque locale for movies. Many films were shot at Silver and June lakes, and the region became a playground for the rich and famous. Moreover between 1920 and 1945, many water and power projects in and around the Basin contributed to its growth.

A major event to entice vacationers occurred in 1940 when June Lake businessmen formed the June Lake Winter Sports Association. As at Mammoth Lakes, skiing on June Mountain became an important commercial venture for the economic health of the community.

After World War II the pace and scope of the Basin's growth slowed down from the boom days experienced during the Los Angeles Water and Power projects. Ironically, electricity came rather late to the village. For a quarter century the Basin's waters were diverted south to supply electricity, but not until 1946 did power lines reach the canyon.

Another boon for the area was the construction of the first June Mountain ski lift which opened in 1961. Other lifts were completed later in the decade. The ski lifts created a winter industry and transformed the horseshoe canyon into a year-round resort center. Over the years more lodging facilities opened for visitors who came to enjoy this spectacular niche in the Sierra Nevada. Fortunately, the village has not lost its quaintness and relaxed, friendly atmosphere.

■ THE HIKE

While in the June Lakes Basin it would be a shame not to sample one or more of its trails. Most trails of the Eastern Sierra involve strenuous hiking, but the hike to Parker Lake is an exception. Climbing from the wide open sagebrush-piñon pine habitat to secluded patches of dense forest, the trail offers great visual interest in a lush glacier-carved canyon.

You need to tackle most of the hike's elevation gain in the first .75 mile as the trail ascends over an intact sagebrush-covered terminal moraine deposited by Parker Canyon's glacier millennia ago. As you near Parker Creek, typical high desert vegetation gives way to stands of aspen and enormous Jeffrey and lodgepole pines. Wildflowers increase in abundance as you near the lake. You pass a trail on the left that descends south to Silver Lake.

Parker Lake's dark green waters nestle in a deep bowl at the feet of colorful, towering peaks. Above the head of the lake, a long waterfall plummets down barren rock before fanning out to leap over a precipice. Pick a spot for a lunch break and enjoy the dramatic scenery. Before retracing your steps, you can explore a trail along the lake's south shore to reach the canyon's headwall.

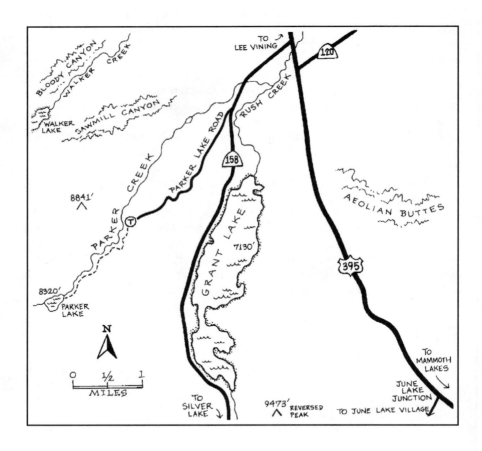

51
Devils Postpile & Rainbow Falls
Basaltic Columns and Waterfalls Near the Sierra Crest

■ THE DETAILS

Getting There: From Lee Vining drive 26 miles south on U.S. Highway 395 to
Mammoth Junction. Turn right on Highway 203, Minaret Summit Road, to
reach the bustling small town of Mammoth Lakes. Continue through town to
the ski area. During summer, day-use visitors must abandon their vehicles and
ride a shuttle bus down the narrow, curvy 13-mile road from Mammoth Resort
to the Monument. The shuttles run seven days a week from the main parking lot
at Mammoth Mountain Ski Area. Unless you are camping up the road, park and
catch the shuttle to the Monument. Check with the Park Service for times and
round-trip fee.

Nearest Campgrounds: Devils Postpile National Monument Campground has 21
sites with piped water, open mid June to late October. Minaret Falls and 3 other
National Forest campgrounds on the spectacular road that winds 13 miles from
Mammoth Resort have 95 more sites.

Lodging: Plan ahead to stay at Red's Meadow Resort 800-292-7758 on the Pacific
Crest Trail near Devils Postpile. Mammoth Lakes has many other choices.

Further Info: Devils Postpile National Monument 760-934-2289. Mammoth Lakes
Visitor Center, Inyo National Forest 760-924-5500.

Hike Distance: One mile round trip to Devils Postpile, 5 miles round trip to
Rainbow Falls.

Difficulty: Easy.

Best Time to Go: Summer, autumn.

Cautions: From about November through mid-June the road closes due to snow.

Starting Elevation: 7600 feet.

Other Maps: USGS Devils Postpile 15 minute topo, Crystal Crag and Mammoth
Mtn. 7.5 minute topos.

Devils Postpile is one of 150 place names in California that mirror the belief of
early settlers who frequently regarded geological oddities and "scenic freaks" as
Satan's handiwork. Eastern Sierra locals around 1900 called the unique setting
Devils Woodpile because it looks like an enormous pile of posts. In reality, Devils

Postpile is a spectacular mass of four- to seven-sided basaltic columns located on the western side of the Sierra Crest not far from Mammoth. Its beginnings, though, can indeed be traced to Lucifer's netherworld.

These striking symmetrical posts were created about 100,000 years ago. Lava erupted from vents in a sprawling earthquake fault along the Eastern Sierra and flowed down the Middle Fork San Joaquin River. As the 400-foot-thick molten basalt uniformly cooled and shrank, it cracked vertically into thousands of columns. The majority of the blue-gray pillars are hexagonal with an average width of two feet.

During the last Ice Age 10,000 years ago, a glacier crept through the valley, bulldozing away most of the volcanic rock which eventually exposed the sheer columns we see today. Further evidence of glacial power can be seen in the parallel grooves cut into the tops of the posts as the rock-laden glacier slowly ground across the formation.

The rubble heap of broken columns at the base of the formation was caused by the weathering effect of frost action, an ongoing process. Frozen water collects in cracks and gradually pries and pushes the columns outward until they fall. Historically a hot bed of seismic activity, earthquakes in the Mammoth region have also toppled the posts.

At an elevation of 7500 feet, the unusual volcanic formation rising 60 to 70 feet from the canyon floor lies 13 miles southeast of Yosemite National Park as the crow flies. Until 1905 it was within Park boundaries. At that time, in response to strong pressure from timber and mining lobbyists, Congress slashed 500 acres from southeastern Yosemite that included Devils Postpile.

Except to locals, Devils Postpile remained a Sierra secret until 1910. Then, public attention focused on this remote, extraordinary global oddity as a plan unfolded to dynamite the Postpile into the nearby Middle Fork San Joaquin River to create a rock-filled dam. Water from the dam was to be used to generate electricity for mining operations.

When the proposal surfaced, various outraged and alarmed champions of the Sierra Nevada, including the district engineer for the U.S. Forest Service, successfully petitioned President William Taft and other federal agencies to protect the area from destruction. By authority of the 1906 Act for the Preservation of American antiquities, President Taft proclaimed Devils Postpile a national monument, safeguarding the area from manipulation and commercial development.

After being set aside as protected land, the Monument was managed by the U.S. Forest Service. However, during the first two decades, visitation was scanty because of its remoteness and poor road access. In 1934 administration of Devils Postpile National Monument was delegated to the Superintendent of Yosemite National Park. Finally, in 1971, responsibilities for Monument lands were transferred to the Superintendent of Sequoia and Kings Canyon National Parks. Today, about 100,000 hikers annually visit Devils Postpile and its beautiful surrounding forest and riparian environment.

■ THE HIKE

You must walk to see the wonderful features of Devils Postpile. From Monument headquarters, an easy 15-minute riverside stroll through the forest takes you to the base of the columnar formation. Take the short side trail leading to the top of the posts to examine the glacial polish and striations on the mosaic-like surfaces.

If you want to extend your hike in this glorious setting, a 2-mile hike from Devils Postpile descends to gorgeous Rainbow Falls created by the river plunging 101 feet over a cliff. To catch the spectacular rainbow captured within the broad cloud of mist, plan to arrive midday.

While you're at Devils Postpile National Monument, especially if it's early summer, consider a visit to Minaret Falls. Just .5 mile north of Monument headquarters along the famous John Muir Trail, the waters of Minaret Creek slip-slide over a wide area of massive, glacier-polished granite. Both falls are dramatically beautiful and exceptionally photogenic.

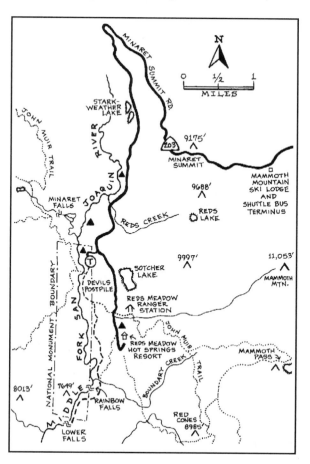

52
Convict Lake
Canyon Rimmed with Towering Peaks

■ THE DETAILS

Getting There: From Highway 395 4.4 miles south of Mammoth Lakes exit, turn west on Convict Lake Road and drive 2.5 miles. As you near the lake, the road splits. The easy hike starts at the end of the left fork, while the strenuous backcountry hike leaves from the spur road on the right.

Nearest Campground: Convict Lake Campground has 88 sites with piped water, open late April through October.

Lodging: Convict Lake Resort has rustic housekeeping cabins set in a lovely stand of aspens not far from the lake. The resort's restaurant has excellent dinners. Convict Lake Resort 800-992-2260. Write Route 1, Box 204, Mammoth Lakes, CA 93546.

Further Info: Inyo National Forest, Mammoth Ranger District 760-934-2505.

Hike Distance: (all round trip) 2 miles around Convict Lake. Wilderness trail: 6 miles to ford, 10 miles to Mildred Lake, 12 miles to Lake Dorothy, 15 miles to Lake Genevieve.

Difficulty: Easy for Convict Lake loop, strenuous for others.

Best Time to Go: Late summer, September through early October for autumn color.

Cautions: Do not attempt to ford the creek unless the flow is low.

Starting Elevation: 7600 feet. Gain to Lake Dorothy: 2675 feet.

Other Maps: USGS Convict Lake and Bloody Mountain 7.5 minute topos.

Large, sparkling Convict Lake nestles at the foot of sheer metamorphic cliffs rising to jagged peaks. Don't let the drab, sagebrush-dotted entrance to this deep glacial canyon mislead you. Enter it to find exposed layers of brightly colored, tilted and folded rock formations ranging from light gray to rich, reddish brown. Hikers, campers and anglers come to this majestic environment to immerse themselves in the relative solitude of a backcountry trail leading to several alpine lakes in John Muir Wilderness.

Called *Witsonapah* by Paiutes and Monte Diablo Lake by early settlers, the lake's tranquil high desert setting offers no hint of its violent moment in history 130 years

Surrounded by towering, colorful peaks, Convict Lake provides access to stunningly beautiful Sierra backcountry locations.

ago, or of how its landmarks were named. The lake, canyon and creek were renamed after one of the West's most dramatic jailbreaks and gun battles ended here.

On Sept. 17, 1871, 29 murderers, horse thieves, and train robbers effectively staged a bloody and deadly prison break from the state penitentiary in Carson City, Nevada. Armed with weapons stolen from prison stores, the inmates split up. Heading south, six of them set off for Arizona where, with other renegades, they "expected to live among the Indians and rob trains." En route they stole horses and brutally murdered and disfigured a teen-aged mail rider from Aurora, Nevada whom they mistakenly identified as a prison guard who had shot two fellow convicts.

Posses from Aurora and Benton quickly assembled and rode off in hot pursuit. Robert Morrison, a merchant and posse member, first spotted the fugitives at Monte Diablo Creek, now Convict Creek, five days after their escape. In true Wild West tradition, a ferocious gunfight erupted in Convict Canyon between the cornered desperados and posse members. Using superior high-powered prison rifles, the outlaws wounded one of the posse, shot four horses out from under them, and killed their Indian guide.

As Morrison dismounted to take cover from wildly flying bullets, he was hit in the side. Outgunned, the posse left him and retreated from the immediate vicinity. When the wounded Morrison attempted to shoot Moses Black, perhaps the most vicious of the six, his pistol misfired, revealing his position in the bushes along the creek. With Morrison exposed and too feeble to try another shot, Black killed him with a bullet through the head. Later that day, his body was taken to Benton where he was given a Masonic funeral. Ironically, Morrison was buried in a new suit he had just bought for his wedding. Lofty Mount Morrison, elevation 12,286 feet, was named in memory of this slain merchant from nearby Benton.

Of the six fugitives, Burke and Cockerill were caught in southern Nevada. The wounded 18-year-old Roberts was arrested at Pine Creek where Black and Morton had abandoned him. Ten days after the breakout, Morton and Black were taken into custody by a Bishop posse in the sand hills near Round Valley. Charlie Jones, convicted murderer, was never captured.

Guarded by Bishop citizens, Roberts, Black and Morton were loaded in a wagon headed back to Carson City when outside town some armed, masked riders commandeered the wagon. Stopping at a cabin in a nearby meadow, the makeshift jury questioned each man for two hours before voting on his fate. The vigilante committee decreed that Black and Morton should hang immediately. Spared the rope by a split vote, young Roberts was returned to prison.

After the so-called trial, the vigilantes hung ropes from a beam at one end of the cabin and placed nooses around the convicts' necks. The wagon served as a portable scaffold, and as it moved forward, the lives of these two dangerous scofflaws ended. In the final analysis, 18 of the 29 escaped inmates were either killed or returned to jail within two months of the breakout. Well over a century has passed since the wild frontier incident occurred, and except for the name, there is nothing to remind us of that violent encounter in Convict Canyon.

■ THE HIKES

Convict Lake attains its ultimate grandeur when its abundant quaking aspens, the West's most flamboyant fall foliage trees, put on their show, but it offers gorgeous hikes all summer as well. Leaf peepers pilgrimage to this mountain shrine in autumn to behold sprawling groves of aspen flowing down the slopes in avalanches of brassy hues and to savor flaming islands of gold, orange, and crimson on canyon floors and along stream banks. The dazzling color display is all the more magical because it is fleeting and unpredictable. Generally, the intensity of fall color in the High Country happens between mid-September and early October, but one heavy windstorm can defoliate a grove.

Two hikes that explore this canyon range from very easy to quite strenuous. By no means do you have to be a long-distance backcountry hiker to witness the magnificent mountain landscape, and the fall foliage show if your timing is right, around the lake. For less conditioned walkers, take the easy, mile-long path at the road end on the left (south) shore of the lake that hugs the lake's shore, circling it to the reach the inlet stream, Convict Creek, at the head of the lake. On the way, watch for the rare copper birch, named for the unusual color of its bark. Where Convict Creek tumbles into the lake, you'll find a great picnic spot at a gravelly beach. If you can safely ford the creek, not likely in early season, head north to meet the Convict Creek Trail along the lake's north shore. On the left the trail ascends steeply toward John Muir Wilderness (see below). To complete the easy walk, turn right and loop around the lake's north shoreline for another perspective of this colorful canyon. If the ford isn't safe, return the way you came.

The more strenuous hike starts near the resort on the north shore, then flanks the lake's north shore to the canyon bisecting its headwall. As you thread the canyon on the steady ascent along Convict Creek, set an easy and enjoyable pace that allows you to appreciate the bountiful wildflowers of summer or the brilliant autumn colors. After a ford of a tributary, you enter John Muir Wilderness. Towering peaks surround you as the trail skirts the base of Laurel Mountain, elevation 11,812 feet. To the west Bloody Mountain, named for its exposed layers of red to reddish-brown rock, dominates the skyline, with the jagged Sierra Crest that flanks it on the left culminating at massive and rounded 13,163-foot Red Slate Mountain, the highest peak for miles. The south rim of this glacial trough you're ascending is topped by Mount Morrison due south and 12,614-foot Mount Baldwin up canyon.

Take note that 3 miles from the trailhead the trail crosses Convict Creek at a tricky and dangerous ford. In early season during snowmelt, do not attempt the hazardous ford of the icy, swift-moving stream. In late summer or autumn, you'll likely have no trouble crossing, though it may require getting wet. If you can safely ford, another 2 miles of hiking up the creek brings you to Mildred Lake below Mount Baldwin. If you got an early enough start to continue, the trail climbs to Lake Dorothy (elevation 10,275) at 6 miles, the largest of the many lakes above Convict Lake, then heads north to reach Lake Genevieve at 7.5 miles. Be sure to leave ample time to complete the hike down before dark.

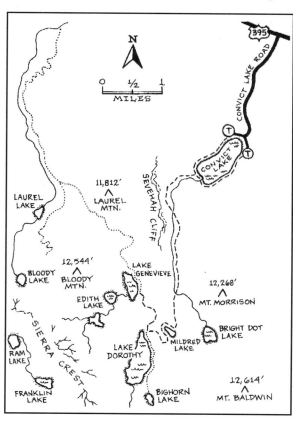

53
Rock Creek Canyon
Heavenly Pie and High Country Lakes

■ THE DETAILS

Getting There: From Highway 395 at Tom's Place, 15 miles south of Mammoth Lakes junction, turn west onto Rock Creek Road and drive 11 miles to road's end and Mosquito Flat trailhead.

Nearest Campgrounds: Rock Creek Lake Campground has 28 sites on the south shore of the lake, open June through September. East Fork Campground, 3 miles down from the lake, opens in May and has 133 sites, with six other campgrounds both up and down the canyon.

Lodging: Rock Creek Lakes Resort, Box 727, Bishop, CA 93515, 760-935-4311.

Further Info: Inyo National Forest White Mountain Ranger District 760-873-2500.

Hike Distance: (all round trip) 4 miles to Long Lake, 5.4 miles to Chickenfoot Lake, 8 miles to Gem Lakes.

Difficulty: Easy.

Best Time to Go: Late summer, early autumn.

Cautions: None.

Starting Elevation: 10,250 feet. Long Lake: 10,543 feet. Chickenfoot Lake: 10,761 feet. Gem Lakes: 10,880 feet.

Other Maps: USGS Mt. Tom, Mt. Abbot 15 minute topos.

Of the many glacier-gouged valleys west of Highway 395 between Bridgeport and Big Pine, Rock Creek Canyon harbors the ne plus ultra of scenic splendor. While the Edenic beauty and lushness of all the Eastern Sierra's numerous lake-filled canyons nurture my soul and refresh my spirit, Rock Creek Canyon's High Country landscape is especially dramatic, poised below the granite amphitheater of the sawtoothed Sierra Crest gleaming in bright, wind-polished air. It's also a great location to witness fall's pyrotechnics. Quaking aspens flaunt themselves like brazen hussies, celebrating the season in an orgy of shimmering colors.

Eleven miles of Rock Creek Canyon are open to automobiles. The remaining three miles through a basin, aptly called Little Lakes Valley, to the canyon headwall are designated wilderness, open only to pedestrians and equestrians. The narrow, paved road provides the highest gateway into Sierra backcountry, higher

Rock Creek Canyon offers a superb and relatively easy introduction to the Eastern Sierra High Country of John Muir Wilderness.

even than Tioga Pass or Whitney Portal. The drive alone paralleling lively Rock Creek in the midst of a rugged and lovely aspen-lined gorge is a stunner.

Climbing westward from Tom's Place on Highway 395, Rock Creek Road first winds by the muted hues of sagebrush and piñon pine-studded slopes. As the road gains altitude, drab tones are soon replaced by the lush greenery of summer or the fiery, autumn-kissed colors of aspen, birch, cottonwood and willow. Meandering past enticing creekside campsites, two small resorts, Rock Creek Lake and a pack station, the scenic byway ends at lofty Mosquito Flat trailhead, elevation 10,200 feet, a little over a mile beyond the lake.

Ringed by several 13,000-foot peaks, Little Lakes Valley sits in a broad, U-shaped glacial trough laced with merry streams and dazzling, flowery meadows. At the head of the canyon, Mounts Mills, Dade, Abbot, Pyramid Peak, and Bear Creek Spire skewer the cobalt-blue sky, while the jagged Wheeler Crest towers to the east. Fabulous cloud sculptures crown these bold, jagged summits that rise like gods above the horizon. Closer to earth, sunlight dances like quicksilver off dozens of glittering lakes necklaced together like beads on a rosary.

Although you don't have to leave your car to appreciate this majestic alpine environment, the best is yet to come if you let your feet lead the way. You don't have to stroll far to reap rewards for abandoning the family flivver. Happily, by the time you arrive at the trailhead, your vehicle has done most of the climbing.

The suggested hike follows what was once a road to a major mining location in the next canyon south. The road from Tom's Place that threads Rock Creek Canyon once turned south at Mosquito Flat, continuing as the primary route to

From the 10,250-foot Mosquito Flat trailhead, hikers pass through lake-filled and flower-spangled Little Lakes Valley.

Pine Creek Tungsten Mine and Mill from the mid-1920s to the 1940s. Before this sublime landscape was protected as John Muir Wilderness, a constant flow of growling ore trucks shattered the valley's tranquility and marred its grandeur.

During World War II a road was constructed directly up Pine Creek Canyon to make access to the country's largest tungsten mine at 11,000 feet easier during winter. The Morgan Pass Road though Rock Creek Canyon was permanently closed at Mosquito Flat in the early 1950s in anticipation of wilderness designation.

John Muir Wilderness protects 580,675 acres, the third largest of 18 designated wilderness areas in the Sierra Nevada. The Wilderness Act of 1964 represented a landmark piece of environmental legislation, setting aside precious ecoregions "where earth and its community of life remain untrammeled, where man is a visitor who does not remain." With no "improvements or developments" other than trails, these unsullied areas of dramatic scenery offer superb hiking, backpacking and horseback riding opportunities.

Rock Creek Canyon, named by mountaineer N.F. McClure circa 1895, has hosted several historical activities besides its role in the Pine Creek Tungsten Mine operations. For thousands of years Native Americans frequented the valley to utilize its plentiful natural resources and to escape sizzling summer temperatures at lower elevations. Inyo National Forest records indicate that from around the turn of the century until the 1930s, sheep and cattle grazed in its verdant meadows. Near the campground at Rock Creek Lake, a sawmill supplied lumber in the 1920s and '30s, some of it used to build the present-day store, resort and cabins.

Having nearly exhausted my reservoir of adjectives in praise of this heavenly Sierra niche, I must confess that besides world class scenery, the other reason I return often to Rock Creek Canyon is the homemade pie at Rock Creek Lakes Resort Cafe. God forbid if I seem to trivialize such a convocation of natural wonders by touting something so earthly, but Sue King, resident Pastry Wizard, gives a whole new meaning to "pie in the sky." Savoring a generous hunk of, say, key lime pie at 10,000 feet is in itself a little slice of heaven and not to be missed if you are anywhere within striking distance of this canyon.

Sue King rises before dawn daily to turn out 15 or so of her delicious creations, but they fly off the shelves around lunchtime. Usually you can expect to choose from French apple, key lime, peach, pumpkin, berry, chocolate, or lemon or coconut or banana cream pies. One year I chatted with a spry elderly couple who drove from Reno to enjoy a slice of mud pie and an autumn stroll in the canyon, a tradition they'd started 20 years before.

Thanks to Janette Cutts, Inyo National Forest archaeologist, we know that Rock Creek Lakes Resort began in 1923 as a one-room structure that primarily sold fishing tackle for its first 30 years. Known then as Rock Creek Lake Store, it was a modest business operation supported mainly by anglers who frequented the canyon's many lakes and streams. In the 1930s the store was enlarged and a kitchen was added. Between 1938 and 1950, owners Aubry and Eleanor Lyons expanded the business by renting boats for use on Rock Creek Lake and selling groceries, gas and oil. The delightful tradition of Rock Creek Canyon pie seems to have been started by Ms. Lyons.

The Colbys and Raders bought the business in 1950 and made significant changes during their 29-year tenure. Construction included an addition to the store to provide living quarters, five guest cabins, and a guest shower and restroom facility. They also considerably expanded the original 1923 store to provide more groceries and supplies for visitors staying in the campgrounds along Rock Creek Road. During this period, the name became Rock Creek Lakes Resort.

Since 1979 the King family has owned the business. Today Jim and Sue King are the owners and operators of this tidy, rustic resort which consists of ten guest cabins, a tiny cafe serving breakfast, lunch and light dinners—and Sue's most excellent pies—a small general store selling groceries, sporting and camping goods, fishing tackle, ice, propane and firewood.

If you crave autumn's annual pageantry, Rock Creek is guaranteed to satisfy. If you want to experience it more intimately on foot, this outing is a great choice for knapsackers of all ages and abilities to sample the High Country with only a modest effort. You'll certainly carry the rich and uplifting images of the canyon's powerful beauty in your mind's eye for a long time.

Experiencing such beauty reinforces the importance and urgency of preserving such stunning ecosystems, home to an intricate, interdependent web of wildlife and plants. Saving what little remains of these wild landscapes is one of the biggest challenges facing us in the 21st century.

■ THE HIKE

Beginning at Mosquito Flat trailhead, follow the broad trail southwest, soon entering John Muir Wilderness. After ascending the brief and moderate Crankcase Grade near the start, the name of which hints at its former usage, the path has little elevation gain for 3 miles until it reaches the switchbacks below 11,040-foot Morgan Pass.

Rest assured that this is no slog-and-pant expedition fit only for strapping Sierra trompers. If you walk no farther than .5 mile to a spectacular viewpoint atop a little rise just before the Morgan Pass and Mono Pass trail junction, you'll have a glorious picture of what classic Sierra High Country is all about. If you turn left at the junction and continue on the gentle trail toward Morgan Pass, you'll ramble past Mack Lake, then Marsh Lake followed by Heart Lake and Box Lake. Just to the east beyond this string of lakes lie another cluster of watery gems. In all, more than 50 lakes are within a two-hour walk or horseback ride from the trailhead.

Your trail skirts the east shore of Long Lake around 2 miles, maybe the most charming of these lakes, an outstanding spot for a lunch break. While you relax on one of the many inviting rocks, let the magic of this extraordinary setting fill your senses. Directly across the lake, many colorfully-banded peaks challenge the skyline. Unless you want to continue .7 mile to Chickenfoot Lake near the headwall, reached by a spur trail that forks left, or continue 2 miles to Gem Lakes, retrace your steps on a leisurely stroll back to the car.

54
Ancient Bristlecone Pine Groves
In Search of Methuselah

■ THE DETAILS

Getting There: From Highway 395 at Big Pine 15 miles south of Bishop, turn east on Highway 168. Drive 13 miles, mostly uphill, then turn north on paved White Mountain Road. The steep, switchbacking route climbs to Schulman Grove in 10 miles. The Patriarch Grove lies 11 miles farther up the mountain on a dirt road.

Nearest Campground: Grandview Campground, elevation 8600 feet, 5 miles south of Schulman Grove on White Mountain Road, has 26 sites with no water. A trail from camp climbs to an old mining site.

Lodging: The small town of Big Pine has the nearest choices.

Further Info: White Mountain Ranger District, Inyo National Forest 760-873-2500, 798 North Main Street, Bishop, CA 93514.

Hike Distance: Discovery Trail is a one-mile loop. Methuselah Trail is a 4.5-mile loop.

Difficulty: Easy to moderate.

Best Time to Go: Summer, early autumn.

Cautions: Come fully prepared to the bristlecone pine area where no gas, water or food is available. Roads are steep and winding, and although adequate for most family cars, not advisable for large RVs or trailers. Be prepared for unpredictable changes in weather and wind velocity.

Starting Elevation: Schulman Grove: 10,100 feet, Patriarch Grove: 11,000 feet.

Other Maps: Inyo National Forest map, USGS Westgard Pass 7.5 minute or White Mountain Peak 15 minute topo.

Clinging tenaciously to life on the 10,000- to 11,000-foot slopes of the White Mountains northeast of Big Pine, the oldest living organisms on earth abide in a harsh and strangely beautiful environment. Here, expansive groves of western bristlecone pines (*Pinus longaeva*), some of them 40 centuries old, thrive in a wind-blasted and rock-strewn landscape. Somewhere in this air that angels breathe, lives the Methuselah Tree, the most ancient, continuously growing life form on the planet. Methuselah has endured for 4700 years, surpassing by 1500 years the oldest giant Sequoia.

Within the Ancient Bristlecone Pine Forest (ABPF) are two groves through which visitors may wander in search of Methuselah. Hiking among these venerable specimens in their alpine-desert homeland offers superb sensory appeal. On a deeper level, a visit to ABPF produces a definite emotional impact. Here in this serenely wild and lofty world, humans and their works are as nothing. It's not at all difficult to become philosophical in the presence of a bristlecone pine. Standing beside a 4000-year-old tree in this remote, timberline region of austere beauty where silence is more than just the absence of noise, offers an extraordinary experience. I find something profoundly moving and humbling about a life form that was already 2000 years old when Christ was crucified.

Weather allowing, ABPF is open from June through October, but summer is the best time for an excursion. During July and early August, high elevation wildflowers splash the stark slopes with brilliant colors. En route to the forest, via White Mountain Road, you'll have heart-stopping panoramas of the Eastern Sierra and the Owens Valley, a dizzying 6000 feet below.

Most people are surprised the first time they view a bristlecone pine. They are not a tall, graceful thing of beauty. More like the squat Humvee of the tree world than an elegant Ferrari, these gnarled and stubby specimens rarely grow taller than 30 feet. Thick, twisted roots dive into ground much too rocky to be called soil. Young bristlecones are slim and symmetrical, but after centuries of battering by the fierce elements at this elevation, they become sculpted into exquisite shapes. Many burly old-timers are mostly dead, but somewhere a thin strip of live tissue nourishes green tufts of needles and a few cones with live seeds.

Bristlecone pines also grow in eastern Nevada and Utah, but California's White Mountains harbor the oldest and most numerous stands. Running parallel to the Sierra Nevada, the Whites comprise the northern portion of the Inyo Mountains, "dwelling place of a great spirit" in the Paiute language. The White Mountains are the westernmost range in the vast Basin and Range Province and are much older than the Sierra. In 1958 the 28,000-acre Ancient Bristlecone Pine Forest was established for scientific research and public enjoyment. Since 1950 the University of California has maintained two high altitude research stations on the upper flanks of White Mountain where scientists study the effects of high elevation on plants, animals and man. White Mountain, elevation 14,246 feet, in addition to the locale of a research natural area, is California's third tallest peak.

There is much to know about the bristlecone pine. The name comes from the appearance of its cones. Rather like a fox tail, a short, curved bristle protrudes from each scale on its three-inch cones. Their needles, five to a bundle, are long-lived and last 35 years or more. A bristlecone's growth must be accomplished during a brief six-week period, but in really dry years, it does not grow at all. If all goes well, the tree will add but one inch to its girth per century, translating to .01 inch each year.

These amazing relics live in a rigorous, alpine world where precipitation rarely totals more than ten inches annually. Shallow rooted bristlecones manage to

Oldest of known living things, scarred and battered bristlecone pines survive in a brutal, high-elevation climate.

survive in thin, nutrient-poor soil where there is virtually no competition from other plant species. Ironically, in locations of the severest duress, a longer life span is possible. In fact, scientists believe that their longevity is related to their inhospitable circumstances. The trees that grow the slowest and are more deprived of moisture and nutrients are "more likely to join the fraternity of 4000-year-old ancients" because their wood becomes more dense and resinous, thus incredibly resistant to disease and decay.

Not all bristlecones live four millennia. Trees established in moister and more sheltered slopes average about 1200 years. Those situated in dry, exposed areas often survive beyond 2000 years. Astonishingly, according to a resident ranger-naturalist at ABPF, some of the dead wood scattered on the ground is nearly 10,000 years old. Even some ghost-like snags have been standing for 1000 years.

Schulman Grove, at the south end of the forest, was named to honor Dr. Edward Schulman of the University of Arizona, pioneer discoverer of the bristle-cones' antiquity. In the late 1950s, Dr. Schulman, an expert in dendroclimatology, an esoteric branch of biology that studies tree rings which very accurately mirror yearly precipitation and summer temperatures, was studying past climate patterns by examining the spaces between tree rings. In his efforts to reconstruct weather history as far back as possible, Dr. Schulman traveled throughout the Southwest seeking old trees, both dead and alive.

In 1957 Schulman's investigations brought him to the White Mountains and the stunning discovery of Pine Alpha, a bristlecone 4300 years old. Using a Swedish increment borer, a long, slender core of wood was removed without harming the tree. Under a microscope the compacted rings were counted and the spaces between them measured. Later, an even older bristlecone was found in the same grove. Schulman determined that the Methuselah Tree had germinated in 2724 B.C., making it 4725 years old in 2001. It's hard to imagine a viable life form that was 1500 years old when the pyramids of Egypt were being built!

■ THE HIKES

On your way to the forest of living monuments, make a rest stop at Sierra Overlook, elevation 9300 feet. Prepare yourself for an overwhelming vista that encompasses more than 100 miles of wild, immense, Eastern Sierra scenery. Stretch your legs on a short trail that leads to a breathtaking, 360-degree panorama that includes Mount Whitney and Mount Williamson, California's two highest peaks.

Continue up the road to Schulman Grove (elevation 10,100 feet), location of the oldest bristlecones. Be sure to check out the two self-guided nature trails, interpretive displays, daily naturalist talks and Visitor Center (open mid-June through mid-September). Picnic tables and toilets are near the grove's entrance, but water is not available. Because ABPF lies far enough off the beaten track, you won't find crowds. During the several hours I spent at Schulman, only five other people were on the trails. Even fewer people visit Patriarch Grove to the north.

Pine Alpha, the first bristlecone dated over 4000 years by Dr. Schulman, stands along the one-mile Discovery Loop Trail. Methuselah, along with hundreds more of the burly giants, grows along the Methuselah Trail, a 4.5-mile loop through the Forest of the Ancients. Primeval Methuselah dwells anonymously among his geriatric kin, unidentified as protection against vandalism. Forest Service officials fear that souvenir hunters or antiquity pirates would peck away at Methuselah until its already tenuous hold on life would be severed.

To explore a higher, even more remote grove, drive 11 miles north from Schulman Grove on a roller-coaster dirt road to the Patriarch Grove where the largest

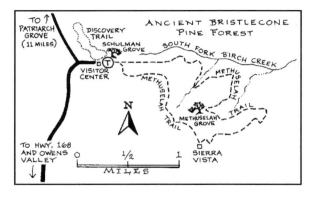

and most contorted bristlecones are anchored to the rocky ground at 11,000 feet just below timberline. The drive, through even more barren and rugged terrain than at Schulman, is other-worldly. The grove sits within a large, exposed amphitheater where wind-driven sand and ice polish and mold the trees into magnificent works of abstract art. It's an utterly dramatic setting, a grand and desolate wilderness of vast open spaces and colorful mountains.

A short, self-guided path leads to the 1500-year-old Patriarch, world's largest bristlecone, with a circumference of nearly 37 feet. Water is not available, but there are restrooms, picnic tables, and a display case. Beyond the Patriarch Grove turn-off, the dirt road continues 4.5 miles to a locked gate at the trailhead for hiking to White Mountain Peak, a very strenuous 15-mile round trip with an elevation gain of 2600 feet. Although not a technical climb, only physically fit trekkers accustomed to high altitude should attempt this journey.

It nurtures the soul to meet something that, compared to our minuscule life span, approaches immortality. In contemplation of this, one begins to question whether humanity is the highest life form. Now and again, we need to see ourselves in proper perspective in the grand scheme of things. Spending time with these twisted, ancient trees can teach us that we are really just a fleeting, minute component of the universe. Sometimes we forget that untold numbers of species existed and became extinct eons before man appeared on the scene, and after we have played our part, we too may disappear. A close encounter with a bristlecone pine provides a healthy reality check.

Further Reading

Adkison, Ron, *Hiking California*, Third edition, Falcon Press, Helena, MT, 2000.

Anderson, Tom, *Black Bear: Season in the Wild*, Voyageur Press, Stillwater, MN, 1992.

Arno, Stephen, *Discovering Sierra Trees*, Yosemite Association, Yosemite, CA, 1973.

Automobile Club of Southern California, *The Mother Lode*, Automobile Club of Southern California, Los Angeles, 1978.

Barhydt, Hap, *Hiking Between Groveland and Yosemite*, Tuolumne Group Sierra Club, Sonora, CA, 1996.

Browning, Peter, *Yosemite Place Names*, Great West Books, Lafayette, CA, 1988.

Cain, Ella, *The Story of Mono County*, Fearon Publishers, San Francisco, 1961.

Centennial Book Committee, *Alpine Heritage*, Alpine, CA, 1987.

Chase, Smeaton, *Yosemite Trails*, Tioga Publishing Group, Palo Alto, CA 1987.

Clark, Ginny, *Guide to Highway 395*, Western Trails Publications, Lake Havasu City, AZ, 1997.

_____ *Mammoth-Mono Country*, Publishers Group West, Berkeley, CA, 1989.

Clark, Ginny & Lew, *High Mountains and Deep Valleys*, Gem Guides, Baldwin Park, CA, 1999.

_____ *Yosemite Trails*, Gem Guides, Baldwin Park, CA, 1999.

Clough, Charles, *Madera Panorama*, Books West, Fresno, CA, 1983.

Deane, Dorothy Newell, *Sierra Railway*, Darwin Publications, Burbank, CA, 1980.

Farquhar, Francis, *History of the Sierra Nevada*, University of California Press, Berkeley, CA, 1965.

Fisher, Vardis and Opal Holmes, *Gold Rushes and Mining Camps of the Early American West*, Caxton Printers, Caldwell, ID, 1990.

Fremont, Jessie Benton, *Mother Lode Narratives*, Lewis Osborne, Ashland, OR, 1970.

Hanna, Jim, *Lundy: Gem of the Eastern Sierra*, Gold Hill Publishing Co., Virginia City, NV, 1990.

Herr, Pamela, *Jessie Benton Fremont*, University of Oklahoma Press, Norman, OK, 1988.

Holliday, J. S., *The World Rushed In*, Simon & Schuster, New York, 1981.

Hoover, Mildred, *Historic Spots in California*, Stanford University Press, Palo Alto, CA 1990.

Hubbard, Douglas, *Ghost Mines of Yosemite*, Awani Press, Fredericksburg, TX, 1958.

Hungry Wolf, Adolph , *Rails in the Mother Lode*, Dawn Press, Burbank, CA, 1989.

Hutchings, James, *In the Heart of the Sierras*, Great West Books, Lafayette, CA, 1990 (reprint of 1880 edition).

Irwin, Sue, *California's Eastern Sierra*, Cachuma Press, Los Olivos, CA, 1993.

Jackson, Joseph Henry, *Anybody's Gold*, Chronicle Books, San Francisco, 1983.

Johnston, Hank, *Shortline to Paradise*, Flying Spur Press, Yosemite, CA, 1986.

_____ *Thunder in the Mountains*, Max Stauffer Publishing, Fish Camp, CA, 1995.

_____ *Yosemite's Yesterdays*, Volume II, Flying Spur Press, Yosemite, CA, 1991.

_____ *Yosemite's Yesterdays*, Flying Spur Press, Yosemite, CA, 1989.

_____ *The Yosemite Grant: 1864-1906*, Yosemite Association, Yosemite, CA, 1995.

Law, Jim, *Memories of El Portal*, Mariposa Heritage Press, Mariposa, CA, 1993.

Leaderbrand, Russ, *Exploring California Byways, Volume VI: Owens Valley*, Westways, Los Angeles, 1972.

Levy, JoAnn, *They Saw the Elephant*, University of Oklahoma Press, Norman, OK, 1992.

Margo, Elizabeth, *Women of the Gold Rush*, Indian Head Books, New York, 1992.

Martin, Don and Betty, *Best of the Gold Country*, Publishers Group West, Berkeley, CA, 1987.

McDonald, Douglas, *Bodie*, Nevada Publications, Las Vegas, 1988.

Mendershausen, Ralph, *Treasures of the South Fork*, Panorama Books, Fresno, CA, 1986.

Morey, Kathy, *Hot Showers, Soft Beds and Dayhikes in the Sierra*, Wilderness Press, Berkeley, CA, 1996.

Morgenson, Dana, *Yosemite Wildflower Trails*, Yosemite Association, Yosemite, CA, 1988.

Muir, John, *Summering in the Sierra*, University of Wisconsin Press, Madison, WI, 1984.

_____ *Yosemite*, Sierra Club Books, San Francisco, 1988.

_____ *My First Summer in the Sierra*, Penguin Books, New York, 1987.

Murphys Old Time Museum, *Ebbetts Pass-Big Tree Route*, Old Timers Museum, Murphys, CA, 1995.

O'Neill, Elizabeth S., *Meadow in the Sky*, Panorama Books, Fresno, CA, 1984.

Parr, Barry, *Hiking the Sierra Nevada*, Globe Pequot Press, Guilford, CT, 1999.

Reynolds, Annie and Albert Gordon, *Stage to Yosemite*, Big Tree Books, El Portal, CA, 1994.

Rose, Gene, *Sierra Centennial*, Three Forests Interpretive Center, Auberry, CA, 1994.

Runte, Albert, *Yosemite: Embattled Wilderness*, University of Nebraska Press, Lincoln, NE, 1990.

Russell, Carl, *100 Years in Yosemite*, Yosemite Natural History Association, Yosemite, CA, 1992.

Salazar, Francisco, *The Gold of Old Hornitos*, Saga West Publishing, Fresno, CA, 1964.

Sanford, Margaret, *Yosemite*, Yosemite Association, Yosemite, CA, 1989.

Sargent, Shirley, *Yosemite and Its Innkeepers*, Flying Spur Press, Yosemite, CA, 1986.

_____ *Foresta and Big Meadow*, Flying Spur Press, Yosemite, CA, 1983.

_____ *Galen Clark: Yosemite Guardian*, Flying Spur Press, Yosemite, CA, 1994.

_____ *Yosemite High Sierra Camps*, Flying Spur Press, Yosemite, CA, 1977.

_____ *Mariposa Guidebook*, Flying Spur Press, Yosemite, CA, 1984.

_____ *The Ahwahnee Hotel*, Sequoia Communications, Santa Barbara, CA, 1990.

_____ *The First 100 Years: Yosemite*, Sequoia Communications, Santa Barbara, CA, 1988.

_____ *Yosemite's Historic Wawona*, Flying Spur Press, Yosemite, CA, 1987.

_____ *Yosemite's Famous Guests*, Flying Spur Press, Yosemite, CA, 1970.

Schaffer, Jeffrey, *Yosemite National Park*, Wilderness Press, Berkeley, CA, 1997.

Schlictmann, Margaret and Irene Paden, *The Big Oak Flat Road to Yosemite*, Awani Press, Fredericksburg, TX, 1986.

Seagraves, Anne, *High Spirited Women of the West*, Wesanne Publications, Hayden, ID, 1992.

Smith, Genny, *Mammoth Lakes Sierra*, Genny Smith Books, Palo Alto, CA, 1980.

Spring, Vicky, *100 Hikes in California's Central Sierra and Coast Range*, The Mountaineers, Seattle, 1997.

Stienstra, Tom, *California Hiking*, Fifth edition, Foghorn Press, Santa Rosa, CA, 2001.

Swedo, Suzanne, *Hiking Yosemite National Park*, Globe Pequot Press, Guilford, CT, 2000.

Trexler, Kenneth, *The Tioga Road*, Yosemite Association, Yosemite, CA, 1980.

Weamer, Howard, *The Perfect Art*, Howard Weamer, Marceline, MO, 1995.

Whitehill, Karen, *Best Short Hikes in California's Northern Sierra*, The Mountaineers, Seattle, 1990.

_____ *Best Short Hikes in California's Southern Sierra*, The Mountaineers, Seattle, WA 1999.

Winnett, Thomas, *Sierra North*, Wilderness Press, Berkeley, CA, 1997.

_____ Sierra South, Wilderness Press, Berkeley, CA, 1993.

Wood, Coke, *Ebbetts Pass and Highway 4*, Old Timers Museum, Murphys, CA, 1985.

_____ *James Sperry of Calaveras*, n.p.

Wurm, Ted, *Hetch Hetchy and Its Dam Railroad*, Trans-Anglo Books, Glendale, CA, 1995.

Illustration Credits

continued from page 6

100	Bower Cave bandstand	Courtesy of Caroline Wenger Korn
103	Muir's mossy boulder	Sharon Giacomazzi
108	Hite's Cove, circa 1881	Courtesy of Leroy Radanovich Collection
119	Bull Buck Tree	Elizabeth Petersen
120	Railway, Nelder Grove	Courtesy of Madera Cty. Historical Society
129	Lower Jackass Lake	Sharon Giacomazzi
132	Doris Lake	Elizabeth Petersen
136	Women at Glacier Pt.	Courtesy of Yosemite Research Library
139	Bear and old car	Courtesy of Yosemite Research Library
142	View from Artist Point	Sharon Giacomazzi
145	Yosemite Falls, 1855	Thomas Ayres/Courtesy, Yosemite Research Library
150	Stage on Big Oak Flat Road	Courtesy of Yosemite Research Library
158	Women at Mirror Lake	George Fiske/Courtesy, Leroy Radanovich Collection
164	CCC crew on Half Dome	Courtesy of Yosemite Research Library
172	Carl Inn, 1920	Courtesy of Yosemite Research Library
177	H. Hetchy before inundation	Courtesy of City of San Francisco
183	Merced Grove	Sharon Giacomazzi
187	Dead Giant, Tuolumne Grove	Courtesy of Yosemite Research Library
193	Big Meadow	Courtesy of Yosemite Research Library
197	Foresta Road	Sharon Giacomazzi
202	Mount Hoffman, 1863	Courtesy of Yosemite Research Library
206	View from Mount Hoffman	Sharon Giacomazzi
210	Half Dome from Snow Cr. Tr.	Sharon Giacomazzi
214	Firefall	Courtesy of Leroy Radanovich Collection
219	Taft Point	Courtesy of Yosemite Concession Services
223	Wawona Hotel	Courtesy of Yosemite Research Library
226	Ice harvesting at Stella Lake	Courtesy of Yosemite Research Library
234	Mount Dana	Courtesy of Yosemite Research Library
241	Bennettville, 1898	Courtesy of Yosemite Research Library
244	Bennettville today	Sharon Giacomazzi
255	May Lundy Mine, 1895	Courtesy of Nevada Historical Society
261	West Lake	Bob Lorentzen
263	Bodie	Sharon Giacomazzi
269	Parker Lake	Sharon Giacomazzi
277	Convict Lake	Sharon Giacomazzi
281	Rock Creek Canyon	Sharon Giacomazzi
282	Little Lakes Valley	Sharon Giacomazzi
287	Bristlecone pines	Sharon Giacomazzi

Index

About the Author

Sharon Giacomazzi is a Sierra hiker who happens to be an avid history buff and a born storyteller. Sharon's love affair with the Sierra Nevada began early, as soon as she learned to walk. She grew up on a large ranch in the foothills below Kings Canyon National Park. When Sharon wasn't asleep or in school, she wandered the hills, wild and free, on foot or horseback. Mountain life got into her blood and stayed, even during years away at college and in the city earning a living as a teacher.

The urban setting always made Sharon feel like an alien, a stranger trapped in a strange land. Finally, in 1980, after 22 years of teaching, she decided to go home to the mountains where her spirit could be nurtured by the Sierra's natural rhythms and cycles.

Sharon bought property close to Yosemite and reconnected with her sense of place and her spiritual home. After building her house, she created ways to eke out a modest living, then began walking, and she hasn't stopped.

In the past 21 years, Sharon has trekked more than 7000 Sierra miles in and around Yosemite National Park. She has been an outings leader for several environmental organizations and community colleges, as well as a leader of her own history hikes. She has read and re-read scores of history books about the Sierra, finding they tremendously enriched her hiking experiences. Treading a trail is certainly rewarding, but Sharon found it a bit one dimensional. Knowing each place's background and nuances takes the hike to another level of intimacy that is very gratifying.

Sharon started writing about the trails and tales of Yosemite and the Central Sierra in 1992. Like walking, once she got going she couldn't stop. Since then, her articles have appeared regularly in the **Yosemite Highway Herald** newspaper and **Sierra Heritage** and **California Explorer** magazines. Much to her amazement and delight, she encountered many people eager for something more than just a hiking guide to get them from point A to B. They wanted some "meat with their potatoes," as one reader chose to put it.

Sharon loves to hike and write about her adventures. Like John Muir, she too feels blessed when she can entice someone to get out there and mingle with the rest of the food chain and "taste the tonic of wilderness."

About Bored Feet

We began Bored Feet in 1986 to publish *The Hiker's hip pocket Guide to the Mendocino Coast*. We've grown our company by presenting the most accurate guidebooks for northern California and the award-winning two-volume series, *Hiking the California Coastal Trail*.

Thank you for supporting quality independent publishing with your purchase, helping us to bring you more information about gorgeous and fascinating California.

We love to hear your feedback about this or any of our other products. Also, if you'd like to receive updates on trails in our books, send your name and address, specifying your areas of interest.

We also offer lightning fast mail / phone order service, offering more than 90 books and maps about California and the West. If you'd like a catalog and / or more of our guides, please send name, address / check or money order, or call one of the numbers below.

Trails & Tales of Yosemite & the Central Sierra	Sharon Giacomazzi	$ 16.00
Geologic Trips: San Francisco & the Bay Area	Ted Konigsmark	13.95
Hiking the CA Coastal Trail, Vol. One: Oregon to Monterey, 2nd edition(Oct.01)	Lorentzen & Nichols	19.00
Hiking the CA Coastal Trail, Vol. Two: Monterey to Mexico	Lorentzen & Nichols	19.00
Great Day Hikes in & around Napa Valley, 2nd edition	Ken Stanton	15.00
Sonoma Picnic: A CA Wine Country Travel Companion	Jack Burton	13.00
Mendocino Coast Glove Box Guide: Lodgings Eateries, Sights, History, 2nd. ed.	Bob Lorentzen	15.00
Mendocino Coast Bike Rides: Roads & Trails, Easy to Advanced	Bob Lorentzen	14.00
Hiker's hip pocket Guide to the Mendocino Coast, 3rd ed.	Bob Lorentzen	14.00
Hiker's hip pocket Guide to the Humboldt Coast, 2nd ed.	Bob Lorentzen	14.00
Hiker's hip pocket Guide to Sonoma County, 3rd ed.	Bob Lorentzen	14.00
Hiker's hip pocket Guide to the Mendocino Highlands	Bob Lorentzen	14.00
Wood, Water, Air & Fire: Anthology of Mendocino Women Poets	Doubiago et al, ed.	19.00

Please add $3 shipping for orders under $30, $5 over $30 ($5 / 7 for rush).
For shipping to a California address, please add 7% sales tax.
Prices subject to change without notice.

BORED FEET PRESS
P.O. BOX 1832
MENDOCINO, CA 95460
888-336-6199
707-964-6629